THE
PRACTICAL
GARDENER

THE COMPLETE GUIDE TO CREATING
AND MAINTAINING EVERY GARDEN

THE PRACTICAL GARDENER

THE COMPLETE GUIDE TO CREATING AND MAINTAINING EVERY GARDEN

DAVID SQUIRE

D

Dealerfield

Published by Salamander Books Limited
129-137 York Way London N7 9LG
United Kingdom

1 3 5 7 9 8 6 4 2

© Salamander Books Ltd. 1996

This edition specially printed for Dealerfield Ltd, 1996

ISBN 1 85927 102 2
Printed in the United Kingdom by
Butler & Tanner Ltd, Frome and London

CREDITS

Managing Editor: Anne McDowall
Designer: Mark Holt
Photographer: David Squire
Photographic Models: Margaret Crowther, Anthony Squire,
Michael Squire, Patricia Squire
Copy Editor: Meg Sanders
Indexer: Hilary Bird
Colour reproduction by: Classic Scan, Singapore
Filmset by: SX Composing Ltd.

Photographs on pages 4/5 Marie-Louise Avery
© Salamander Books Ltd. (Chelsea Flower Show 1992;
Designer: Douglas G Knight); page 143 © G.P.L./Brian Glover.

ACKNOWLEDGEMENTS

The author wishes to thank the following for their generous
help in the preparation of this book:

All Exterior Designs (Builders), Hassocks, West Sussex;
Do-it-All Limited (Burgess Hill, West Sussex); Jim Clowes;
Frank and Jean Cooper; Margaret Crowther; Michael Gibson;
John and Vana Haggerty; Halls Garden Products Limited (for
providing transparencies and their Halls Popular 86 model
greenhouse); Hozelock Aquatics; Nikki King and the staff of
King's Garden Centre, Hassocks, West Sussex; Sheila Marshall;
Ray and Val Marshe; Peter McHoy; Bob Morley (bricklayer and
builder); Neill Tools Limited for providing a wide range of
Spear and Jackson garden tools; Plumpton Horticultural
College, Plumpton, East Sussex; Rosslow Roses (Alan Staples),
Hailsham, East Sussex; Royal Horticultural Society's Garden,
Wisley, Surrey; Ian Hill of Supersheds Limited; A. W. Thomas
Limited (Builder's Merchant), Wivesfield Green, Sussex;
Thompson & Morgan (seed merchants) of Ipswich.

THE AUTHOR

David Squire studied botany and horticulture at the Hertfordshire College of Horticulture and at the Royal Horticultural Society's Garden at Wisley, England, where he gained the Wisley Diploma in Horticulture. For several years he worked as a sub-editor, writer and reporter for two well-known garden magazines before moving to book publishing with an international publishing house.

David has written more than fifty books and contributed to several major gardening part-works. *The Scented Garden* (also published by Salamander) won the Garden Writers of America Quill and Trowel Award. Additionally, he acts as a gardening consultant and is involved in the photography of plants; he took the majority of the pictures featured in this book.

David lives in West Sussex with his wife and two sons, together with their dog and six cats.

Contents

Introduction

Successful gardening is based on a combination of inspiration, planning and practical information. The inspiration often comes from looking at other people's gardens or by visiting botanical gardens, where it is possible to see plants growing in situations that show them to perfection. To grow such plants yourself, you need access to practical information, that vital know-how that enables plans to be implemented with confidence. This can range from preparing the soil for sowing seeds or planting shrubs and trees, to building a wall, laying a patio, or growing plants in a greenhouse. It is the purpose of this comprehensive and abundantly illustrated book to provide this information and guide readers through the many practical tasks involved in creating a garden. Additionally, because it is essential to be able to identify plants when planning a garden, more than two hundred and seventy of them are illustrated, with many more described. These range from annuals, biennials and herbaceous plants to climbers, shrubs and roses, with vegetables, herbs and fruit as well.

The book is divided into eleven chapters and includes features on constructing patios, drives, fences and pergolas, cultivating the soil by digging, hoeing and mulching, increasing plants by sowing seeds, taking cuttings, layering, budding and grafting, and growing plants in containers for display on patios.

Gardening is a hobby that creates fresh challenges each year and although some parts of a garden may cause disappointment one year, the following season inevitably presents an opportunity to correct mistakes or to try something else. It is this continual renewal that makes *The Practical Gardener* an invaluable aid to have at your elbow, year after year.

PROTECTING THE ENVIRONMENT

Throughout this book we have indicated the use of peat in seed and potting composts and as a mulch around plants, but the extensive and continual removal of this material from peat beds is increasingly leading to the destruction of the environments of animals, insects and plants. Therefore, whenever possible choose substitutes for peat, especially when preparing seed and potting composts; these are created from renewable sources, such as coconut fibres. In the garden, decayed garden compost created from decomposed vegetable waste is an ideal and inexpensive material for creating a mulch. Shredded woody garden waste and bark are other materials that can and should be used as mulches around plants.

Right: Borders packed with herbaceous plants can be ablaze with colour throughout summer. Colourful shrubs and trees create bright backgrounds.

Below: Garden ponds enable a wide range of water plants to be grown, as well as moisture-loving plants that can be planted around the edge.

GARDEN CONSTRUCTION

Permanent features, from paths, steps and drives to fences, pergolas, and trellises, are vital in a garden. They are all functional elements of a garden design – providing all-weather surfaces which allow access throughout the year, separating a garden from its surroundings or one part of a garden from another, or supporting plants. But as well as being functional, they must be attractive and harmonize with their surroundings.

Summerhouses, sheds and greenhouses are also incorporated into many gardens and to ensure their long life they must be erected on a firm, strong base that will not later subside or crack. The repair and maintenance of garden buildings is important, and, if done as soon as a problem is noticed, prevents further deterioration.

Laying gravel paths and drives

Gravel paths, drives and standing areas for cars can be attractive features in their own right and have a more natural and informal appearance than those made from asphalt, crazy-paving or flexible concrete pavers.

Gravel drives are relatively inexpensive to construct and their shape can vary to suit any size and outline. The noise of gravel underfoot can also be a security feature, alerting home-owners – and dogs – to someone's approach.

Paths and small drives are best formed of 6mm/¼in pea shingle. (This is frequently sold as 9mm/⅜in washed shingle and includes 6mm/¼in shingle up to the above size.) Gravel is slightly larger and better suited to bigger areas. It is also less likely to spread sideways and is not so easily picked up on shoes and scattered by car tyres as pea shingle.

Gravel will eventually settle and will need to be topped up, but this is not an onerous task. Weeds can be a problem and although sodium chlorate soon kills them and prevents the growth of further ones, it is likely to be washed sideways, when it might kill near-by grass and plants. It is

therefore best kept 1m/3ft away from plant borders and grass edges. There are weedkillers that do not have a residual effect and these can be safely used near plants and lawns. Avoid splashing them by placing a piece of thin boarding (which you can carry in your hand) against the edging and apply the chemicals using a fine-rosed watering-can. Regularly rake the surface of the gravel to keep it level.

CONSTRUCTING A DRIVE

The first task is to ensure that the area is well drained and does not become boggy in winter. If necessary, install drains (see pages 42-3).

Install the edging (see right), ensuring that its height is correct in relation to the finished height of the gravel when laid. Dig out the roots of perennial weeds. If left, weeds will continue to grow and will create unwelcome plants that will push up through the gravel.

A firm base is essential and its depth depends on the amount of traffic expected, its weight, and whether vehicles are continually stopping and starting. Most bases need be no more than

Right: Pea-shingle forms an attractive and natural path that is ideal alongside shrub and mixed borders. Allow plants to slightly spread over the edge of the path, so that its sides are 'softened' and do not appear to create a rigid outline.

CONSTRUCTING A SHINGLE DRIVE

1 Dig out an area 90cm-1.2m/3-4ft wide and 10cm/4in deep where the path is to be sited. Friable topsoil can be spread over the surface of shrub borders.

2 Strong side constraints are essential. Preferably, use those made of concrete; cement them into position so that their tops are slightly above the surface of the surrounding lawn or soil. Place broken bricks under the side constraints to hold them in position while the cement hardens.

3 Consolidate clean, broken rubble between the constraints.

4 Spread pea shingle over the rubble, so that its surface is about 2.5cm/1in below the top of the side constraints.

CONSTRUCTING EDGES

It is essential that gravel does not spread from the drive on to flowerbeds and garden lawns, or on to pavements and roads. This can be prevented in several ways:

- Grass edges create attractive, inexpensive and practical edgings for gravel drives, especially where the sides meander and are gently curved. The surface of the grass should be about 5cm/2in above the gravel's surface. If it is too high, the edges will dry out and crumble if trodden upon.

- If you are creating a lawn alongside a gravel path, it is essential to put in a temporary edge while it becomes established, especially if it is being seeded rather than formed from turves. Corrugated plastic edging, 15cm/6in or 20cm/8in wide, can be secured with 20cm/8in-long wood stakes (which you can remove once the lawn is established).

- Where a gravel drive abuts a path alongside a road, you will need to restrain the gravel to prevent it spreading and becoming a nuisance. This is best done by concreting a row of bricks along the edge, with the top about 18mm/^{3}/$_4$in above the gravel's surface. To ensure that car tyres are not damaged when passing over the road side of edging bricks, consider using those with a chamfered top on one edge.

- If the edge of the drive is straight (and not adjacent to a pavement or road), concrete slabs about 15cm/6in high, 36-50mm/1^1/$_2$-2in thick and 90cm/3ft long can be concreted into position. Using slabs with rounded tops instead of square ones helps to create a softer outline. When positioned, their tops should about 2.5cm/1in above the gravel.

7.5cm/3in thick and formed of compacted rubble. Use the end of a large beam to repeatedly ram the surface.

Spread gravel over the surface, initially to a depth of about 5cm/2in. It will settle in the first few months and you will then need to top it up.

COUNTRY DRIVES

An easy and economical way to construct a long gravel drive is to hire a rotavator. Dig up the soil to a depth of 15-20cm/6-8in, then spread cement over the surface and rotavate it in. It is essential to consolidate this loose soil; either drive a car over the surface or use the end of a stout beam to ram the soil. Spread gravel over this and water the surface.

If you cannot hire a rotavator, use a fork to dig the soil and to mix in the cement powder. For this system to work the soil must not be of a type that becomes boggy after a few showers of rain. Additionally, side constraints are essential.

SHINGLE PATHS

Shingle paths do not need the same depth of foundation as drives and standing areas. Dig out the area to about 10cm/4in deep, then concrete side constraints into position. Consolidate a 5cm/2in-thick layer of rubble in the base, then add pea-shingle.

Gravel paths about 1.2m/4ft wide can be made even more attractive by letting paving stones (60cm/24in square, or 60cm/24in wide and 75cm/30in long) into them so that they act as large stepping stones. The top of the paving stones should be level with the surface of the gravel and about 2.5cm/1in below the top of the side constraints.

Laying paving slabs

Pre-cast paving slabs are ideal for creating a firm, all-weather patio. They can be used on their own or combined with other materials, such as bricks and pebbles, to create more decorative patterns.

TYPES OF SLABS

The range of sizes and shapes of pre-cast paving is wide; their thickness is also variable, but is usually 42-50mm/1¾-2in (thinner ones are likely to crack. The most common size is 45cm/18in square, with quarter and half sizes available so that patterns can be formed. Other standard sizes are 60cm/24in square and 75cm/30in long by 60cm/24in wide (but these can be difficult for one person to manipulate). Hexagonal slabs are popular and are good for forming interesting and attractive patterns.

Paving slabs are available in a good choice of finishes. A plain surface can seem uninteresting, but smooth paving slabs harmonize with modern settings. They are available in a range of colours and are less expensive than most other finishes.

Textured slabs have an interesting surface, which is resistant to slip during wet weather. Some are grooved while others look as though they have been brushed with a stiff broom.

Riven slabs, which have the appearance of natural stone, are very popular, and are available in several colours.

Various types of patterned paving slabs are available, most simulating other materials, including crazy-paving, parquet flooring and cobbles. Their colours are often brighter than, for example, those of the riven type; but they do enable you to form interesting patterns.

STORING SLABS

Do not leave slabs in a heap as this will damage them. To store slabs before use, position two strong boards on a firm surface (but not where the patio is to be laid), 30cm/12in apart and at a right angles to a wall. Then stand the slabs on the boards on their sides so that they lean at a slight angle towards the wall. Place a piece of wood against the wall to protect it from being scratched by the slabs. Storing slabs in this way prevents them being stained, and protects edges from becoming knocked and chipped.

Right: Unlike grass paths, which become bare and unsightly at their edges when plants spread over them, those formed of paving slabs create a firm, attractive surface throughout the year. Here, Lady's Mantle (*Alchemilla mollis*) looks especially attractive when spilling over a path formed of paving slabs.

LAYING PAVING SLABS

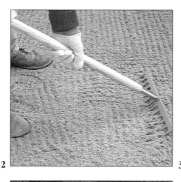

1 Remove the topsoil and add and compact a 10cm/4in-thick layer of clean rubble over the site. Spread a 5cm/2in-thick layer of sharp sand over this.
2 Use a metal garden rake to level the sand; rake the sand in several directions.
3 Mark out on the sand the area of the first slab and place five blobs of mortar on it – near each corner and in the centre.
4 Gently place the slab in position and check it has a gentle slope so that water drains away.
5 Position the next slab and check its position relative to the first slab. If the slabs have straight edges, place 12mm/½in-thick spaces between them.
6 When the mortar holding the slabs is hard, fill the joints with a stiff, dry mortar mix and ram it in.

LAYING A PATIO FROM PAVING SLABS

Where a patio adjoins a building it is essential that the patio surface is at least 15cm/6in below the damp course. If this is impossible, leave a 10cm/4in-wide, 15cm/6in-deep gap between the slabs and the building. After you have laid the slabs, fill this space with 6mm/¼in pea-shingle.

CUTTING PAVING SLABS

If you are fitting a patio around a building, you may need to cut slabs. This is not difficult and although professionals use a powered masonry saw it is possible to cut them with a bolster (type of cold chisel) and a club hammer (a heavy hammer is used with one hand).

- A bolster and club hammer are easy to use, but you should wear gloves and an eye mask for protection. Mark the line to be cut in pencil on the slab, then place the slab on a firm, flat surface such as a lawn. Place a straight-edged board along the line and with the edge of the bolster score a line around the slab, on all sides and edges. Then, using the bolster and club hammer, work around the slab, several times. When complete, place the slab on a board, so that the scored line is above its edge. Use the wooden handle of the club hammer to sharply knock the slab so that it breaks along the line.

- If you have a large number of slabs to cut, you may decide to hire a powered masonry saw. Make sure that you observe all safety requirements: use a circuit-breaker, wear an eye and face mask, keep children and pets indoors, and do not wear loose clothing that could become entangled with the saw.

Ensure that this gulley allows water to drain freely, otherwise there is a risk of damp passing into the building.

Thorough preparation of the site is important if the patio is not to subside, causing paving slabs to crack after a few years.

First you will need to remove the topsoil from the site and consolidate the sub-soil. Ensure that there are no tree roots near the surface or immediately below. If you need to dig these out, consolidate the sub-soil afterwards.

Assessing the levels of the site is essential. The finished patio will need to slope slightly, and uniformly away from the house. Use pegs and a spirit-level placed on top of a 2.4m/8ft-long straight-edged plank to check the levels.

Mark out an area about 15cm/6in larger (on all sides) than the planned size of the patio and form a 10cm/4in-thick layer of compacted clean rubble. Use the end of a stout piece of timber to ram it. Cover the rubble with a 5cm/2in-thick layer of sharp sand.

Start laying the slabs from the edge of the building; this should be the highest point. Mark in the sand the area of the first slab, then use a mixture of one part cement to five parts builder's sand to form a bed for each slab. This mortar can be spread in two patterns – in ridges 36-50mm/1½-2in high just inside the slab's four edges, or as five blobs, one in each corner and the fifth in the centre.

Position the slab and gently bed it on the mortar. Check with a spirit-level that it has a slight slope in the right direction to shed water away from the house. Lay the next slab so that you are starting to form a line along the side of the house (or the highest side). Check that it lines up with its neighbour and has the same slight slope away from the house.

If the edges of the slabs are at right angles to the surface you will need to place 12mm/½in-thick spacers between each slab. However, some slabs have slightly bevelled edges and this enables them to be positioned close together while still leaving space for joints to be filled afterwards.

Once you have laid the patio, leave it alone for about a week, then fill the joints with a stiff, dry, weak mortar mixture, avoiding the surface of the slabs, and ram this into place. The finished level should be just below the surface of the slabs.

Laying crazy-paving and natural stone paths

Crazy-paving patios, paths and drives can be laid to suit any outline as well as gentle contours that would be impossible for paving slabs (see pages 14-5) and concrete pavers (see pages 18-9).

Crazy-paving surfaces are formed from broken paving slabs, usually plain coloured and with a smooth surface. If you wish, you can add a few coloured broken pieces to the area. When buying crazy-paving, make sure you specify the colour – and check that you have a mixture of large and small pieces.

Natural stone can also be used, but it is expensive and is most suitable for paths or small patios, and then only in cottage-like situations where it harmonizes with the rustic surroundings.

LAYING CRAZY-PAVING PATHS AND PATIOS

To ensure a long life for crazy-paving it must be laid on a strong foundation.

Use strings to mark the edges of the area to be laid. Dig out the topsoil from this area and spread it over borders. If the sub-soil is soft, dig this out to about 13cm/5in deep and form a 10cm/4in-thick layer of compacted, clean rubble. Ram it

with the end of a stout piece of timber. Over this lay a 5cm/2in-thick layer of sharp sand. If you need to stand on the prepared area, place a wide plank on it.

Where the sides of the area to be crazy-paved are not constrained by a firm edge, such as a wall or part of a building, use shuttering 10-13cm/4-5in wide and 12mm/½in thick to mark the edge. After excavating the soil, position this shuttering so that the top edge will be level with the top of the crazy-paving, to restrain the sand at the sides.

When installing the shuttering, knock in supporting pegs on the outer edge of the paving area. You may be able to remove this shuttering later if a lawn is butted next to the path.

Spread out the pieces of crazy-paving, so that you can see easily those with straight edges. These are best for the outer edges, while completely broken pieces are positioned on the inside.

When laying a path, begin by positioning about 1m/3½ft of edging on each side. Set stones on mortar formed of one part cement and five of soft sand. For a patio, lay edging along one nar-

LAYING A CRAZY-PAVING PATH

1 Use strings to mark the area of the path. Then, dig out the topsoil. Also, remove the subsoil to about 13cm/5in deep. Install wooden side constraints (their tops level with the surrounding lawn or soil).
2 Form a 10cm/4in-thick layer of compacted, clean rubble in the base.
3 Cover this with a 5cm/2in-thick layer of sharp sand, so that the surface is about 5cm/2in below the top of the side constraints.
4 Spread a layer of mortar over the sand and lay straight-edged pieces of broken crazy-paving along the sides, about 1m/3½ft at a time.
5 Spread mortar in the centre and fit in other pieces.
6 Fill the gaps between the stones with mortar, finishing it slightly below the surface so that water runs off.

Above: Crazy-paving forms natural-looking paths in gardens and can be laid to any width and to suit most contours. Crazy-paving paths are ideal in semi-formal gardens, where they meander from one feature to another, forming all-weather surfaces. Ensure they are constructed on a strong, firm base.

row end and about 1m/3½ft down the two sides.

Select and provisionally position pieces of crazy-paving to fit into the inside area. This is like assembling a jigsaw and may take a little time. When this initial area is arranged satisfactorily, lift each piece and bed it on mortar. It is essential that the surface is even, although it may slope in several directions. This is achieved by placing a piece of 5-7.5cm/2-3in-square timber about 90cm/3ft long over the area and gently tapping it with a club (heavy) hammer.

Continue to form the edgings, about 1m/3½ft at a time, then filling in the centre, until the path or patio is complete.

Fill the gaps between the pieces of paving with mortar. Try not to get any on the slabs as it may mark them. Use a trowel and ensure that mortar is worked well between the pieces and until level with the surface but with the centre slightly below. This assists water to drain from the path.

Do not put any weight on the paving while filling the joints; if the area is too wide for you to reach the centre from the sides, wait until the mortar on which the stones are bedded is hard.

If you are laying crazy-paving for a drive, you will need to dig deeper foundations. Because of the weight it will be expected to support – as well as the repeated stopping and starting of cars –

you will need to increase the layer of compacted rubble from 10cm/4in-thick to 15cm/6in. You will also need to ensure that each piece of crazy-paving is on an overall bed of mortar.

LAYING A NATURAL STONE PATH OR PATIO

Natural stone forms attractive paths and patios, where it creates an all-weather surface while allowing plants to be grown between the stones.

Use strings to mark out the area of the path or patio. Dig out the topsoil. If the sub-soil is not firm, dig this out to 13cm/5in deep and fill with compacted rubble, then 5cm/2in of sharp sand.

Because of its uneven thickness, natural stone is more difficult to lay than crazy-paving. The pieces of stone (unless sawn, which eliminates their natural appearance) do not have clean-cut edges. For the path or patio's edges, choose pieces of stone with relatively straight edges.

Position the stones at the edge of the path, and then place them on blobs of mortar. Arrange other pieces in the inside of the path and also place these on mortar. Dig out the sand and rubble under the joints between some of the pieces of stone, and fill these areas with soil-based compost. Later, you can plant small plants in them. Compact mortar in cracks between the slabs, except where plants are to be set.

Laying concrete pavers

Concrete pavers are relatively new and are increasing in popularity for paths, patios and drives. Each paver is about the size of a house brick. They are sometimes known as 'flexible' pavers because they are laid on a bed of sand and, if necessary, can later be lifted and re-laid. Pavers can be laid in attractive patterns; some of these are suitable for paths, where the area is narrow, others for wider areas such as patios and drives.

Pavers are available in a range of colours and textures and should be selected to harmonize with the house and the nature of the garden. There are several types, but the most common one has a bevelled edge at the top. Some have wavy edges and are known as fishtails.

LAYING PAVERS

Because pavers are just bedded into sharp sand it is essential to provide a firm base. The thickness of the base will be dependent on the type of sub-soil and whether the surface will be used as a path or as a drive for cars. You will also need to construct a restraining edge to prevent sand collapsing sideways.

Use strings to mark out the edges of the path, patio or drive. Assess the levels; pavers are best laid on a flat surface, although a slight incline is acceptable if it is uniform and covers the width of the path, patio or drive.

Dig out the topsoil and spread it on borders. If the sub-soil is firm and only a path is being constructed, you can lay the pavers on a 5cm/2in-thick bed of sharp sand. However, if the sub-soil is soft, dig it out to allow for a 7.5cm/3in-thick layer of compacted rubble, then place a 5cm/2in-thick layer of sharp sand on top of this.

If you are constructing a drive, increase the thickness of the compacted rubble base to at least 10cm/4in and place a 5cm/2in-thick layer of sharp sand on top.

Install constraints along the edge. The tops of constraints (concrete strips or strong wood) should be level with the surface of the pavers when laid and compacted (when they drop about 9mm/^{3}/$_8$in). Concrete constraints can be concreted into position, while wooden ones need stout pegs about 1m/3^1/$_2$ft apart and secured to the outside edge.

CONSTRUCTING A PATH

1 Use strings to mark the area of the path. Dig out the soil to a depth of a total of 15cm/6in. Install constraints along the sides.
2 Form a 7.5cm/3in-thick layer of rubble in the base.
3 Spread sharp sand over the rubble. Ensure its surface is evenly below the top of the side constraints (see text). 4. The pavers can then be positioned on top of the sand. Choose a pattern that suits a path and does not involve cutting the pavers, such as the parquet bond.
5 To compact the pavers, place a flat piece of wood on the surface and repeatedly tap with a club hammer.
6 Brush dry, sharp sand over the surface, then again compact the pavers. Repeat this then water the surface of the path with a fine-rose watering-can.

PATTERNS FOR PAVERS

Some complex patterns are best left to professional constructors, but several are very simple and, if you design the path or patio with measurements to suit multiples of the widths of pavers, little cutting is needed.

- **Herringbone** pattern is popular because the pavers interlock and form a strong surface that is ideal as a drive or hard standing for vehicles. However, you will need to cut pavers that are laid diagonally to the edges. If you lay the pavers parallel, you will need to cut only to create half-bricks.
- **Parquet** pattern is the easiest design for a rectangular area or a straight path. However, it is not strong enough to support the weight of cars.
- **Cane-weave** pattern is formed of rows of three parallel blocks. The rows are staggered so that crossing pavers meet other blocks half-way along them. It is an easy solution for paths, but is not suitable for drives.
- **Running bond** is easy to lay but you will need to cut half-blocks. It is laid across the path or drive, with the pavers in staggered lines.
- **Squared** design is ideal for rectangular or square areas, for paths or patios. It is made up of whole pavers forming a square, with a half-brick in the centre.
- **Fishtail** design is used with fishtail blocks, which have wavy edges. When used in a parquet design of two blocks one way and two others at right angles these create a strong surface.

Below: Pavers with wavy edges create a stronger and less formal surface than those with straight sides. Position spreading plants at the junctions of paths to 'soften' sharp corners and to help create focal points within small areas.

To ensure that the 5cm/2in-thick layer of sharp sand is uniform, select a piece of wood about 15cm/6in deep, 12-18mm/^{1}/$_2$-^{3}/$_4$in thick and slightly wider than the area to be laid and cut the ends so that the centre of the board leaves a 5cm/2in-thick layer of sharp sand when scraped along the base. At this stage, the distance between the surface of the sand and the top of the constraint should be the thickness of the paver less 9mm/^{3}/$_8$in (the amount by which the sand later compacts). Do not stand on the sand.

Start laying the pavers from one end, selecting one of the patterns listed (see left). After the first few rows of pavers are in position, place a long, flat plank on them and progressively move it along. Stand on it to lay the pavers.

To cut blocks, hire a hydraulic stone splitter. Use this with care, wear protective glasses to prevent splinters and dust getting into eyes.

Use a motorized plate compactor (sometimes known as a plate vibrator) to bed the pavers into the sharp sand. Alternatively, on paths use a wide, flat piece of wood and repeatedly tap its surface with a club hammer.

After the pavers have compacted, brush a thin layer of dry, sharp sand over the surface. Then, pass the plate compactor over the entire area again. Add further dry sand and use the compactor again so that the sand works between the pavers; this stage further compacts the base, while sand between the blocks holds them extra firm. Lastly, water the surface with a fine-rose watering-can.

Constructing garden steps

Garden steps should be pleasing to the eye as well as functional, providing an all-weather surface leading from one level to another. There are several elements to consider:

Width of the steps To be practical for two people to walk alongside each other when negotiating steps, they need to be at least 1.3m/4½ft wide. For one person, a width of 75cm/2½ft is sufficient. However, keep the width in proportion to the feature from which the steps lead; a wide patio with a narrow, central flight of steps leading to a lower level will look out of proportion, and vice versa.

Flight That is the complete run of steps.

Tread This should be 30-45cm/12-18in deep and with a fall of 6-12mm/¼-½in from the back to the front edge so that water drains freely.

Riser The vertical distance between steps is usually 10-18cm/4-7in.

Overhang Also known as the 'nosing', this is the area of the edge of the tread which overhangs the riser. It creates a neat and professional appearance and reduces the risk of people tripping over the steps.

Landing Occasionally, extra long areas are left between large flights of steps; when wide, this is an ideal place for positioning plants in pots and tubs. Flights with more than ten steps are best broken up with a landing so that people can rest. It also makes long flights more attractive.

Base stone Positioned at the bottom of a flight of steps and essential where the steps lead to a lawn. If omitted, the grass at the base becomes worn and will be difficult to cut close to the steps. A similar stone can be positioned at the top of a flight. If base and top stones are made slightly wider than the steps, plants in tubs and urns can be positioned on either side.

CALCULATING THE NUMBER OF STEPS

Garden steps must be functional as well as harmonizing with the garden. It is important to ensure that the treads and risers are in proportion with each other.

To assess the number of steps needed, measure the vertical height between the top and bottom of the flight. Divide this by the height of the risers (including the thickness of the treads) to

Right: Log steps with the treads formed of shingle or gravel are ideal in informal gardens; they look especially attractive in spring when edged in daffodils. An alternative method of construction is to have grass forming the treads. However, in winter the surface can be slippery when wet.

CONSTRUCTING CUT-IN STEPS

1 Use strings to mark out the area of the flight, and the positions of each step. Use a spade to cut out the shape of the steps. At the base, excavate 15cm/6in deep.

2 At the base, form a 7.5cm/3in-thick layer of rubble, then cover with sharp sand.

3 Spread mortar over the sand and lay the first paving stone. Check it is level, then, complete the base area.

4 Use bricks to form the riser for the first step. Cement them into position.

5 Form a 5cm/2in-thick layer of broken rubble where the first step is to be positioned, then add and firm sharp sand to the top of the riser (use a long piece of wood to level the surface).

6 Use mortar to secure the first step into position. The following steps are formed in the same way.

TYPES OF STEPS

The range of steps – and materials used in their construction – is wide.

- **Cut-in steps**, built into slopes or banks, are easily made from bricks and paving slabs. Rubble is generally for foundations and mortar to secure them together.

- **Free-standing** steps are constructed on a flat surface to link one level with another. Because these steps are not dug into an existing slope, stronger and more elaborate construction is needed to retain and support them, especially at their sides.

- **Log** steps are popular in rustic and informal situations. They can be used with gravel as well as grass paths. Use logs 10-15cm/4-6in thick. Start from the base of the slope and secure the first log in place with two stout stakes, driven in on the lower side and about 10cm/4in in from each end of the log. Consolidate a level area of gravel behind the log, then install and secure a further log.

- **Grass** steps are picturesque and unusual and can be informal when combined with logs, or given a semi-formal nature when edged with bricks positioned lengthways to the flight of steps. Use a strip of grass 15-38cm/6-15in to form each main tread. Cut the grass regularly to ensure the steps remain attractive.

give the number of treads. The measurements for the base stone (which can be added later) will be in addition to this figure.

Before deciding on the exact measurements, look at paths in other gardens and measure the treads and risers of those that are comfortable to use. If the risers are too high and the treads narrow, the steps will be tiring to climb. Conversely, if the treads are long and the risers shallow, there is an increased chance of tripping over them.

When you have calculated the number and width of the treads, measure back from the top of the slope and mark the position where the steps are to begin.

While assessing the flight, take into account the materials to be used; for example, paving slabs 45cm/18in deep used as a treads will, if a brick riser is positioned on them, create treads 35cm/14in deep, including the overhang. Slabs 60cm/24in deep create treads 50cm/20in deep.

Erecting a trellis to support a climber

Many climbers are self-supporting, but for those that naturally twine or have tendrils or twisting leaf stalks, support from a trellis is essential.

A trellis can be secured to a wall or left free standing so that it forms a screen, perhaps concealing rubbish bins, making a patio secluded or screening a neighbouring garden.

SECURING A TRELLIS TO A WALL

Check that the brickwork or rendering is sound before securing a trellis to a wall. Vigorous climbers have masses of leafy growth which when buffeted by strong wind will soon dislodge poorly secured trelliswork.

Position the trellis against a wall so that its base is 23-30cm/9-12in above the ground. Do not set it directly on the ground, as this encourages the onset of decay. Use a spirit-level to ensure the trellis is upright and level, especially if the ground slopes. Mark on the wall the position of each corner of the trellis, so that later it can be relocated in the same place. Then mark the trellis at the positions where it is to be drilled (usually near the corners), again checking that the brickwork

is sufficiently sound to support it. Place the trellis on the ground or blocks of wood.

Use an ordinary timber drill to make holes in the trellis, taking care not to split the wood by forcing the drill through it too quickly. Slightly countersink the holes so that the heads of the fixing screws will be flush with the surface.

Insert screws into the holes and reposition the trellis against the wall. Gently tap the heads of the screws to mark the drilling positions in the wall. Use a masonry drill to make holes and insert a wall-fixing plug in each one.

Reposition the trellis and insert the screws, tightening each a few turns at a time, so as not to strain the trellis if the wall surface is irregular.

FREE-STANDING TRELLISES

Both diamond- and square-holed prefabricated trellis panels can be bought and secured between strong, 10-15cm/4-6in square, upright posts. Several panels create an attractive screen when clothed with climbers.

Mark a straight line (using a garden line) where the trellis is to be erected. Lay out the posts and

Right: Large-flowered clematis hybrids need the support of a strong trellis well secured to a wall or fence. There are many varieties of these beautiful clematis to choose from; most have 'single' flowers, but a few are 'double'. Their colours range from white to purple and some have a bar of a different colour on each petal.

SECURING A TRELLIS TO A WALL

1 Position the trellis on the wall and with its base above the ground. Use a spirit-level to ensure that the trellis is level. Mark the corners so that later it can be replaced in the right position.
2 Mark the trellis where it is to be drilled.
3 Drill holes in the trellis. Countersink them to ensure the head of each screw will be flush with the surface of the wood.
4 Position the trellis on the wall, insert the screws into the holes and gently tap to mark their positions on the wall. Drill the wall, using a masonry drill, and insert wall fixings into the holes. Replace the trellis and screw into place. Initially, only partially tighten the screws; when they are all in position, tighten them fully.

MAKING A JOINTED TRELLIS

Prefabricated square-hole trelliswork invariably has cross-members nailed on top of vertical timbers. However, when making a trellis at home, you can recess the timbers into each other by using cross-halving joints. This type of trellis is ideal as a free-standing unit, but don't use it against a wall unless you can create space behind it for shoots to clamber around.

- Use 2.5cm/1in-square pieces of wood and cut half of them to the desired width. If the trellis is to be square, place all the timbers together, side by side, and secure with adhesive tape. Use sufficient timbers to create 18-23cm/7-9in squares.

- Next, use a ruler to mark the wood 2.5cm/1in in from each end and then at equal spaces between, remembering to allow the width of the crosswise timber at each position. Use a try-square to mark around each timber to ensure the joints will be perfectly square.

- Use a saw to cut half-way through each joint, and a sharp chisel to cut out half the width of the wood.

- Place the timbers on a large, flat surface and slot them together. If some joints are tight, use a coarse file to remove some wood.

- When they fit, smear the surface of each joint with a waterproof outdoor glue and use 2.5cm/1in-long galvanized nails to secure them. If, after insertion, a nail is slightly too long, place the protruding point on a piece of metal and hit the head with a hammer.

trellis on the ground and mark the positions where you will secure the posts in the ground.

Square-holed trellis invariably has a timber frame and this can be nailed directly to the posts. Trellis formed of thin wood with diamond-shaped holes may not have a wood frame and

you will therefore need to construct one from 2.5cm/1in-square timber.

Dig holes 38-45cm/15-18in deep. The top of the trellis should be 12-25mm/^{1}/$_2$-1in below each post's top, and the base 7.5-25cm/3-10in above the soil. If it rests on the ground it will rot.

Use guy-lines or long pieces of wood to hold the posts upright while the trellis is nailed to them. Adjust the depths of the holes if necessary to ensure the trellis is level. After checking the position of the trellis and using a spirit-level to ensure posts are upright, pour concrete around their bases. Leave the supports in place for two or three days until the concrete is firm.

Alternatively, you can use metal post supports. These are formed of a long spike with a square socket at its top into which a wooden post is slotted and secured. Drive a metal support into the ground by slotting a short off-cut of post timber into the metal socket and hitting it with a large hammer. When at the right depth, remove the off-cut and slot in and secure a post.

Nail a cap to the top of each post. This helps to prevent water entering the end grain and causing wood to rot. Also, if the style of trellis permits, nail a strip of 5cm/2in-wide and 18mm/^{3}/$_4$in-thick timber along its top. Use a plane to slightly slope the top edges of this wooden strip – it makes it look more professional and helps to shed water.

Constructing a screen from rustic poles

Few garden features create such nostalgia and old-fashioned country-garden charm as those made from rustic poles. They can be used to great effect for pergolas, screens, pillars and tripods, which create ideal homes for many climbers, including roses, honeysuckle and clematis.

CHOOSING POLES

Most rustic poles are larch or pine. They are available in varying thicknesses, usually 7.5-10cm/3-4in, occasionally 13cm/5in. For constructing pergolas, poles with a uniform width of 7.5-10cm/3-4in are best, while thicker poles are better for pillars. For rustic arches over a 1.2m/4ft-wide path, poles 5-7.5cm/2-3in are suitable (poles that are too thick would dominate the feature).

Poles are mostly sold with their bark attached and to many gardeners this is part of their charm. Poles peeled of bark and pressure treated with a wood preservative are also available. These are usually sold in 2.4m/8ft lengths and are generally 5-7.5cm/2-3in wide.

JOINING POLES

Arches and other features made from rustic poles can be bought in parts ready for assembly; all that is then needed is to nail or bolt them together. However, it is not difficult to construct your own arch, pergola or screen from poles bought from a garden centre or timber merchant.

The joints used to secure one pole to another are simple to make – and there are few of them. The only tools you will need are a panel-saw, sharp wood-chisel, and a coping-saw or pad-saw.

Galvanized nails can usually be driven directly into the wood, but if the top piece of wood shows any sign of splitting as you drive in a nail, it is safer first to drill a hole the same diameter as the nail. Do not drill the lower piece of wood.

If you are using bolts to secure pieces of wood, you will need to drill both pieces with holes slightly larger than the shank of the bolt.

Cross-halving joints are used to secure cross members together. This involves cutting away half of each pole so that the two parts fit snugly. Mark the width of the join and use a panel-saw to make two cuts halfway through the wood on

JOINING RUSTIC POLES

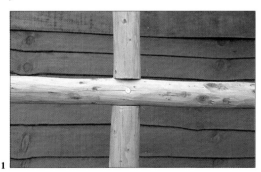
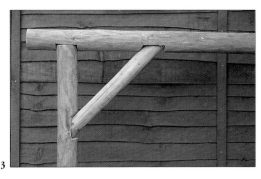

1 Cross-halving joints are used to secure cross members; cut away half of the diameter of each pole, so that they fit snugly. Use a galvanized nail to secure them together.
2 Bracing corners is important; the simplest method is to cut the end of the diagonal bracing pole at a 45° angle.
3 An alternative way to secure corners is to cut a notch out of the horizontal and upright poles. Use galvanized nails to secure them.
4 When securing a horizontal pole to the top of an upright, cut one-third through the horizonal pole. Cut the sides of the joint with a saw, and use a chisel to remove the wood between them. Secure the poles with galvanized nails.

ROSES FOR RUSTIC PILLARS AND TRIPODS

Pillars and tripods made from rustic poles can be used to support climbing plants, and roses look especially effective. Tripods create a firm support and are well suited to windy areas. Rose varieties suitable for growing on pillars and tripods include:

- **'Aloha':** A Modern Shrub Rose with large, cupped, clear pink, fragrant flowers.

- **'Compassion':** A Modern Climber with salmon pink, Hybrid Tea-like flowers amid glossy, dark green foliage.

- **'Galway Bay':** A Modern Climber with large, Hybrid Tea-like, salmon pink flowers.

- **'Golden Showers':** A Modern Climber with large, semi-double, golden yellow flowers that fade to cream.

- **'New Dawn':** A Modern Climber with silvery blush pink flowers that deepen towards the centre and that have a fresh, fruity fragrance.

- **'Pink Perpetué':** A Modern Climber with medium-sized, bright rose-pink flowers with a slight fragrance.

- **'White Cockade':** A Modern Climber with fragrant, pure white, beautifully shaped blooms with a Hybrid Tea-like shape.

- **'Zéphirine Drouhin':** A Bourbon Climber with fragrant, deep rose-pink flowers.

each pole. Then use a sharp wood-chisel to chop out the wood. If you cut the joint halfway through in several places between the two initial cuts you will find it easier to chisel out the wood.

Bracing corners with diagonal poles provides extra strength. The easiest and simplest way to do this is to cut the ends of the bracing pole at 45° angles, so that when positioned the ends fit flush against the vertical and horizontal poles.

Joining a horizontal rail and upright post is best achieved by cutting a V-shaped notch a third of the way through the side of the upright. Then cut a V-shape on the end of the horizontal pole and use a galvanized nail to secure them.

Securing a horizontal pole to the top of an upright pole can be done by cutting the horizontal pole one-third of the way through so that it sits on top of the upright. Drill the horizontal pole to prevent splitting then secure the poles with nails.

Alternatively, cut and file the top of the vertical pole so that it is cupped and place the cross member in it. The advantage of this joint is that it does not weaken the horizontal pole.

SECURING POLES IN THE GROUND

The bases of rustic poles soon decay if they are in holes full of water throughout much of the year. If the soil is light, sandy and well drained this risk is diminished, but in clay soil careful preparation of the hole and the base of the pole is essential.

Dig a hole about 75cm/30in deep and fill the base with 15cm/6in of rubble. Remove bark from the lower 60cm/24in of pole and stand it in plant-friendly wood preservative for twenty-four hours. Then, stand the pole in the hole and fill around it with compacted rubble. This allows water to drain from around the post's base.

Alternatively, after digging a hole and preparing the pole as detailed above, stand the pole in a drainage pipe (ideally one that fits the pole tightly. Then stand the pipe and pole in the hole and compact rubble around them.

Right: Rustic trellises support plants, create an attractive and natural-looking screen, and help to fuse one part of the garden with another. As well as providing attractive homes for climbing plants, they can also be used to support hanging-baskets, which create additional colour and interest throughout summer.

Constructing a screen-block wall

Screen-block walling is formed of large, pre-cast concrete blocks 30cm/12in square and 10cm/4in thick. Some blocks create a pattern within themselves, while others require combinations of four blocks. The best way to judge the pattern that suits you is to have a look in a builder's yard or at completed walls in other gardens. Remember that blocks cannot be cut, and there are neither half nor quarter sizes.

Unlike ordinary bricks, which are bonded by being overlapped, screen walling blocks are stacked one on top of the other. This does not give the wall a great deal of strength and supporting piers are therefore needed every 3m/10ft along a wall. These supports can be formed from bricks, or from piers (known as pilasters) made of pre-cast, hollow blocks, which can be stacked and held together with mortar. The blocks can also be reinforced with iron rods to give additional strength.

BUILDING A SCREEN-BLOCK WALL

The construction method described here is for using pre-formed blocks to construct the piers (pilasters). The first step is to make strong footings for the piers and wall.

Dig a trench 30cm/12in deep and 38cm/15in wide. Form a 15-20cm/6-8in-thick layer of compacted rubble in the base, then pour in a 10cm/4in-thick layer of one part cement, two and a half of sharp sand and three and a half of 18mm/³⁄₄in aggregates.

Walls over 90cm/3ft high need additional support. Provide this by cementing a reinforcing rod into the central hole created by the pilaster blocks. Insert the base of the reinforcing rod into the concrete base before it sets; ensure that it is upright and half the width of the block away from the end. If each end of the wall has a pilaster, assess the distance between the reinforcing rods, allowing for an additional 12mm/³⁄₄in between each block to be placed in between.

Each pilaster block is 20cm/8in deep and therefore before constructing the wall and deciding on its height, draw a detailed plan so that when the wall is complete the top of the pier will be level with the blocks. Often – and especially if the wall's base is slightly below ground-level –

CONSTRUCTING A SCREEN-BLOCK WALL

1 At the base, lay two rows of bricks; this looks better than bedding the screen-blocks directly on the base.
2 Ensure pillars constructed next to walls are secured to them every 15-20cm/6-8in.
3 Use pieces of galvanized wire to 'tie' the screen-blocks to the pillar, at every course (30cm/12in).
4 Regularly check that the screen-blocks are upright. Use a long builder's spirit-level as this is more accurate than a short one.
5 Also, regularly check that the pillars are level.
6 Position capping stones along the top of the screen-blocks, as well as on the pillars. Cement them into position. These help to prevent water penetrating the brickwork.

Above: Screen-blocks can be used to create an attractive background for plants. Additionally, a screen-block wall helps to separate one part of a garden from another, and if positioned on the prevailing wind side can be used to protect tender plants. The background can be further enhanced by allowing climbers such as clematis to scale the wall.

bricks or concrete blocks are used as a base. Allow for their depth when judging the height.

Start at one end and, using one part cement and five of building sand, set a couple of pilaster blocks in position. If the base is formed of concrete blocks or bricks, lay these also, up to the level of the base of the screen blocks. If the other end is formed of a pier of pilaster blocks, cement these into position too. Use a spirit-level and line to check that the piers and bricks are upright and in a straight line. As the piers are constructed, pour mortar inside the central hole.

Cement the screen blocks into position, forming an even bed of mortar – about 12mm/¹/₂in thick – under and around each block. While the mortar is still relatively soft, tidy up the joints between the screen blocks by using a trowel or

running the end of a small piece of hosepipe along them. When you reach the top, cement copings to the wall and piers.

Do not put any pressure on the wall for at least two weeks after construction. Remember that the wall does not have the constructional strength of one made of traditional bricks.

If the wall is to be longer than 3m/10ft, you can use special pilaster blocks with slots on either side so that you can slot the screen blocks into them. If the wall turns a corner, use pilaster blocks with recessed channels on adjacent sides.

USING ORNAMENTAL BRICKS AS PILLARS

Although more expensive to construct, walls formed of a combination of bricks and screen-block walling can be very attractive, especially if you use decorative-faced blocks instead of normal bricks to form the piers and a low wall at the base of the screen-blocks. These decorative-faced blocks are sold in a wide range of sizes; usually 10cm/4in wide, up to 45cm/18in long and 5-10cm/2-4in thick. They are strong enough to support a wall up to 1.8m/6ft high.

Construct piers 30-38cm/12-15in square at the wall ends, unless one of the piers is butted on to an existing house wall, in which case make it 15-20cm/6-8in wide and 30-38cm/12-15in deep. (Changing the size in this way helps to blend the screen block wall with the house, and reduce the visual dominance of the pier next to the wall.)

The foundations will need to be slightly thicker than for blockwork pilasters – about 15cm/6in deep. Walls up to 3m/10ft long will need only a pier at either end. For longer walls, introduce additional piers. Start by constructing one of the piers. Then build a low wall between this pier and the position of the next one. Allow 30cm/12in for each screen block, plus 12mm/¹/₂in between them for mortar.

To produce a professional appearance, centre the low wall on each pier, so that the edges of the pier can be clearly seen. Build up the wall to the desired height.

Cement the screen blocks into position before constructing the next pier. This will allow you to make slight positional adjustments if your calculations were less than completely accurate.

Build the second pier, centring it on the low wall and screening blocks. Finally, add copings to the wall and piers.

CONSTRUCTING A DUSTBIN SCREEN

Dustbin screens are quickly and easily made from screen-block walling. They do not have to encircle dustbins totally; screening on two sides is usually all that is necessary.

- A strong foundation is essential and this can be created in the same way as described for screen-block walls. Alternatively, cement two or three 60cm/24in-square paving slabs on a firm base.

- Cement three rows of screen-block walling around the base or on the foundations. It is usually necessary to turn a corner but you can do this without using a corner pier. Instead, as you position and cement each row, use short pieces of galvanized wire, bedded into the mortar, to link the tiers.

- Coping is not needed, although it will enhance the feature.

Erecting a wooden fence

Fences are essential to all gardens; they separate one garden from another, create privacy, contain family pets and keep out vagrant animals. As well as being functional, however, they should also be pleasing to the eye and suit the style of the garden. For example, wattle hurdling is ideal in rural areas, but would look wrong in towns where boarded fences may be more suitable.

The legal maximum height of a fence depends on local rules and regulations; if you are in doubt consult your local planning department.

Incidentally, there is no height limit on hedges, so if you need or want an extra-high barrier, you could plant a hedge about 90cm/3ft from the fence. This will ensure that the area is animal proof as well as creating a high barrier.

ERECTING PANEL FENCING

The first task when erecting a fence is to clear the site and to check the position.

Mark the line of the fence using a garden line, then dig out the first post hole to a depth of 60cm/24in. Make it about 30cm/12in square, or even just the width of the spade's blade. (If you make it too large you will need more concrete.)

Put 5-7.5cm/2-3in of clean rubble in the hole's base, then compact it. Stand the post in position and prop it vertically by using long, thin pieces of wood as guys. Use a spirit-level to ensure the post is upright. Place the first panel in position, standing it on two bricks (one at each end) so that it is 5cm/2in above the ground. This will help to prevent the base of the panel rotting.

Check that the top of the post is 18-25mm/³/₄-1in above the panel's top. Adjust the height of the post by removing or placing rubble under it.

Remove the panel and place it on the ground, so that the bottom edge is level with the post. Mark the position of the second post, remove the panel and dig a hole to the same dimensions as those of the first.

Place and compact rubble in the hole and position the next post as before. Ensure that its top is 18-25mm/³/₄-1in above the panel's top. Put the panel in position, standing it on bricks. Check that the posts are upright and, using galvanized nails, nail the panel to the posts.

Re-check that the posts are upright. Then,

Right: The tops of fences can be made more attractive by securing trelliswork to them. These can be integrated when the fence is constructed (as shown here), when longer supporting posts are installed, or added later and nailed or screwed to the existing posts. The Mountain Clematis (*Clematis montana*), seen here, harmonizes with the wallflowers at the fence's base.

ERECTING PANEL FENCING

1 Use strings to mark out the position of the fence. Start from one end; if a corner post is being installed, mark the positions of both posts. Dig the hole about 60cm/24in deep and 30cm/12in square.
2 Place clean rubble in the hole, then position the post; ensure it is vertical by using a spirit-level.
3 To gauge the distance between each post, rest the panel on the ground. Dig a hole and insert the post.
4 Stand the panel on bricks and use galvanized nails to secure it to the post. Use long pieces of wood to guy the post upright. When all of the panels are nailed to the posts, concrete them into position. Before the concrete sets, re-check that the posts are upright.

using a mixture of one part cement to three of ballast, pour 15cm/6in of concrete around each post's base. Slope the top of the concrete in each hole away from the post to prevent water collecting around the wood. Use pieces of wood to hold the post upright while the concrete dries. When dry, fill over the concrete with soil.

Use the same sequence – laying a panel on the ground to estimate the post's position, digging, checking heights and concreting – for all the other posts.

When all posts are in position and the cement has dried, add a cap to each post. This makes the fence look more professional and also prevents water entering the top of the post.

An alternative to adding a cap to each post is to cut them at a slight angle. However, this is more difficult than buying ready-made caps and just nailing them (with two galvanized nails in each one) to the tops of posts.

The life of a fence can be extended if it is painted annually. Also, as fencing ages it assumes a bland colour, but a coat of presevative creates a warmer and more attractive appearance.

RANGE OF FENCES

There are many and varied types of fencing panel available, including several types that are easy to construct. The range includes:

- **Close-boarded** This type is usually constructed on site by fencing companies and creates a strong boundary. Vertical posts are positioned 1.8-3.6m/6-12ft apart and arris rails (longitudinal, usually triangular-section rails on which the overlapping vertical planks will be nailed) are inserted into them. The posts are then concreted into position and, when secure, boards are nailed to them. Eventually, arris rails rot at their ends, but these can be repaired by the use of proprietary fittings.

- **Overlapping, wavy edged boards** These are sold as panels in a range of sizes, from 90cm/3ft to 1.8m/6ft high and usually 1.8m/6ft long. Horizontal wavy-edged boards are nailed to a framework to form a panel, which is then nailed to vertical posts. This fencing has a less formal appearance than close-boarded types.

- **Interwoven panels** These have a rustic look; thin, horizontal strips of pine or larch, about 7.5cm/3in wide, are woven with vertical strips to create a basket-like pattern. Like other panels, they are available in a range of sizes, and are secured to vertical posts.

- **Wattle hurdling** This has a country-like appearance; thin strips of wood are woven to form panels about 1.8m/6ft long and in several heights. To continue the informality, the panels are then secured to rustic poles.

- **Picket fences** These have both formality and a rural appearance and are ideal for creating elegant and traditional-looking boundaries in towns and villages. They are constructed on site; arris rails are secured to upright posts and then vertical pieces of wood, usually 5-6cm/2-2^1/$_2$in wide and known as pales, are nailed to the arris rails. Gaps of about 5cm/2in are left between the pales, and their tops are either rounded or cut to a point. These fences are usually no more than 1.2m/4ft high and look especially attractive when painted white although they are some times left unpainted.

- **Chestnut paling** This rustic fencing is formed of split chestnut stakes strung about 10cm/4in apart between galvanized wires at their tops and base. It is sold in heights ranging from 90cm/3ft to 1.8m/6ft, and in rolls about 9m/30ft long. It is secured to stout poles at either end with intermediate ones to prevent sagging.

- **Ranch-style fencing** This is increasingly popular and creates a bright, formal fence for towns and villages. It is formed of pieces of 12-18mm/^{1}/$_2$-^{3}/$_4$in-thick wood, 7.5-15cm/3-6in wide, nailed horizontally to well-secured posts. Gaps of 7.5-10cm/3-4in are left between the planks, which are usually painted white.
  These fences range in height from 90cm/3ft to 1.8m/6ft. For extra privacy, planks can be secured to both sides of the upright posts, with the gaps between the planks on one side being covered by planks secured to the other side.

Making a picnic table

Garden furniture is an essential part of outdoor leisure activities. The range of tables, chairs and benches which you can buy is wide, but it is also possible to construct your own. This picnic table is a robust model which combines a table with two benches.

Making this picnic table is not difficult and requires neither a lot of carpentry skills, nor a wide range of tools. It is best to buy softwood (hardwood is a possibility, but is more expensive) planed to the size required. Then all that you need to do is to cut it to length and to secure the parts together.

You will need a saw; an electric drill; a countersink, to enable screw heads to be finished flush with the wood's surface; a bradawl to mark where holes are to be drilled; a screwdriver; sandpaper, to smooth sawn edges, and two spanners (which could be the adjustable type), to tighten the bolts and nuts. You may also find it useful to have a drill stand, which secures the drill in a vertical position and enables you to drill holes at right angles to the wood's surface. This ensures that bolts, when inserted, fit easily.

CONSTRUCTING A PICNIC TABLE

The ideal length of the table and benches is likely to be between 1.2m/4ft and 1.8m/6ft; lengths over 1.5m/5ft are best supported on six legs and for that reason the bench described here is 1.2m/4ft long.

The table top is formed from five 1.2m/4ft-long planks, each 8cm/3$\frac{1}{2}$in wide and 30mm/1$\frac{1}{4}$in thick. Two pieces of wood, each 53cm/21in long and 30mm/1$\frac{1}{4}$in square, are used to secure the table planks together. They are screwed to the planks, 7.5cm/3in from their ends. This creates a strong top that will even take the weight of someone sitting on it!

Each of the two benches is formed of two planks, both 1.2m/4ft long, 7.5cm/3in wide and 30mm/1$\frac{1}{4}$in thick. These are held together by two pieces of wood, 21cm/8$\frac{1}{2}$in long and 30mm/1$\frac{1}{4}$in square, which are screwed to the planks, about 11cm/4$\frac{1}{4}$in from their ends.

The legs and cross supports resemble an A-frame with the top cut off. Each of the A-frames is formed of two pieces of wood, 75cm/30in long, 10cm/4in wide and 30mm/1$\frac{1}{4}$in thick; the base

MAKING A PICNIC TABLE

1 First, use bolts to secure together the four pieces of wood that form each A-frame.
2 Use rust-resistant screws to secure two pieces of wood to the undersides of the planks that form the table-top.
3 Similarly, screw two pieces of wood to the undersides of the two planks that form each bench.
4 Turn the table-top upside down and bolt an A-frame assembly to each end.
5 Stand the A-frames – and table-top – upright and bolt the seat assemblies into place.
6 Turn the complete assembly upside down to screw a cross-bracing piece of wood to the underside of the table-top and A-frames.

Above: Picnic tables are an essential part of outdoor living. After construction, thoroughly paint the wood several times and during winter stand each of the legs on a brick and cover the entire table and legs with polythene.

of the frame is a piece of timber 1.3m/50in long, 10cm/4in wide and 30mm/1¼in thick. These are positioned so that they support the benches 38cm/15in above the ground. The top of each A-frame is formed of a piece of wood 53cm/21in long, 2¼in wide and 30mm/1¼in thick. These provide a support for the table top.

Each A-frame is secured to the table top as well as to the benches, with angled wooden struts – 55cm/22in long, 6cm/2½in wide and 30mm/1¼in thick – securing the lower part of the A-frame to the underside of the table top.

ASSEMBLING THE TABLE

The first task is to assemble the two A-frames. At each of the 'corners', use two 5mm/³⁄₁₆in coach bolts in holes spaced about 5cm/2in apart. Use

large washers to prevent the nuts tearing into the wood. Before fully tightening the nuts, ensure all the coach bolts, washers and nuts are in position.

Assemble the top of the table by screwing the two 53cm/21in-long supports to the five 1.2m/4ft long planks. Space the planks 18mm/³⁄₄in apart and position each support 7.5cm/3in from the ends. Use galvanized screws.

Next, screw the tops of each bench unit to the 21cm/8½in-long pieces, leaving 36mm/1½in between each plank and positioning the support 7.5cm/3in from each end. Again, use galvanized screws.

The first step in securing these three units together is to turn the table top upside down. Then, bolt an A-frame to each end. Again, use 5mm/³⁄₁₆in coach bolts, one for each leg. Turn the bench the correct way up and bolt each bench unit to the A-frame – one at each end. You will then need to again turn the bench over so that you can screw the two cross-bracing pieces of wood to the underneath of the table as well as to the A-frame.

When the table is complete, paint it with a wood preservative and repeat this every spring. During winter, stand the table on bricks and cover it with polythene.

As well as buying wood from a timber supplier, it is also possible to buy picnic tables in 'flat packs' at garden centres and do-it-yourself stores. Indeed, for many people this is the most efficient way to buy a picnic table.

GARDEN SEATS

These are essential in any garden as resting places and as vantage points from which to admire the results of your work. Buy ready-made benches or construct your own.

- **Construct two brick piers,** about 45cm/18in high and 30cm/12in square, set 1.2-1.5m/4-5ft apart. Use masonry fixings to secure a 30cm/12in-long piece of 36-50mm/1½-2in-thick, 10cm/4in-wide timber to the top; strong planks that form the bench can then be secured to these pieces.

- **Old railway sleepers** create ideal benches in wild gardens; ensure they are well secured to a wood or brick base.

- **A wheeled bench,** with two wheels at one end and two legs at the other, creates an interesting feature. It has the advantage of being easily moved under cover during winter, and its position can be adjusted to gain the most sun in summer.

31

Forming a base for a shed or summerhouse

To ensure long life for a shed or summerhouse it is essential that it is erected on a firm base. If, after construction, the base subsides, it will direct stress over one area and can cause the framework to distort and the roof to buckle. A flow of air under the structure's base helps to prevent the onset of decay if it becomes wet.

The floor of a shed or summerhouse is formed of boards (usually tongued and grooved to add strength and to eliminate draughts entering the building) nailed to timbers 5-6cm/2-2½in deep and 25-36mm/1-1½in wide, depending on the size of the building. The floor is then supported on wooden bearers, again ranging in size according to the size of the building, but usually from 5cm/2in square to 5cm/2in deep and 6cm/2½in wide. These timbers must be strong and have been pressure treated with a preservative to ensure long life. Check, too, that they are not warped and that they are of even thickness.

Enough bearers are needed to enable them to be spaced 38-45cm/15-18in apart; and they should be positioned at right angles to the structural timbers that hold the floor together.

PREPARING THE BASE

The base must be firm and level. A firm base ensures that the building will not subside, while a level base enables doors and windows to be opened properly.

If the soil is firm and has not been disturbed through digging up tree roots, you may be able to position the bearers directly on the ground. However, it is safer to create a firm base to prevent the risk of the building collapsing.

Spaced out paving slabs are an economical way to create a base. Flat-surfaced (not ribbled) paving slabs 60cm/24in square should be positioned 38cm/15in apart. You can use slightly larger paving slabs, but these are more difficult to handle on your own.

Measure and mark the corners of the area needed for the base. Measure across the diagonals (the distances should be equal) to check that the sides are parallel and the corners square.

Rake the area, firm the soil and use a spirit-level on top of a long, straight-edged board to check the overall level. Spread a 25-36mm/ 1-1½in-thick layer of sharp sand over the area –

Right: Summerhouses and ornamental sheds can be used as focal points in a garden, as well as for storing garden chairs and collapsible tables and tools and other equipment.

ERECTING A SUMMERHOUSE OR SHED

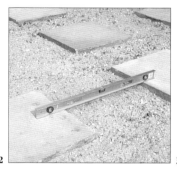

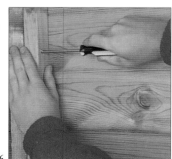

1

2

3

4

5

6

1 Use large, smooth-surfaced paving slabs to form a base and use a spirit-level to check that each one is level.
2 Continue laying paving slabs, checking that each one is level and that they are all level with each other.
3 Place bearers in position, at right angles to the main supporting framework at the floor's base. Check that they are level.
4 Thoroughly paint all parts of the building with a wood preservative.
5 Put the floor in place and again check the levels.
6 Screw or bolt the sides together.

1½-2in-thick layer of sharp sand over the base. Cement flat-surfaced, 60cm/24in-square slabs into position by dabbing five cement blobs (about 5cm/2in high and 7.5cm/3in wide) on the sand and placing a slab on top. Use a spirit-level to check the slabs are level. Leave about 12mm/½in between each slab and later brush a dry mixture of one part cement and three of sand into the cracks between them.

The main problem with this type of base is that water that runs under the shed floor tends to linger there causing damp problems, as there is no space into which it can drain.

ERECTING THE BUILDING

Before erecting the building, paint the inside and outside walls with a wood preservative. Place the bearers on the base, then position the floor on the bearers. Sometimes, if the shed is large, or if a verandah is added to a summerhouse, the base is in two parts. If this is the case, nail a piece of thin wood along the side to hold the parts together during construction.

Put one of the ends in its place and either prop it so that it is vertical or ask a companion to hold it. Then position one of the long sides on the base and either bolt or screw these two sides together. Don't fully tighten bolts or screws at this stage. Next, position and secure the other end in the same way. The last side to be secured should be the one with the windows and door. Check that the sides sit evenly on the base and that the door opens and closes without touching its frame before you tighten up screws and bolts. Use 5cm/2in-long galvanized nails to nail the base of each wall to the floor – knock in the nails at a distance of 20cm/8in from each other.

Some sheds – especially large ones – have roof trusses, which you will need to put in place before you attempt to add the roof. It is not an easy job to put the roof on and you will need the help of a strong companion and two step-ladders. If there is no space on one side of the building, you will need to lift up the two parts of the roof from the same side. If this is so, place the nearside one on first, so that the other side can be slid over it. Secure it in position with the fixings provided.

Covering the roof with felt and glazing the windows are necessary both initially and for maintenance and are described on pages 34-5.

and to 10cm/4in beyond. Again, use a rake to level the area. Position a slab at each corner and use a spirit-level to check their individual levels, and that they are level with each other. Add further slabs and ensure they are level.

Alternatively, you could construct a continuous base. However, although this will be strong, it is expensive and time consuming to construct. Mark out and level the area and form a 36-50mm/

ASSESSING LEVELS

Judging levels in a garden over distances up to 2.4m/8ft is fairly easy; all that you need is a spirit-level and a long, straight-edged plank. Above this distance, knock short stakes into the ground and progressively work along in 2.4m/8ft lengths.

For long distances apart you can use a hosepipe to assess differences in height as follows:

● Insert a piece of clear plastic tubing into each end of a hosepipe, so that about 20cm/8in protrudes. Mark each piece of tubing about 5cm/2in from its end.

● Tie one end of the hosepipe to a short stake at the highest point, so that the end is 30cm/12in above the ground. Then take the other end to the position to be assessed and fill the hosepipe with water.

● Lift the lower end until the water in the hosepipe is at the same distance from the pipe's ends. Measure the distance from the ground to assess the difference in height between the two points.

Maintaining sheds and summerhouses

Sheds and summerhouses made of wood need regular attention to prevent them becoming unsightly and rotting prematurely. The amount and nature of the work needed to maintain a wooden shed or summerhouse depends on the type of wood. Teak, which is prohibitively expensive for most people, has a long life, while western red cedar is also resistant to rot. All you should need to do to maintain these woods is to rub down the wood with sandpaper, wipe the surface with a clean cloth and coat with teak or cedar oil.

The wood most commonly used in garden buildings is deal. This is an all-embracing term for a type of softwood timber and now mainly refers to wood from firs and pines; it is soft and vulnerable to decay. Before buying a building made from deal, check that it has been pressure treated with a wood preservative; this will add a few years to the building's life.

Even if the wood has been pressure treated, it is a good idea to paint all surfaces with a preservative before you assemble the parts, so that you can get into all the nooks are crannies, especially at the ends, which later may be hidden.

RENEWING ROOFING FELT

The life of roofing felt is usually no more than eight years – sometimes less if it is thin and the shed is in strong sunlight. Strong winds also rip thin felt, especially at the edges and if the overlaps were not properly glued or if the barge board (which secures the ends) was loosely nailed in position.

Small holes and tears can be patched by cutting a piece of felt and sticking it over the area; but do not expect this to last more than a couple of seasons. If the damage is extensive, do not try to patch it up, as leaks soon cause the wood underneath to rot. Wait for a dry day, then pull off all the old felt, as well as the large-headed galvanized nails used to secure it.

Check that the planks of wood (or plywood) that form the roof are secure; if they are decaying, replace them. Paint the roof with a wood preservative.

Buy a fresh roll of heavy-duty roofing felt. This is sold in varying widths; you will need to decide whether to buy enough to provide two strips for each side, with a narrow strip to go over the ridge and to overlap the two side pieces, or to have just one piece on each side, and a further piece of the same width over the ridge. Measure the width of the roof and allow about 15cm/6in for each overlap and a further 7.5cm/3in for each of the eaves.

When cold, felt cracks and readily tears so keep it indoors for a couple of days before using it, and choose a warm day for the job. Cut a piece of felt to the length of the roof, plus 10cm/4in at either end. Roll it up loosely. With great care – and help from a friend – place the felt on one side of the roof and position it so that it overlaps the eave by 7.5cm/3in and each end by 10cm/4in. Then use galvanized, large-headed, 12-18mm/$^1\!/_2$-$^3\!/_4$in-long nails (known as clouts) to secure the felt to the roof. Knock them in 15cm/6in apart and 36-50mm/$1^1\!/_2$-2in from the upper edge of the felt. Fold over the felt at the eave and nail it to the roof's edge. It may be necessary to trim it back – but ensure it allows water to drip off, rather than running back on to the shed's side. Do not secure the two ends at this stage.

Right: When selecting a garden shed or summerhouse, choose one that suits the garden and, perhaps, fits into a small area. Hexagonal summerhouses create interesting features and because windows can be fitted into doors as well as front-facing sides, plenty of light can enter the building.

RENEWING ROOFING FELT

1   2   3

1 Use a claw hammer to remove the large headed, galvanized nails (clouts) that secured the old felt.
2 Position the first strip of roofing felt, so that the lower side overlaps an eave by about 7.5cm/3in. Then, use clouts to secure it on the upper edge.
3 Where a strip of roofing felt overlaps another, coat the area with a roofing adhesive.

REPAIRING A BROKEN WINDOW

At some time, windows in sheds are sure to be broken. Replace the glass as soon as possible, but make a temporary repair immediately.

Remove the broken glass and cut a piece of plywood or stiff cardboard to fit the area. Then, stretch a double layer of polythene (a black dust-bin liner is ideal) over the plywood. Secure it in place by using several wood battens, each 15-20cm/6-8in long, 12-18mm/¹/₂-³/₄in thick and 5cm/2in wide, in which you have partially knocked two 36mm/1¹/₂in-long nails. Position these battens over the polythene – and the wood around the window – and knock the nails about 6mm/¹/₄in into the wood, or until they feel secure, leaving the heads exposed.

Have a piece of glass cut to size. Use an old wood chisel to remove old putty and pull out old sprigs or glazing pins that were used to secure the glass. When clear and clean, coat the wood with a preservative.

Roll a piece of putty into a sausage about 12mm/¹/₂in thick and bed it into the wood by pressing with a thumb. Create a uniform bed of putty all the way around the wood. Position the glass in the frame and carefully press the edges of the glass so that they rest on a uniform bed of putty. It may be necessary to go around the edges six or more times. Use a putty knife or a wide-bladed wood chisel to cut off excess putty.

Finally, use a small hammer to knock in four brass sprigs to secure the glass. Knock a sprig about 5cm/2in from the top and the same distance from the bottom, on each side. If you do not have a small hammer, position a pair of pliers between the hammer and sprig.

Secure a similar piece of felt on the other side of the roof in the same way. Next, cover the ridge with felt. Use a strip that straddles the ridge and overlaps the two side pieces by 15cm/6in. Mark the overlap on the side pieces and coat the surface in roofing adhesive. Use the clouts to secure the felt at 7.5-10cm/3-4in intervals.

At the ends – and especially at the corners – carefully fold over the felt and nail it at 7.5cm/3in intervals to secure it to the gable ends. Usually, there are barge boards and these should finally be nailed in place.

REPLACING A BROKEN WINDOW

1 Wear strong gloves when removing broken glass from a window. For extra safety, also wear protective glasses.
2 Remove the old putty, then paint the wooden framework. Use a putting knife to spread an even line of putty around the frame.
3 Place the new glass in position and press its edges so that it beds into the putty. Use four brass sprigs to hold the glass in place.

SOIL CULTIVATION

The regular and routine preparation of land to enable plants to be grown and seeds sown is a major aspect of gardening. Digging the soil in late autumn or early winter is part of this routine and one that cannot be neglected, especially when preparing land for the creation of new borders for shrubs, annuals or herbaceous plants. Vegetable plots also need yearly digging, especially if the land is heavy.

The installation of land drains can be essential when making a new garden or, perhaps, improving and renovating an established one. The careful selection of tools such as spades, forks, rakes and hoes also makes a major contribution to happy and easy gardening; they should not be awkward to handle or too heavy.

Single-digging

It may appear anomalous that plants in the wild grow from one year to another without the soil in which they are growing being dug annually, whereas the ground for vegetables and summer-flowering bedding plants requires yearly digging. Part of this conundrum is explained by the fact that gardeners expect a more colour-packed display or a greater concentration of food plants than that occurring in the wild.

A few soil-care schemes have been introduced to enable gardeners to forgo regular digging and although for short periods and on light soils these have been successful, most soils – and especially heavy clay ones – will benefit from annual digging.

Digging aerates soil, improves its drainage, buries annual weeds and exposes the surface to weathering that breaks down large lumps. It also enables decayed compost and manure to be mixed into the ground. Additionally, the larvae of some soil pests, such as cockchafer grubs, are exposed to frost and birds.

Digging is best performed between autumn and mid-winter, whenever soil is workable and has not been saturated by winter rains, and while there is time for frost to break it down by spring. Light, sandy soils can be dug later than clay types; they are naturally better aerated than clay and therefore nutrients in manure or compost are soon leached by winter rains. Dig light soils in late winter or early spring.

The two main methods of digging are single-digging and double-digging. Single-digging involves cultivating soil to the depth of a single spade blade (25-30cm/10-12in), while double-digging is to twice that depth (see pages 40-1).

SINGLE-DIGGING

The first task is to dig a trench 25-30cm/10-12in deep and 30cm/12in wide at one end of the plot. Barrow the soil from this to the other end. If the plot is very wide and long, divide it lengthways into two equal parts and instead of barrowing soil to the far end, move it to the other side. However, it is usually better and less involved just to move soil to the other end of the plot.

Start digging the next trench by skimming off grass and annual weeds and placing them upside

SINGLE-DIGGING

1 Take out a trench 25-30cm/10-12in deep and 30cm/12in wide across one end of the plot. Move the soil to the other end.
2 Skim off weeds and grass and place upside down in the trench. Spread well-decayed compost or manure in the trench's base.
3 Insert the spade a few inches into the soil, at a right-angle to trench.
4 Insert the spade to the full depth of the blade, lift out the block of soil and place it upside down in the far side of the trench. Continue in this way until the digging is complete, placing the soil previously placed at the end of the plot into the final trench.

Above: Annually digging borders for summer-flowering bedding plants ensures that roots do not have to force their way through compacted soil. It also enables uniform development of the plants, which is essential to the attractiveness of the border.

down in the first trench's base, together with compost or manure. Thrust the spade just a few inches into the soil at right-angles to the trench. Then insert the spade to the full depth of the blade so that you turn over a block of soil about 10cm/4in thick. Place this upside down in the trench. Continue in this way until the digging is complete right across the plot.

Remove and burn perennial weeds such as Dock, Bindweed and Horsetail.

SOIL INSECTS – FRIEND OR FOE?

Many insects live in the soil – some are beneficial, naturally attacking and killing plant pests; others are harmful to plants. When digging, many of these are exposed and can be readily popped into a jar — but which are a gardener's friend and best left in the soil?

Beneficial soil insects:

- **Ladybird beetle larvae,** as well as centipedes and slow-worms, are found in soil as well as in compost heaps. Take care not to kill them.

- **Rove beetles,** including the Devil's Coach-horse, have powerful jaws and eat cabbage root fly eggs, strawberry aphids, red spider mites and many other plant pests.

- **Violet ground beetles** are agile, 18-30mm/^{3}/4-1in long and have a purplish black sheen. They feed on aphids, small slugs and snails, insect eggs, springtails, mites and ants.

Harmful pests found in soil and rubbish:

- **Cockchafer grubs** are the larvae of May Bugs or June Bugs.

- **Leatherjackets** are the larvae of Crane Flies and prevalent in newly-cultivated grassland and moist soil.

- **Slugs and snails** are readily identified and quickly decimate plants if left unchecked.

- **Wireworms** are the larvae of Click Beetles and are most active in gardens newly converted from grassland.

- **Woodlice, millepedes and earwigs** are often found in compost and rubbish dug into soil.

When digging in autumn and early winter, do not break down large clods of soil, but leave them exposed to frost, rain, wind and snow during winter. When digging soil in late winter or early spring, break down large lumps.

TESTING THE SOIL FOR LIME

Soils are derived from a wide range of materials; some mineral, such as sand, clay, silt and chalk; others organic, and as the remains of animals and plants. All of these influence the acidity or alkalinity of soil. Alkaline soils, for instance, are usually found where there is underlying chalk. Acid soils are mainly found in areas where there is a mass of dead organic material, such as peat. Between these two, there is a range of soils, their alkalinity or acidity influencing the types of plants that can be grown.

Acidity or alkalinity is measured on a pH scale from 0 to 14, with 7.0 being neutral. Soils below pH 7.0 are increasingly acid down the scale, whereas those above pH 7.0 are increasingly alkaline up the scale. Most plants grow best in slightly acid soil, at pH 6.5.

Proprietary soil-testing kits are widely available. To use them, mix a soil sample with water and compare its colour with a chart to indicate the pH reading. Also available are pH meters and these are ideal for gardeners who are red/green colour blind.

If your soil is alkaline, dig in plenty of well-decomposed garden compost or manure and use acidic fertilizers such as sulphate of ammonia. Grow chalk-loving plants.

If your soil is acid, you can correct it by dusting the surface of newly dug soil with hydrated lime or ground limestone. The amount needed depends on the pH, the soil type and whether you use ground limestone or hydrated lime. The following amounts decrease acidity by 1.0 pH.

Soil	Hydrated lime	Ground limestone
Clay	612g/sq m 18oz/sq yd	815g/sq m 24oz/sq yd
Loam	405g/sq m 12oz/sq yd	545g/sq m 16oz/sq yd
Sand	205g/sq m 6oz/sq yd	270g/sq m 8oz/sq yd

Double-digging

Double-digging involves cultivating land to the depth of two spade blades and is beneficial when converting grassland into a garden, especially if the lower soil is compacted and poor draining.

Double-digging has the same virtues as single-digging – aeration, drainage, removal of weeds and incorporation of compost and manure. It is performed in autumn or early winter, so that the soil has time to weather and settle before spring.

DOUBLE-DIGGING

The first task is to dig a trench 25-30cm/10-12in deep and 60cm/24in wide across the plot and to barrow the soil to the other end. If the plot is long and wide, divide it lengthways into two equal parts and instead of barrowing soil to the far end, move it to the other side. However, it makes digging easier and simpler if the soil is just moved to the other end.

Use a garden fork to dig the base of the trench to a depth of 25-30cm/10-12in. At the same time mix in annual weeds and grasses, well-decomposed compost and manure. Never dig in perennial grasses such as Couch Grass.

If the area has been pasture land, skim off the grass and place it upside-down in the trench, using a spade to break it up.

Mark off a 60cm/24in-wide area along the plot and parallel with the trench. Then, use a spade to systematically turn this upside-down into the trench. Insert the spade's blade a few inches into the ground at a right-angle to the trench. Then press the spade to its full depth to remove a vertical slice of soil about 10cm/4in thick. Invert this into the trench. Continue doing this until all the soil from this 60cm/2ft wide strip is in the trench. The soil will probably bulk up and form a mound higher than the ground not yet dug.

In the base of the newly dug trench, continue the process of digging with a fork, adding manure and covering with the soil from a further 60cm/24in wide trench. Finally, place the soil from the first trench in the last one.

WHAT IS SOIL?

Soil is a complex mixture of mineral particles, animals and plants in varying stages of decay, air and water in varying quantities.

Right: Shrub and herbaceous borders, as well as those formed of a mixture of these plants together with annuals, biennials and bulbs, need thorough preparation to ensure the plants grow strongly for several years. Ensure all perennial weeds are removed; if left, they sprout up among cultivated plants, suffocating them as well as stealing plant foods and making the border unsightly.

DOUBLE-DIGGING

1 Take out a trench 25-30m/10-12in deep and 60cm/24in wide across one end of the plot; barrow the soil to the other end.
2 Use a garden fork to dig the trench's base 25-30cm/10-12in deep. At the same time, fork compost or well-decayed manure into soil.
3 Mark out a further 60cm/24in-wide strip of soil and dig this area, turning it over and placing in the trench. The soil will mound up higher than the surrounding area, but will settle during winter .
4 Continue down the plot, turning over the soil into the trench, until the end of the plot is reached and soil from the first trench can be put into the last one.

There are also soil organisms – from the microscopic fungi and bacteria that break down complex compounds to simple ones that plants can absorb, to the worms that play an important part in the aeration of soil and distribution of organic material, especially from the surface to lower levels. Warmth, which is partly due to this organic activity, and partly a result of air temperature and radiant heat, is vital for the germination of seeds and growth of roots.

The mineral part of soil is formed of fine and coarse sand, clay and silt, and it is the proportions of these that influence a soil's ability to grow plants.

SOIL TYPES

Clay soils are stiff and notoriously difficult to work, slow to warm up in spring and likely to become baked hard and cracked in summer. However, their virtue is that their small clay particles retain plant foods better than sandy soils. There are clay particles in most soils and it is only when they form 35 per cent or more that problems arise.

Silty soils have particles slightly larger than clay types but smaller than those of sand. In general, soils with a high silt content are poorly drained, lack the chemical-retentive qualities of clay and tend to be acid. Also, after rain the surface often forms a cap, preventing the entry of air.

Sandy soils are easily worked and warm up rapidly in spring so that early crops can be grown. Unfortunately, they are so free-draining that plant foods are rapidly leached. Strong winds can cause erosion of surface particles in very sandy soil.

Water is essential for the growth of plants. Clay soils remain wetter than sandy types, but are reluctant to release the water to plants. For instance, if heavy clay soil is compared with a sandy type – both containing 10 per cent moisture – the sandy one will appear moist and release water to plants, whereas clay types appear dry and do not provide plants with water.

Air is vital to enable roots to breath, as well as for the existence of many soil organisms. Soil temperature is closely related to the amount of water and air present. Sandy soils retain less water than clay types and invariably are warmer, especially in spring. Clay soils are often saturated with water, and this keeps the temperature low.

ASSESSING SOIL

There are several easy ways to judge if a soil's composition is light, medium or heavy:

- Pick up a handful of soil and rub some between your thumb and forefinger. If it creates a smooth, slippery, greasy surface, it contains clay; if rough and gritty, it is predominantly sandy.

- Slightly moisten some soil, roll it into a thin sausage and curl it to form a ring. The smaller the ring it is able to form without breaking, the higher its clay content.

- Fill a screw-top jar a quarter to half full of soil. Then, fill to three-quarters full with tap water and shake vigorously for several minutes. After being left for an hour the mixture will have settled in layers – stones at the base, followed by coarse and light sand, then silt and clay. Organic material will float on the surface. The proportions of these layers indicate the nature of the soil.

- Although not scientific, the 'boot' test is infallible – if soil sticks to your boots after you have walked over wet soil in winter, you can be sure that the soil contains plenty of clay. Incidentally, clay soil does not necessarily have an acid nature, so assess its pH before you apply lime.

Draining soil

Ideally, soil should be well-draining yet able to retain moisture. When soil is totally saturated with water, air is unable to permeate it and roots and soil organisms are unable to 'breathe'. Conversely, if the soil is too well drained, it dries out rapidly and plant growth ceases.

You can prevent light, sandy, freely draining soil from drying out by adding well-decayed compost, manure and peat, as well as by forming a mulch over the surface of the soil to conserve moisture. But where soil is naturally saturated, this needs to be improved by installing drains.

Winter is the best time to check if drains are needed. Puddles of water on the surface of the soil indicate the need for drains. Rushes, sedges and mosses are also good indicators that drainage is needed. For confirmation, in autumn dig a 1.2m/4ft-deep hole and during winter monitor the level of water. If it remains level with the surface or within 23cm/9in of the rim for long periods, you will definitely need to install drains.

There are several ways to drain land. On large areas, such as farmland and playing fields predominantly formed of clay, 'mole' drains are often used. A tractor draws a metal, bullet-headed spike, 45-75cm/18-30in deep, through the soil and the tube-like tunnel it forms acts as a drain. In suburban gardens, however, this is obviously not practical and rubble or tile drains are usually installed. Another, recent, alternative is a plastic core surrounded by porous fabric, which is supplied in lengths several metres long. It is easy to lay by digging a trench a spade's blade wide and 30-45cm/12-18in deep and positioning the drain in the base. Other plastic drains (see below) are formed of perforated 7.5cm/3in or 10cm/4in-wide tubes (sold in 25m/82ft-long coils).

RUBBLE AND TILE DRAINS

Both of these types of drain involve digging trenches across the waterlogged area to lead the water to a drainage ditch or soakaway. Usually, only one main drainage pipe is needed, with secondary drains radiating at an angle from it in a herringbone pattern. The spacings between the side drains will depend on the nature of the soil – 3.6-4.5m/12-15ft for clay soils to 12m/40ft on light, sandy ones.

INSTALLING PLASTIC DRAINS

1 Use strings and canes to mark out the lines of the main drain and side drains.
2 Dig out the trenches, with a slight slope towards the sump or drainage ditch.
3 Spread a 5cm/2in-thick layer of shingle in the base of each trench, and place the perforated plastic tubing on top.
4 Where each side drain meets the main one, cut the side one at an angle that fits snugly against the main pipe. Do not cut the latter.
5 Cover the joint with double-thickness strong polythene.
6 Spread a 7.5-10cm/3-5in-layer of shingle over the pipes, then a double thickness of polythene to prevent soil blocking the shingle. Then, add topsoil.

Above: Raised beds are an ideal way to grow plants when the surrounding soil is poorly drained. Here, *Hakonechloa macra* 'Albo-aurea', with cascading narrow, golden leaves creates a vibrant feature at the corner of a bed and alongside a path. It is also ideal for growing in a large pot on a patio.

Whether you are making drains of rubble or pipes, it is essential to dig trenches 60-75cm/24-30in deep and 30-45cm/12-18in wide, with a minimum slope of one in 90 towards the outlet. The width of the trench will very much depend on its depth and on whether you are digging it by hand, or by machine (in which case it can be deeper and narrower).

Rubble drains are less expensive to install than pipe ones, but do not last so long. Invariably, soil eventually seeps among the rubble and clogs up the spaces through which water could drain. Because digging trenches is the most laborious part of installing drains – and as it is a task common to both systems – it is generally better to lay pipes. Nevertheless, if you have inherited a small garden strewn with rubble, and if drainage is not a major problem, rubble drains could be the better choice.

Pipe drains are formed of unglazed clay pipes; those about 30cm/12in long and 13cm/5in wide are used as the main pipes, with 10cm/4in wide ones used as feeder pipes.

LAYING TILE DRAINS

Dig out the trenches and use a builder's spirit-level to check that the base slopes towards the outlet. Fill the base of the trench with 7.5-10cm/3-4in of gravel and place the pipes on top so that their ends closely butt.

Where side drains meet the main one, cut away part of the side pipe and ensure it meets the main pipe at a join. This allows water easily to enter the main drain without having to make a hole in it. Place large pieces of broken tile, or pieces of double-thickness polythene over the joins to prevent soil entering the pipes and blocking them. Cover the pipes with 15cm/6in of gravel – more under a lawn where there is no risk that digging will disturb the pipes – then topsoil, until the excavated area over the pipes is level with the surface of the surrounding soil. Within a few months, the soil will settle slightly and you may need to add more soil.

CREATING RUBBLE DRAINS

After using a builder's spirit-level to check the slope, fill the trench to within 30-38cm/12-15in of the surface with clean rubble. Place a double layer of polythene over the whole surface, to help prevent soil becoming washed into the rubble and causing blockages. Then fill up with top-soil. Allow time for the soil to settle and top up the level before creating a lawn or any other permanent feature on top.

GETTING RID OF THE WATER

Few gardeners are fortunate enough to have a stream or drainage ditch into which excess water can be drained. Therefore it is usually necessary to form a drainage sump.

You can create a sump by digging a hole about 1.2m/4ft square and deep at the lowest point (it needs to be at least 30cm/12in deeper than the end of the pipe that drains into it).

Fill the sump to half its depth with clean, broken bricks or large stones, then to within 30cm/12in of the surface with gravel. Cover this with inverted turves or a double thickness of polythene, and fill to the surface with top soil.

You will need to cover the ends of pipes draining into ditches with wire-netting to prevent vermin passing into them and using them as homes. If you neglect to do this, pipes will soon become clogged.

Gardening tools

Well-made garden tools that suit your height and build are an investment for life and a pleasure to use. Always buy the best you can afford: stainless-steel types are expensive and durable, but others are just as long-lasting if cleaned after use and stored in a dry, well-ventilated shed.

DIGGING AND FORKING TOOLS

Garden spades are mainly used to dig soil in autumn and winter, although throughout the year they have uses from shovelling soil to trimming lawn edges (if you don't have an edging-knife, earlier known as an edging-iron).

Spades are made in several sizes. Always buy one you can use easily without tiring: digging types have blades about 27cm x 19cm (11in x 7½in), while border models are 23cm x 14cm (9in x 5½in) and are often sold as 'lady's spades'.

Some spades have blades with tread-like ledges at the top of the blade. This enables you to put more pressure on the blade in heavy soil without making an indent in the sole of your shoe or boot. However, these spades are heavier and more difficult to clean.

Most spades are sold with 72cm/28in-long handles (the distance from the top of the blade to the tip of the handle), although some are 82cm/32in. There are three different types of handle and the one you choose is a matter of personal preference: T-shaped, D-outlined, and D-Y. The D-Y shape is the most popular and differs from the D-outlined type in having a Y-shape where the D joins the shaft.

Garden forks are often used to dig extremely heavy clay soil in winter. They are also ideal for breaking down large lumps of soil in spring when preparing ground for sowing or planting. A fork is also useful for shallowly scarifying surface soil in shrub borders and between herbaceous plants.

There are several sizes of forks: digging types (often known as garden forks) have four prongs, or tines, 27cm/11in long, while border forks also have four prongs but only 23cm/9in long. Potato forks are similar in size to digging types, but with flat rather than round tines. The lengths and types of the handles are similar to those available on spades.

GARDENING TOOLS

1 **Planting tools** are essential and include hand trowels and hand forks (both short and long handles), dibbers, garden lines, bulb planters and watering-cans.
2 **Pruning tools** include secateurs, strong knives and saws.
3 **Soil cultivation tools** include spades, forks, hoes and rakes.
4 **Lawn tools** encompass rakes – spring-tined rakes, those with plastic-tines and others with rubber tines – edging knives, edging shears and hand shears.

HOEING TOOLS

Hoes are used to cultivate surface soil, creating a tilth and severing weeds.

Draw hoes are mainly used to form shallow drills for sowing seeds, although often they are employed to sever weeds at ground-level. They can also be used to form drills 15cm/6in deep for planting potato tubers. Draw hoes have a goose-necked head that angles a sharp-edged blade towards the user. The metal head is attached to a 1.5m/5ft long wood or plastic handle.

When forming a drill you walk backwards, drawing the hoe towards you; when using the hoe to remove weeds, you move forwards.

Dutch hoes are ideal for severing weeds at ground-level and creating a tilth that reduces moisture loss from the soil's surface. A Dutch hoe is formed of a wood or plastic handle about 1.5m/5ft long attached to a 10-15cm/4-6in-wide flat metal head sharpened on its leading edge. To use a Dutch hoe you walk backwards, pushing the blade through the soil.

Onion hoes are like miniature draw hoes – a 7.5cm/3in-wide blade fitted to a goose-shaped neck, with a 30-38cm/12-15-long handle. They are used to sever weeds around seedlings.

RAKING

Rakes are essential for levelling soil, removing debris from borders and lawns, and preparing ground for sowing lawn seed or laying turves.

Iron rakes have 25-30cm/10-12in-wide heads with ten to fourteen teeth, each 6-7.5cm/2½-3in long. The head is fitted to a wood or plastic handle 1.5m/5ft long. This type of rake is ideal for levelling soil.

Landscape rakes are essential for levelling large areas of soil. These have a 72cm/28in-wide wooden head with 7.5-10cm/3-4in-long tines spaced 36mm/1½in apart.

LAWN TOOLS

Spring-tined rakes have heads formed of twenty wire tines that fan to about 50cm/20in wide – ideal for removing leaves and dead grass.

Plastic-tined lawn rakes are a variant on the spring-tined type but instead of wire tines have plastic ones. Heads fan to about 60cm/24in wide.

Rubber lawn rakes are ideal for pulling out dead grass and scattering worm-casts and are formed of a wood or plastic handle about 1.5m/5ft long and a 45cm/18in-wide head formed of about thirty-three flexible rubber tines. Some heads are only 30cm/12in wide, with eighteen rubber tines.

Edging knives, earlier known as edging-irons, resemble half-moon metal heads, sharpened on their lower and rounded edges. They are used to straighten neglected lawn edges.

Edging shears cut grass along lawn edges . Strong, tubular, 81cm/32in-long metal handles open and close shears 18-20cm/7-8in long.

Hand shears can be used to trim long grass as well as to cut hedges. Long-handled shears, known as lawn shears, enable you to cut long grass without having to bend down.

CUTTING AND SAWING

Secateurs are used for many pruning and cutting jobs. There are two types: the 'Anvil' type, where blade cuts against a firm, flat metal anvil; and the 'Bypass' form, where two parrot-shaped blades cross each other.

Saws are essential for cutting thick branches. Some saws cut on a push stroke, while others, such as Grecian saws with curved blades, have teeth that cut on a pull stroke.

PLANTING TOOLS

Hand trowels, formed of a metal scoop with a handle 15-30cm/6-12in long, are ideal for planting small plants.

Hand forks, similarly sized to hand trowels, have heads formed of four metal tines. They are ideal for digging out shallowly rooted weeds and cultivating surface soil.

Dibbers are simple tools used to make planting holes and often re-cycled from broken spade and fork handles. They initially are 30-38cm/2-15in long, but become worn down through use.

Bulb planters help in planting bulbs in grass by removing a core of turf and soil to a given depth.

Mulching soil

A traditional mulch is a layer of well-decayed organic material, such as garden compost or farmyard manure, placed over soil to prevent the growth of weeds and to conserve moisture in the ground. It also prevents rain falling on bare ground and then splashing on plants, while during summer it insulates roots from strong sunshine. Organic mulches also add to a soil's fertility and improve structure, reducing the risk of soil erosion during heavy rain storms. Certain mulches can also be used to control a few pests: placing lawn clippings around carrots deters carrot flies, for example.

Over the last few years, several types of mulches formed of plastic sheeting and other non-organic materials have become popular. Pea-sized shingle is also used.

ORGANIC MULCHING MATERIALS

These are derived from plants and animals and include the following:

Garden compost can be created by systematically forming kitchen and garden plant waste into layers. When fully decomposed, garden compost it is friable and brown, has a sweet smell and is pleasant to handle.

Farmyard manure, increasingly difficult to obtain, is best dug into soil during winter, especially if it is not fully decayed. It is only used as a mulch when well decomposed.

Peat is frequently recommended as a mulch but its extraction from peat beds destroys the natural habitats of many animals, birds and insects and it is therefore environmentally unfriendly. In any case, unless kept moist it is soon blown about and disturbed by birds.

Bark chippings create an effective mulch and are especially useful in ornamental gardens and around shrubs and trees. Unfortunately, because the chippings are light, birds invariably disturb them when seeking insects in the damp soil beneath, as well as using them to line nests.

Wood chippings, formed of chopped woody waste such as stems and twigs, are ideal as a mulch. Electrically powered shredders can be bought or hired and woody garden waste converted into useful material. Unfortunately, like bark chippings, this form of mulch is easily disturbed by animals, birds and strong wind.

Grass cuttings can either be composted or applied fresh around plants. However, when used direct from a lawn, ensure the turf has not recently been treated with a weedkiller, form a mulch only 2.5cm/1in thick and keep it away from the stems of plants. This is because as it decays it warms up and may then damage plants. It may also attract snails and slugs.

Straw is sometimes considered as a mulch, but in dry summers it does not readily decay, it blows about, and considerable bacterial action is needed to break down its structure, often leading to nitrogen deficiency in some soils.

NON-ORGANIC MULCHES

These consist mainly of black polythene as well as a few household materials:

Black polythene has been increasingly used to form a mulch to conserve moisture and suppress weeds. Additionally, when placed on the ground early in the year it helps soil to warm up, which means that you can sow seeds, and plant young plants earlier than normal.

CREATING AN ORGANIC MULCH

1 Use a hoe to remove annual weeds and to create a crumbly tilth. Use a hand trowel to dig out perennial weeds.
2 Thoroughly water the soil to at least 10cm/4in deep.
3 Form a 5-7.5cm/2-3in-thick layer of well-decomposed compost.

CREATING A COMPOST HEAP

No garden or kitchen waste should be thrown away; rather, it can be composted. You can form free-standing heaps, but an improvement is to have three ventilated bins placed about 90cm/3ft apart – each 1-1.2m/3½-4ft square and high – with provision for air to pass through the heap. These bins are used in rotation: one still being filled, another completely filled and the contents left to decay, and the last one yielding decayed compost ready for use.

Filling the container:

- Choose a sheltered, well-drained piece of ground and spread coarse material such as straw loosely to a depth of 23-30cm/9-12in. Tread it firm.
- Form a 15cm/6in-thick layer of vegetable waste, annual weeds, soft hedge-clippings, vacuum-cleaner emptyings and soft leaves. If you use grass cuttings, make the layers thinner, as when the grass compacts, air is excludedand the heepwill not rot down well.
- Place a 5cm/2in-thick layer of soil over the heap, thoroughly water and dust with sulphate of ammonia at 14g/½oz per square metre/yard. Alternatively, use a proprietary compost activator. Continue building up the layers.
- When the heap is 1.2m/4ft high, cover with 2.5-5cm/1-2in of soil, then a plastic sheet to prevent the heap becoming too wet or too dry. After about six months in winter (three in summer), either dig the decayed material into soil or use as a mulch.

Always hoe soil before watering it. Hard, dry, crusty soil repels water, so that it just runs off the surface rather than penetrating the ground. Additionally, it is less messy to hoe dry soil than soil which is newly watered.

Form a 5-7.5cm/2-3in-thick mulch around herbaceous plants, trees and shrubs. When forming mulches around grafted fruit trees, leave a small gap between the stem and mulch to prevent roots developing from the union.

During summer, organic mulches decay – and birds scatter them – and by autumn little may be left. In early winter, lightly fork the remainder of the mulch into the soil.

CREATING PLASTIC MULCHES

Plastic mulches are very effective at smothering weeds, conserving moisture and warming up the soil, but they but do not add to a soil's fertility. The soil preparation for creating a mulch from a plastic sheet is the same as for organic mulches.

When forming mulches on bare soil to warm it up in preparation for early planting of vegetables, form a slight ridge about 45cm/18in wide along the row. Place the black polythene over this and secure its edges by using a spade to make slits 7.5-10cm/3-4in deep in the soil. Press the edges of the polythene into the slits. Then close up the slits to trap and secure the polythene.

FORMING SHINGLE MULCHES

Pea-shingle creates a superb non-organic mulch, especially in rock gardens. Clear the soil of weeds and rubbish, water it thoroughly and then add a 2.5cm/1in-thick layer of clean, 6mm/¼in shingle. This keeps the surface dry and cool for alpines.

Newspapers when laid in several thickness create an excellent mulch. However, layers of wet, decaying newspapers are not attractive and are therefore best reserved for vegetable gardens. Unfortunately, during hot summers the paper quickly dries out and blows about.

Old carpets are mainly used in vegetable gardens, but take care that they do not create a haven for slugs, snails, earwigs and millepedes, especially when continually wet.

FORMING MULCHES OF ORGANIC MATERIAL

Most mulches are formed in spring or early summer. First, hoe the soil to sever annual weeds at ground-level and use a trowel or garden fork to dig up perennial weeds. Make sure that you dig deep enough to remove their roots; if left, they grow and will be awkward to remove later unless the mulch is lifted. Then water the soil, ensuring that it is soaked at least 10cm/4in deep.

FORMING A POLYTHENE MULCH FOR STRAWBERRIES

1 Remove all weeds and form a slightly rounded ridge. Thoroughly water the soil. Secure the polythene by using a garden spade to form slits along each side of the ridge; press the edges of the polythene into them. Use a sharp knife to form cross-slits at the planting positions.
2 Spread the roots in the planting hole, and firm them.
3.Water the soil.

LAWNS

A well-manicured lawn forms a traditional part of a garden, creating a play area for children and a sward which unifies the garden and forms a permanent backcloth for plants. A lawn is also a restful and directional part of a garden; it is undemanding on the eye, yet, if well planned, can draw attention to features which, perhaps, are not initially apparent.

Lawns need not be flat – they can be terraced, or formed into steep banks or gentle slopes, and they can be bounded by regular, straight lines or irregular curving edges.

Once formed, lawns are often the most neglected parts of a garden, yet with only a little regular attention they can be transformed from a broken-edged, uneven-surfaced and weed-ridden feature to one that is a joy to look at and walk upon, and enhances the entire garden.

Creating lawns from seed

Whether you are laying turves or sowing seeds, thorough soil preparation is essential. If this part of the work is neglected or skimped, the final appearance of the lawn may disappoint you.

PREPARING THE SITE
First of all, you will need to clear the area of weeds – dig out perennial ones intact and hoe off annual types. Ensure the drainage is satisfactory (see pages 46-7), checking during winter by digging the soil to the depth of a spade's blade (see pages 38-9). If you are converting heavy pasture land into a lawn, you will need to double-dig the soil (see pages 40-1). If the soil is waterlogged install land drains (see pages 42-3).

If the soil is well-drained, relatively light and previously cultivated, you can leave preparation until early spring and use a rotavator to prepare the soil. However, you will need to remove all perennial weeds first, as even if their roots are chopped up they will grow again and create a big problem that willbe difficult to eradicate.

A few weeks before sowing or turfing, rake the surface level (or with an even gradient) and remove large stones; leave small ones as they prevent soil compaction and encourage moisture retention during dry seasons. Firm the surface by systematically shuffling sideways across the plot. Firm the entire surface in this way; do not use a garden roller as this causes excessive and uneven compaction. Then rake the soil again to create its final levels and an even tilth.

SOWING LAWN SEED
About a week before sowing seeds – usually in late spring or late summer to early autumn – rake in a dressing of a general fertilizer at 50g per sq m/1½oz per sq yd.

Wait until a dry day and sow seeds at 50g per sq m/1½oz per sq yd. Do not economize on the amount of seed, as this produces a thin and sparse lawn that takes a long time to develop an overall sward. Conversely, excessive amounts of seed produce a dense coverage of young seedlings susceptible to diseases. It is essential to sow seeds evenly and this is best achieved by using strings to section the area into metre- or yard-wide strips. Then, by using a metre- or yard-

LAWNS FROM SEED

1 About a week before sowing seed, rake in a general fertilizer at 50g/sq m or 1½ oz/sq yd.
2 Use strings to mark yard or metre strips. Use two bamboo canes to form yard- or metre-squares.
3 Evenly scatter lawn seed at the rate of 50g/sq m 1½ oz/ sq yd, into each square. Once one square has been sown, move one of the canes to form a fresh square.
4 When the area has been sown, gently and lightly rake the surface. Cover the surface with wire-netting or strings to prevent birds and cats scratching and disturbing the soil.

ADVANTAGES AND DISADVANTAGES OF A LAWN FROM SEED

The main choice when creating a new lawn is between sowing seeds or laying turves (see pages 52-3). Other ways include improving existing pasture land by levelling and general lawn care over several years (see pages 56-7), or in warm countries by dibbling tufts of grass into the soil.

Advantages of sowing seeds:

- Cheaper than laying turves.

- Easy to create intricately shaped areas.

- Lighter work than laying turves.

- Once you have prepared the area and bought seed, you don't have to commence sowing immediately – bad weather or lack of time to sow seeds within a few weeks does not create problems; (though you may need to rake the surface again if children or pets have trodden on it).

- The range of lawn seed is wide and it is easier to select the type of grass required.

Disadvantages of sowing seeds:

- You will need to wait between three and four months before you can use the lawn.

- If you do not prepare the area well, perennial grasses can be a problem before fine ones are established.

- To protect the seeds from birds, you will need to cover the whole area with wire netting, which is an expense and a nuisance. Stretching black cotton over the area, though inexpensive, is still time consuming.

- Cats tend to dig up newly sown soil and toddlers and young children are certain to tread on it.

long measuring rod and a couple of bamboo canes, each strip can be sectioned off into metre or yard squares. Mark out the first metre or yard area and sow it with the correct amount of seed. Then move one of the canes a metre or yard down the strip to form a further square area and sow more seeds. Stand on a flat plank to avoid compacting the soil with your feet.

Mechanical seed-sowing appliances are available, but unless the area is large it is best to rely on systematically sowing seeds by hand. Even though it appears laborious, it does ensure that the seed is sown evenly.

When you have sown the whole area, lightly and shallowly rake the surface to cover the seeds. This aids germination and helps to hide seeds from birds. If the soil is dry – especially in spring and when there is little chance of rain within a few days – gently but thoroughly soak the soil with water. Ensure the seed is not washed about over the surface.

Cover the ground with wire-netting or black cotton tightly stretched across the area – 7.5-10cm/3-4in above the surface – to prevent birds and cats disturbing seeds. Some seed is treated with a bird repellant, but this does not prevent birds initially touching the seeds or using the area as a dust-bath. However, ensure the cotton cannot become entangled around legs and bodies of animals and birds; and remove it as soon as grass seedlings are established.

Small areas can then be covered with clear polythene. As well as protecting the area from birds and cats, polythene ensures even germination by keeping the area uniformly moist. It also keeps the soil warm. Germination takes seven to ten days and when grass seedlings are 18-25mm/³/₄-1in high, remove the polythene. (If you have used black, rather than clear, polythene, you should remove it immediately grass seed germinates.

Do not cut the grass until it is 36-50mm/1¹/₂-2in high, and then set the mower's blades to cut off the top 12mm/¹/₂in. For the next two or three mowings, allow the grass to grow to 6.5-7.5cm/2¹/₂-3in high and cut off the top 2.5cm/1in. Thereafter, cut it to 2.5cm/1in high if a surface tolerant of wear is needed, or only 12mm/¹/₂in for a neater appearance and for sitting on.

Make sure the mower's blades are sharp, so that the grass seedlings are cleanly severed and not ripped out of the soil.

SELECTING LAWN SEED

The range of types of grass seed is wide and you should select it to suit the expected wear given to the area. For example, ornamental mixtures usually contain two types of fine grasses, perhaps a blend of 80 per cent (by weight) of red fescue and 20 per cent bent grass. Lawns created from this mixture are suited to front gardens and other areas where there is little wear.

Harder-wearing (sometimes known as wear-tolerant) lawn seed mixtures have 40 to 60 per cent ornamental grasses, with the rest formed of coarser grasses such as smooth-stalked meadow grass and perennial ryegrass. Dwarf ryegrasses are also ideal as they have fine leaves and do not need to be cut as frequently as other ryegrasses. There are also seed mixtures specially prepared for shady areas.

Lawn seeds are widely available from garden centres and hardwear outlets as well as seed catalogues. Lawn seed is mainly sold in 500g, 1kg and 2kg packets; sometimes in larger units such as 10kg. A 500g packet is sufficient to sow 10 sq m/12 sq yards.

Many garden centres offer advice on seed mixtures and will prepare ones suitable for your garden and its function. Often, this is the most economical way to buy lawn seed.

Creating lawns from turves

When laying turves the soil will need the same thorough preparation and attention for lawns from lawn seed (see pages 50-1). Also, ensure the drainage is good (see pages 42-3) and check that perennial weeds have been dug out.

LAYING TURVES

Turves can be laid from spring to autumn, but ensure irrigation is available during dry periods. Early autumn is the most popular time, as the soil is warm and usually moist.

About a week before laying turf, evenly scatter and rake in a general fertilizer at 70g per sq m/ 2oz/per sq yd.

Mark out the area to be turved, stretching a garden line down one of the long sides. Make the area about 7.5cm/3in larger (on all sides) than the desired finished lawn size – turves shrink slightly and you can cut back excess later, once the lawn is established. Laying a slightly larger area of turf also allows you to trim back any damaged edges.

Preferably, lay turf immediately after delivery; if this is impossible, roll out the turves – grass-side uppermost – and water them using a fine-rosed watering can lightly but thoroughly.

Start laying the lawn by rolling out a turf and positioning it alongside a garden line. Then, lay another turf, closely butted to its end, and continue until you have formed a complete row. Place a flat plank, about 20cm/8in wide and 2.4-3m/8-10ft long, on the newly laid turf and stand on it while positioning a further row. Butt the turves close together, ensuring that the joints are staggered. If the turves differ in thickness, you will need to either to add or remove soil from under them.

As well as ensuring each turf is butted close to its neighbour, firm it gently to make sure the root-side is in close contact with the ground. Placing a plank on top of the turves as they are laid helps to firm them but you can also attach a 45cm/18in square of thick wood to a 1.2-1.5m/ 4-5ft-long stout pole and use this to firm them.

Even if you have managed to position turves so close together that there are no gaps between them, it is wise to scatter a mixture of equal parts sieved soil and fine peat along the cracks and

LAYING TURVES

1 About a week before laying turf, rake a general fertilizer into the surface.
2 Stretch a garden line down one side, making the area slightly larger than eventually needed. Excess turf can be cut back after it is established. Roll out a turf and ensure it aligns with the garden line. Place another turf in position, butting the ends close together.
3 When the first row is complete, place a plank on top to stand on while laying the next row. Stagger joints.
4 Ensure the turves are in firm contact with the soil. Use a 45cm/18in-square piece of wood secured to a 1.2-1.5m/4-5ft-long pole to gently firm the surface.
5 Trickle a mixture of peat and friable soil into the cracks between the turves.
6 Gently brush the compost into the cracks.

Above: Grass is ideal for creating paths as well as lawns. Both have a natural and non-dominant appearance that helps to highlight plants and to unify a garden. Ensure the plants do not greatly overhang the lawn's edges, or the grass will eventually die and the area become unsightly.

brush it in. When the area is complete, water the turves with a sprinkler and keep it damp until they are established.

Apart from watering it, leave the lawn alone for about a month before treading on it. In any case, you should wait until the joints between the turves cannot be seen. You can then cut the grass, but not initially shorter than 2.5cm/1in high. Later, reduce the height of the cut to 12mm/¹/₂in high, unless the grasses are exceptionally coarse when they are best left to grow slightly longer.

TYPES AND SOURCES OF TURF

There are two basic sources of turf:

Meadow turf is cut from disused pasture and is often the cheapest type available, but is often formed of coarse, rapid-growing ryegrass that

needs frequent mowing. Usually, the turves are cut 90cm/3ft long and 30cm/12in wide and about 36mm/1¹/₂in thick, although this is variable. Sometimes these are sold flat rather than rolled, which means that they sometimes fall apart.

Cultivated turf (sometimes known as seeded turf) is specially sown and grown by turf merchants, with seed mixtures selected to suit the lawn's use. It costs more than turf cut from meadows but does enable you to select grass for either a well-used or ornamental lawn.

A hard-wearing type is ideal for most lawns, while an ornamental one is more expensive and better suited to front gardens. However, it reveals neglect more quickly than the hard-wearing type.

Cultivated turf is sold in rolls, either forming one square yard (pieces 40 x 205cm/16 x 81in) or two-thirds of a square yard (40 x 137cm/16 x 54in). Pieces 75cm/2¹/₂ft x 3m/10ft are also available but the precise size will depend on the supplier. Each turf is about 12mm/¹/₂in thick. When ordering turf, buy about five per cent more than you need to allow for wastage.

BUYING TURF

Turf is mainly available from garden centres or direct from national or local suppliers. A few large DIY stores also stock turves. If possible, inspect turves before buying them. Check they are free from weeds, are of the desired quality and that pests or diseases are not present. Check, too, that each turf is evenly covered with grass.

Delivery charges usually depend on the amount of turf ordered and the distance travelled. They vary enormously and therefore always check what the total cost will be and if it includes all taxes. It is possible to collect your own turf, but ensure your car is both large and strong enough to transport it. As soon as turf is delivered, check it to ensure you have received the quality and amount ordered.

ADVANTAGES AND DISADVANTAGES OF A LAWN FROM TURVES

Rapid establishment and cost are often the main reasons for choosing to create a lawn from turves, but here are a few other factors to consider before you make your choice.

Advantages of laying turves:

- Creates an instant sward, but will take up to four weeks before it can be used.
- Eliminates problem of birds and cats disturbing grass seeds.
- Ideal where there are young children who might disturb the surface of a newly sown lawn.
- Turves can be laid at almost any time from spring to autumn, (though irrigation must be provided during dry periods).

Disadvantages of laying turves:

- More expensive than sowing seeds.
- Turves have to be laid within twenty-four hours of delivery. If left, exposed sides begin to dry and the grass becomes yellow.
- It involves much heavier work than sowing seeds.
- Ideally, the soil the turves were stripped from should be the same type as that which they are to be laid on.

Renovating lawns

Lawns invariably become worn with use and time. Lawn edges are frequently trodden upon, especially in winter when borders are dug or lightly forked. Also, when the grass is covered with snow the edges are obliterated and even more vulnerable to a misplaced boot. Additionally, border plants may spread over lawn edges and suffocate grass, dogs tear up the surface and bitches, when urinating on grass, cause yellow patches. Lawn games compact turf, while a lawn mower sometimes shaves an edge. Remedying these problems need not be radical or expensive, usually takes only an hour or so, and is well worth tackling promptly.

REPAIRING HOLES IN LAWNS

Dogs and children are adept at digging holes in lawns. Also, supports for lawn game equipment are often hammered into turf and if they are rocked back and forth, either by the wind or in the course of play will eventually make large holes. These holes are best filled in late spring or early summer, or failing this, in early autumn.

The best way to do this is to use a piece of wood about twice the size of the hole. For example, if the hole is 10-15cm/4-6in wide, select a piece of wood 25-30cm/10-12in square and 12-18mm/1/2-3/4in thick and place it over the damaged area. Use an edging knife to cut around the edges of the wood. Then use a spade to cut under the turf to remove it. Use the same piece of wood to cut another piece from an out-of-the-way corner in a lawn, using it to replace the piece you have taken out. Brush friable soil into the gap around the square, then water the area regularly until the edges knit.

MENDING BROKEN LAWN EDGES

Repair broken lawn edges in spring and early summer or early autumn, when the soil is relatively moist. Repair is easy and quick.

Most casual damage to lawn edges never exceeds 15cm/6in in width and 7.5cm/3in in depth. Therefore, cut a piece of wood 20-23cm/8-9in wide, 30cm/12in long and 12-18mm/1/2-3/4in thick. Place this over the damaged area and with one end alongside with lawn's edge.

Use an edging knife to cut around the wood, then a spade to cut underneath. Ensure that you cut the turf to an even thickness. Gently lift out the damaged turf and reverse it, so that the damaged end is towards the lawn's centre and the good end flush with edge. Fill and firm the damaged area with friable soil or compost and dust the surface with seeds. Also brush compost into the gap around the turf and keep the area moist until the edges knit together.

LEVELLING BUMPS AND DEPRESSIONS

Bumps and depressions – if not more than 1.5m/5ft wide – can be easily corrected. Stretch a garden line over the centre of the depression or mound and use an edging knife to cut down through the turf to about 5cm/2in deep. Then, measure out 30cm/12in-wide strips on either side and also cut along these.

Stretch a garden line at a right-angle to these cuts and use an edging knife to cut the turf, 5cm/2in deep. Then use a spade to cut underneath the turf from the centre outwards and roll sections of turf back to level ground. You can then remove or add soil to make the area level. Rake and lightly consolidate the soil, then roll

REPAIRING LAWN EDGES

1 Place a piece of wood 20-23cm/8-9in wide, 30cm/12in long and 12-18mm/1/2-3/4in thick over the damaged area and flush with the lawn's edge.
2 Use an edging knife to cut around the board, then cut evenly under it with a spade.
3 Lift out the turf and reverse it, so that the broken end is inwards. Fill up and firm the broken part with compost and sow lawn seed.

CONTENDING WITH TREE ROOTS

In an ornamental lawn, an aged tree with roots pushing up the turf around the trunk is unsightly. Also, the blades of a mower may be damaged by the roots. The easiest way to overcome this problem is to cut a bed around the tree's trunk, so that raised roots are then set in soil.

In informal areas where, perhaps, the grass is not cut frequently, use a strimmer to trim long grass around trees.

back and firm the turf. Brush compost into the joins and keep the area moist until they knit firmly together.

BARE AREAS

Bare patches are often the result of too much foot traffic at one point. Sometimes grass can be encouraged to re-grow by fencing off the area in late spring, early summer or autumn and keeping it regularly watered. However, the soil in such areas is usually seriously compacted, preventing the entry of air and water. If this is the case, fork the soil to about 15cm/6in deep, refirm it and sprinkle seed across the area at 50g per sq m/1¹/₂oz per sq yd. Lightly rake this into the surface, then gently water, but not so heavily as to cause the seed to be washed over the surface. Allow the surface to dry slightly, then cover the seeded area with clear polythene.

The polythene serves several purposes. It prevents birds and animals from disturbing the area, keeps the soil moist and retains warmth in the ground. Remove the polythene when the seedlings are 18-25cm/³/₄-1in high but keep the area sectioned off to prevent anyone walking on it until the grass is well established and has been cut several times.

SUNKEN STEPPING STONES

Stepping stones in lawns invariably settle and every few years need to be lifted and repositioned slightly higher. Place a straight-edged board across each stepping stone to check how much it has settled. Lift each stone individually, place sharp sand underneath and replace it.

Ensure it is level and firm, with its surface just below the surrounding ground. This is especially important if the mower used to cut the grass is a cylinder type; hover mowers naturally glide over stones that are just slightly too high.

BARE LAWN EDGES

Where the grass alongside an herbaceous or mixed border has become suffocated and killed by overhanging plants, the choice is either to plant less lax and rampant plants close to the edge, or to position a row of paving slabs alongside the border. Let them into the lawn, with their surface flush with the surrounding grass. This also prevents plants being damaged by the lawn mower.

YELLOW PATCHES

Yellow patches in lawns are usually caused by bitches constantly urinating in the same position. If the area is unsightly, remove turf from it and replace with a fresh piece taken from else where in the garden. Alternatively, dig out the soil to about 15cm/6in deep, replace with fresh loam, firm the area and scatter seed over it.

If the area is only slightly yellow, use a garden fork to spike the ground, then water it copiously. Later, apply a nitrogenous fertilizer to encourage the rapid growth of grass.

REPAIRING HOLES IN LAWNS

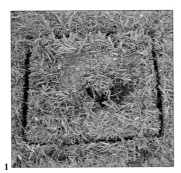  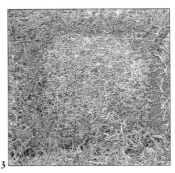

1 Place a piece of wood 25-30cm/10-12in square and 12-18mm/¹/₂-³/₄in thick over the hole and use an edging knife to cut around it. Cut under it and remove.
2 Use the wood to cut another piece of turf from an out-of-the-way position, and place it in the hole.
3 Brush compost between the cracks and keep the area moist until the new piece of turf is established.

Lawn care thoughout the year

Lawns tend to be neglected in most gardens. Each summer they are expected to be lush, green and healthy and usually remain attractive even with only a little maintenance, but with regular care throughout the year they can be even better.

MOWING LAWNS

Regular and frequent mowing is essential when grass is growing strongly, from early spring to early or mid-autumn. In mild areas, the need for mowing sometimes continues into early winter.

Precisely how often the lawn needs to be cut depends on its nature and on its growth; during late spring and early summer, when the soil is moist and the weather warm, twice a week may be necessary. Later in the year – and especially if the weather is dry – perhaps a mowing once a week or even only every fortnight is sufficient. Less nutrients are taken from the soil by cutting grass frequently than by letting it become excessively high between each cut. Also, the longer the grass the faster it grows. Many mowers are unable to cope with tall grass and, if long, several cuts – with the blades set at different heights –

may be necessary to reduce the lawn's height. This all takes more time than just cutting the lawn at regular and frequent intervals throughout summer.

The height established lawns are cut depends on whether you require an ornamental lawn or a hard-wearing surface. For an ornamental appearace, cut 12mm/¹/₂in high, but for a hard-wearing surface 2.5cm/1in is better. During dry, hot summers leave the grass longer, about 30-36mm/1¹/₄-1¹/₂in high and avoid cutting grass frequently during hot periods.

Although ornamental lawns appear neat and tidy when cut close, this weakens the turf and anything closer than 6mm/¹/₄in is harmful. Also, unless the lawn is exceptionally level, cutting the grass too close inevitably results in the mower's blades scalping the surface and leaving bare patches.

In general it is best to have a grass-box fitted to the mower. If left, the mowings create an untidy surface, especially on an ornamental lawn. They also encourage the presence of pests and diseases and greater activity of worms, and can

LOOKING AFTER A LAWN

1 The blade on a hover mower can be adjusted by moving the thick washers to either above or below the blade.
2 Ensure that the blade on a hover mower is sharp; a new one is easily fitted by undoing the central bolt.
3 Keep lawn edges trimmed by using long-handled shears.
4 Feed lawns, ensuring the fertilizer is evenly distributed by stretching string across the surface and by using two canes to form metre or yard squares.
5 Aerate lawns by pushing the prongs of a garden fork into the surface. Alternatively, use a hollow-tined type that removes cores of soil. Rake these off the lawn's surface.
6 Spread a mixture of finely sieved peat, loam and sharp sand over the surface of the lawn.

Above: Specimen trees, such as the Judas Tree (*Cercis siliquastrum*), are ideal for creating focal points in lawns. Water is essential to keep lawns green and attractive: as soon as a lawn starts to lose its springiness, and if there has been no appreciable rain for a week, water the lawn thoroughly. Do not just dampen the surface.

impede aeration. Provided you have not applied weedkillers to the lawn, you can place mowings on a compost heap. However, during dry periods lawn mowings left on the surface will protect the grass, acting as a light mulch and conserving soil moisture.

FEEDING LAWNS

Regularly mowing grass removes nutrition from the soil and therefore feeding is essential. During spring and summer, use fertilizers that are quick-acting and apply them every six to eight weeks, except during periods of drought. Proprietary lawn fertilizers containing nitrogen, phosphate and potash are available. Apply at about 70g per sq m 2oz per sq yd, but follow the manufacturer's instructions exactly.

In late summer and early autumn, use slow-acting fertilizers containing less nitrogen, a medium amount of potash and a large quantity of phosphate to encourage root development rather than leaf growth. Give only one application of this autumn treatment, at about 70g per sq m/2oz per sq yd or according to directions.

Before applying fertilizers, ensure that the entire lawn is thoroughly watered, especially if the weather is dry. But the foliage itself should be dry before any application of fertilizers. And after feeding, if no rain appears within two days, lightly but thoroughly water the area.

There are three main ways to apply fertilizers: in a granular or powdered form applied by hand; diluted and given through a watering can or hose-end dilutor which enables a large area to be treated quickly; and through a mechanical distributor (which can be bought or hired).

Even distribution is essential, so use strings spaced a metre or yard apart to section off the lawn, and then two canes to systematically form squares within which to apply the correct amount of fertilizer.

AERATING AND TOP-DRESSING LAWNS

The organic content of lawns usually becomes depleted and in late summer or early autumn this should be replaced at the same time as aerating the lawn. Use a garden fork to make 10cm/4in holes over the surface. Alternatively, use a wheeled lawn spiker, preferably with hollow tines that remove cores of soil. Rake off the cores, together with dead grass, then rake in a mixture of finely milled peat, loam, and sharp sand (it should not contain lime and the particle size should not be too coarse). On lawns created on heavy soil, use a mixture of one part peat, two of loam and four of sand. For lawns formed on loamy soil, use a mixture of one part peat, four of loam and two of sand on sandy soil, a mixture of two parts peat, four of loam and one of sand.

Spread the mixture – at about 1.35kg per sq m 3lb per sq yd – over the surface and into the spike holes. Use a birch broom or the back of an iron rake to spread the mixture – or for large areas, a 1.5-1.8m/5-6ft-long and 15-20cm/6-8in-wide plank attached to a central handle. Small depressions in the surface can be filled in, but deep holes need other treatment (see pages 54-5).

BRUSHING, RAKING AND SCARIFYING

Throughout the year, dead grass, worm casts and, in autumn, fallen leaves from nearby trees and shrubs accumulate on the surface of lawns. If left, they suffocate young grasses and eventually kill them.

In autumn, regularly use a lawn brush, besom or mechanical sweeper to remove leaves, ideally within a few days of them falling. If left, leaves are pulled into the soil by the activity of worms, and once leaves are wet they stick to the lawn's surface and are difficult to remove. Spring-tine wire rakes are useful for raking up leaves that have become embedded in a wet lawn.

In spring, use a spring-tine wire rake to remove dead grass and other debris that has accumulated during winter.

In early autumn, use a spring-tine wire rake or a scrake (like a rake, but with a series of knife-like cutting tines) to scarify the surface and to remove the thatch-like covering, or mat, which is formed of fibrous material on top of the soil's surface. If very thick (more than 12mm/½in) it will prevent the entry of water into a lawn and encourage the presence of diseases.

TREES, SHRUBS AND HEDGES

Trees and shrubs have a permanency that is essential in gardens, where they often form backgrounds for bulbous and herbaceous plants, as well as creating colourful and shapely features on their own. Hedges are often used to form backcloths for herbaceous plants, which in spring and when young are soon damaged by cold and blustery winds. Some hedging plants, however, have a diminutive nature and are more suited to creating small decorative flowering or foliage hedges within a garden.

A few shrubs, such as *Buddleja (Buddleia) alternifolia*, are ideal for creating lawn features, while trees grown for their attractive bark are especially suitable as focal points at the end of a garden. Some of these are further enhanced by crocuses naturalized in the grass around them.

Preparing and planning a shrub border

A shrub border offers the opportunity to create a permanent, labour-saving part of a garden. It can produce a wide range of flowers in varying shapes, colours and scents, as well as leaves in many colours, shapes and sizes. Some shrubs have coloured bark and berries, and you could also include a few trees with attractive bark to create additional height.

RANGE OF SHRUBS

The range of shrubs is wide and shrub borders can have flowers throughout the year. The plant profile pages in this chapter describe and illustrate a number of different winter-flowering shrubs (pages 64-5), spring-flowering types (pages 78-9), and ones that flower in summer (pages 82-7). Evergreen shrubs are featured on pages 94-5, those with rich autumn colours on pages 90-1, and those with attractive barks, stems or berries on pages 68-71.

Plan borders to contain both deciduous and evergreen shrubs. Evergreen types can be positioned to screen unattractive backgrounds, to filter wind and to provide shelter for less hardy plants. Deciduous types, are good for their fresh new growth in spring, range of flower colours and kaleidoscope of rich leaf colours in autumn.

Richly coloured barks and stems, as well as berries and attractively shaped twigs, can be just as interesting as flowers – and they are present for a long period. More interest is now shown in planting shrubs in groups so that they highlight and complement each other. Contrasting leaf colours and shapes, complementary flower colours and varied outlines, as well as overall shapes and sizes, help to bring extra interest to borders. A few of these planting combinations are suggested opposite.

Scent is important in gardens and can be achieved throughout the year. Position fragrant plants near paths; this makes the scent readily detectable and avoids the problem of people walking over a border to find out from where the fragrance is coming.

SIZE AND GROWTH OF SHRUBS

The speed at which individual shrubs grow, together with their ultimate height and spread,

PLANNING A SHRUB BORDER

1 Measure the border and draw it to scale on paper.
2 Using the same scale, cut out pieces of paper to represent individual shrubs. Position these on the plan to create an attractive border.
3 Use sand to mark out the border, indicating the extent of each shrub and its planting position. At this stage, the plan can still be changed.
4 Plant the shrubs. To ensure shrubs become established quickly, water the soil thoroughly and then apply a mulch to conserve moisture in the soil.

COMPANION PLANTING

Planting shrubs in groups creates a more exciting garden. Here are a few associations to try:

- *Ribes sanguineum* 'Brocklebankii' and *Cotinus coggygria* 'Foliis Purpureis'.

- *Philadelphus coronarius* 'Aureus' and Lavender or Rosemary.

- *Potentilla fruticosa* 'Elizabeth' and *Perovskia atriplicifolia* 'Blue Spire'.

- *Tamarix ramosissima* 'Pink Cascade', *Buddleia fallowiana* 'Alba' and *Caryopteris* x *clandonensis*.

- Lavender, *Hebe armstrongii* and *Berberis thunbergii* 'Atropurpurea'.

- *Cotoneaster frigidus* 'Cornubia', *Choisya ternata*, *Skimmia japonica* and *Viburnum davidii*.

invariably influences their selection. A shrub's size is critical in a small garden. The height and spread indicated for each shrub illustrated and described elsewhere in this chapter are those the plant will reach when grown in ideal conditions. In cold areas and where soil is poor, growth is less. Conversely, grown in exceptionally fertile, moisture-retentive soil, in good light and when sheltered from cold winds, they will be larger. It is worth looking at similar plants in neighbours' gardens, as well as in parks and gardens open to the public, to check the heights and spreads of plants in your area.

In botanic gardens and those open to the public, shrubs are often planted in bold, dominant groups of three or five plants. This technique is clearly suitable for large borders, but in suburban gardens it is usually impossible, although low, ground-hugging shrubs such as ericas and callunas are always better when in groups than if planted singly.

Below: Shrubs introduce permanency into a garden and once established create a wealth of flowers, colourful leaves or berries for many years.

Do not position large shrubs all together; rather, space them out along the border, with some at the back and others towards the middle and front. Instead of planting large shrubs in a continuous line at the back of a border, allow for some surprises – perhaps a choice and slightly tender plant within the protection of a larger one. To create contrasts of height, consider planting small trees with attractive winter bark - such as birches and some acers – among heathers.

PLANNING THE BORDER

Even though you may be impatient to plant shrubs in a border, it is worth spending a few days planning it and considering what it will be like in five or ten years time or more.

Measure the area of the border and draw it to scale on a sheet of graph paper. Mark in the shrubs to scale, as they will be in ten years. The best way to do this is to cut small pieces of paper to scale and move them around on the plan. When they are in the right position, you can paste them on the graph paper.

When the plan is complete, use sand to trace out on the border itself the area each shrub will eventually fill. This is the moment for a final check on their positions. How to plant container-grown and bare-rooted shrubs is described on pages 62-3 and 66-7.

Planting a container-grown shrub

Looking around a garden centre, choosing a container-grown plant that appeals to you and planting it on the same day is very satisfying. It creates an instant feature that was not possible in earlier years when deciduous shrubs and trees were sold only as 'bare-rooted' plants during their dormant period, from early to late winter. Shrubs with an evergreen nature were dug up from their nursery bed, their roots wrapped in hessian, and sold in late spring and early summer, or late summer and early autumn, when the soil is warm. Container-grown trees and shrubs offer the possibility of instant gardening, but soil preparation must still be thorough if plants are to become established quickly and have a long life.

INSPECTING THE PLANT

It is essential to inspect a plant before buying it. Small plants usually become established faster than large ones, but it is vital that the plant is healthy and has a good root system. A weak and sickly shrub – however cheap – is not a bargain as it never develops into a healthy plant that will give you enjoyment over many years.

Before buying a plant, always check that:
• The compost is moist – neither dry nor waterlogged. If dry, this indicates that the plant has been neglected. If excessively wet, this may have caused roots to decay.
• Moss is not present on the compost, as this indicates the plant has been in the container for too long.
• Roots are not coming out the container. If they are, it is likely that they are matted and will not readily grow outwards and into new soil when planted.
• The plant is well secured in the container and has not recently been potted up.
• The plant is labelled.
• The plant is not lop-sided; often the result of being displayed in an exposed, windy area. However, if the plant is only slightly lop-sided, you can position it in a shrub border so that its unattractive side faces away from the path.

PLANTING A CONTAINER-GROWN PLANT

The first job is to prepare the soil. Dig the area thoroughly and add well-decomposed organic

Right: The Hardy Plumbago (*Ceratostigma willmottianum*) is a half-hardy deciduous shrub that grows to about 90cm/3ft high and wide and needs the protection of a wall or fence, especially during the first few years after being planted. Small, rich blue flowers appear during mid-summer and in autumn the foliage usually turns red.

PLANTING A CONTAINER-GROWN SHRUB

1

2

3

4

5

6

1 About a week before planting, fork a light dressing of a general fertilizer into the planting area.
2 The day before planting the shrub, water its compost several times.
3 Dig a hole to accomodate the root-ball, placing the soil on sacking if planting in a lawn. Form and firm a slight mound in the hole's base.
4 Remove the container and place the root-ball on top of the mound. Adjust the height of the mound, so that the top of the root-ball is slightly lower than the surrounding soil.
5 Firm soil in layers around the root-ball. Do not completely fill the hole with soil and only then firm it. Use the heel of your shoe or boot to firm the soil.
6 Rake or fork the surface level and thoroughly water the whole area.

material, such as garden compost and manure. When preparing the soil for just one plant, ensure that the whole area is well drained; if not, there is a risk of creating a sump for excess water in the rest of the border to drain into. It is better to prepare the entire border in winter, digging deeply (pages 38-41), checking drainage (pages 42-3) and adding organic material.

ADVANTAGES OF CONTAINER-GROWN SHRUBS

Since the birth of garden centres in the early 1960s, plants have increasingly been grown and sold in containers. Before then, deciduous trees, shrubs and hedges were traditionally sold with bare roots, while evergreen types had their roots 'balled' (wrapped in hessian) to keep soil moist and around them. The advantages of buying container-grown shrubs, as opposed to bare-rooted ones, are as follows:

- They can be planted at any time when the soil is not frozen or waterlogged. (However, spring and early summer are the best planting times, as this enables plants to become established before the onset of winter).
- You can select the plant and check that it is healthy.
- They create a more instant garden, as bare-rooted shrubs are planted during their dormant period.
- Plants in containers receive less of a check to their growth than when 'balled' or 'bare-rooted'.

About a week before planting, sprinkle a general fertilizer at a rate of about 70g per sq m/ 2oz per sq yd over the entire area and fork it lightly into the surface of the soil.

Water the plant the day before planting it to ensure that its compost is moist; allow excess to drain before setting the plant in the soil. Dig out a hole large enough to accommodate the container. (When planting in a lawn, put the soil on sacking rather than directly on the grass). Form a slight mound of soil in the base of the hole, then firm it down gently.

Remove the container and place the root-ball on top of the mound, checking that its top is slightly below the surface.of the soil Adjust the height of the mound accordingly. If the shrub is in a border, turn the plant so that its best side is facing towards the path.

When the plant's depth is established, use a garden trowel or fork to spread soil around the root-ball, gently firming it in layers rather than filling the hole to its top and only then pressing it down. Finally, use the heel of your shoe or boot to ensure the soil is firm around the root-ball. Rake or lightly fork the surface level and water the soil to settle it around the roots.

Winter-flowering shrubs

PLANT NAME AND DESCRIPTION	SITUATION AND CULTIVATION	PROPAGATION

Calluna vulgaris
Heather (UK/USA)
Ling (UK/USA)
Scotch Heather (USA)
Height: 7.5-60cm/3-24in (range)
Spread: 13-60cm/5-24in (range)

Hardy, low-growing evergreen shrub with scale-like leaves ranging from green to shades of orange and red. From mid-summer to early winter plants bear spires of small, single or double flowers. Colours include white, pink and purple.

Plant in peaty, acid, moisture-retentive soil. Lighten heavy ground with sharp sand. Select an open, sunny position. In spring, use sharp shears to trim off dead flowers.
Early winter-flowering varieties include 'David Eason' (red), 'Durfordii' (pale pink), 'Goldsworth Crimson' (deep crimson), 'H.E. Beale' (bright rose-pink), 'Hibernica' (mauve), 'Peter Sparkes' (deep pink), 'Serlei' (white), 'Underwoodii' (silvery white) and 'White Gown' (white).

Take 2.5-5cm/1-2in-long cuttings from sideshoots from mid- to late summer. Remove the lower leaves and insert about 12-18mm/^{1}/2-^{3}/4in deep in pots containing equal parts moist peat and sharp sand, then place in gentle warmth. When rooted, transfer into individual pots and place in a cold frame until large enough to be planted into a garden.

Chimonanthus praecox
(syn. *C. fragrans*)
Winter Sweet (UK/USA)
Height: 1.8-3m/6-10ft against a wall
Spread: 2.4-3m/8-10ft against a wall

Bushy deciduous shrub has spicily scented, cup-shaped flowers with pale, waxy, yellow petals and purple centres from mid- to late winter. They are borne on bare stems, the mid-green leaves appearing later. 'Grandiflorus' has larger flowers, with red centres.

Well-drained but moisture-retentive soil and a warm, south- or west-facing position, preferably against a wall. It grows well in chalky soils.
Little pruning is needed, other than thinning out congested and old shoots in spring, after the flowers fade. However, when growing it against a wall, cut back all flowered shoots to within a few inches of their bases in early spring.
Young plants do not bear flowers.

Layer low-growing shoots in late summer. Rooting takes about two years. Then, sever from the parent and plant into a garden or nurserybed.
Alternatively, sow seeds in late summer or early autumn, in seed pans or pots in a cold frame. It takes five or more years to produce a flowering plant from seed and therefore most plants are bought or raised by layering shoots.

Cornus mas
Cornelian Cherry (UK/USA)
Sorbet (USA)
Height: 2.4-3.6m/8-12ft
Spread: 1.8-3m/6-10ft

Hardy, densely branched, twiggy and bushy deciduous shrub which bears golden yellow flowers in small clusters on naked stems from mid-winter to spring. Occasionally trees bear edible, red, semi-translucent fruits. The leaves become reddish purple in autumn.

Fertile, moisture-retentive but well-drained soil in full sun.
No regular pruning is needed, other than cutting out damaged shoots, or those that block paths or encroach on other plants in spring.
The deciduous nature of this shrub allows bulbs to be planted under it to create further colour in late winter and spring.

Sow seeds in late summer in sandy loam-based compost in seed pans or pots. Place in a cold frame. Germination is slow – up to one-and-a-half years. When the seedlings are large enough to handle, transfer them into individual pots. Later plant into a garden.

Daphne mezereum
February Daphne (USA)
Mezereon (UK/USA)
Mezereum (UK/USA)
Height: 90cm-1.5m/3-5ft
Spread: 60-90cm/2-3ft

Hardy, small deciduous shrub with fragrant, purple-red flowers from late winter to spring. The flowers cluster tightly on the stems and are followed in autumn by poisonous, scarlet berries. There is a white-flowered form.

Moisture-retentive but well-drained soil in full sun or light shade suits it, as well as soils containing lime. Many gardeners say it does best in cool, moist positions.
No regular pruning is needed, other than occasionally cutting out damaged or misplaced shoots in spring.
Plant small bulbs around it to create extra interest in spring.

Most daphnes are increased by layering shoots or taking cuttings. This daphne, however, is propagated by sowing seeds. These must be harvested as soon as the fruits show colour; sow them immediately in seed-trays and place in a cold frame. When the seedlings are large enough to handle, transfer them to small pots. Take the seeds only from healthy, vigorous plants.

Daphne odora
Winter Daphne (UK/USA)
Height: 1.5-1.8m/5-6ft
Spread: 1.5-1.8m/5-6ft

Bushy, slightly tender, rather lax evergreen shrub with shiny, mid-green leaves. From mid-winter to mid-spring it bears crowded heads of pale purple flowers.
The form 'Aureomarginata' has leaves with creamy white edges. It is slightly hardier than the normal species.

Erica x darleyensis
Erica (UK)
Heather (UK)
Height: 45-60cm/18-24in (range)
Spread: 45-75cm/18-30in (range)

Hardy evergreen shrub, a cross between *E. carnea* and *E. mediterranea*. From early winter to late spring it develops flowers in clusters up to 13cm/5in long in colours including white, pink and purple.

Erica erigena
(syn. *E. hibernica/E. mediterranea*)
Irish Heath (UK/USA)
Height: 1.8-3m/6-10ft
Spread: 90cm-1.2m/3-4ft

A slightly tender evergreen shrub with mid-green leaves arranged in whorls. The purple-pink flowers, borne in terminal clusters, often appear in mid-winter and continue until early summer. There are several varieties.

Lonicera fragrantissima
Height: 1.8-2.1m/6-7ft
Spread: 1.5-1.8m/5-6ft

A bushy shrub which can be evergreen, partially evergreen or deciduous, depending on the climate. Creamy white, very fragrant flowers are borne in pairs from mid-winter to early spring. It is best grown in a shrub border, rather than as a specimen on its own.

PLANT NAME AND DESCRIPTION	SITUATION AND CULTIVATION	PROPAGATION

Erica carnea
(syn. *E. herbacea*)
Erica (UK)
Heather (UK)
Snow Heather (USA)
Height: 5-30cm/2-12in (range)
Spread: 15-60cm/6-24in (range)

Hardy, prostrate or low-growing evergreen shrub with terminal flower clusters in white, pink, red and purple from late autumn to late spring; many create magnificent displays in winter.

Most heathers demand peaty, acid, moisture-retentive soil. Winter-flowering ericas, however, are tolerant of lime. Lighten heavy ground with sharp sand.
Plant ericas in open, sunny positions away from overhanging deciduous trees that will cast their leaves in autumn. Trim off dead flowers in spring.
Winter-flowering varieties include 'December Red', 'King George', 'Myretoun Ruby', 'Pink Spangles', 'Ruby Glow', 'Springwood Pink' and 'Springwood White'.

Take 2.5-5cm/1-2in-long cuttings from sideshoots from mid- to late summer. Remove the lower leaves and insert about 12-18mm/^{1}/$_2$-^{3}/$_4$in deep in pots containing equal parts moist peat and sharp sand and place in gentle warmth. When rooted, transfer into individual pots and place in a cold frame until large enough to be planted into a garden.

Hamamelis mollis
Chinese Witch Hazel (UK/USA)
Height: 1.8-3m/6-10ft
Spread: 2.1-3m/7-10ft

Hardy deciduous shrub or small tree with spreading branches. During early and mid-winter, sweetly scented, rich golden yellow, spider-like, flat-petalled flowers are borne in clusters along naked stems. In autumn, the mid-green leaves turn rich yellow. 'Pallida' has pale yellow flowers with claret-red centres.

Moisture-retentive but well-drained, neutral or slightly acid soil suits it. Heavy, wet soil needs to be improved with sharp sand and plenty of decayed compost and manure. Choose a sheltered, sunny or slightly shaded position.
No regular pruning is needed other than cutting out misplaced and straggly stems and branches in spring.

Layer low-growing stems in late summer. Rooting takes several years, after which sever the rooted part from the parent plant and set it in a nurserybed or garden.
Alternatively, take 10cm/4in-long cuttings from the current season's shoots in late summer, preferably as heel cuttings. Insert them in pots of equal parts moist peat and sharp sand and place in a cold frame. Unfortunately, they do not readily develop roots.

***Mahonia x media* 'Charity'**
(syn. *Mahonia* 'Charity')
Height: 1.8-2.4m/6-8ft or more
Spread: 1.5-2.1m/5-7ft or more

Hardy, evergreen shrub with leathery leaves formed of up to twenty-one dark green, spine-toothed leaflets. From early to late winter it bears cascading, 23-30cm/9-12in-long spires of fragrant, deep lemon yellow flowers that create a magnificent display at a time when they are best appreciated.

Moisture-retentive but well-drained, preferably slightly acid and peaty soil is desirable, although it survives lightly chalky conditions.
Little pruning is needed, other than cutting back straggly stems to ground level in spring.

Take 7.5-10cm/3-4in-long tip cuttings from sideshoots in mid-summer. Insert in pots of equal parts moist peat and sharp sand and place in a propagating frame with gentle bottom heat. When rooted, pot up into individual pots and place in a garden frame. During the following spring or early summer, plant into a nurserybed or garden.

Viburnum tinus
Laurustinus (UK/USA)
Height: 2.1-2.7m/7-9ft
Spread: 1.5-2.1m/5-7ft

Hardy, densely leaved and stemmed evergreen shrub with mid- to dark green leaves. From early winter to late spring it bears flat heads, up to 10cm/4in wide, of white flowers, pink when in bud.
There are several superb forms, including 'Eve Price', with carmine buds and pink-tinged white flowers.

Fertile, deeply prepared, moisture-retentive soil and a bright position sheltered from early-morning sun. Also, select a position sheltered from cold north and east winds.
No regular pruning is needed other than cutting out misplaced, dead, weak and straggly shoots in spring.

Take 7.5-10cm/3-4in-long cuttings, preferably heel cuttings, from the current season's shoots in mid-summer. Insert them in pots of equal parts moist peat and sharp sand and place in a propagating frame with gentle warmth. When rooted, pot up into individual pots and place in a cold frame. During the following spring or early summer, plant into a nurserybed for a couple of years.
Alternatively, layer low-growing shoots in late summer. They take about a year to develop roots.

Mahonia bealei
Height: 1.5-2.1m/5-7ft
Spread: 1.5-2.1m/5-7ft

Hardy, slow-growing evergreen shrub with leathery leaflets, grey-green above and yellowish green beneath. During mid- and late winter, lemon yellow flowers appear in 10-15cm/4-6in-long clusters at the tips of the stems.

Mahonia japonica
Height: 2.1-3m/7-10ft
Spread: 2.1-3.6m/7-12ft

Hardy evergreen shrub with leathery leaves formed of glossy, tooth-edged, dark green leaflets. From mid-winter to early spring it develops lily-of-the-valley scented, lemon yellow flowers in drooping clusters up to 23cm/9in long. This shrub is often confused with the closely related *M. bealei*.

Viburnum x bodnantense
Height: 2.4-3.6m/8-12ft
Spread: 1.8-3m/6-10ft

Hardy, large and upright deciduous shrub with clusters of sweetly scented, rose-tinted white flowers on bare stems from early to mid-winter. The flowers are remarkably tolerant of frost. The form 'Dawn' has richly fragrant flowers, rose-red when in bud and becoming white with a hint of pink.

Viburnum farreri
(syn. *V. fragrans*)
Height: 2.4-3m/8-10ft
Spread: 2.1-2.4m/7-8ft

Hardy, upright deciduous shrub with bright green, toothed leaves, which are tinted bronze when young. From early to late winter – and sometimes into early spring – it reveals richly scented white flowers, tinged pink, borne in pendent clusters up to 36mm/1^1/$_2$in long.

Planting a bare-rooted tree or shrub

Bare-rooted shrubs and trees can be bought directly from nurseries and garden centres, as well as through nursery mail-order catalogues. Usually, shrubs and trees are ordered in winter and arrive several months later.

If you are going to plant the shrub or tree within a week of its arrival, leave it in its wrapping and place it in a cool lobby or shed. However, if you have to delay planting because the weather is frosty or the soil excessively wet or frozen, the roots must be 'heeled-in'. Take out a 30cm/12in-deep trench in a sheltered, out-of-the-way corner of the garden, place the roots in it, cover them with soil and gently firm.

STAKING AND SUPPORTING TREES
Trees invariably need staking, especially when young and until their roots are established and the trunk is able to withstand strong winds. (Heavy snow falls can also bend the trunks of young trees when branches are laden with snow.) Always use stout – ash, chestnut or spruce – stakes which have had their lower end treated with a preservative.

There are several ways to support trees. One is to insert an upright stake into the planting hole prior to planting the tree. The top of the stake should be about 5cm/2in below the lowest branch and positioned on the windward side of the tree to reduce the chance of the trunk rubbing on the stake.

This is the best method to support an ornamental tree, especially one with a long, clear trunk; the stake is less obtrusive and it is possible, if the tree is in a lawn, to cut grass close to it.

Alternatively, you can insert a stake at a 45° angle, so that its top crosses the trunk just below the crotch. The top of the stake must face into the prevailing wind. This is an ideal method of re-staking a tree if an earlier stake has broken.

Another method is to create an H-shaped support by knocking two stakes into the soil, one each side of the tree, and securing a cross-stake to them to which the trunk is tied. Again, this is an ideal way to support trees where the original stake is broken.

Whichever method of staking you choose, it is essential that you tie the trunk securely to the

Right: The Mount Etna Broom (*Genista aetnensis*), a native of Sicily and Sardinia, forms a tall, elegant, rather sparse deciduous tree or large shrub with golden-yellow flowers during mid and late summer. When positioned against a dark background the richly coloured flowers create a beacon of colour that brings vitality to borders.

PLANTING A BARE-ROOTED TREE

1 Place the roots in a bucket of water overnight. Also, cut off any that are damaged or excessively long and thin.
2 Dig a hole, ensuring it is wide enough to accommodate the roots. Form and firm a slight mound in its base.
3 Knock a strong stake into the soil. Place the tree on top of the mound and spread out its roots. Place a straight piece of wood across the hole and check that the tree is slightly deeper than before. This allows for soil settlement.
4 The top of the stake should be just below the tree's crotch.
5 Cover and firm soil over the roots, in layers.
6 Use a couple of tree-ties to secure the stem to the stake. Ensure that the ties do not constrict the stem.

stake. Proprietary plastic ties are readily available; once they are in position, check them regularly to ensure that the trunk is not constricted and that they are still sound.

PLANTING A BARE-ROOTED TREE

Thoroughly dig the soil in late autumn, removing perennial weeds and adding well-decomposed organic material such as compost or manure (see pages 38-41). Also, ensure that the area is well drained (see pages 42-3). About a week before planting, lightly fork or rake a general fertilizer into the surface soil at about 70g per sq m/2oz per sq yd.

Check the roots and use secateurs or a sharp knife to cut off those that are damaged. If the roots are dry, place them in a bucket of water for several hours.

Dig a hole large enough to accommodate the roots and form a slight mound in its base. Temporarily place the tree in the hole and adjust its orientation so that the most attractive side faces the direction from which it will be mainly seen. Position a vertical stake so that it avoids the main roots and is on the windward side; remove the tree and hammer the stake 30-45cm/12-18in into the soil so that its top will be 5cm/2in below the lowest branch.

Replace the tree, spread its roots over the mound and adjust the height so that the old soil mark on the trunk is 18-25mm/³/₄-1in below the surface. Check this by laying a piece of straight wood across the hole, then add or remove soil as necessary. Positioning the trunk slightly lower than the surrounding soil allows for the inevitable soil settlement after planting.

Put the tree into the hole, spread out the roots and add friable soil in stages. Gently lift the plant up and down several times to enable the soil to work in between the roots, and firm the soil in layers in the planting hole as you go.

When the hole is filled – and the soil is firmed – to the level of the surrounding ground, tie the tree to the stake in a couple of places using tree-ties. Ensure that the top of the stake is just below the crotch. Gently water the soil to settle it around the roots.

Inspect the ties several times in the first few months after planting; as the soil settles the trunk may drop slightly causing it to be strangulated unless the ties are loosened.

ADVANTAGES OF BARE-ROOTED SHRUBS AND TREES

Although you cannot inspect bare-rooted plants to check their health and must plant them in winter immediately (or heel them in) to prevent roots drying out, there are advantages in buying some trees and shrubs with bare roots rather than as container-grown specimens.

- They are usually slightly cheaper than container-grown types.

- Because these plants are raised in nurserybeds, their roots are not constricted in small containers. Relatively small plants do not suffer when grown in containers, but the roots of large trees invariably become contorted and take longer to become established after planting than bare-rooted types. Indeed, if too twisted they seldom recover.

- Rarer and more unusual species and varieties of trees and shrubs are not always sold as container-grown plants, but are usually available as bare-rooted types from specialist nurseries.

Barks, stems, seed heads and berries

PLANT NAME AND DESCRIPTION	SITUATION AND CULTIVATION	PROPAGATION

Acer griseum
Paperbark Maple (UK/USA)
Height: 3.6-4.5m/12-15ft
Spread: 2.4-3m/8-10ft

Slow-growing deciduous tree with buff-coloured bark that peels to reveal orange-brown under bark. The mid-green leaves, formed of three leaflets, assume rich scarlet and deep red shades in autumn and create a magnificent display, especially when highlighted by the low rays of the sun.

Wind-sheltered position in sun or light shade, and slightly chalky or neutral, well-drained but moisture-retentive soil. Support young trees to prevent damage from wind.
No pruning is normally needed, except initially to shape the tree, removing crossing, misplaced and damaged shoots and branches.
It is superb as a focal point in a lawn. Alternatively, position in a border of low-growing, shade-tolerant herbaceous plants. Avoid obscuring the trunk.

Buy trees from a nursery. This acer readily produces fruits, although seeds rarely germinate. Indeed, their germination rate is seldom more than five percent and this accounts for the relative scarcity of this superb tree. There is no readily available rootstock onto which it can be grafted.

Araucaria araucana
Chile Pine (UK)
Chilean Pine (USA)
Monkey Puzzle (UK/USA)
Height: 6m/20ft after twenty years
Spread: 3-3.6m/10-12ft after twenty years

Distinctively shaped evergreen conifer with stiff, shiny, rigid and spine-tipped dark green leaves closely overlapping each other. Eventually the branches · droop and the lower ones fall off, leaving an attractive bare trunk.

Moisture-retentive, fertile soil suits it best, although it grows in most situations, other than those that are badly drained. Stake young plants to ensure that they are upright.
Best planted in spring so that plants are well established by the onset of winter. No pruning is required.

Sow seeds singly in small pots of loam-based compost in spring and place in a cold frame. Gradually transfer plants into larger pots of loam-based compost. After three or four years, they can be planted ·into a garden.
Alternatively, take 10cm/4in-long cuttings from vertical shoots in mid-summer and insert into pots of equal parts moist peat and sharp sand. However, removing shoot tips spoils a plant's shape.

Arbutus x andrachnoides
(syn. *A.* x *hybrida*)
Height: 3-4.5m/10-15ft
Spread: 2.1-2.7m/7-9ft

Hardy deciduous tree with cinnamon-red bark and slightly leathery, dark green leaves. In late autumn or spring it bears ivory-white, pitcher-shaped, nodding flowers. Unlike its parents, the Grecian Strawberry Tree (*A. andrachne*) and Killarney Strawberry Tree (*A. unedo*), it seldom bears strawberry-like fruits.

Slightly acid or lightly alkaline soil and a sunny aspect sheltered from cold winds. It tolerates shallow, limy conditions. Young trees are susceptible to damage from cold winds, but with age they become hardier.
No regular pruning is needed, other than cutting off straggly shoots in early spring. Occasionally, remove lower branches to further expose the attractive bark. This tree is especially attractive when positioned where the low light of evening glances off the leaves and bark.

Take 7.5-10cm/3-4in-long heel cuttings of half-ripe shoots during early to mid-summer. Trim the heel, remove lower leaves and insert in pots of equal parts moist peat and sharp sand in a propagation frame with a bottom heat of 16°C/61°F. When rooted, pot up the cuttings individually into small pots and place in a cold frame until large enough to be planted into a nurserybed or permanent position.

***Betula utilis* 'Jacquemontii'**
(syn. *B. jacquemontii*)
Height: 6-9m/20-30ft
Spread: 3-4.5m/10-15ft

Hardy deciduous tree with dazzling stems and peeling bark, usually white but light pinkish brown and ochre-cream forms are known.
It is closely related to the Himalayan Birch (*B. utilis*), which has magnificent orange-brown or dark coppery brown peeling bark.

Sun or shade and deep, well-drained, slightly acid loam suits it. Stake newly planted trees. No regular pruning is needed, other than occasionally cutting out a misplaced or damaged branch.
It is usually planted as a specimen tree in a lawn and looks especially attractive when surrounded by a sea of naturalized, small, spring-flowering crocuses. Remember not to cut the grass until the bulbs have died down naturally.

Raised from seed, but takes several years to produce a tree ready for planting into a garden. Therefore, buy strong, healthy trees from a nursery.

Acer davidii
Snakebark Maple (UK/USA)
Height: 4.5-6m/15-20ft
Spread: 2.4-3m/8-10ft

Hardy deciduous tree with dark green leaves; they are red-bronze when unfolding and in autumn assume tints of yellow, red and purple. The grey bark is striped white; this is especially noticeable when the tree is grown in light shade.

Acer pensylvanicum
Moosewood (UK/USA)
Snakebark Maple (UK)
Height: 5.4-7.5m/18-25ft
Spread: 3-4.5m/10-15ft

Hardy deciduous upright tree with its trunk and branches striped with jagged white lines. The young wood, however, is first green, then reddish brown, later striped. Other Snakebark Maples include *A. davidii* and *A. grosseri*.

Arbutus andrachne
Grecian Strawberry Tree (UK)
Height: 3.6-4.5m/12-15ft
Spread: 2.4-2.7m/8-9ft

Slightly tender – especially when young – half-hardy evergreen shrub. The dark green leaves are leathery, but the most attractive feature is the smooth, cinnamon-red, peeling bark. White flowers in spring are followed by strawberry-like, orange-red fruits.

Arbutus menziesii
Madrona (UK/USA)
Madrone (USA)
Height: 4.5-5.4m/15-18ft
Spread: 2.8-4.5m/8-15ft

Evergreen tree with glossy, dark green leaves and small, white, pitcher-like flowers in terminal clusters up to 23cm/9in long in mid- and late spring. The trunk and large branches have smooth, terracotta bark.

PLANT NAME AND DESCRIPTION	SITUATION AND CULTIVATION	PROPAGATION

Calocedrus decurrens
(syn. *Libocedrus decurrens*)
California Incense Cedar (USA)
Incense Cedar (UK/USA)
Height: 6-7.5m/20-25ft
Spread: 2.4-3.6m/8-12ft

Usually slender, slow-growing evergreen conifer with dense, dark green and glossy leaves crowded in flattened, vertical, fan-like sprays. Attractive, reddish brown, scaly and roughly textured bark.

Sunny, sheltered position and fertile, well-drained but moisture-retentive soil. Plant young trees in spring. No regular pruning is needed, other than cutting out double stems when young.

This distinctive columnar conifer looks best when in a small group, where it can create a superb focal point at the end of a long path and when highlighted against the sky. When planting just one specimen, consider 'Aureovariegata' with yellow-splashed foliage.

Sow seeds in late autumn in pots of loam-based seed compost and place in a cool greenhouse or outdoors in a garden frame. By the following spring the seeds will have germinated and the young seedlings can be transferred into a nurserybed. Keep the soil free from weeds and after three or four years set the plants into permanent positions.
C.d. 'Aureovariegata' is raised from 7.5cm/3in-long cuttings taken in mid- to late summer and inserted in sandy compost. Place in a cold frame.

Chaenomeles speciosa
Japanese Quince (UK/USA)
Japonica (UK)
Height: 1.5-1.8m/5-6ft
Spread: 1.5-1.8m/5-6ft

Hardy, deciduous, twiggy shrub with a tangle of spiny stems and dark green, glossy leaves. Clusters of bowl-shaped flowers, in shades of red, appear mainly in late winter and spring, sometimes into early summer. In late summer and autumn it bears yellow-green fruits.

Full sun and well-drained but moisture-retentive soil. When planted against a south- or west-facing wall it flowers earlier than normal.

Little pruning is needed when grown as a bush, other than thinning out congested shoots after the flowers fade. When grown against a wall, it grows higher and needs regular pruning in late spring or early summer. Cut back the previous season's shoots to two or three buds from its point of origin.

Layer low-growing stems in late summer. However, rooting is slow and it takes two or three years for plants to develop roots. When rooted, sever plants from the parent and plant in a nurserybed until growing strongly. Alternatively, take 10cm/4in-long cuttings – preferably heel cuttings – of the current season's shoots in mid-summer. Insert in pots of equal parts moist peat and sharp sand and place in gentle warmth. Pot up individually when rooted and place in a cold frame.

Clematis vitalba
Old Man's Beard (UK)
Traveller's Joy (UK)
Height: 4.5-6m/15-20ft or more
Spread: 4.5-6m/15-20ft or more

Vigorous, deciduous, somewhat sprawling climber with a country-like appearance; too large for most gardens but ideal in a wild garden. Its main attraction is the glistening, silky seed heads that appear in autumn and remain throughout winter.

Full sun or very light shade, but the roots must not be in direct sunlight. Deeply prepared, slightly alkaline and moisture-retentive but well-drained soil is needed.

Cut out dead and straggly shoots in spring. If neglected, this climber becomes a tumbling mass of stems; neglected plants can be cut hard back in spring.

Low, straggly stems often layer themselves – cut away rooted plants in spring and replant into their growing positions. Alternatively, take 10cm/4in-long cuttings from the current season's shoots in mid-summer. Insert them in pots of equal parts moist peat and sharp sand and place in gentle warmth. When rooted, pot up into individual pots and overwinter in a cold frame. Plant into a border in spring.

***Cornus stolonifera* 'Flaviramea'**
Dogwood (UK/USA)
Height: 1.8-2.4m/6-8ft
Spread: 2.1-3m/7-10ft

Deciduous, vigorous, suckering, spreading shrub with dark green, oval to lance-like leaves, 5-13cm/2-5in long. This well-known variety has eye-catching bright greenish yellow young shoots in winter and is especially attractive when planted at the side of a pond.

Sun or partial shade and fertile, moisture-retentive soil. To encourage the growth of young stems, cut back all shoots to within 5-7.5cm/2-3in of soil level in spring.

The form 'Flaviramea' is closely related to the bright crimson-stemmed Westonbirt Dogwood (*C. alba* 'Sibirica'), with which it forms a superb colour association when planted with it in a group.

Remove and replant rooted suckers in late autumn or early spring. Alternatively, layer long shoots in late summer, severing and planting them a year later when rooted.

Betula albo-sinensis septentrionalis
Height: 4.5-5.4m/15-18ft
Spread: 2.4-3m/8-10ft

Hardy deciduous tree mainly grown for its attractive bark, which is shiny, orange-brown with a grey and pink bloom. The ordinary species is known as the Chinese Red Birch and has bright orange to orange-red bark, which peels off in thin sheets.

Betula ermanii
Erman's Birch (UK)
Russian Rock Birch (UK)
Height: 5.4-7.5m/18-25ft
Spread: 2.4-3.6m/8-12ft

Slightly tender – especially if subjected to spring frosts in exposed gardens – deciduous tree, widely acclaimed for its peeling, creamy white bark, tinted pink on the trunk. Branches are orange-brown.

Betula papyrifera
Canoe Birch (UK/USA)
Paper Birch (UK/USA)
White Birch (UK/USA)
Height: 6-9m/20-30ft
Spread: 3-4.5m/10-15ft

Hardy deciduous tree with gleaming white bark, which, on old trees, peels off in large strips. It is one of the whitest of all birches and very smooth.

Cornus alba
Red-barked Dogwood (UK)
Tartarian Dogwood (USA)
Height: 1.2-1.5m/4-5ft
Spread: 1.2-1.8m/4-6ft

Hardy, vigorous, suckering and spreading deciduous shrub with rich red young stems in winter. *C.a.* 'Sibirica', the Westonbirt or Siberian Dogwood, has brilliant crimson stems in winter. Cut back all stems in spring.

69

Barks, stems, seed heads and berries

PLANT NAME AND DESCRIPTION	SITUATION AND CULTIVATION	PROPAGATION

Cortaderia selloana
Pampas Grass (UK/USA)
Height: 1.5-2.4m/5-8ft
Spread: 1.5-2.1m/5-7ft

Perennial evergreen grass with slender leaves and tall, woody stems that bear silvery plumes up to 45cm/18in long from late summer to late winter. There are several forms: 'Pumila' (1.2-1.8m/4-6ft high) and 'Sunningdale Silver' (2.4-3m/8-10ft and with extra-large plumes).

Full sun and fertile, moisture-retentive soil. It is ideal as a focal point in a lawn, or when planted in a shrub border. However, do not crowd other plants around it in this situation. In winter, when covered with frost or a light coating of snow, it looks particularly attractive.
In spring, cut down the old flower stems, as well as dead leaves. Wear gloves to prevent the leaves tearing your hands.

Lift and divide large clumps in spring, replanting the young parts. However, this usually results in spoiling the mother plant's shape.

Corylopsis sinensis
Winter Hazel (UK/USA)
Height: 3-4.5m/10-15ft
Spread: 2.4-3.6m/8-12ft

Hardy, deciduous, twiggy and branching shrub. The somewhat pear-shaped leaves are heart-shaped at their base. During late winter and early spring, fragrant, primrose-yellow, catkin-like flowers appear on bare branches. There are several superb forms, including 'Spring Purple' with purple-violet young stems.

Plant in well-drained but moisture-retentive soil. Preferably, the soil should be lime-free, but if alkalinity is only slight, mix plenty of peat into the topsoil. Plant in full sun or partial shade, and away from cold winter and spring wind.
No pruning is needed, other than occasionally cutting out dead shoots at ground level when flowering ceases.

Layer low-growing stems in autumn or early winter; they take up to two years to develop roots. Sever rooted stems in spring and plant them into a nurserybed or garden.

Cotoneaster horizontalis
Fishbone Cotoneaster (UK)
Rock Cotoneaster (USA)
Height: 60-90cm/2-3ft
Spread: 1.2-1.8m/4-6ft

Hardy, deciduous shrub with branches initially horizontal but with age slightly upright. The branches form a herringbone-like framework, and in summer are covered with small, dark green, glossy leaves. In autumn, branches are smothered in red berries.

Full sun or very light shade and well-drained but moisture-retentive soil. No pruning is needed, other than shaping young plants in spring.

Layer low-growing stems in late summer or autumn. Rooting takes up to two years, when young plants can be severed from the parent and moved to a nurserybed until large enough to be set in a garden. Alternatively, put them directly into a garden border. Plants can also be raised from seeds, but the seedlings are usually variable and do not totally resemble the parents.

Cotoneaster lacteus
Height: 3-4.5m/10-15ft
Spread: 2.4-3.6m/8-12ft

Hardy evergreen shrub with shiny, deep green, leathery leaves and creamy white flowers borne in 5-7.5cm/2-3in-wide heads during early summer. These are followed in autumn by clusters of red berries which last well into winter.

Full sun or very light shade and well-drained but moisture-retentive soil. No pruning is needed, other than shaping young plants in spring.

Layer low-growing stems in late summer or autumn. Rooting takes up to two years, when young plants can be severed from the parent and moved to a nurserybed until large enough to be set in a garden. Alternatively, put them directly into a garden border. Plants can also be raised from seeds.

Cornus stolonifera
American Dogwood (UK/USA)
Red Osier Dogwood (UK/USA)
Height: 1.8-2.4m/6-8ft
Spread: 2.1-3m/7-10ft

Deciduous, vigorous, suckering, spreading shrub with dark green, oval to lance-like leaves, 5-13cm/2-5in long. This well-known shrub has dull red stems in winter. These are encouraged by cutting back all stems in spring.

***Corylus avellana* 'Contorta'**
Corkscrew Hazel (UK)
Harry Lauder's Walking Stick (UK)
Height: 2.4-3m/8-10ft
Spread: 1.8-2.4m/6-8ft

Hardy, slow-growing shrub with branches curiously twisted in a spiral. When seen against a blue sky in winter it is very attractive. This is a form of the larger and more vigorous Hazel or Cob-nut.

Dipelta floribunda
Height: 2.4-3.6m/8-12ft
Spread: 2.1-3m/7-10ft

Deciduous shrub, hardy in most temperate regions, with mid-green leaves and attractive, peeling, light brown bark. During late spring and early summer it bears sweetly scented, foxglove-like, pale pink flowers flushed yellow in the throat.

Pernettya mucronata
(now known as *Gaultheria mucronata*, but invariably sold as *Pernettya*)
Height: 60-90cm/2-3ft
Spread: 90cm-1.5m/3-5ft

Bushy, hardy evergreen shrub with small, glossy, dark green leaves. Clusters of round fruits, varying in colour from white to pink, purple and red, appear in autumn and remain throughout winter. Old bushes become leggy.

PLANT NAME AND DESCRIPTION	SITUATION AND CULTIVATION	PROPAGATION

Eucalyptus pauciflora
Cabbage Gum (UK/USA)
Ghost Gum (UK/USA)
Height: 7.5-10.5m/25-35ft
Spread: 4.5-6m/15-20ft

Hardy evergreen tree with leathery, bright glossy-green, sickle-shaped adult leaves. When young the leaves are oval to circular. When first exposed the bark is white, darkening to grey. It is one of the hardiest eucalyptus species.

Full sun and well-drained but moisture-retentive fertile soil – it tolerates slight chalkiness. Plant small trees in early summer, staking them to prevent damage from strong winds, as wind often causes more damage than severe frost. Rapid establishment depends on adequate moisture during summer. As long as the tree is not damaged by frost, it will develop a single trunk. However, if wind or frost damage does occur, cut back to within 45cm/18in of soil level in late spring.

New Cabbage Gum trees are normally raised from seeds. They germinate rapidly when sown in late winter or early spring, 3mm/^{1}/sin deep in seed trays of loam-based compost kept at 13°C/55°F. After germination, reduce the temperature and prick out the seedlings, either into wider spacings in seedboxes or into individual pots. Overwinter in a cold frame and plant into a nurserybed or garden during the following spring.

Prunus maackii
Amur Cherry (UK)
Manchurian Cherry (UK)
Height: 7.5-10.5m/25-35ft
Spread: 4.5-6m/15-20ft

Tall, deciduous, broadly pyramidal tree with attractive smooth, brownish yellow bark that peels like that of a birch. The form 'Amber Queen' has glossy, honey-coloured, flaking bark and white, scented flowers.

Plant in well-drained but moisture-retentive, friable soil. Good light is essential. Ensure that the tree is well staked when young to produce a straight trunk and so that roots are not loosened by strong winds.
No pruning is needed, except during its formative years to remove a misplaced branched. Prune this tree in early spring.

Can be raised from cuttings, but it is better to buy an established tree from a nursery.

Pyracantha rogersiana
Firethorn (UK/USA)
Height: 1.5-2.4m/5-8ft
Spread: 1.2-1.8m/4-6ft

Hardy evergreen shrub with narrow, mid-green leaves. It is ideal for planting against a wall. In early summer it develops white flowers in clustered heads 5cm/2in wide, while in autumn, and throughout much of winter, it bears reddish orange fruits. The form 'Flava' has bright yellow fruits.

Full sun or light shade and fertile, deeply prepared, well-drained soil. It grows well in slightly acid, as well as lightly alkaline, soil. If growing it as a wall shrub, ensure that the supporting framework is strong.
No pruning is necessary unless the plant is grown as a wall shrub; then, cut out excessively long shoots from late spring to mid-summer.

Take 7.5-10cm/3-4in-long cuttings from the current season's shoots in mid-summer. Insert them in pots of equal parts moist peat and sharp sand and place in gentle warmth. When rooted, pot up into individual pots and overwinter in a cold frame. In spring, either transfer young plants into large pots or plant into a nurserybed.

Trachycarpus fortunei
(*T. excelsa/Chamaerops excelsa*)
Chinese Windmill Palm (USA)
Chusan Palm (UK)
Height: 1.8-3.6m/6-12ft
Spread: 1.8-3m/6-10ft

Slow-growing evergreen palm with large fans, often 90cm/3ft wide, of glossy, mid-green leaves borne on stalks up to 90cm/3ft long. Its trunk is clothed in black, coarse, hairy fibres.

Sun or light shade and sheltered from cold winds. Well-drained but moisture-retentive soil, neither strongly acid nor strongly alkaline, is essential. Plant in mid- to late spring, initially staking to prevent damage from strong winds.
It is ideal for introducing a Mediterranean atmosphere to patios, especially those with a southerly aspect and sheltered from cold winds. Alternatively, plant it as a specimen tree at the side of a sunny lawn.

In late spring, cut off large suckers from around the plant's base and pot up into loam-based compost. Place in a greenhouse where 10-13°C/50-55°F can be maintained. When rooted, lower the temperature and plant into a nurserybed during the following spring.
Alternatively, in spring, sow seeds 2.5cm/1in deep in seed trays of sandy compost kept at 24°C/75°F. After germination, reduce the temperature to 10°C/50°F and prick off the seedlings into individual pots.

Phyllostachys nigra
Black Bamboo (UK/USA)
Black-stemmed Bamboo (UK)
Height: 3-6m/10-20ft
Spread: Forms large clumps

A superb bamboo, hardy once established. In warm areas, and when moisture is available to it, it is spreading and very vigorous. The hollow stems are initially green, but later become very black.

Prunus serrula
Height: 6-7.5m/20-25ft
Spread: 4.5-5.4m/15-18ft
Birch-bark Tree (UK)

Hardy deciduous tree with narrow, slender-pointed, willow-like leaves and clusters of white flowers during mid- and late spring. The tree, however, is mainly grown for its bright reddish brown, mahogany-like peeling bark, which is especially noticeable on young trees.

Rubus cockburnianus
(syn. *R. giraldianus*)
Ornamental Bramble (UK/USA)
Height: 2.1-2.7m/7-9ft
Spread: 1.5-1.8m/5-6ft

Hardy, vigorous deciduous shrub with upright stems that have a white, waxy bloom tinged blue during winter. The stems are sparsely covered with stiff spines up to 12mm/^{1}/2in long. In early summer it bears small, purple flowers.

***Salix matsudana* 'Tortuosa'**
Dragon's-claw Willow (UK/USA)
Height: 3-4.5m/10-15ft
Spread: 2.4-3.6m/8-12ft

Hardy, slow-growing and erect deciduous shrub with contorted and twisted branches. The leaves are narrow, pointed and mid-green. In spring it bears greenish yellow catkins.

Planting a hedge

At one time, fortress-like, solid and near-impenetrable hedges dominated most front gardens. They were planted to create privacy, keep out wandering animals, provide a windbreak and mark the property's boundary. But hedges can be more than protective, or mere definers of boundaries. They should be integral parts of a garden's design and their selection and position given as much consideration as other features.

FORMAL OR INFORMAL HEDGES
Some hedges are clipped and therefore have a formal appearance, with vertical sides and flat or castellated tops, whereas others are informal, with a softer outline. The choice between hedges is largely a matter of personal preference; to many gardeners, a neatly trimmed Privet (*Ligustrum ovalifolium*), Yew (*Taxus baccata*), Chinese Honeysuckle (*Lonicera nitida*) or Dwarf Box (*Buxus sempervirens* 'Suffruticosa') hedge represents all that is desirable in a formal setting. To others there is nothing more spectacular than a lax outline formed, perhaps, of the evergreen *Berberis* x *stenophylla* or deciduous *Forsythia* x *intermedia* 'Spectabilis'. Both of these hedging shrubs have superb flowers.

PLANTING A HEDGE
Once planted, a hedge will be a feature for many decades. It therefore deserves the same thorough soil preparation as that given to other shrubs. In autumn or early winter, dig the soil and mix in well-decayed compost or manure (see pages 38-41). Also, check that the drainage is satisfactory: if areas remain wet, install drains (see pages 42-3).

The exact time for planting a hedge depends on the plants. Deciduous hedges formed of bare-rooted shrubs are planted from early to late winter, whenever the soil is not frozen or excessively wet. Evergreen 'balled' shrubs (carefully dug up from a nurserybed and their roots wrapped in hessian) are planted in late spring and early summer, as well as late summer and early autumn, when the soil is warm and moist and the weather not too hot. Container-grown shrubs, both evergreen and deciduous, can be planted any time when the soil is not frozen or very wet.

PLANTING A CONIFEROUS HEDGE

1 Dig out a trench about 30cm/12in deep and 30-45cm/12-18in wide.
2 A few hours before planting the hedge, thoroughly water the individual plants.
3 Space out the plants in the trench and check that the surface of the compost will be slightly deeper than before. This allows for subsequent soil settlement.
4 Remove the containers and gently spread top-soil around the roots. Firm it in layers, rather than all at once when the trench is full.
5 In windy areas tie each plant to an individual cane. In especially blustery areas, tie each cane top to a wire strained between posts at either end. Take care not to constrict the stems.
6 Thoroughly water the soil. several times and apply a mulch.

Below: The Dwarf Box (*Buxus sempervirens 'Suffruticosa'*) is ideal for creating a dwarf, evergreen hedge. Here it is seen as an edging for the Arum Lily *Zantedeschia aethiopica* 'Crowborough'.

Whatever the hedge, the way to plant it is the same. Dig out a trench about 30cm/12in deep and 30-45cm/12-18in wide, depending on the spread of each plant's roots. It is better to dig out a trench, rather than to create individual planting holes. On pages 74-5, many hedging plants are illustrated and described, with detailed notes given about their planting distances. In general, however, plants in low-growing hedges are spaced 23-30cm/9-12in apart; medium-height types 30-45cm/12-18in apart; and plants for tall hedges 45-75cm/18-30in apart. Plants in high windbreaks (usually large conifers) are spaced 90cm/3ft (or more) apart.

Where a wide, sound-deadening hedge is required, use a double row of plants. Dig out a wide trench (about twice the normal width) and stagger the plants, with a space between the rows equal to about half or three-quarters the distance between plants in the row.

Check that when planted each shrub will be 18-25mm/$3^3/_4$-1in deeper than previously planted to allow for subsequent ground settlement. The soil mark on the stem indicates the previous depth. Spread and firm soil in layers around the roots.

In exceptionally windy areas you will need to stake young plants. Insert a cane by each plant and tie its top to a wire tensioned between stakes at either end of the row.

To encourage deciduous plants to develop shoots near to ground level, and to ensure that the hedge's base is clothed in leaves during later years, cut back each plant by one-third to a half immediately after planting.

Hedges for all gardens

PLANT NAME AND DESCRIPTION	SITUATION AND CULTIVATION	PROPAGATION

X *Cupressocyparis leylandii*
Leyland Cypress (UK)
Height: 6-9m/20-30ft as a hedge
Spread: 1.2-1.8m/4-6ft as a hedge

Hardy, exceptionally fast-growing, evergreen conifer with grey-green foliage. It is a cross between two distinctive conifers, *Chamaecyparis nootkatensis* and *Cupressus macrocarpa*. Although frequently grown as a hedge, it is better as a windbreak and left to grow 15m/50ft or more.

Full sun and ordinary well-drained soil. When growing plants as a hedge, space them 75-90cm/2½-3ft apart; but set them 1.5-2.4m/5-8ft apart and in staggered rows when planting as a large windbreak. Forms a large hedge which becomes difficult to clip.

Take 10cm/4in-long cuttings from lateral shoots during late summer and early autumn. Trim off the lower leaves and insert them in pots of equal parts moist peat and sharp sand; place them in a cold frame. When rooted, transfer into individual pots and place outdoors. Alternatively, plant into a nurserybed until large enough to be planted into a garden.

Cupressus macrocarpa
Monterey Cypress (UK/USA)
Height: 1.8-3m/6-10ft as a hedge
Spread: 1-1.2m/3½-4ft as a hedge

Hardy, vigorous, fast-growing evergreen conifer with bright green foliage in densely packed sprays. Although hardy, young plants can be damaged in exceptionally cold and exposed positions. With age, the hedge tends to broaden. 'Golden Cone' (illustrated) has golden foliage: there are other golden forms.

Full sun and well-drained but moisture-retentive soil. When growing plants as a hedge, set them 45-60cm/18-24in apart. Clip established hedges in mid-summer.

Take 7.5cm/3in-long cuttings from the tips of shoots in late summer and insert them in pots of equal parts moist peat and sharp sand. Place in a cold frame. When rooted, plant into a nurserybed until large enough to the put in a garden.

Fagus sylvatica
Beech (UK)
European Beech (USA)
Height: 2.4-3.6m/8-12ft as a hedge
Spread: 1-1.5m/3½-5ft as a hedge

Hardy, vigorous deciduous tree that can be grown to form a large boundary hedge, ideal for filtering strong, cold, north winds. The broadly oval, wavy-edged leaves are bright green when young, later becoming mid-to deep green and yellow and russet in autumn.

Full sun or light shade and fertile, well-drained soil. Avoid heavy and badly drained ground. When growing plants as a hedge, position them 45-60cm/18-24in apart in a single row. Alternatively, create a wider hedge by planting a double row, with the plants staggered. Plant them firmly and immediately cut off the top one-quarter to one-third to encourage branching and the development of shoots from the hedge's base. Trim beech hedges every year in mid-summer.

Sow seeds outdoors in a sheltered, slightly shaded seedbed in autumn. Germination is not rapid and it is two or three years before young plants can be planted into a garden.

***Lavandula angustifolia* 'Hidcote'**
(syn. *L. nana atropurpurea*)
Lavender (UK/USA)
Height: 30-60cm/12-24in
Spread: 45-60cm/18-24in

Hardy evergreen shrub; forms a low-growing, relatively short-lived hedge that is ideal for separating one part of a garden from another, or even alongside a path. The narrow and silvery grey leaves are surmounted by deep purple-blue flowers from mid- to late summer.

Full sun and well-drained soil in a sheltered position. It is ideal for planting in coastal areas as it is tolerant of salt-spray. When growing plants as a hedge, set them 23-30cm/9-12in apart in a single row. In spring, pinch out the growing tips to encourage bushiness, and annually clip established hedges in early to mid-spring.

Take 7.5cm/3in-long cuttings from non-flowering shoots in mid-summer and insert them in pots of equal parts moist peat and sharp sand. Place in a cold frame. When rooted, transfer them individually into small pots and overwinter in a cold frame. Plant into a garden in spring.

Berberis* x *stenophylla
Height: 1.5-1.8m/5-6ft as a hedge
Spread: 1.3-1.5m/4½-5ft as a hedge

Hardy evergreen shrub with arching stems that bear sprays of yellow flowers during spring and into early summer. Untrimmed hedges bear berries, but become larger than the size indicated above. Creates a hedge with an informal outline. Space the plants 45-60cm/18-24in apart.

***Buxus sempervirens* 'Suffruticosa'**
Edging Box (UK/USA)
Height: 20-38cm/8-15in as a hedge
Spread: 15-23cm/6-9in as a hedge

Hardy, dwarf evergreen shrub with small, shiny, dark green leaves. It is ideal for creating miniature hedges within a garden. However, it needs to be regularly clipped to keep it small. Space the plants 15-20cm/6-8in apart.

Cotoneaster lacteus
Height: 1.5-2.1m/5-7ft as a hedge
Spread: 75-90cm/2½-3ft as a hedge

Hardy evergreen shrub with oval, leathery, deep green leaves. Their undersides are hairy and grey. Creamy white flowers are borne in early and mid-summer.
  It is excellent for creating an evergreen hedge in cold regions. Space the plants 38-45cm/15-18in apart.

***Escallonia* 'Donard Seedling'**
Height: 1.5-1.8m/5-6ft as a hedge
Spread: 1.2-1.5m/4-5ft as a hedge

Slightly tender evergreen shrub with long, arching branches bearing glossy, dark green leaves. Apple-blossom-pink flowers are borne in early and mid-summer on arching branches. Space the plants 38-45cm/15-18in apart and prune off the top quarter of all stems to encourage bushiness.

PLANT NAME AND DESCRIPTION	SITUATION AND CULTIVATION	PROPAGATION

Ligustrum ovalifolium
California Privet (USA)
Privet (UK)
Height: 1.2-1.8m/4-6ft as a hedge
Spread: 60-75cm/2-2½ft as a hedge

Hardy, bushy shrub, usually evergreen, but in exposed areas and during exceptionally cold winters it can become only partially evergreen. With its oval, mid-green leaves it creates a dominant feature and well-grown plants produce an attractive screen.

Full sun to shade and ordinary garden soil. Avoid very light or heavy soils. When growing plants as a hedge, space them 30-45cm/12-18in apart, in single or double rows. In double ones, stagger the plants across the rows.
Set the plants in position in autumn or early spring, and in late spring cut them back by about a half to encourage bushiness. The following spring, cut back all shoots by one-third. Regularly clip established hedges in both late spring and late summer.

Take 25-30cm/10-12in-long hardwood cuttings in autumn and insert them 15cm/6in deep in sandy soil in a nurserybed. The following autumn, move the cuttings to their growing positions.

***Lonicera nitida* 'Baggeson's Gold'**
Height: 90cm-1.2m/3-4ft as a hedge
Spread: 75-90cm/2½-3ft as a hedge

Hardy, bushy evergreen with small, golden leaves which become yellowish green in autumn. It is fractionally less vigorous and hardy than the all-green form, and tends to produce strong, irregular stems. If planted as a hedge against a sheltered and sun-blessed wall it grows slightly higher.

Any ordinary, well-drained but moisture-retentive soil suits it. A position in full sun is preferable; when in shade the leaf colour is not so bright. When growing plants as a hedge, space them 25cm/10in apart. After planting, cut back all shoots by about a half, and during the second spring by one-third. This ensures a bushy nature and a base full of stems and leaves.

Take 10cm/4in-long cuttings during mid- and late summer. Remove the lower leaves and insert them in equal parts moist peat and sharp sand in pots. Place in a cold frame and when roots have formed transfer into individual pots or plant into a nurserybed.
Another way to increase this plant is to take 23cm/9in-long hardwood cuttings in autumn and to insert them about 10cm/4in deep in a well-drained nurserybed.

Taxus baccata
Yew (UK/USA)
Height: 1.8-2.4m/6-8ft as a hedge
Spread: 90cm-1.2m/3-4ft as a hedge

Hardy, slow-growing, long-lived evergreen conifer with narrow, dark green leaves, yellowish green beneath. It can be grown as a densely leaved hedge and used mainly as a boundary. In very large gardens it can also be planted as an internal hedge, perhaps to form a background screen to herbaceous plants.

Full sun to deep shade and moist soil. It grows well in slightly alkaline soil, as well as in neutral and lightly acid types. When growing plants as a hedge, set them 38-45cm/15-18in apart, in single or double and staggered rows. To encourage bushiness, and plentiful shoots growing from the hedge's base, cut off the growing tips. Use hedging shears to trim established plants in early summer.

Take 7.5cm/3in-long cuttings, with heels, in late summer. Insert them in pots of equal parts moist peat and sharp sand, and place in a cold frame. When rooted, set the young plants in a nurserybed for two or three years until large enough to be planted into a garden. Alternatively, the ordinary species can be raised from seeds sown in seed-trays in sandy seed compost in autumn and placed in a cold frame. When the seedlings are about 5cm/2in high, put them in a nurserybed for two to three years.

Thuja plicata
Western Red Cedar (UK/USA)
Giant Cedar (USA)
Height: 2.1-2.4m/7-8ft as a hedge
Spread: 1-1.2m/3½-4ft as a hedge

Hardy, evergreen, fast-growing and long-lived conifer with bright, glossy green foliage, which when crushed emits a fruity fragrance. When grown as a hedge, it forms a dense screen for the perimeter of a garden. 'Atrovirens' (illustrated) has bright green foliage.

Full sun and deeply prepared, well-drained but moisture-retentive soil. When growing plants as a hedge, space them 45-60cm/18-24in apart. Trim established hedges in mid-summer.

Take 7.5cm/3in-long cuttings from the tips of shoots in late summer and insert them in pots of equal parts moist peat and sharp sand. Place in a cold frame. When rooted, plant into a nurserybed until large enough to be planted in a garden.

Griselinia littoralis
Height: 1.2-2.4m/4-6ft as a hedge
Spread: 75-90cm/2½-3ft as a hedge

Slightly tender, slow-growing evergreen shrub with leathery, shiny, apple green leaves. 'Variegata' has leaves with white edges, while 'Dixon's Cream' has leaves splashed and marked in creamy white. Both of these variegated forms are less vigorous than the all-green type. Space the plants 45-50cm/18-20in apart.

Ilex aquifolium
Common Holly (UK/USA)
Height: 2.4-4.5m/8-15ft as a hedge
Spread: 1.2-1.5m/4-5ft as a hedge

A hardy evergreen and somewhat variable shrub; it is mainly the variegated forms that are grown as hedges as they are more decorative than the all-green type. Space the plants about 45cm/18in apart. In the following spring, cut back the growing tips to encourage bushiness.

***Ligustrum ovalifolium* 'Aureum'**
Golden Privet (UK/USA)
Height: 1.2-1.5m/4-5ft as a hedge
Spread: 60-75cm/2-2½ft as a hedge

Hardy, bushy shrub, usually evergreen, but in exposed areas and during exceptionally cold winters can become only partially evergreen. The oval, rich yellow leaves are usually green centred. Space the plants 30-38cm/12-15in apart, in single or double rows.

***Lonicera nitida* 'Fertilis'**
Height: 1.2-1.5m/4-5ft as a hedge
Spread: 45-50cm/18-20in as a hedge

Hardy, bushy shrub with box-like, glossy leaves crowded on erect branches. Space plants 30cm/12in apart and cut back by half to encourage bushiness. During the following season, cut back all shoots by one-third. Thereafter, trim at least twice a year to maintain its shape.

Pruning deciduous shrubs

Of all the skills required in a garden, pruning ornamental shrubs is usually the least understood. Too frequently it is cloaked in unnecessary mystique. Basically, the purpose of pruning shrubs is four-fold:

• To improve the appearance and shape of a plant.
• To enhance the quantity and quality of flowers.
• To maintain vigour and encourage long life.
• In a few instances, such as with the Red-barked Dogwood (*Cornus alba*), to encourage yearly development of young, attractive stems.

Part of the purpose of pruning is to improve the appearance and shape of a shrub, but it is not intended to be a way of greatly restricting its size. Rather than each year drastically cutting back a shrub, which may not need radical pruning, it is far better to plant a shrub whose ultimate height and spread are right for the position.

TYPES OF PRUNING TREATMENT

For convenience, deciduous shrubs can be divided into three main types for pruning purposes, but it is worth remembering that, in temperate regions, the time of year when each shrub is pruned is dictated by its flowering time in relation to winter: pruning is normally done at such a time as to allow the shrub the longest possible period of new growth before it again bears flowers. This implies that all shrubs are pruned immediately their flowers fade, but this is not so; if late-summer flowering shrubs were pruned directly after flowering, this would encourage the development of young shoots which would then be killed by frost during winter. Pruning is therefore delayed until spring or early summer.

Information about pruning specific deciduous shrubs is given throughout this chapter, covering winter-flowering shrubs (pages 64-5); barks, stems, berries and seed-heads (pages 68-71); spring-flowering shrubs (pages 78-9); summer-flowering shrubs (pages 82-7); and autumn-coloured shrubs.

The three main groups of deciduous shrubs and their pruning treatment are:
Spring and early summer-flowering deciduous shrubs. These encompass a wide range or shrubs, including forsythia, Flowering Currants (*Ribes*) and Mock Orange (*Philadelphus*). Prune

Right: From China and the Himalayas, *Hydrangea aspera* has a rounded, shrubby habit and during early and mid-summer bears flowers formed of lilac-pink outer florets and porcelain-blue inner ones. Remove dead flower heads after flowers. Also, cut out weak and damaged shoots.

PRUNING A WEIGELA

1 Weigela (earlier known as Diervilla) flowers in early summer and is pruned immediately the flowers fade.
2 Cut out twiggy growths, as well as old and crossing stems. Keep the shrub's centre clear to encourage a good circulation of air.
3 Each year, cut out a few of the old, flowered stems to their base. This encourages the development of fresh, young shoots.
4 Cutting out flowered and old stems encourages the development of young shoots later in the same season. These will bear flowers during the following season.

centre of the shrub, close to their point of origin. The aim is to enable light and air to penetrate into the shrub. Plants suffocated by a mass of old shoots will only produce weak and soft growth. As well as encouraging the shrub to develop a good display of flowers, pruning ensures that it is growing evenly and is not misshapen and lopsided. Inevitably, after a few years the shrub may develop a thick base and it may then be necessary to cut out branches that are quite thick. This may result in an imbalanced amount of growth on one side and you will need to take this into consideration.

Late summer- and early autumn-flowering deciduous shrubs. These include the Butterfly Bush (*Buddleia davidii*), caryopteris, potentilla, hibiscus and hardy fuchsias. Because they flower too late in the year to produce ripened shoots before the onset of winter frosts, they are best left until the following spring before being pruned. Most of these shrubs respond to hard pruning; that is, cutting back all shoots that flowered during the previous year.

As with deciduous shrubs that flower early in the year, make sure that you cut out dead, crossing and diseased shoots.

Winter-flowering deciduous shrubs. Most of these winter-brightening shrubs, such as Witch Hazels (*Hamamelis*), Winter Sweet (*Chimonanthus*), Cornelian Cherry (*Cornus mas*) and winter-flowering viburnums, require very little pruning, other than in spring to cut out weak and diseased shoots, as well as those that are straggly and cross the shrub's centre.

Winter-flowering shrubs are often more easily restricted to a small area than spring and summer-flowering types, and this should also be done with the main pruning in spring.

SHRUBS GROWN FOR COLOURED STEMS

These include the Red-barked Dogwood (*Cornus alba*), Westonbirt Dogwood (*C. a.* 'Sibirica'), which displays bright crimson shoots, *C. a.* 'Kesselringii' with purplish black stems, and *C. stolonifera* 'Flaviramea' with yellow to olive-green-coloured young stems.

To encourage these shrubs, which have a suckering habit, to develop fresh shoots each year, cut them down to soil-level in mid-spring. By the time the following winter arrives they will have developed masses of attractive stems.

PRUNING TOOLS

Traditionally, gardeners used very sharp knives to prune shrubs, but there is no doubt that most people prefer less lethal and more easily used equipment. The range is wide and includes:

- **Secateurs** are easily used; most of them cut stems 15mm/⅝in thick, while heavy-duty types can cut 25mm/1in-thick stems. There are two types of secateurs: one has a scissor-like action in which one blade passes the other, and is often known as a 'bypass' type (earlier it was called a parrot-type) secateur. The other model has a sharp blade that cuts when in contact with a firm, flat surface called an anvil. Left- as well as right-handed models are available.

- **Long-handled loppers** (also known as long-handled secateurs or pruners) have either a 'bypass' or 'anvil' cutting action. They have handles 38-45cm/15-18in long and cut stems up to 5cm/2in thick. Some models have a double cutting-action which enables thick stems to be cut with greater ease and accuracy.

- **Pruning saws** are ideal for cutting branches and thick stems. Grecian saws with pointed ends cut on the pull stroke and are ideal for cutting awkward branches. Other saws have coarse teeth and are better for thick branches. Depending on their size, saws cut wood up to 18cm/7in thick – or even thicker in the case of bow-saws.

---

these immediately after they flower, cutting back selected flowered shoots to fresh, young growths that will develop into flowering shoots for the following year. At the same time, cut out dead or diseased shoots, as well as those that cross the

Spring-flowering trees and shrubs

PLANT NAME AND DESCRIPTION	SITUATION AND CULTIVATION	PROPAGATION

Amelanchier lamarckii
June Berry (UK/USA)
Shadbush (UK/USA)
Snowy Mespilus (UK)
Height: 4.5-7.5m/15-25ft
Spread: 3.6-6m/12-20ft

Hardy, deciduous, large shrub or small tree that creates a wealth of pure white, star-shaped flowers during mid-spring. At the time of flowering, the leaves are starting to unfold. In autumn they assume soft yellow and red tints.

Moisture-retentive but well-drained lime-free soil and a position in full sun or light shade. It is essential that the soil does not dry out in summer.
   No regular pruning is needed, other than cutting out damaged branches in spring.
   Plant a carpet of golden faced daffodil bulbs under the tree to create extra colour in spring.

Layer low-growing stems in late summer. They take about a year to develop roots, when the stem is severed from the parent and planted into a nurserybed or garden. Alternatively, detach rooted suckers in spring or autumn. Plant into a nurserybed until large enough to be set into a garden.

Choisya ternata
Mexican Orange Flower (UK/USA)
Height: 1.5-1.8m/5-6ft
Spread: 1.5-2.1m/5-7ft

Slightly tender evergreen shrub with a rounded, bushy habit and terminal clusters of sweetly scented, orange-blossom-like white flowers mainly during mid- and late spring but often intermittently through summer. The glossy green leaves emit a bouquet reminiscent of oranges when crushed.

Fertile, deeply cultivated, well-drained soil and a sheltered position in full sun suit it, although it is tolerant of light shade. Avoid positions open to cold northerly and easterly winds. In northerly areas grow against a south-facing wall.
   No regular pruning is needed, other than removing frost-damaged shoots in spring, cutting them out to their bases to encourage the development of fresh ones.

Take 7.5cm/3in-long cuttings from the current season's shoots in mid-summer. Insert them in pots of equal parts moist peat and sharp sand, and place in gentle warmth. When rooted, transfer to individual pots and place in a cold frame. Later, when a plant fills its pot with roots, transfer to a nurserybed until large enough to be put into a garden.

Forsythia x intermedia
Golden Bells (UK/USA)
Height: 1.8-2.4m/6-8ft
Spread: 1.5-2.1m/5-7ft

Vigorous, deciduous shrub that in early and mid-spring bears masses of golden yellow flowers up to 30mm/1in across in clusters of up to six on shoots produced during the previous year. There are several superb forms, including 'Lynwood', with large, yellow flowers, and 'Spectabilis', also yellow.

Fertile, deeply prepared and moisture-retentive soil in full sun or light shade suit it. Forsythias grow equally well in neutral and slightly alkaline soil.
   Regular pruning is essential to encourage the development of flowers. As soon as flowering is over, cut out all shoots that bore flowers to within an inch or so of the old wood. This encourages the development of fresh shoots. Also cut out damaged wood.

Take 25cm/10in-long cuttings of the current season's shoots in early autumn and insert them 10-15cm/4-6in deep in a nurserybed outdoors. Sprinkle sharp sand in the base of the trench so that each cutting's base rests on it. This encourages the development of roots and helps to prevent the cutting's base decaying. The following autumn, the cuttings will have rooted and can be planted into a border or given wider spacings in a nurserybed.

***Magnolia liliiflora* 'Nigra'**
(syn. *M.* x *soulangiana* 'Nigra')
Height: 1.8-2.4m/6-8ft
Spread: 1.5-2.1m/5-7ft

Spectacular, hardy deciduous shrub with straggly growth and oblong to pear-shaped mid-green leaves up to 20cm/8in long. During mid-spring and into early summer it bears dark, reddish purple, chalice-shaped flowers up to 10cm/4in wide, upright at first and creating an eye-catching display.

Deeply prepared, loamy, well-drained but moisture-retentive soil and a position sheltered from cold north and east winds ensures success. Preferably, the site should be rich in leaf-mould, peat or compost. If it is not, form a mulch of these materials over the soil in spring . No regular pruning is needed.
   Naturalize bulbs under this deciduous shrub, but avoid vivid yellows, which distract attention from the magnolia – whites and soft yellows are a better choice.

The easiest way to increase it is by layering low-growing branches in early summer. Rooting takes up to two years, when the young plant should be severed from the parent and planted into either a nurserybed or garden.

Berberis darwinii
Darwin's Berberis (UK/USA)
Height: 1.8-2.4m/6-8ft
Spread: 1.8-2.4m/6-8ft

Hardy evergreen shrub with small, holly-like, dark green and glossy leaves. In late spring it produces masses of deep yellow flowers, followed by blue berries. 'Prostrata' is a smaller form, 90cm-1.2m/3-4ft high, and with orange flower buds that open to golden yellow.

***Chaenomeles speciosa* 'Nivalis'**
Japanese Quince (UK/USA)
Height: 1.5-1.8m/5-6ft
Spread: 1.5-1.8m/5-6ft

Hardy, deciduous, twiggy shrub with a tangle of spiny stems and dark green, glossy leaves. From late winter to spring – and sometimes later – it bears pure white flowers. There are many other superb varieties, in rosy pink, crimson-red and orange-red.

Lonicera fragrantissima
Height: 1.5-1.8m/5-6ft
Spread: 1.5-1.8m/5-6ft

An evergreen shrub – sometimes only partially evergreen in cold areas – with oval, rather stiff and leathery mid-green leaves. From mid-winter to spring it produces fragrant, creamy white flowers.

***Malus purpurea* 'Lemoinei'**
(syn. *M.* x 'Lemoinei')
Height: 4.5-5.4m/15-18ft
Spread: 3.6-4.5m/12-15ft

A superb flowering crab apple, with purple leaves that assume a bronze tinge in autumn, and masses of single, purple-crimson flowers during mid- and late spring. The fruits are also purple-bronze.

PLANT NAME AND DESCRIPTION	SITUATION AND CULTIVATION	PROPAGATION

Magnolia stellata
(syn. *M. kobus stellata*)
Star Magnolia (UK/USA)
Height: 2.4-3m/8-10ft
Spread: 2.4-3m/8-10ft

Hardy, slow-growing deciduous shrub with a rounded but compact habit and mid-green, lance-like leaves up to 10cm/4in long. During early and mid-spring it bears fragrant, white, star-shaped flowers up to 10cm/4in wide. 'Rosea' has pink flowers.

Deeply prepared, loamy, well-drained but moisture-retentive soil and a position sheltered from cold north and east winds ensure success. Preferably, the site should be rich in leaf-mould, peat or compost. If it is not, in spring form a mulch of these materials over the soil. No regular pruning is needed.
  Naturalize bulbs under this deciduous shrub. Yellow daffodils harmonize with the white flowers.

The easiest way to increase it is by layering low-growing branches in early summer. Rooting takes up to two years, when the young plant is severed from the parent and planted into either a nurserybed or garden.

***Prunus* 'Accolade'**
Height: 4.5-6m/15-20ft
Spread: 4.5-7.5m/15-25ft

Hardy, deciduous, graceful, open and spreading ornamental cherry tree with masses of blush pink, semi-double flowers, deep rosy pink when in bud, borne in pendulous clusters during early and mid-spring.
  It is a hybrid between the Sargent Cherry (*Prunus sargentii*) and the erect *P. subhirtella*.

Well-drained but moisture-retentive garden soil, preferably slightly chalky, suits it. No regular pruning is needed, other than cutting out dead or damaged shoots in early summer, when the tree's sap is starting to rise.
  Securely stake the tree when young to avoid damage from wind.

Buy a healthy, strong tree from a nursery.

Rhododendron luteum
(syn. *R. flavum/Azalea luteum*)
Height: 1.8-3m/6-10ft
Spread: 1.5-2.1m/5-7ft

Hardy, deciduous, free-flowering shrub, a parent of many azaleas but also worth growing for its own undemanding nature and wealth of fragrant, rich yellow flowers borne in rounded clusters during late spring and early summer. In autumn, the leaves assume rich shades of orange, purple and crimson.

  Dappled light and fertile, moisture-retentive, slightly acid, light soil. Enrich both heavy and extremely sandy soils with decomposed compost or manure. Avoid exposed positions – a sheltered position under tall deciduous trees is suitable, as long as the soil does not dry out. It is ideal for planting on a bank alongside a stream.
  No regular pruning is needed, other than occasionally cutting out a damaged or frosted shoot. Remove dead flower heads by bending them sideways.

Layer low-growing stems in autumn. Rooting takes about two years.

Spiraea* x *arguta
Bridal Wreath (UK)
Foam of May (UK)
Height: 1.8-2.4m/6-8ft
Spread: 1.5-2.1m/5-7ft

Hardy, dense, twiggy and bushy shrub with graceful, slender branches that from mid- to late spring bear masses of pure white flowers. It is a superb shrub, seldom failing to create an eye-catching display. The mid-green leaves create a foil to the flowers.

  Fertile, deeply prepared, moisture-retentive but well-drained soil and a position in full sun suit it.
  No regular pruning is needed, other than trimming back long shoots in mid-summer. If your spiraea is trained around the side of a garden gate or other feature, use hedging shears to trim it lightly as soon as the flowers fade.

Take 7.5-10cm/3-4in-long cuttings from the current season's shoots in mid-summer. Insert them in pots of equal parts moist peat and sharp sand, and place in a cold frame. When rooted, pot up into individual pots and plant into a nurserybed or border when established and large enough.

***Prunus* x *amygdalo-persica* 'Pollardii'**
Height: 5.4-6m/18-20ft
Spread: 5.4-6m/18-20ft

A hardy and vigorous hybrid with mid-green leaves and masses of almond-like, rich pink, 5cm/2in-wide flowers borne on bare branches during early and mid-spring. This variety is a cross between a peach and an almond.

Prunus padus
Bird Cherry (UK/USA)
Hagberry (USA)
Height: 6-7.5m/20-25ft
Spread: 4.5-6m/15-20ft

Hardy, distinctive deciduous tree with lax, 7.5-13cm/3-5in-long tassels of almond-scented white flowers in late spring. The form 'Grandiflora' (also known as 'Watereri') has longer flower tassels, up to 20cm/8in long.

***Prunus subhirtella* 'Pendula'**
Weeping Spring Cherry (UK)
Height: 3.6-4.5m/12-15ft
Spread: 3-6m/10-20ft

A magnificent, spreading and weeping, deciduous, spring-flowering cherry with cascading branches packed with pinkish white flowers. 'Pendula Rosea', often sold as 'Pendula', has flesh pink flowers, while 'Pendula Rubra' has deep rose flowers, carmine when in bud.

***Ulex europaeus* 'Plenus'**
Double-flowered Gorse (UK/USA)
Height: 1.5-2.1m/5-7ft
Spread: 1.5-2.1m/5-7ft

Hardy, spiny evergreen, which becomes drenched in honey-scented, golden yellow, pea-type flowers during spring and into early summer. Often the flowering continuous sporadically until the following winter or early spring.

Pruning trees and evergreen shrubs

Trees and evergreen shrubs need less regular and systematic pruning than deciduous shrubs, but they do benefit from a yearly inspection. If neglected, branches of deciduous trees can become entangled or hang too low to allow plants underneath them to grow healthily, while evergreen shrubs become packed with weak, crossing and contorted shoots.

PRUNING TREES
Trees need little pruning, but as they are long-lived it is essential to create an evenly shaped, attractive outline – and you should begin to do this while the tree is young. Part of training and pruning is to ensure the trunk is upright, so regularly check the stake and ties securing it. Prune the head of the tree while it is young to create an even, attractive shape. Most trees are best pruned in winter while the tree is dormant, but flowering cherries and other members of the *Prunus* family are best pruned in late spring or early summer, when the sap begins to flow.

During a tree's early years it needs regular inspection, but the need to check it decreases as

it matures. When a tree is young it is easy to select young stems that will develop into main branches and to cut out those that are weak, misplaced or just not required. Also, pruning cuts heal over quickly at an early stage.

With age, and as a tree broadens, there is a likelihood that some of its branches will bend downwards and smother plants growing underneath, as well as preventing people passing by. Heavy snowfalls frequently weigh down and damage branches; where this happens cut back to an upward and outward-pointing shoot. Some trees have a pendulous habit by nature and these should be planted where they will not become a problem in later years.

PRUNING EVERGREEN SHRUBS
Once established, evergreen shrubs need no more attention than is necessary to shape them and to cut out weak, diseased or straggly shoots. This is best done in spring, or in cold areas, in early summer. It is essential not to prune evergreen shrubs during winter, as pruning encourages the development of young shoots, which

PRUNING EVERGREENS

1 Use secateurs to prune evergreen shrubs with large leaves. Cut the stems to just above a leaf joint.
2 Heavy-duty, long-handled lopping shears are ideal for cutting branches which are too thick to be cut by secateurs, yet too thin to warrant the use of a saw.
3 Use a Grecian saw to cut thick branches. This saw curves to a point and cuts on the pull stroke. It is ideal for cutting branches in narrow, constricted positions.
4 Secateurs are ideal for cutting out twiggy shoots. Cut close to the main stem.

Above: The hardy evergreen shrub *Berberis* x *stenophylla* creates a wealth of golden yellow flowers during mid-spring. Very little pruning is needed, other than cutting out dead and misplaced shoots, which should be done immediately flowers fade. Eventually it forms a large and spreading shrub.

will then be killed by frost. If an evergreen shrub blooms in spring (*Berberis* x *stenophylla* for example), delay pruning until its flowers have died.

Sometimes major surgery is needed when evergreen shrubs become too large and spreading, and this is best tackled as soon as growth begins in spring; this allows the maximum period before the onset of winter. In such instances, you will have to sacrifice a season's flowers.

Remember that the older the wood that is cut, the more difficult it is for the shrub to develop fresh shoots.

Never use hedging shears to cut evergreens (except privet), as they mince leaves and make them visually unappealing. Instead, use secateurs or long-handled lopping shears and cut just above a leaf joint.

REJUVENATING OLD TREES

When taking over an established garden you may well inherit a tree, possibly one that is large and neglected. Although your initial instinct may be to cut it down and to plant another, first examine it and compare its favourable characteristics with the disadvantages of keeping it.

If it is near to the house, consider the volume of water it absorbs from the soil and whether the roots might eventually cause subsidence. Conversely, if a large tree is removed from an area of soil that is constantly moist, it may initiate ground-heave, when instead of shrinking through lack of water the soil rises as a result of the large amount of water in it (formerly consumed by the tree). If in doubt about a tree's removal, call in expert opinion before taking any action.

Do not decrease the height of a tree by just lopping off branches at the desired height. This will result in an outline that resembles a brush. Instead, remove complete limbs without upsetting its uniform outline.

PRUNING HEATHERS AND ERICAS

Callunas, ericas and daboecias are kept tidy and given a neat outline by lightly trimming them with hedging shears. Brush the trimmings off the plants using a soft broom.

Trim callunas and summer-flowering ericas in spring, before growth starts, using shears to create a neat, undulating outline and to remove dead flowers. Winter- and spring-flowering types are trimmed in the same way, as soon as their flowers fade. Trim off the old flower heads of daboecias in late winter or early spring.

PRUNING CONIFERS

The range of conifers is wide; most of them are evergreen, a few deciduous. Evergreen types can be planted to create screens of foliage and are used as hedges, or as specimen trees in lawns. Deciduous conifers invariably are grown as specimen plants and include the Swamp Cypress (*Taxodium distichum*), Dawn Redwood (*Metasequoia glyptostroboides*) and European Larch (*Larix decidua*).

When grown as hedges, evergreen conifers are planted in single or double rows and allowed to grow naturally, although some are clipped and, when too large, their growing tops are removed. However, cutting out the terminal shoot frequently spoils their shape. Specimen conifers, whether evergreen or deciduous, must be inspected when young to ensure they do not have two main stems, known as double leaders. If they do, cut out one of them.

Summer-flowering trees and shrubs

PLANT NAME AND DESCRIPTION	SITUATION AND CULTIVATION	PROPAGATION

Buddleja (Buddleia) alternifolia
Height: 3-4.5m/10-15ft
Spread: 3-4.5m/10-15ft

Hardy deciduous shrub clothed in narrow, pale green leaves. From early to mid-summer its cascading stems are drenched with 2.5cm/1in-wide clusters of sweetly scented, lavender-blue flowers. Usually it is grown as a shrub, but occasionally as a standard tree, when it forms a superb focal point in a lawn.

Full sun and deeply prepared, friable, well-drained but moisture-retentive soil. It grows well in slightly alkaline conditions. When grown as a standard, it need the support of a stout stake secured to the stem in several places.
To maintain a neat shape, prune immediately the flowers fade. Cut back stems by two-thirds. Do not delay with the pruning, as this shrub flowers on wood produced during the previous year.

Take 10cm/4in-long cuttings from the current season's growth in mid-summer. Preferably, use cuttings with heels (parts of the older wood). Insert them in equal parts moist peat and sharp sand and place in a cold frame. Overwinter in the frame and plant into a nurserybed in early summer of the following year.

***Ceanothus* 'Gloire de Versailles'**
(syn. *Ceanothus* x *delilianus* 'Gloire de Versailles')
Californian Lilac (UK/USA)
Height: 1.8-2.4m/6-8ft
Spread: 1.8-2.4m/6-8ft

Hardy deciduous shrub with a lax and open habit. From mid- to late summer it bears 15-20cm/6-8in-long clusters of fragrant, soft powder-blue flowers at the ends of long stems.

Full sun and light, moderately fertile, deeply prepared, moisture-retentive soil. Choose a warm position, sheltered from cold winds. Regular pruning is essential; in spring, cut back the previous year's shoots to within 7.5cm/3in of the old wood. This encourages the development of fresh shoots that will bear flowers later in the same year.

Take 7.5-10cm/3-4in-long cuttings in mid-summer. Insert them in pots of equal parts moist peat and sharp sand and place in gentle warmth. When rooted, transfer them into individual pots and overwinter in a cold frame. It is usually necessary to re-pot plants when roots fill a pot; plant them into a garden during the following year.

Ceratostigma willmottianum
Chinese Plumbago (USA)
Hardy Plumbago (UK)
Height: 60-90cm/2-3ft
Spread: 60-90cm/2-3ft

Half-hardy, deciduous, twiggy shrub with dark green, diamond-shaped leaves that assume rich red tints in autumn. During mid- and late summer – and often into early autumn – it displays small, rich blue flowers in terminal clusters up to 6.5cm/2¹/₂in wide.

Full sun and light, fertile, well-drained but moisture-retentive soil. Either plant it in the protection of a wall, or among shrubs or herbaceous perennials. Indeed, because it benefits from being cut hard back in early spring it is often treated as an herbaceous plant. Fresh shoots develop in late spring and these bear flowers later in the year.

Take 7.5cm/3in-long cuttings from the current season's growth in mid-summer. Insert them in a pot of equal parts moist peat and sharp sand and place in gentle warmth. When rooted, pot them up individually and overwinter in a frost-proof garden frame or greenhouse. In spring, plant them into a garden.

Cistus* x *lusitanicus
Rock Rose (UK/USA)
Sun Rose (UK)
Height: 30-60cm/12-24in
Spread: 45-60cm/18-24in

Evergreen shrub with narrow, lance-shaped, dark green leaves. During early and mid-summer it develops white flowers about 5cm/2in wide, spectacularly splashed with crimson at the base of each petal. Other superb Rock Roses include *C.* 'Silver Pink'.

Well-drained, light, rather poor soil suits it, and a position in full sun. Cistus are not hardy in extremely cold areas and therefore must always be given a position sheltered from cold winds. Cistus are excellent for planting in coastal areas, as they are tolerant of salt-spray. Always buy plants growing in containers, as they dislike root disturbance.
No regular pruning is needed, other than cutting out straggly, dead and winter-damaged shoots in spring.

Take 7.5cm/3in-long cuttings from the current season's growth in mid-summer and insert them in pots of equal parts moist peat and sharp sand. Place them in gentle warmth in a propagating frame. When rooted, pot up the cuttings into individual pots and place in a cold frame during winter.

Buddleja (Buddleia) davidii
Butterfly Bush (UK/USA)
Orange-eye Buddleia (USA)
Summer Lilac (USA)
Height: 1.8-2.4m/6-8ft
Spread: 1.8-2.4m/6-8ft

Hardy deciduous shrub, well known for its long, often arching stems that bear large, plume-like, terminal heads of fragrant, lilac-purple flowers during mid- and late summer.

Buddleja (Buddleia) fallowiana
Height: 1.5-3m/5-10ft
Spread: 1.5-1.8m/5-6ft

Bushy deciduous shrub – slightly tender in temperate regions – with grey leaves and terminal clusters of sweetly scented lavender flowers from mid-summer to early autumn. The form 'Alba' has creamy white flowers.

Buddleja (Buddleia) globosa
Orange-ball Tree (UK)
Height: 2.4-3m/8-10ft
Spread: 2.4-3m/8-10ft

Evergreen shrub, semi-evergreen in severe climates. In sheltered and mild areas it grows larger than the above measurements. It has dark green, lance-shaped leaves and globular, scented, orange-yellow flowers borne in lax, terminal clusters during early summer.

Caryopteris* x *clandonensis
Height: 60cm-1.2m/2-4ft
Spread: 60-90cm/2-3ft

Bushy deciduous shrub with aromatic grey-green leaves. During late summer and into autumn it produces clusters of blue flowers. There several varieties, all slightly hardier than the normal species. These include 'Arthur Simmonds' (bright blue), 'Heavenly Blue' (deep blue) and 'Kew Blue' (rich blue).

PLANT NAME AND DESCRIPTION	SITUATION AND CULTIVATION	PROPAGATION

Eucryphia x *nymansensis*
Height: 2.4-4.5m/8-15ft
Spread: 1.8-2.4m/6-8ft

Evergreen, slender, vigorous, fast-growing shrubby tree with shiny green leaves and beautiful cream flowers about 6.5cm/2½in wide during late summer and into early autumn. The flowers are borne singly or in small clusters. In cold regions the leaves can be damaged by frost. *E. glutinosa* is hardier, and deciduous or partially evergreen.

Full sun or light shade and neutral to slightly acid, moisture-retentive, peaty soil. Protection from cold, searing winds is essential. Support young plants with strong stakes.
   No regular pruning is needed, other than nipping out the growing tips of young plants to encourage bushiness.

Take 7.5-10cm/3-4in-long cuttings from the current season's shoots in mid- to late summer. Cuttings with heels (part of the older wood) root more quickly than normal types. Insert them in pots of moist peat and sharp sand and place in gentle warmth. When rooted, pot up into individual pots and place in a cool greenhouse or frost-free garden frame. In spring, place outside and, later, pot up into larger pots. Plant into a garden during the following year.

Genista aetnensis
Mt. Etna Broom (UK/USA)
Height: 4.5-6m/15-20ft
Spread: 4.5-5.4m/15-18ft

Large, tall deciduous shrub with a lax habit and light green, rush-like branches sparsely clothed with mid-green leaves. During mid- and late summer it develops terminal clusters of golden yellow flowers. Fortunately, even small, young plants flower and therefore a wonderful display is created over many years.

Full sun and light, well-drained soil. It grows best in poor soil. Always buy plants that are already growing in containers as it does not like root disturbance. No staking is needed.
   No regular pruning is required, other than cutting out winter-damaged stems in spring. Thin out plants with densely arranged stems.

Take 7.5cm/3in-long cuttings of the current season's shoots in mid-summer and insert in pots of equal parts moist peat and sharp sand. Place in a cold frame. When rooted, pot them up into individual pots and plant into a garden the following spring.
   Sow seed in spring in pots of sandy loam-based compost and place in a cold frame. When the seedlings are large enough to handle, move them into individual pots. Later, when large and established, plant into a garden.

Genista cinerea
Height: 2.4-3m/8-10ft
Spread: 1.8-2.4m/6-8ft

Hardy, deciduous, slender-stemmed, elegant shrub from the broom family, with small, grey-green leaves and arching stems bearing sweetly scented flowers in clusters up to 7.5cm/3in long during early and mid-summer. It is ideal for creating a dominant splash of yellow. After the flowers fade it develops silky seed pods.

Full sun and light, well-drained soil. It grows best in poor soil. Always buy plants that are growing in containers as it does not like root disturbance. No staking is needed.
   No regular pruning is needed, other than cutting out winter-damaged stems in spring. Also, thin out plants with densely arranged stems.

Take 7.5cm/3in-long cuttings of the current season's shoots in mid-summer and insert in pots of equal parts moist peat and sharp sand. Place in a cold frame. When rooted, pot up into individual pots and later plant into a garden.
   Sow seeds in spring in pots of sandy loam-based compost in pots and place in a cold frame. When the seedlings are large enough to handle, move them into individual pots. Later, when established and growing strongly, plant into a garden.

Genista hispanica
Spanish Broom (USA)
Spanish Gorse (UK)
Height: 60-90cm/2-3ft
Spread: 1.5-2.4m/5-8ft

Spreading deciduous shrub, densely spined and covered in narrow, deep green leaves. During early and mid-summer it is often totally smothered with clusters of deep yellow flowers. When in flower it creates a dominant feature that often eclipses displays of nearby plants.

Well-drained, light soil, with a position in full sun, suits it best. It thrives in slightly poor soil, so do not mulch or feed this plant.
   A warm, sheltered position is essential; in cold climates select an area protected from cold winds.
   No regular pruning is needed, although to create bushy plants is it essential to nip out the growing points of young plants in mid-summer. Thin out congested plants after their flowers fade.

Sow seeds in spring in pots of sandy, loam-based compost; place in a cold frame. When the seedlings are large enough to handle, move them into individual pots. Later, plant into a garden.
   Take 7.5cm/3in-long cuttings of the current season's shoots in mid-summer and insert in pots of equal parts moist peat and sharp sand. Place in a cold frame. When rooted, pot up into individual pots and later plant into a garden.

Cercis siliquastrum
Judas Tree (UK/USA)
Love Tree (USA)
Height: 3-5.4m/10-18ft
Spread: 2.4-3.6m/8-12ft

Hardy, bushy deciduous tree or large shrub, spreading with age, with heart-shaped leaves. Pea-shaped, rose-purple flowers crowd on naked branches in early summer. Purple-tinted seed pods from mid-to late summer.

Cistus ladanifer
Laudanum (USA)
Height: 1.5-1.8m/5-6ft
Spread: 1.2-1.5m/4-5ft

Hardy evergreen shrub, with dull green and leathery leaves. During early summer it produces white flowers up to 6cm/2½in wide and with a maroon blotch at the base of each petal. The stamens are bright yellow.

Cornus florida 'Rubra'
Flowering Dogwood (UK/USA)
Height: 3-4.5m/10-15ft
Spread: 4.5-5.4m/15-18ft

Hardy, well-branched deciduous shrub or small tree with dark green leaves that turn brilliant orange and scarlet in autumn. This form has pink and white, petal-like bracts during late spring and early summer; the normal species has white bracts.

Corokia cotoneaster
Wire Netting Bush (UK)
Height: 1.5-1.8m/5-6ft
Spread: 1.5-1.8m/5-6ft

Distinctive and unusual, slightly tender evergreen shrub with masses of slender but stiff, intertwined shoots that resemble wire netting. During early summer it develops star-like, 12mm/½in-wide, bright yellow flowers. Red, round fruits, about 6mm/¼in wide, appear later.

Summer-flowering trees and shrubs

PLANT NAME AND DESCRIPTION	SITUATION AND CULTIVATION	PROPAGATION

***Hebe* 'Autumn Glory'**
Shrubby Veronica (UK)
Height: 60-75cm/2-2¹/₂ft
Spread: 60-75cm/2-2¹/₂ft

Hardy, sparsely branched, erect evergreen shrub with glossy green leaves, edged in red when young, and deep purplish blue flowers from mid-summer to autumn. 'Midsummer Beauty' is another hybrid hebe, with tassels about 13cm/5in long and packed with lavender-purple flowers. It grows to about 1.2m/4ft.

Full sun and well-drained soil. Plants succeed in neutral as well as slightly acid or alkaline conditions, and especially thrive in coastal areas.
  No regular pruning is needed, other than cutting back leggy plants in spring to encourage the development of fresh shoots from their bases.

Take 7.5-10cm/3-4in-long cuttings from non-flowering shoots of the current season's growth in mid-summer. Insert them in pots of equal parts moist peat and sharp sand; place in a cold frame. When rooted, pot up into individual pots; later, when established and growing strongly, plant them into a garden.

Helichrysum italicum
(syn. *H. angustifolium*)
Curry Plant (UK)
White-leaf Everlasting (USA)
Height: 30-38cm/12-15in
Spread: 38-60cm/15-24in

Dwarf deciduous shrub with narrow, silvery grey, needle-like leaves that emit a strong bouquet reminiscent of curry. Heads of mustard yellow flowers appear in small clusters above the foliage during early and mid-summer.

Light, well-drained soil, with a position in full sun, suits it. Avoid excessively fertile soils, as well as those that are poorly drained and remain wet and cold.
  No regular pruning is needed, other than trimming back old shoots in spring. Also in spring, cut back stems damaged by severe winter frosts.

Take 7.5cm/3in-long cuttings from the current season's growth in mid-summer and insert in pots of sandy compost. Place in a cold frame and pot up into individual pots in spring.

Hibiscus syriacus
Shrubby Mallow (UK)
Height: 1.8-3m/6-10ft
Spread: 1.2-1.8m/4-6ft

Hardy deciduous shrub with a bushy, upright stance and rich green, three-lobed and coarsely toothed leaves. From mid-summer to early autumn it bears 7.5cm/3in-wide flowers in a range of colours: 'Blue Bird' (violet-blue), 'Red Heart' (white with red centres) and 'Woodbridge' (rose-pink).

Full sun and fertile, well-drained but moisture-retentive soil. Select areas sheltered from cold winds. In exposed areas, plant it in the shelter of a wall.
  No regular pruning is needed, other than shortening long shoots immediately the shrub finishes flowering. Also, cut out frost-damaged shoot-tips in spring.

Take 7.5-10cm/3-4in-long cuttings from the current season's non-flowering shoots in mid-summer. Cuttings with heels (parts of the older wood) develop roots more quickly than normal types. Insert them in pots of equal parts moist peat and sharp sand, then place in gentle warmth. When rooted, pot them into individual pots and overwinter in a cold frame.

Hydrangea arborescens
Hills of Snow (USA)
Height: 1.2-1.8m/4-6ft
Spread: 1.2-1.8m/4-6ft

Hardy deciduous shrub with bright green leaves and dull white flowers borne in flat heads up to 15cm/6in across during mid- and late summer – and sometimes into early autumn. With maturity, these flowers fade to bronze-brown. The form 'Grandiflora' has larger, pure white flower heads.

Full sun or light shade and fertile, moisture-retentive soil enriched with well-decomposed compost. Regular pruning is essential; in late winter or early spring, cut back by half the shoots that flowered during the previous year.

Take 10-15cm/4-6in-long cuttings from the current season's shoots in mid- to late summer. Insert them in pots of equal parts moist peat and sharp sand, then place in gentle warmth. When rooted, transfer them into individual pots and place in a cold frame. In spring, set the plant in a nurserybed until large enough to be put in a garden.

Cytisus battandieri
(now properly known as *Argyrocytisus battandieri*)
Moroccan Broom (UK)
Pineapple Broom (UK)
Height: 3-4.5m/10-15ft
Spread: 3-3.6m/10-12ft

Large, bushy shrub with golden yellow, pineapple-scented flowers borne during early summer. In cold, temperate regions it is best grown against a warm wall.

Cytisus* x *beanii
Broom (UK/USA)
Height: 45-60cm/18-24in
Spread: 75-90cm/2¹/₂-3ft

Hardy, bushy, dwarf, deciduous and semi-prostrate shrub, often spreading to more than the suggested width. Deep golden yellow, pea-shaped flowers are borne on slender branches during late spring and early summer.

Cytisus* x *kewensis
Height: 30-60cm/12-24in
Spread: 90cm-1.2m/3-4ft–or more

Sprawling, deciduous shrub with mid-green leaves. During late spring and early summer it produces masses of pale yellow flowers.

Cytisus* x *praecox
Warminster Broom (UK/USA)
Height: 1.5-1.8m/5-6ft
Spread: 1.5-1.8m/5-6ft

Hardy, bushy and vigorous deciduous shrub with arching stems bearing creamy white, pea-shaped flowers during late spring and early summer. The form 'Allgold' has sulphur yellow flowers.

PLANT NAME AND DESCRIPTION	SITUATION AND CULTIVATION	PROPAGATION

Hydrangea macrophylla
Common Hydrangea (UK)
French Hydrangea (USA)
Height: 1.2-1.8m/4-6ft
Spread: 1.2-1.8m/4-6ft

Hardy deciduous shrub with a rounded outline and coarsely toothed, light green leaves. Hortensias have have mop-like flower heads, 13-20cm/5-8in wide (shown), while Lacecaps have flat heads, 10-15cm/4-6in across. Flowers from mid-summer to early autumn.

Dappled light and fertile, slightly acid, moisture-retentive soil enriched with well-decomposed compost. Acid soil ensures that blue varieties remain blue. However, the use of aluminium sulphate (or a proprietary bluing powder) reduces the influence of alkaline soils.
Little pruning is needed, other than cutting out two- or three-year-old shoots at ground level in early spring to encourage the development of strong, young shoots. Remove dead flower heads in autumn or spring.

Take 10-13cm/4-5in-long cuttings from the current season's shoots in mid- to late summer. Insert them in pots of equal parts moist peat and sharp sand, and place in gentle warmth. When rooted, pot up into individual pots and place in a cold frame. In spring, plant them in a nurserybed until large enough to be put in a garden.

Hydrangea paniculata
Height: 2.4-3m/8-10ft
Spread: 2.4-3m/8-10ft

Large deciduous shrub with long, arching stems bearing mid-green leaves and magnificent pyramidal heads, up to 20cm/8in long, of white flowers during late summer and into early autumn. With age, the flowers turn pink. The form 'Grandiflora' has massive flower heads, up to 45cm/18in long; flowers become purplish pink, later brown.

Full sun or light shade and fertile, moisture-retentive soil enriched with well-decomposed compost.
Regular pruning is essential: in late winter or early spring, cut back by half shoots that flowered during the previous year. If exceptionally large flowers are wanted, thin out the flowering shoots. However, this drastic pruning invariably reduces the plant's lifespan.

Take 10-15cm/4-6in-long cuttings from the current season's shoots in mid- to late summer. Insert them in pots of equal parts moist peat and sharp sand; place in gentle warmth. When rooted, pot up into individual pots and place in a cold frame.
In spring, set them in a nurserybed until large enough to be put in a garden.

***Hypericum* 'Hidcote'**
(syn. *H. patulum* 'Hidcote')
Rose of Sharon (UK/USA)
St. John's Wort (UK)
Height: 90cm-1.5m/3-5ft
Spread: 1.5-2.1m/5-7ft

Almost evergreen, hardy, bushy shrub with dark green, lance-shaped leaves. From mid-summer to autumn it develops spectacular, saucer-shaped, waxy, golden yellow flowers up to 7.5cm/3in wide.

Full sun and fertile, well-drained but moisture-retentive soil. Avoid dry soil in total shade, as this markedly reduces the plant's ability to flower.
Little pruning is needed, but plants benefit from long shoots being cut back close to their base in spring.

Take 10-13cm/4-5in-long cuttings, preferably with a heel, and from the current season's shoots, in mid-summer. Insert them in pots of equal parts moist peat and sharp sand; place in a cold frame. When rooted, plant into a nurserybed until large enough to be set in a garden.

Kalmia latifolia
Calico Bush (UK/USA)
Mountain Laurel (UK/USA)
Height: 1.8-3m/6-10ft
Spread: 1.8-2.4m/6-8ft

Hardy evergreen shrub with lance-shaped, leathery, glossy, mid-green leaves and saucer-shaped, pale blue to rosy red flowers borne in rounded clusters up to 10cm/4in across during early summer. The variety 'Clementine Churchill' has rich, rosy red flowers.

Partial shade and light but moisture-retentive, lime-free soil. Cool, moist soil is essential and therefore regularly mulch the area around plants. No regular pruning is needed, but remove the old flower heads.

Layer young, low-growing stems during late summer or early autumn. Shoots take about a year to develop roots. When rooted, sever the stems from the parent and plant in a nurserybed until large enough to be set in a garden.
Alternatively, take 10cm/4in-long cuttings from the current year's growth in mid-summer and insert in pots of equal parts moist peat and sharp sand. Place in a cold frame. When rooted, plant into a nurserybed for a couple of years until large enough to be put in a garden.

Davidia involucrata
Dove Tree (UK/USA)
Ghost Tree (UK)
Handkerchief Tree (UK/USA)
Height: 4.5-7.5m/15-25ft
Spread: 3-5.4m/10-18ft

Hardy deciduous tree, famed for its large creamy white bracts (modified leaves) which appear during early summer and obscure the rather insignificant flowers.

Deutzia scabra
Height: 1.8-2.4m/6-8ft
Spread: 1.2-1.8m/4-6ft

Hardy deciduous shrub with peeling, brown bark on erect branches. During early and mid-summer it bears white flowers often flushed pink. Several superb forms, including 'Pride of Rochester' (double white flowers, tinged pink) and 'Plena' (double white flowers suffused rose-purple).

Fuchsia magellanica
Lady's Eardrops (UK/USA)
Height: 1.2-1.5m/4-5ft
Spread: 60cm-1.2m/2-4ft

Slightly tender, bushy and spreading shrub; it is the hardiest of outdoor fuchsias and widely grown in warm, coastal areas as a hedge. From mid-summer to autumn it bears crimson and purple pendent flowers up to 5cm/2in long.

***Kerria japonica* 'Pleniflora'**
Bachelor's Buttons (UK)
Japanese Rose (USA)
Jew's Mallow (UK)
Height: 1.8-2.4m/6-8ft
Spread: 1.8-2.1m/6-7ft

Hardy deciduous shrub with long, slender stems and bright green, tooth-edged leaves. This form has double orange-yellow flowers up to 5cm/2in wide during late spring and early summer.

Summer-flowering trees and shrubs

PLANT NAME AND DESCRIPTION	SITUATION AND CULTIVATION	PROPAGATION

Kolkwitzia amabilis
Beauty Bush (UK/USA)
Height: 1.8-3m/6-10ft
Spread: 1.5-2.4m//5-8ft

Hardy, deciduous, somewhat twiggy and dense shrub with arching branches and broadly oval, dark green leaves. The branches are attractive, with peeling, brown bark. During early summer it bears foxglove-like pink flowers with yellow throats. The variety 'Pink Cloud' develops a profusion of pink flowers.

Well-drained but moisture-retentive soil and a position in full sun or light shade suit it.

It needs regular pruning to encourage the development of flowers each year. As soon as the flowers fade, cut out some of the older shoots. This creates space for the development of further shoots.

The Beauty Bush looks superb in a border with other shrubs, as well as combined with a foreground of Foxgloves (*Digitalis purpurea*).

Take 10-13cm/4-5in-long cuttings from the current season's shoots in mid-summer. Insert them in pots of equal parts moist peat and sharp sand, then place in a cold frame. When rooted, plant into a nurserybed until large enough to be put into a garden.

***Laburnum* x *watereri* 'Vossii'**
(syn. *L.* x *vossii*)
Golden Chain Tree (UK/USA)
Golden Rain Tree (UK)
Height: 3-4.5m/10-15ft
Spread: 3-3.6m/10-12ft

Hardy deciduous tree, well-known for its fragrant, golden yellow flowers borne in slender, pendulous clusters (botanically known as racemes) up to 60cm/2ft long in early summer. It attracts bees.

Full sun or light shade and moisture-retentive but well-drained soil. Support young trees with strong stakes, especially in exposed positions or windy areas. No regular pruning is needed, other than shaping the tree when young.

All parts including the seeds and pods of the plant are poisonous; therefore, do not plant it near children's play areas or fish ponds. However, this hybrid does not set seed freely.

This hybrid – raised from a cross between *Laburnum alpinum* and *L. anagyroides* – does not come true when raised from seeds. Therefore, it is increased in late winter by grafting the species on to rooted plants.

***Lavatera olbia* 'Rosea'**
Tree Lavatera (UK/USA)
Height: 1.5-2.1m/5-7ft
Spread: 1.8-2.4m/6-8ft

Hardy, vigorous, soft-stemmed, branching, cottage-garden shrub with large, lobed grey-green leaves and masses of rose-coloured flowers about 6.5cm/2¹/₂in wide from mid-summer to autumn. The rather lax and spreading nature of this shrub creates a wonderful display over several months.

Full sun and light, well-drained but moisture-retentive soil. Choose a warm, sheltered position, away from cold northerly winds. It is ideal for planting in coastal areas, where it withstands salt-spray.

In autumn, cut back the long shoots to half their length to reduce the risk of wind damage in winter. In spring, trim the plant to maintain a regular and even shape.

Take 7.5-10cm/3-4in-long cuttings from non-flowering shoots of the current season's growth in mid- to late summer. Insert them in pots of equal parts moist peat and sharp sand, and place in a cold frame. When rooted, transfer them into individual pots and overwinter in a cold frame. Plant into a nurserybed in spring, or direct into a border.

***Philadelphus coronarius* 'Aureus'**
Golden-leaved Mock Orange (UK)
Height: 1.5-2.1m/5-7ft
Spread: 1.5-1.8m/5-6ft

Hardy deciduous, upright but bushy shrub with orange-blossom-scented, creamy white flowers during early and mid-summer. It is, however, the bright golden yellow leaves, slowly becoming greenish yellow, that distinguish it. They create a dramatic effect and capture attention throughout summer.

Light shade or dappled light – full sun tends to bleach the leaves. Deeply prepared, well-drained but moisture-retentive garden soil suits it.

Regular pruning is needed to ensure the development of flowers each year and to prevent the shrub becoming a jungle of old shoots with flowers produced only at the ends of shoots. As soon as the flowers fade, thin out the old wood, taking care to retain young shoots that will bear flowers during the following season.

Take 25-30cm/10-12in-long cuttings from mature shoots in autumn. Insert them in a sheltered nurserybed. Take out a straight-sided trench, about 15cm/6in deep, sprinkle a layer of sharp sand in its base and stand the cuttings on it. Firm soil around them. By the following autumn roots will have formed and the cuttings can be transferred to a nurserybed until large enough to be planted in a garden.

Magnolia sieboldii
Height: 3-4.5m/10-15ft
Spread: 3-3.6m/10-12ft

Hardy deciduous shrub or small tree with dark green, lance-shaped leaves and white, pendent, bowl-shaped flowers about 7.5cm/3in wide appearing (a few at a time) from early to late summer. The fragrant flowers have conspicuous rosy crimson or maroon stamens at their centres.

Olearia* x *haastii
Daisy Bush (UK/USA)
Tree Aster (USA)
Height: 1.8-2.1m/6-7ft
Spread: 2.1-2.7m/7-9ft

Hardy evergreen shrub with glossy, mid-green leaves with grey-white, felted undersides. During mid- and late summer it bears 7¹/₂in-wide, terminal clusters of white, daisy-like flowers.

***Paeonia suffruticosa* 'Rock's Variety'**
Height: 1.5-1.8m/5-6ft
Spread: 1.5-1.8m/5-6ft

Slightly tender deciduous shrub with pale to mid-green leaves. During early summer it bears white flowers, richly and prominently blotched in maroon-crimson.
There are many other forms of *P. suffruticosa* (Moutan Paeony), including

***Philadelphus* hybrids**
Mock Orange (UK/USA)
Height: 90cm-3m/3-10ft (range)
Spread: 90cm-3.6m/3-12ft (range)

Hardy deciduous shrub with a lax nature and arching branches bearing single or double, sweetly fragrant, white, cup-shaped flowers during early and mid-summer. Hybrids include 'Avalanche' (90cm-1.5m/3-5ft high/single) and 'Virginal' (2.4-2.7m/8-9ft high/double).

PLANT NAME AND DESCRIPTION	SITUATION AND CULTIVATION	PROPAGATION

Potentilla fruticosa
Shrubby Cinquefoil (UK/USA)
Height: 1-1.2m/3¹/₂-4ft
Spread: 1-1.2m/3¹/₂-4ft

Deciduous, bushy but compact shrub with mid-green leaves and masses of buttercup yellow flowers about 2.5cm/1in across from early to late summer and often into early autumn. Hybrids include 'Elizabeth' (soft yellow), 'Red Ace' (glowing red), 'Sunset' (orange to brick-red) and 'Tangerine' (tangerine-red).

Light, well-drained but moisture-retentive garden soil and a position in full sun suit it. Avoid shaded areas as this decreases the shrub's normal prolific flowering.
No regular pruning is needed, but to ensure plants remain bushy cut out weak and old stems to soil-level in spring. Also, clip off dead flowers as soon as they fade.

Take 7.5cm/3in-long cuttings from the current season's shoots in late summer and insert in pots of equal parts moist peat and sharp sand. Place in a cold frame. When rooted, plant into a nurserybed until large enough to be put into a garden.

Romneya coulteri trichocalyx
California Tree Poppy (UK)
Matilija (USA)
Tree Poppy (UK)
Height: 90cm-1.2m/3-4ft
Spread: 90cm/3ft

Hardy, semi-woody shrub with herbaceous-like stems bearing deeply lobed, blue-green leaves and slightly fragrant, poppy-like, white flowers up to 13cm/5in wide from mid- to late summer – and often into early autumn.

Full sun and deeply prepared, light, well-drained soil enriched with peat or well-decomposed compost. Plant this shrub in a warm, wind-sheltered position. It is sometimes difficult to establish, but once growing is very vigorous.
In autumn, cut the stems down to within a few inches of the soil.

Sow seeds evenly and thinly, 3-6mm/ ¹/₈-¹/₄in deep, in seed-trays or pots in late winter or early spring. Place in gentle warmth. After germination and when large enough to handle, move the seedlings into individual pots. When established and growing strongly, place the pots in a cold frame. Plant out into a garden during the following spring.

Syringa meyeri
Height: 1.5-1.6m/5-6ft
Spread: 1.2-1.5m/4-5ft

Hardy, small-leaved lilac – a rounded, deciduous shrub with oval, dark green leaves and violet-purple flowers in small, rounded clusters up to 10cm/4in long during early summer. Occasionally, a second flush of flowers appears in late summer. Like another small-leaved lilac, *S. microphylla* 'Superba', this is well suited to small gardens.

Deeply prepared, fertile, well-drained but moisture-retentive soil and a position in full sun or light shade suit it.
No regular pruning is needed, other than cutting out dead shoots in spring.

Take 7.5cm/3in-long cuttings with heels during mid-summer and insert in pots of equal parts moist peat and sharp sand. Place in gentle warmth until rooted, then pot up and put in a cold frame. In spring, plant into a nurserybed for a couple of years before planting into a garden.

***Weigela* hybrids**
Height: 1.5-1.8m/5-6ft
Spread: 1.5-2.4m/5-8ft

Hardy, deciduous, wide-spreading shrub with arching branches bearing finely wrinkled, oval, mid-green leaves. During early summer it produces crowds of flowers, each about 2.5cm/1in long. Varieties include 'Abel Carrière' (soft rose), 'Bristol Ruby' (ruby red), 'Eva Rathke' (bright red), 'Avalanche' (white) and 'Newport Red' (bright red).

Fertile, well-drained but moisture-retentive soil and a position in full sun or light shade suit it. Avoid places where the soil dries out in summer.
Regular pruning is needed to encourage the yearly development of flowers. After the flowers fade, thin out and cut back all flowered shoots to within a few inches of the old wood.

Take 25-30cm/10-12in-long cuttings from mature shoots of the current season's growth in autumn. Insert them in a sheltered nurserybed. Take out a straight-sided trench, about 15cm/6in deep, sprinkle a layer of sharp sand in its base and stand the cuttings on it. Firm soil around them. By the following autumn roots will have formed and the cuttings should be transferred to a nurserybed until large enough to be planted in a garden.

Sorbaria arborea
(now know as *S. kirilowii*)
False Spiraea (UK/US)
Height: 2.4-4.5m/8-15ft
Spread: 2.4-3.6m/8-12ft

Hardy deciduous tree with ash-like, deeply- toothed, mid-green leaflets. During mid- to late summer it develops large pyramidal heads – often 30cm/12in long of creamy white flowers.

Spartium junceum
Spanish Broom (UK/USA)
Weever's Broom (UK/USA)
Height: 1.8-2.4m/6-8ft
Spread: 1.5-2.1m/5-7ft

Hardy deciduous shrub with green, rush-like stems; these bear narrow, mid-green leaves that fall off after maturity. From early to late summer it develops fragrant, pea-shaped, golden yellow flowers borne in terminal clusters.

***Viburnum opulus* 'Sterile'**
Snowball Bush (UK/USA)
Height: 2.4-3.6m/8-12ft
Spread: 2.4-3.6m/8-12ft

Hardy, deciduous, bushy shrub with white flowers – first green – borne in large, round, flower heads during early summer. This variety is a form of the well-known Guelder Rose (*V. opulus*).

***Viburnum plicatum* 'Mariesii'**
Height: 2.4-3m/8-10ft
Spread: 3-4.5m/10-15ft

Hardy deciduous shrub with dull green, toothed leaves and white flowers borne in tiers during early summer. The variety 'Lanarth' is similar, but less spreading and with smaller flowers.

Establishing, clipping and pruning hedges

Neglected hedges mar a garden: they are frequently the first features to be seen and if ragged, bare-based or over-grown are an eyesore that detracts from the rest of the garden.

ESTABLISHING NEWLY PLANTED HEDGES

If newly planted hedges are left alone, establishment will be slow, and they may become deformed or, if the weather is very extreme, die. The first year after being planted is the most critical time for hedges – ice, frost, snow, wind, dry soil and hot weather soon cause damage.

Dry weather is damaging, especially in spring and early summer when plants are responding to higher day temperatures and demanding more activity from their roots. To keep roots moist, remove all weeds, thoroughly water the soil and spread a 5cm/2in-thick mulch of well-rotted compost around the plants and over an area 38-45cm/15-18in on either side. The mulch may be disturbed by birds as well as blown by swirling wind, but the chance of this happening can be reduced by keeping it moist. (See pages 46-7 for more on mulching soil.)

Weeds choke plants and rob them of food. Also, lawns too close to hedges often spread, intrude on hedges and deprive them of food, especially of nitrogen, which is the main plant nutrient for leaf and stem growth. Regularly hoe off or pull up weeds, and trim back lawn edges.

Feed hedges with a general fertilizer at 70g per sq m/2oz per sq yd in spring and again during mid-summer. Lightly fork or rake the fertilizer into surface soil, taking care not to damage roots. In spring, apply the fertilizer before forming a mulch.

Strong wind is a problem before roots are established and able to support the hedging plants. Newly planted evergreen hedges are especially vulnerable as they present a large area of foliage to blustery wind. Inspect individual plants regularly, replacing broken canes and ties as necessary. (In blustery areas, tie each plant to an individual care.)

Frost loosens soil, so use the heel of your shoe or boot to refirm soil around and over the roots in spring. When doing this, re-check the ties securing plants to canes.

CARING FOR HEDGES

1 In spring, remove weeds from around both newly planted and established hedging plants.
2 Frost often loosens soil around the roots of young plants; firm it with the heel of your shoe.
3 Water the soil and add a mulch of decayed compost or moist peat.
4 Use hedging shears to trim small hedges. Ensure the shears are sharp.
5 Use secateurs to trim large-leaved hedges, cutting to slightly above a leaf-joint.
6 Cut large hedges by using electric hedging trimmers. Ensure a power-breaking device is fitted into the circuit and trail the cable over your shoulder so that it cannot be inadvertently cut. If the hedge is dusty, wear a pair of protective goggles.

Above: Beech (*Fagus sylvatica*) forms a dominant and long-lived deciduous hedge. In spring the young leaves are bright green, becoming mid-to deep green in summer and in autumn assuming yellow and russet tints. Trim the hedge so that the top is slightly angled to encourage snow to fall off easily.

CLIPPING AND PRUNING HEDGES

The treatment required to create an attractive hedge differs according to the hedge's nature. Formal, deciduous hedges must be initially pruned when planted as the first stage in creating a hedge covered with foliage from its base to the top. Use secateurs to cut back the hedge's height by one-third to a half and also to cut back long sideshoots. This severe pruning encourages the development of sideshoots during the first season of growth.

During the following spring, cut back the previous year's growth by a half. By the end of the third year the hedge will be bushy and packed with shoots.

When the hedge starts to take shape, use hedging shears or electric clippers to cut it several times a year. It is better – and easier – to cut the hedge frequently than to leave it until growth is long.

Coniferous hedges, which naturally develop shoots from their bases, should not be pruned when planted, although long shoots can be trimmed back in spring.

When a coniferous hedge reaches 15-20cm/ 6-8in above its desired height, cut off the tops of the leading shoots. During the following year the hedge will thicken and you can then use garden shears or electric clippers to trim the side growths as necessary.

Informal deciduous hedges, like formal types, must be cut back when planted to encourage bushy shoots from ground level. This is especially important as many informal hedges are grown for their flowers and if the hedge is initially neglected these may eventually appear only high up. Cut plants back by one-third to a half. During subsequent years, you can leave informal hedges to develop naturally unless they are not making much side growth, in which case cut back the top shoots, removing about half of the previous year's growth. You may need to do this again during later years. Always cut just above a leaf joint, and in spring or autumn.

Many informal hedges have large leaves. To avoid chopping up the leaves use secateurs or long-handled lopping shears rather than hedging shears to prune.

RENOVATING OLD HEDGES

Eventually, hedges that are not regularly pruned may become too large and will have to be reduced in height and width.

- If the hedge is both too wide and too high, correct this over two or three years rather than all at once. In early spring, just before growth begins, use long-handled lopping shears to cut back the top; the following year (or two years) cut the sides.

- Not all hedging plants can be drastically cut back but those that can include aucuba, Beech, Box, elaeagnus, forsythia, Gorse, Hawthorn, hippophaea, Hornbeam, *Lonicera nitida*, Privet, pyracantha, rhododendron, roses, Sweet Bay and Yew.

- Large, straggly hedges formed of Lavender and Rosemary are best replaced by new plants.

- Conifers, with the exception of Yew, should not be cut hard back, and are best replaced. However, the tops of tall conifer hedges can be cut off, although the result is not always attractive.

Autumn-coloured trees and shrubs

PLANT NAME AND DESCRIPTION	SITUATION AND CULTIVATION	PROPAGATION

Acer cappadocicum
Height: 7.5-9m/25-30ft
Spread: 3-5.4m/10-18ft

Large deciduous tree, ultimately up to 15m/50ft or more, with five- or seven-lobed green leaves 7.5-13cm/3-5in wide. In autumn, they assume rich butter yellow shades. There are several superb forms of this tree, including 'Aureum', with leaves that are yellow when young, later becoming green and returning to yellow in autumn.

Plant in cool, moisture-retentive but well-drained soil; preferably, it should be neutral, although this acer is tolerant of slight alkalinity. Full sun or slight shade suits it, preferably sheltered from cold winds. Avoid situations where the prevailing autumn wind could rapidly blow off the leaves.
    Although attractive throughout the year, it is at its best in autumn. Therefore, ensure that it is positioned where it can be readily admired.

Sow seeds in autumn in seed-trays or pots of sandy, loam-based compost and place in a cold frame. When the seedlings are large enough to handle, transfer them into individual pots. Later, plant them into a nurserybed until large enough to be planted into a permanent position.

Cornus florida
Flowering Dogwood (UK/USA)
Height: 3-4.5m/10-15ft
Spread: 3-5.4m/10-18ft

Hardy, deciduous, spreading, well-branched shrub or small tree with dark green leaves which, in autumn, turn brilliant shades of scarlet and orange. Additionally, in late spring and early summer it develops green flowers surrounded by large, white, petal-like bracts. There are several varieties.

Full sun and light, deeply prepared, well-drained but moisture-retentive neutral or slightly acid soil suit it. It does not grow well in shallow, chalky soil. No regular pruning is needed.

Layer low-growing shoots in late summer or early autumn. Rooting takes up to two years. Sever the rooted stems from the parent and plant into a border. Alternatively, take 10cm/4in-long cuttings from the current season's shoots in mid-summer. Insert them in pots of equal parts moist peat and sharp sand, then place in gentle warmth. Transfer cuttings into individual pots when rooted and overwinter in a cold frame. In spring, plant into a nurserybed and leave for two or three years.

Fagus sylvatica
Common Beech (UK)
European Beech (USA)
Height: 7.5-10.5m/25-35ft
Spread: 6-9m/20-30ft

Large deciduous tree, eventually growing to 30m/100ft or more. Often, however, it is grown as a hedge up to 3.6m/12ft tall. The broadly oval, mid-green leaves, bright green when young, assume rich yellow and russet tones in autumn before falling.

Light to medium soil in a bright, sunny position. Avoid heavy and wet ground. When growing it as a hedge, space the plants 45-60cm/18-24in apart, either in a single row or staggered in two rows to create greater density.
    When grown as a tree, it needs no pruning; but when planting it as a hedge cut down all plants by about one-third as soon as they are planted to encourage bushy growth. Trim hedges to shape in mid-summer.

Sow seeds in a seedbed outdoors in autumn. When seedlings are large enough to handle, transplant them to a nurserybed and later into permanent positions.

Fothergilla major
Height: 1.8-2.4m/6-8ft
Spread: 1.5-1.8m/5-6ft

Deciduous, slow-growing shrub with white, sweetly scented, bottle-brush-like flowers in heads up to 5cm/2in long during late spring. They appear before the dark green leaves, which in autumn assume rich red and orange-yellow tints.

Full sun and acid, fertile, moisture-retentive peaty soil enriched with well-decomposed compost suit it.
    No regular pruning is needed, other than occasionally cutting out damaged shoots in spring. .

It is easily increased by layering low-growing shoots in late summer or early autumn. They take up to two years to develop roots.

Berberis thunbergii
Japanese Berberis (UK/USA)
Height: 1-1.2m/3½-4ft
Spread: 1.2-1.5m/4-5ft

Hardy deciduous shrub with pear-shaped, pale to mid-green leaves that in autumn turn brilliant red. This shrub has the bonus of bearing pale yellow flowers followed by small, round, scarlet berries.

Cercidiphyllum japonicum
Katsura Tree (UK/USA)
Height: 6-7.5m/20-25ft
Spread: 4.5-6m/15-20ft

Deciduous tree, eventually growing to 9m/30ft or more, with rounded and somewhat heart-shaped leaves, red when unfolding in spring but later turning rich green. In autumn they assume red and yellow tints. On still days in autumn it has the aroma of burnt sugar.

Enkianthus campanulatus
Height: 1.8-2.7m/6-9ft
Spread: 1.2-1.8m/4-6ft

Hardy deciduous tree with erect branches and dull green, finely tooth-edged leaves that turn brilliant red in autumn.
    During late spring and early summer it bears creamy white, bell-shaped flowers with red veins.

Gingko biloba
Maidenhair Tree (UK/USA)
Height: 6-9m/20-30ft
Spread: 2.4-3m/8-10ft

Distinctive, hardy deciduous conifer with leathery, somewhat fan-shaped, pale green leaves which in autumn become soft golden yellow. It is an ideal tree for planting on either side of a wide path.

PLANT NAME AND DESCRIPTION	SITUATION AND CULTIVATION	PROPAGATION

***Hamamelis mollis* 'Pallida'**
Chinese Witch Hazel (UK/USA)
Height: 1.8-3m/6-10ft
Spread: 2.1-3m/7-10ft

Deciduous spreading shrub with roundish to slightly pear-shaped, mid-green leaves that in autumn assume rich yellow tints. The leaves, which fall in late autumn, are followed in mid- and late winter by sweetly scented, wavy-petalled, spider-like, sulphur yellow flowers that cluster on the naked twigs.

Moisture-retentive but well-drained, fertile, neutral or slightly acid soil. Lighten heavy ground by digging in plenty of well-decayed organic material such as compost and manure. Choose a sunny or lightly shaded site, sheltered from cold north and east winds.
 Little pruning is needed, other than cutting out dead branches after the flowers fade.

In autumn, peg low-growing branches into the soil to encourage the formation of roots. Rooting takes about two years, after which, sever the stem from the parent and either plant directly into a border or put in a nurserybed for two or three years.

Hydrangea paniculata
Height: 2.4-3m/8-10ft
Spread: 2.4-3m/8-10ft

Large, spreading deciduous shrub with mid-green leaves that assume yellow shades in autumn. During late summer and into early autumn it develops large, pyramidal clusters of white flowers.
 'Grandiflora' is a superb form with masses of heads, up to 45cm/18in long, packed with white flowers.

Rich, moisture-retentive but well-drained soil and a position in full sun or light shade suit it. Avoid exposed positions.
 In late winter or early spring, cut back the previous season's flowering stems by half. This encourages the development of fresh shoots that will bear flowers later in the same season.
 Plant this shrub 1.5-1.8m/5-6ft from the front of a border; if too close, it soon obstructs the lawn, especially when the long stems are bent over by the weight of the flowers.

Take 13-15cm/5-6in-long cuttings from the current season's shoots in mid- to late summer. Insert them in equal parts moist peat and sharp sand; place in gentle warmth. When rooted, pot up into individual pots and place in a cold frame. In spring, set the young plants in a nurserybed until large enough to be put in a garden.

Juglans nigra
Black Walnut (UK/USA)
Height: 7.5-10.5m/25-35ft
Spread: 6-7.5m/20-25ft

Large, deciduous, fast-growing tree, eventually maturing to well over 24m/80ft high. The huge leaves, up to 60cm/24in long, are formed of eleven to twenty-three leaflets and are fragrant when rubbed. In autumn, the foliage turns a beautiful yellowish green. The tree's has a slightly pyramidal shape.

Plant in well-drained but moisture-retentive loamy soil. When young, plants are rather tender and can be damaged by severe frost. If a leading shoot is damaged, select and tie in a shoot to replace it. As this tree eventually creates a dominant outline, position it where it can be left for many years.

Raise new plants from seed and transplant young trees to their growing positions as early as possible. This is because it is difficult to transplant them successfully when old.

Parrotia persica
Height: 3-5.4m/10-18ft
Spread: 3-4.5m/10-15ft

Deciduous, slow-growing tree or large shrub with a bushy and spreading habit. In autumn, the oval to pear-shaped mid-green leaves assume handsome shades of gold, amber and crimson. These shades vary from one year to another. On older trees the bark flakes to create attractive patterns. Eventually, trees reach 9m/30ft or more.

Fertile, well-drained but moisture-retentive, slightly acid soil is best, although it tolerates lime. For the best autumn colours, it needs an open position in full sun or very light shade. No regular pruning is needed, other than trimming to shape while young. Remove misplaced, damaged and crossing branches.
 Position this tree towards the bottom of your garden, so that it forms a dominant focal point in autumn. Avoid positioning large shrubs in front of it.

Raise new plants from seeds sown in pots of sandy, loam-based compost in late summer or autumn and placed in a cold frame. Germination takes up to eighteen months. When the seedlings are large enough to handle, transfer them into individual pots. When larger, plant into a nurserybed and leave for four or five years before planting into a permanent position. Alternatively, layer low-growing branches in late summer. When roots have formed, after about two years, sever from the parent.

Liquidambar styraciflua
American Sweet Gum (USA)
Red Gum (USA)
Sweet Gum (UK/USA)
Height: 5.4-7.5m/18-25ft
Spread: 2.4-3.6m/8-12ft

Large deciduous tree, eventually 24m/80ft or more high, with deeply divided, five- or seven-lobed, shiny green leaves that in autumn assume shades of crimson, purple and orange.

Liriodendron tulipifera
Tulip Poplar (USA)
Tulip Tree (UK/USA)
Yellow Popular (USA)
Height: 5.4-7.5m/18-25ft
Spread: 3-4.5m/10-15ft

Hardy deciduous tree with distinctively shaped leaves; they are saddle-shaped, with the top of the central lobe cut off almost square. The leaves are mid-green and in autumn turn butter yellow.

Rhus typhina
Stag's Horn Sumach (UK/USA)
Velvet Sumac (USA)
Height: 2.4-3.6m/8-12ft
Spread: 2.4-3.6m/8-12ft

Hardy, deciduous shrub with mid-green leaves up to 45cm/18in long and formed of thirteen to twenty-six leaflets. In autumn, the leaves assume rich shades of orange, red and purple. The stems are densely covered with reddish hairs.

Taxodium distichum
Bald Cypress (UK/USA)
Swamp Cypress (UK/USA)
Height: 7.5-9m/25-30ft
Spread: 3.6-4.5m/12-15ft

Hardy deciduous conifer with narrow, yellow-green leaves which in autumn become rich brown before falling. This superb conifer has the bonus of attractive bark.

Looking after trees and shrubs

Most trees, once established, continue to grow healthily and vigorously for many years, becoming part of a garden's landscape. Shrubs need slightly more attention, especially those that flower during summer and yearly develop fresh shoots which bear new flowers.

For how to prune deciduous shrubs and trees see pages 76-7 and for pruning evergreen ones, pages 80-1; other aspects essential to their care are described below.

MULCHING
As well as providing plants with food, a mulch helps to suppress the growth of weeds, conserve moisture and keep the soil cool during summer. Additionally, as the mulch is usually lightly forked into the ground in autumn, it improves the soil's structure and encourages soil organisms.

Form a mulch in spring; first remove all weeds and thoroughly water the soil, then create a 5cm/2in-thick layer of well-rotted compost or manure around the plant. Keep it about 5-7.5cm/2-3in from the trunk or stems that arise from ground level to prevent rotting.

REMOVING WATERSHOOTS
Some trees produce thin shoots on their trunks and branches; these are known as watershoots. If left, they create an eyesore and use up the tree's energies in excess growth.

They are easily removed by cutting them out close to the tree. Spring is the best time – especially if the tree is a member of the *Prunus* family – as at that time the sap is rising. In winter, when the tree is dormant, the chance of disease spores entering the tree through cuts is greater.

Use a sharp saw to cut the shoots close to the trunk. If you have to remove clusters of watershoots, you may cut a large area of bark. Use a sharp knife to smooth the surface and cover it with a fungicidal tree paint.

TRANSPLANTING SHRUBS AND TREES
If you are taking over or re-planning an existing garden, it is likely that you may want to move a shrub or tree; this is not an easy or quickly accomplished task. Clearly, large trees or shrubs are more difficult to move successfully than small ones, so unless the plant is relatively small – and this applies especially to trees – it is better to scrap it and to buy a fresh one.

Transplant evergreen types in late spring and early summer, or late summer and early autumn; deciduous ones should be moved in winter, when they are dormant.

Large specimens can be moved over two or three seasons: in the first year, dig around and under half the plant, then replace the soil. The second year, do the same to the other side. This breaks the main roots and encourages development of fibrous ones. During the third year, dig under the complete plant and move it.

Before you actually move the tree or shrub you will need to prepare the new planting hole. Mix damp peat with the soil excavated from the hole as this helps to retain moisture around the roots. Then, with several people to help, lift the root-ball on to a large, strong piece of canvas and drag it to its new position. Carefully position the plant in the hole and place a stick across the top of the hole to check that the top of the root-ball is slightly below the surrounding ground. Work in

Right: Rhododendrons create a wealth of flowers that can dominate a garden. They prefer light, acid soil which has plenty of peat or leaf mould added to it. Remove dead flowers, snapping them off the faded flower clusters adding them to and using the compost heap.

CUTTING OFF A LARGE BRANCH

1

2

3

1 Cut off the branch 45-60cm/18-24in from its point of origin.
2 Use a sharp saw to make a cut on the underside of the remaining part of the branch. Cut half to two-thirds of the way through it. Then saw through the branch from the top side.
3 Use a sharp knife to smooth the surface of the cut, then cover with a fungicidal paint.

and firm the peat and soil mixture around the roots. Water the soil thoroughly and continue this during the first summer, especially if the weather is dry.

If necessary, support the stem or trunk with an oblique stake. In windy areas, erect a screen of canvas on the windward side of the plant. Alternatively, use a shelter formed of straw packed between two layers of wire netting and secured between two stakes. Form a mulch around the plant to help conserve moisture in the soil.

REMOVING DEAD FLOWER HEADS
Shrubs that produce large flowers benefit from having the old flower clusters removed. As well as improving the shrub's appearance, 'dead-heading' prevents the development of seeds and directs the plant's energies into growth. Place old flower heads on a compost heap.

REMOVING A LARGE LIMB
Occasionally you will need to cut off a large branch. In most cases, this is best performed in winter, but late spring or early summer is better for ornamental cherries. Rather than cutting off the branch close to the trunk in just one operation, it is better to remove it in stages until only 45-60cm/1-2ft is left on the tree. This prevents the weight of the branch ripping the bark.

For the final operation, use a sharp saw to make a cut on the underside of the branch, close to the trunk. Then make a cut from above to complete the amputation. Use a sharp knife to smooth the surface of the cut, then cover with a fungicidal tree paint.

GROWING ACID-LOVING PLANTS IN CHALKY SOILS

In chalky soils it is difficult to grow acid-loving plants such as camellias, ericas, hydrangeas, pieris, rhododendrons and azaleas. Holes dug out and filled with acid soil have an initial benefit, but soil water soon turns the soil alkaline again. Creating raised beds is one solution that will have a longer lasting effect. Use concrete or stout wood surrounds to create a bed 23-30cm/9-12in deep, above the general level of the soil, and fill it with slightly acid soil.

Another way to grow acid-loving plants in chalky soil is to overcome the problem chemically. Chalk in soil 'locks up' iron – as well as a few other chemicals – and prevents plants absorbing it. Iron is essential to plants; lack of it causes leaves to become yellow and symptoms are worse at the shoot bases and on the oldest leaves. Two or three applications a year of chelated iron will keep plants green, but it is not practical, and certainly not economical, to treat the entire garden in this way, so apply the treatment only to choice plants.

CREATING A SCREEN

1 Until established, newly planted or transplanted shrubs need protection against cold winds. Take wire netting 3-3.6m/10-12ft long and fold it in half.
2 Pack straw or hay evenly between the two pieces of wire netting.
3 Weave string or wire around the sides to hold them closed, then secure the netting to strong stakes on the windward side of the shrub.

Evergreen shrubs for year-through colour

PLANT NAME AND DESCRIPTION	SITUATION AND CULTIVATION	PROPAGATION

***Elaeagnus pungens* 'Maculata'**
Thorny Elaeagnus (USA)
Height: 1.8-3m/6-10ft
Spread: 1.8-3m/6-10ft

Hardy evergreen shrub with a rounded but spreading outline and oval, leathery, glossy green leaves splashed with gold. The stems are slightly thorny, while silvery white, fragrant flowers appear in autumn. It is a superb shrub for creating colour in winter, when gardens are often at their blandest.

Deeply prepared, fertile soil and a position in full sun or light shade suit it. Avoid shallow, chalky soils. It is tolerant of salt-spray in coastal areas, and withstands exposed positions.
No regular pruning is needed, other than cutting back long and straggly stems in late spring. At the same time, shoots that have reverted to producing all-green leaves should be cut out to their points of origin.

Take 7.5-10cm/3-4in-long cuttings from the current season's growth during mid- to late summer. Insert them in pots of equal parts moist peat and sharp sand, then place in a cold frame. Pot them up into individual pots when rooted, later transferring to a nurserybed or a border when established and filling pots with roots.

***Euonymus fortunei* 'Emerald 'n' Gold'**
Height: 30-45cm/12-18in
Spread: 45-60cm/18-24in

Dwarf, bushy, hardy evergreen shrub, densely covered with brightly golden variegated leaves that turn bronzy pink in winter. Other forms include 'Emerald Gaiety' (creamy white and green), 'Golden Prince' (young leaves tipped bright gold) and 'Sheridan Gold' (bright green leaves suffused golden yellow).

Ordinary garden soil in full sun or light shade; full sun encourages the best leaf colours. Variegated forms are less hardy than all-green types and succeed best in bright, warm positions on the south sides of banks and in the lee of walls. No regular pruning is needed.
Several forms of this shrub will climb, as well as forming a spreading and bushy shrub. These include 'Silver Queen' (cream, white and green leaves). They grow about 1.8m/6ft high when planted against a warm wall.

Layer low-growing stems in autumn. Rooting takes about a year; when rooted, plants can be moved to a nurserybed or planted directly into a border.
Take 7.5cm/3in-long cutting of the current season's growth and insert them in pots of equal parts moist peat and sharp sand. Place them in a cold frame. When rooted, plant into a nurserybed until large enough to be put into a garden.

***Ilex x altaclarensis* 'Lawsoniana'**
Variegated Holly (UK)
Height: 3.6-5.4m/12-18ft
Spread: 2.4-3.6m/8-12ft

Hardy evergreen shrub with thick, leathery, dark green leaves prominently splashed in bright yellow. Unlike most hollies, the leaves are generally spineless. During winter it produces clusters of large, orange-red berries. There are several other forms, including 'Golden King' (golden edged leaves).

Deeply prepared, moisture-retentive but well-drained loamy soil and a position in full sun suit it. Variegated hollies rapidly lose their colouring when planted in shade.
Hollies are ideal for planting in coastal and exposed areas.
No regular pruning is needed.

The easiest way to increase it is by layering low-growing stems in autumn. Rooting takes about two years, when rooted plants can be severed from the parent and planted into a nurserybed or a garden.
Alternatively, take 7.5cm/3in-long cuttings from the current season's growth in mid- to late summer and insert them in pots of equal parts moist peat and sharp sand. Place them in a cold frame. Plant rooted cuttings into a nurserybed before planting into a garden.

***Ilex aquifolium* 'Madame Briot'**
Variegated Holly (UK)
Height: 3-5.4m/10-18ft
Spread: 1.8-3m/6-10ft

Hardy evergreen shrub with purple stems and leathery, spiny, green leaves edged in dark yellow. Their centres are mottled in gold and light green. Others include 'Ferox Argentea' (spiny, with creamy white edges), 'Golden Van Tol' (leaves edged in gold) and 'Silver Queen' (creamy white edges).

Deeply prepared, moisture-retentive but well-drained, loamy soil and a position in full sun suit it. Variegated hollies rapidly lose their colour in shade.
Hollies are ideal for planting in coastal and exposed areas.
No regular pruning is needed.

The easiest way to increase it is by layering low-growing stems in autumn. Rooting takes about two years. Sever the rooted plants from the parent and plant into a nurserybed or garden.
Alternatively, take 7.5cm/3in-long cuttings from the current season's growth in mid- to late summer and insert them in pots of equal parts moist peat and sharp sand. Place in a cold frame. Plant rooted cuttings into a nurserybed for a couple of years before planting into a garden.

***Aucuba japonica* 'Variegata'**
(syn. *A. j.* 'Maculata')
Gold-dust Tree (USA)
Spotted Laurel (UK)
Height: 1.8-3m/6-10ft
Spread: 1.8-2.4m/6-8ft

Distinctive evergreen with leathery, narrowly oval, shiny, dark green leaves spotted in yellow. It creates a dominant feature and is an especially welcome sight in winter.

***Euonymus japonicus* 'Aureus'**
(syn. *E. japonicus* 'Aureo-pictus')
Height: 1.2-1.5/4-5ft or more
Spread: 90cm-1.2m/3-4ft or more

Hardy, bushy, densely branched evergreen shrub with glossy, dark green leaves strongly marked bright yellow in their centres. Other variegated forms include 'Albo-marginatus' (white edges) and 'Ovatus Aureus' (creamy white edges; also known as 'Aureovariegatus').

***Lonicera nitida* 'Baggeson's Gold'**
Height: 1.2-1.8m/4-6ft
Spread: 1.2-1.5m/4-5ft

Hardy, bushy, densely leaved evergreen shrub with small, rich golden leaves that turn yellow-green in autumn. It is useful as a hedging plant, as well as in a border, where it creates a bright beacon of colour throughout the year.

***Pachysandra terminalis* 'Variegata'**
Japanese Spurge (USA)
Height: 25-30cm/10-12in
Spread: 45cm/18in

Hardy, spreading and ground-covering evergreen shrub with deep green leaves edged in white. Small white flowers appear in mid-spring. It is an ideal plant to create an attractive backdrop for other plants, as well as to smother weeds.

PLANT NAME AND DESCRIPTION	SITUATION AND CULTIVATION	PROPAGATION

Salvia officinalis 'Icterina'
Height: 45-60cm//18-24in
Spread: 38-45cm/15-18in

A relatively short-lived, slightly tender shrub that in cold regions may become only semi-evergreen. Nevertheless, its green-and-gold variegated leaves make it a superb garden plant. Other variegated sages include 'Purpurascens' (young leaves suffused purple) and 'Tricolor' (grey-green leaves splashed creamy white and suffused purple and pink).

Full sun and light, well-drained garden soil in a warm position sheltered from cold winds suit it. Pinch off flowers to encourage better leaf development. In spring, cut out shoots damaged by frosts, as well as those that have become straggly.

Take 7.5cm/3in-long cuttings, preferably with a heel, in late summer. Insert them in pots of equal parts moist peat and sharp sand and place in a cold frame. Pot them into individual pots when rooted and overwinter in a cold frame. Nip out the growing tips of young plants to encourage bushiness. In spring, plant them into a garden.

Senecio 'Sunshine'
(syn. *Brachyglottis* 'Sunshine')
Height: 60cm-1.2m/2-4ft
Spread: 90cm-1.5m/3-5ft

Mound-forming, evergreen shrub with silvery grey leaves, white-felted beneath. During early and mid-summer it develops daisy-like, bright yellow flowers about 2.5cm/1in wide. The naming of this plant is confused and often plants named as *S. greyi* and *S. laxifolius* are sold as the same species.

Deeply prepared, well-drained but moisture-retentive soil and a position in full sun suit this shrub. It also grows well in coastal areas exposed to salt-spray.
No regular pruning is needed, other than to cut out straggly stems in spring.

Layer young, low-growing stems in late summer. Rooting takes a year, when young plants can be severed from the parent and planted into a nurserybed until large enough for the garden.
Alternatively, take 7.5-10cm/3-4in-long cuttings from the current season's growth in late summer and insert them in pots of equal parts moist peat and sharp sand. Place them in a cold frame. When rooted, during the following spring, plant into a nurserybed until large enough to be planted into a garden.

Vinca major 'Variegata'
(syn. *V. major* 'Elegantissima')
Variegated Greater Periwinkle (UK/USA)
Height: 15-38cm/6-15in
Spread: 90cm-1.2m/3-4ft

Hardy, spreading and sprawling variegated evergreen shrub with glossy, mid-green leaves edged in creamy white. During spring and summer it bears bright blue flowers, about 2.5cm/1in wide.

Ordinary, well-drained garden soil and a bright, sunny position suit it. Avoid excessively fertile soils and positions in deep shade, as these encourage rapid growth and a tendency for the plant to lose its attractive variegations.
No regular pruning is needed, other than to cut back long shoots in spring and summer.

The trailing stems root naturally into the soil and rooted sections can be detached in spring and planted directly into their growing positions.
Alternatively, lift and divide congested plants in autumn or spring, replanting young pieces into a border.

Yucca filamentosa 'Variegata'
Variegated Adam's Needle (UK/USA)
Height: 60-75cm/2-2¹/₂ft
Spread: 90cm-1.2m/3-4ft

Slightly tender evergreen shrub with rosettes of deep green leaves edged in whitish yellow. In mid-summer it develops bell-shaped, plume-like heads of creamy white flowers on stems 1.8m/6ft tall. These stems are often cut off as they detract from the variegated leaves.

Well-drained soil is essential; even light, sandy types are suitable. Plant it in a warm, wind-sheltered position. It is native to the south-east states of North America and will not thrive in extremely cold areas.
No pruning is needed.

In spring, cut off rooted suckers and plant them directly into a garden. Unrooted, small suckers are inserted into a sandy nurserybed until they form roots – up to three years.

Phormium tenax
New Zealand Flax (UK/USA)
New Zealand Hemp (UK/USA)
Height: 1.5-3m/5-10ft
Spread: 1.2-1.8m/4-6ft

Half-hardy evergreen shrub with strap-like, leathery, mid- to deep green leaves. It is the variegated forms that create most interest and these include 'Purpureum' (bronze-purple) and 'Variegatum' (striped green and yellow).

Pieris japonica 'Variegata'
Height: 1.8-2.4m/6-8ft
Spread: 1.8-2.1m/6-7ft

Hardy, slow-growing, evergreen shrub with shiny, grey-green leaves with creamy white edges, flushed pink when young. It has the bonus of producing terminal clusters of white flowers during spring, and is an ideal shrub for planting in a lightly shaded wild garden.

Pittosporum tenuifolium
Height: 1.5-3.6m/5-12ft
Spread: 1.5-2.1m/5-7ft

Half-hardy evergreen shrub with variable vigour depending on the warmth of the area. The species has wavy-edged, pale green leaves borne on almost black stems. But it is the variegated forms that are most attractive. These include 'Silver Queen' (silvery grey), 'Irene Paterson' (young leaves creamy white).

Vinca minor
Lesser Periwinkle (UK/USA)
Height: 5-10cm/2-4in
Spread: 90cm-1.2m/3-4ft

Hardy, evergreen, ground-covering and spreading shrub with glossy, dark green leaves. However, it is the variegated forms that are mainly grown; these include 'Aureovariegata' (leaves blotched in yellow) and 'Variegata' (leaves variegated creamy white).

ORNAMENTAL GARDENING

The range of plants that brighten gardens is wide and, apart from shrubs and trees, includes bulbs, hardy and half-hardy annuals, biennials, herbaceous perennials, roses and rock garden plants, while climbers drench walls and pergolas with richly coloured flowers or attractive leaves.

While the annuals and biennials have an ephemeral nature, the herbaceous perennials and rock garden plants are longer lived and need only be lifted and young parts replanted after three to five years. Roses and climbers have a long life-span, often of ten or more years. Dahlias and chrysanthemums create colourful displays in summer and into early autumn; they come in a blaze of colours, with a good choice of flower shapes and sizes.

Growing hardy and half-hardy annuals

Hardy and half-hardy annuals are some of the most popular of all garden plants. Each year they are raised from seeds and create a rich range of brightly coloured flowers throughout summer.

Hardy annuals can be sown in the positions where they are to flower, while half-hardy types should be raised in gentle warmth and later planted out when all risk of frost has passed.

SOWING HARDY ANNUALS
Prepare the site by thoroughly digging the soil in late autumn or early winter; single-digging (see pages 38-9) is sufficient in borders that have been cultivated during earlier years, while land newly converted from pasture needs double-digging (see pages 40-1).

It is a waste of time and seeds to sow hardy annuals too early in the year, when the soil is still cold and wet; the seeds will not germinate and may even start to decay before conditions are right for germination. The earliest time for sowing seeds depends entirely on the weather; even within a distance of one hundred miles the optimum time may vary by seven to ten days. Also,

gardens on warm, sunny slopes can be sown earlier than those with a cold and wind-blown aspect.

While waiting for the soil to warm up and dry out slightly, avoid walking upon it as this causes uneven compaction. Wait until the surface of the soil is dry and crumbly – usually during mid- and late spring. Prepare the soil by first raking the surface level, then systematically shuffling sideways across the plot, at each crossing firming a strip about 25cm/10in wide. Then use a rake to level the surface again.

Some gardeners sow hardy annuals simply by scattering the seeds and then lightly raking the surface. Although this is an easy method it will not enable you to readily identify and remove weeds while they are still young. Nor will you be able to thin seedlings easily. Instead of just scattering seeds, sow them in drills.

Mark out the border into sections in which to sow different species and varieties of annuals. Do not make all of these areas the same shape and size; those towards the front of the border should be smaller and shallower than those at

SOWING HARDY ANNUALS

1 In late autumn or early winter dig the soil. During mid to late spring, rake the surface and then systematically shuffle sideways over the soil to consolidate it evenly. Then rake the surface level and use trickles of sand to mark out the sowing positions; make them different sizes.
2 Use a straight-edged stick to mark the positions of the drill and use a pointed stick to form drills 6-12mm/ $^1/_4$-$^1/_2$ in deep and about 23cm/9in apart.
3 Sow seeds evenly and thinly along the base of each drill in each sowing area.
4 Use the back of a metal rake to draw and push soil over the seeds. Firm the surface by pressing downward with the head of a metal rake.

Above: Hardy and half-hardy annuals create some of the brightest flowers in a garden during summer. Hardy annuals are sown where they will flower, while half-hardy types are sown in a greenhouse and planted outdoors as soon as risk of frost has passed.

the back, where you will want to sow taller species. Use the point of a stick, or a thin trickle of sharp sand, to mark out the sowing areas. Then use a garden line or a long, straight stick as a guide for a draw hoe when taking out 6-12mm/¹/₄-¹/₂in-deep drills about 23cm/9in apart.

Sow seeds thinly and evenly along the base of each drill. There is always a temptation to sow all the seeds in a packet, but sowing seeds thickly encourages the presence of diseases, is a waste of money and makes thinning seedlings difficult.

Cover the seeds by using the back of a metal rake head and both pushing and drawing soil over them. Take care not to push the seeds sideways so that they are moved out of a straight line. Alternatively, straddle the row, position your feet in a V-shape and shuffle forwards, so that soil is directed over the seeds. However, when rows are close together, or short, this is not a practical method to adopt.

Firm soil over the seeds by using the head of a metal rake and pressing downwards with it. The soil should be in close contact with the seeds.

Birds like seeds and often scratch at the surface to get at them. Traditionally, thin pea-sticks were laid on the soil until the seeds germinated.

Alternatively, you can tightly stretch white cotton across the bed, about 10cm/4in above the soil, but make sure that birds are not harmed by it.

When the seedlings start to touch each other in the row they must be thinned. If left, they become congested, etiolated and more susceptible to diseases. The optimum spacings to which seedlings should be thinned varies from one species to another (these are indicated on pages 100-7). Preferably, thin seedlings in two stages; first to half the recommended spacing, and later to the full distance. After each thinning re-firm soil around the seedlings, then lightly but thoroughly water the area

SOWING HALF-HARDY ANNUALS

Half-hardy annuals are widely grown in summer-flowering bedding schemes as well as in hanging-baskets, windowboxes and other containers. If you have a greenhouse or conservatory that can be kept warm in late winter and early spring, it is possible to raise your own plants.

Fill a seed-tray and gently firm the compost, especially around the edges. Compost that is left loose and unfirmed dries quickly and does not encourage rapid germination. Re-fill the seed-tray with compost and use a straight-edged piece of wood to strike the surface level. Use a compost presser (13-15cm/5-6in wide and 18mm/³/₄in thick) to firm the surface to about 12mm/¹/₂in below the tray's rim.

Tip some seeds into a V-shaped piece of stiff paper and lightly tap its end so that seeds fall evenly over the surface. Do not sow seeds closer than 12mm/¹/₂in to the edges. Use a horticultural or domestic sieve to spread compost evenly over the seeds. The thickness of the covering varies: some seeds are pressed into the surface, while others are covered with 3-6mm/¹/₈-¹/₄in of compost. (The depth of sowing a wide range of half-hardy annuals is indicated on pages 100-7.)

Water the compost by placing the seed-tray in a bowl filled with 2.5cm/1in of water. When moisture seeps to the surface, remove the seed-tray and allow excess to drain. Do not water the seeds from overhead, as this disturbs them.

Place the seed-tray in gentle warmth and cover with a polythene lid or sheet of glass. Most seeds need darkness to encourage germination, but a few germinate best when given light. Add a sheet of newspaper to those that need darkness.

Hardy annuals, half-hardy annuals and biennials

PLANT NAME AND DESCRIPTION	SITUATION AND CULTIVATION	PROPAGATION

***Agrostemma githago* 'Milas'**
Corn Cockle (UK/USA)
Purple Cockle (USA)
Height: 90cm-1.2m/3-4ft
Spread: 38-45cm/15-18in

Hardy annual with slender, light green leaves and masses of delicately veined, lilac-pink flowers borne at the tops of upright stems from mid-summer to autumn. The flowers deepen in colour towards their edges. It gains it name from Milas in Turkey, where it originated.

Full sun and ordinary garden soil. It grows well in poor soil, as long as it is moisture-retentive – the display declines dramatically during droughts.

It creates attractive plant associations when positioned behind scarlet poppies and orange and red nasturtiums.

From mid- to late spring sow seeds in the positions where they are to flower. Form drills 6mm/^{1}/4in deep and 25-30cm/10-12in apart and sow seeds evenly and thinly. Germination takes about two weeks. When large enough to handle, thin the seedlings 15-20cm/6-8in apart.

***Amaranthus caudatus* 'Viridis'**
Love-Lies-Bleeding (UK/USA)
Tassel Flower (USA)
Height: 90cm-1.2m/3-4ft
Spread: 38-45cm/15-18in

Hardy annual with light green leaves and long, drooping tassels packed with pale lime green flowers from mid-summer to autumn. It is attractive both in a garden and in flower arrangements indoors. The normal species has crimson tassels. Its leaves turn bronze in autumn.

Full sun and deeply prepared, fertile, well-drained soil.

With its pale colouring, 'Viridis' is ideal for highlighting other plants, while the species, with its bold splashes of colour, can be used to form dominant areas in a mixed border.

After the flowers fade, pull up the plants and place on a compost heap.

From mid- to late spring sow seeds in the positions where they are to flower. Form drills 3mm/^{1}/8in deep and 25-30cm/10-12in apart and sow seeds evenly and thinly. Germination takes two to three weeks. When large enough to handle, thin the seedlings 30-38m/12-15in apart.

Alternatively, sow seeds earlier in seed-trays and keep at 15°C/59°F. Prick out seedlings into seed-trays when large enough to handle, harden off in a cold frame and plant into a border in late spring.

Bellis perennis
Common Daisy (UK/USA)
Height: 2.5-10cm/1-4in
Spread: 7.5-10cm/3-4in

Hardy perennial, invariably grown as a biennial, with mid-green leaves and bright-faced, well-known white flowers, tinged pink and with a central yellow disc. They appear from early spring to autumn. There are several varieties, in colours including white, carmine, pink, salmon and rich cherry.

Full sun or light shade and fertile, moisture-retentive but well-drained soil. Set the plants 13-15cm/5-6in apart. After they finish flowering, pull up and discard.

Bellis perennis 'Monstrosa' creates a pleasing partnership with the blue-flowered Grape Hyacinth *(Muscari armeniacum)*.

Sow seeds thinly and evenly, 6mm/^{1}/4in deep, in a seedbed outdoors during late spring and early summer. Germination takes ten to fourteen days. When the seedlings are large enough to handle, thin them to 7.5cm/3in apart. In late summer, move the plants to their flowering positions, setting them 15-20cm/6-8in apart.

Some varieties, such as 'Rob Roy' and 'Dresden China' do not produce seed and are therefore best lifted and divided in mid-spring.

Calendula officinalis
English Marigold (UK)
Pot Marigold (UK/USA)
Height: 45-60cm/18-24in
Spread: 25-30cm/10-12in

Hardy annual with light green leaves and masses of daisy-like, bright yellow or orange flowers about 7.5cm/3in wide from early summer to autumn. There is a wide range of varieties, many double-flowered. Some are dwarf, and only to 30cm/12in high.

Full sun and well-drained, even poor, soil. It is ideal for growing in mixed and country-style borders, where it creates bright pools of colour that contrast well with blue flowers.

It grows well with little attention; regularly remove dead flowers to encourage more to grow. This also prevents the development of self-sown seedlings which, if left, can dominate borders during the following year.

From early to late spring, sow seeds in positions where they are to flower. Form drills, 12mm/^{1}/2in deep and 25cm/10in apart, and sow seeds evenly and thinly. Germination takes ten to fourteen days. When large enough to handle, thin the seedlings to 25-30cm/10-12in apart.

Adonis aestivalis
Pheasant's Eye (UK)
Height: 30cm/12in
Spread: 25-30cm/10-12in

Hardy annual with deep crimson, cup-shaped flowers amid mid-green, feathery foliage from early summer.

Adonis annua is also known as Pheasant's Eye; it is taller, up to 40cm/16in, and more upright and branching.

Ageratum houstonianum
Flossflower (USA)
Pussy-foot (USA)
Height: 13-30cm/5-12in (range)
Spread: 15-30cm/6-12in (range)

Half-hardy annual with clusters of bluish mauve flowers throughout summer and into early autumn. There are many varieties and these extend the colour range to bright blue, mauve, pink and white.

Alcea rosea
(syn. *Althaea rosea*)
Hollyhock (UK/USA)
Height: 1.8-2.4m/6-8ft
Spread: 50-60cm/20-24in

Hardy perennial, usually grown as a biennial, occasionally grown as an annual. Tall stems bear pink flowers from mid-summer to autumn. There are many varieties, in yellow, pink, red and white, and some with double flowers.

Antirrhinum majus
Snapdragon (UK/USA)
Height: 23cm-1.2m/9in-4ft (range)
Spread: 23-45cm/9-18in (range)

Usually grown as a half-hardy annual – but also as a hardy annual and even a hardy perennial – this well-known plant creates masses of irregularly shaped flowers in a wide colour range from mid-summer to late autumn.

PLANT NAME AND DESCRIPTION	SITUATION AND CULTIVATION	PROPAGATION

Campanula medium
Canterbury Bell (UK/USA)
Height: 38-90cm/15-36in
Spread: 23-30cm/9-12in

Hardy biennial with upright stems bearing hairy and wavy-edged, green leaves surmounted by blue, white, purple or pink bell-shaped flowers up to 36mm/1¹/₂in long from late spring to mid-summer. The 38cm/15in-high variety 'Bells of Ireland' is especially suitable for planting in small gardens.

Full sun and moderately fertile, well-drained soil. Set plants about 30cm/12in apart in late summer or early autumn. In windy and exposed areas, insert small, twiggy sticks around the plants in early spring, so that stems and leaves can grow up and through them. After flowering, pull up and place the plants on a compost heap.

Sow seeds thinly and evenly from mid-spring to early summer in drills 6mm/¹/₄in deep. Germination takes two to three weeks. When the seedlings are large enough to handle, thin them to 23cm/9in apart. In late summer or early autumn, transfer the plants to their flowering positions.

Cheiranthus* x *allionii
(syn. *Erysimum* x *allionii*)
Siberian Wallflower (UK)
Height: 30-38cm/12-15in
Spread: 25-30cm/10-12in

Hardy, bushy perennial, invariably grown as a biennial, with dark green leaves and scented, orange flowers borne in terminal clusters from mid-spring to early summer.

Full sun, fertile, well-drained and slightly alkaline soil. If acid, dust the surface with ground limestone at 115g/4oz per sq yd/sq m. Set the plants 25-38cm/10-15in apart. Keep the soil free from weeds and re-firm it in spring if loosened by frost. When plants are about 13cm/5in high, pinch out their growing tips to encourage bushiness. After flowering, pull up and discard plants.

Sow seeds thinly and evenly, 6mm/¹/₄in deep, in a seedbed outdoors during late spring and early summer. Germination takes ten to fourteen days. When the seedlings are large enough to handle, thin them to 13-15cm/5-6in apart. In late summer, move the plants to their flowering positions, setting them 25-38cm/10-15in apart, depending on their vigour.

Chrysanthemum carinatum
(syn. *C. tricolor*)
Annual Chrysanthemum (UK)
Tri-coloured Chrysanthemum (USA)
Height: 50-60cm/20-24in
Spread: 30-38cm/12-15in

Hardy annual with stiff, bright green leaves and upright stems bearing flat-faced, daisy-like flowers with contrasting circular bandings, in a medley of colours, from early to late summer.

Full sun or light shade and fertile, light, well-drained soil. In exposed areas, support this annual chrysanthemum with twiggy sticks, inserted when the plants are small so that they grow up and through them. When growing plants to produce flowers for room decoration, pinch out their growing tips when they are young. This encourages branching and the development of long sideshoots. In autumn, pull up and compost the plants.

From early to late spring, sow seeds in positions where they are to flower. Form drills, 6mm/¹/₄in deep and 23cm/9in apart, and sow seeds evenly and thinly. Germination takes ten to fourteen days. When large enough to handle, thin the seedlings 23-30cm/9-12in apart, depending on the vigour of the variety.
In mild areas, seeds can also be sown in their flowering positions in late summer and covered with cloches. This encourages the development of larger plants and earlier flowers.

Cleome spinosa
Spider Flower (UK)
Height: 90cm-1m/3-3¹/₂ft
Spread: 45-50cm/18-20in

Half-hardy annual with an erect habit, mid-green leaves divided into several leaflets, and lax, rounded heads, up to 10cm/4in wide, of white, pink-flushed flowers from mid-summer to late autumn. 'Colour Fountain Mixed' has flower heads in pink, rose, lilac, purple and white; 'Helen Campbell' is white.

Full sun and fertile, well-drained but moisture-retentive soil, which has had plenty of well-decomposed organic material added to it. Set the plants 38cm/15in apart. Support them with twiggy sticks, inserted early, so that stems and leaves grow up and through them. In autumn, pull up and discard the plants.

Sow seeds in seed-trays, thinly and evenly, 3mm/¹/₈in deep, during late winter and early spring. Keep at 18-20°C/64-68°F. Germination takes two to four weeks. When the seedlings are large enough to handle, prick them out into fresh seed-trays, so that they are spaced 36-50mm/1¹/₂-2in apart. Alternatively, move the seedlings into individual pots. When established, slowly acclimatize plants to outside conditions. Plant them into a border when the risk of frost has passed.

Arctotis* x *hybrida
African Daisy (UK/USA)
Height: 30-60cm/12-24in
Spread: 30cm/12in

Half-hardy annual with narrow, grey-green leaves and long-stemmed flowers up to 10cm/4in across in brilliant shades of white, cream, yellow, orange, apricot and red from mid-summer to autumn.

Asperula orientalis
Annual Woodruff (UK)
Height: 30cm/12in
Spread: 7.5-10cm/3-4in

Hardy annual with whorls of narrowly lance-shaped, mid-green, hairy leaves and clusters of small, fragrant pale-blue flowers during mid-summer.

Begonia semperflorens
Fibrous Begonia (UK)
Wax Begonia (UK/USA)
Height: 15-23cm/6-9in
Spread: 20-25cm/8-10in

Tender perennial usually grown as a half-hardy annual and used in summer bedding schemes. The glossy, bright green or purple leaves are surmounted from early to late summer by red, pink or white flowers.

Callistephus chinensis
Annual Aster (USA)
China Aster (UK/USA)
Height: 38-45cm/15-18in
Spread: 25-30cm/10-12in

Half-hardy annual, rather erect and with mid-green, toothed leaves. Large, daisy-like flowers appear from mid-summer until the frosts of autumn. There are many varieties, in a range of colours, including pink, red, purple and white.

PLANT NAME AND DESCRIPTION	SITUATION AND CULTIVATION	PROPAGATION

Consolida ambigua
(syn. *C. ajacis/Delphinium consolida*)
Larkspur (UK/USA)
Height: 75cm-1.2m/2½-4ft
Spread: 30-38cm/12-15in

Hardy annual with finely cut, mid-green leaves and sparsely branched, upright stems bearing spires of blue, purple, red, pink, or white flowers from early to late summer. Strains include the tall and stately Giant Imperials, ideal for garden decoration, and Stock-flowered types.

Full sun or light shade and fertile, well-drained but moisture-retentive soil. Support Larkspurs with twiggy sticks, inserted while the plants are small so that they grow up and through them. Cut off faded flowers to encourage more to develop. In autumn, pull up and discard the plants.
It is an ideal cottage-garden annual and creates a wonderful display in a mixed border, as well as in one solely confined to hardy annuals.

From early to late spring, sow seeds in positions where they are to flower. Form drills 6mm/¼in deep and 23-30cm/9-12in apart, and sow seeds evenly and thinly. Germination takes two to three weeks. When large enough to handle, thin the seedlings to 23-38cm/9-15in apart depending on their vigour.
Seeds can also be sown in their flowering positions in autumn and covered with cloches. They do not like being transplanted and therefore must be sown where they are to flower.

Dianthus barbatus
Sweet William (UK/USA)
Height: 30-60cm/12-24in (range)
Spread: 20-38cm/8-15in (range)

Short-lived perennial, invariably grown as a biennial, with 7.5-15cm/3-6in wide, flattened heads densely packed with sweetly scented, single or double flowers during early and mid-summer. Their colour range includes crimson, scarlet, salmon-pink and cerise-pink. Flowers are often marked with other colours.

Full sun and well-drained soil. Set the plants 20-25cm/8-10in apart. Keep them free from weeds and after their flowers fade, pull up and discard.
Sweet Williams are very much cottage-garden plants and can be planted in mixed borders, amid shrubs and border perennials. They combine well with the shrub Bridal Wreath (*Spiraea* x *arguta*), see page 79.

Sow seeds thinly and evenly, 6mm/¼in deep, in a seed bed outdoors during late spring and early summer. Germination takes ten to twenty-one days. When the seedlings are large enough to handle, thin them to 13-15cm/5-6in apart. In late summer, move the plants to their flowering positions, setting them 20-25cm/8-10in apart, depending on their vigour.

Didiscus coeruleus
(syn. *Trachymene coerulea*)
Blue Lace Flower (UK)
Queen Anne's Lace (UK)
Height: 38-45cm/15-18in
Spread: 23-30cm/9-12in

Half-hardy, bushy annual with light green, deeply divided leaves and long stems that bear umbrella-like, lightly scented, lavender-blue flower heads up to 5cm/2in wide during mid-summer.

Sheltered position in full sun and moderately fertile, deeply prepared, well-drained soil. Set the plants 23cm/9in apart. Support them – especially in exposed areas – with twiggy sticks, inserted when plants are put into the soil, so that their leaves and stems grow up and through them. In autumn, pull up and discard the plants.

Sow seeds thinly and evenly, 3mm/⅛in deep, in seed-trays during late winter and early spring. Keep at 15-20°C/59-68°F. Germination takes ten to fourteen days. When the seedlings are large enough to handle, prick them out into seed-trays, so that they are spaced 36-50mm/1½-2in apart. Alternatively, move the seedlings into individual pots. When established, slowly acclimatize plants to outside conditions by first putting them in a cold frame. Plant into a border as soon as all risk of frost has passed.

Dimorphotheca pluvialis
'Glistening White'
Cape Marigold (UK/USA)
Rain Daisy (UK)
Height: 23-30cm/9-12in
Spread: 15-23cm/6-9in

Half-hardy annual with short, branching stems that bear silky, pure-white, glistening flowers about 5cm/2in wide during early and mid-summer. The flowers appear above the dark green, hairy leaves, which are slightly scented.

Full sun and light, well-drained but moisture-retentive soil. Choose a warm, sheltered position. It is ideal for the front of a border. Set the plants in position, about 15cm/6in apart, in spring, as soon as the risk of frost has passed. Remove dead flowers throughout summer and pull up and discard plants in late summer. No staking is needed.

Sow seeds thinly and evenly in drills 6mm/¼in deep and 15-23cm/6-9in apart in late spring, in positions where they are to flower. Germination takes two to three weeks. When large enough to handle, thin the seedlings 15-23cm/6-9in apart. Alternatively, sow seeds in seed-trays in a greenhouse during early spring. When large enough to handle, prick out the seedlings to about 5cm/2in apart in seed-trays, acclimatize to outdoor conditions and plant into a garden when there is no further risk of frost.

Centaurea cyanus
Bluebottle (UK/USA)
Cornflower (UK/USA)
Height: 23-90cm/9-36in
Spread: 23-38cm/9-15in

Hardy annual with grey-green leaves and button-like flower heads in pink, red, purple, blue or white from early summer until the frosts of autumn. Range of varieties and heights.

Centaurea moschata
(now known as *Amberboa moschata*)
Sweet Sultan (UK/USA)
Height: 60cm/2ft
Spread: 30cm/12in

Hardy annual with thin stems and narrow, grey-green leaves. From early summer until the frosts of autumn it bears scented, tooth-edged flowers about 7.5cm/3in wide in white, yellow, pink or purple.

Cheiranthus cheiri
(syn. *Erysimum cheiri*)
Wallflower (UK/USA)
Height: 20-60cm/8-24in
Spread: 25-38cm/10-15in

Hardy perennial usually grown as a hardy biennial, with dark green leaves. During late spring and early summer it bears clusters of sweetly scented flowers in many shades, including yellow, red, orange and pink, as well as white.

Clarkia elegans
(syn. *C. unguiculata*)
Farewell-to-Spring (USA)
Height: 45-60cm/18-24in
Spread: 30cm/12in

Hardy annual with mid-green leaves and double flowers up to 5cm/2in wide from mid-summer to autumn. There are many varieties, in white, salmon pink, lavender, orange or purple.

PLANT NAME AND DESCRIPTION	SITUATION AND CULTIVATION	PROPAGATION

Eschscholzia californica
Californian Poppy (UK/USA)
Height: 30-38cm/12-15in
Spread: 15-23cm/6-9in

Hardy annual with delicate, finely cut blue-green leaves and masses of saucer-like, bright orange-yellow flowers up to 7.5cm/3in wide from early to late summer. These are followed by blue-green seed pods. The colour range now also includes scarlet, crimson, rose, orange, yellow, white and red.

Full sun and light, poor and well-drained soil. Fertile soil, heavy soil and a position in shade dramatically reduce the colour intensity and abundance of the flowers. Remove the seed pods to encourage the development of further flowers.
    To get the best from Californian Poppies as cut-flowers indoors, cut them still in bud.

From early to late spring, sow seeds in the positions where they are to flower. Form drills 6mm/¼in deep and 23cm/9in apart and sow seeds evenly and thinly. Germination takes ten to fourteen days. When large enough to handle, thin the seedlings to 15-23cm/6-9in apart, depending on the vigour of the variety.
    In mild areas, seeds can also be sown in their flowering positions in late summer and covered with cloches.

Heliotropium arborescens
(earlier known as *H.* x *hybridum*)
Cherry Pie (UK)
Heliotrope (UK/USA)
Height: 38-45cm/15-18in
Spread: 30-38cm/12-15in

Half-hardy perennial, invariably treated as a half-hardy annual, with dark-green, finely wrinkled leaves and fragrant, forget-me-not-like flowers from early summer to autumn. Colours range from dark violet, through lavender, to white.

Full sun and fertile, well-drained but moisture-retentive soil. In borders, plant them 30-38cm/12-15in apart. When grown as bushy border plants no staking is needed, but when as half-standards strong stakes are required. Plants to be grown as standards are raised from cuttings.

Sow seeds thinly and evenly, 6mm/¼in deep, in seed-trays from late winter to early spring. Keep at 16-18°C/61-64°F. Germination takes two to four weeks. When large enough to handle, prick out the seedlings. When established, slowly acclimatize plants to outside conditions by putting them in a cold frame. Plant them into a border when all risk of frost has passed. Alternatively, raise plants from 7.5cm/3in-long cuttings taken in late summer; insert in pots of moist peat and sharp sand. Keep in gentle warmth.

Hesperis matronalis
Sweet Rocket (UK/USA)
Height: 60-90cm/2-3ft
Spread: 38-45cm/15-18in

Hardy but short-lived perennial invariably grown as a biennial. It has an upright nature, with dark green, lance-shaped leaves and long spires of fragrant, cross-shaped, white, mauve or purple flowers during early summer. 'Purpurea' has purple flowers, while 'Candidissima' is white and dwarf.

Full sun or light shade and light, moisture-retentive but well-drained soil. It can be naturalized in a wild garden. Set the plants 38-45cm/15-18in apart. Plants often produce self-sown seedlings, but usually do not breed true. Unless in a naturalized setting, plants are usually pulled up and discarded when their flowers fade.

Sow seeds thinly and evenly, 6mm/¼in deep, in a seedbed outdoors from mid-spring to early summer. Germination takes seven to ten days. When the seedlings are large enough to handle, transplant them to a nursery bed, setting them 20cm/8in apart. In late summer or early autumn, move the plants to their flowering positions, setting them 38-45cm/15-18in apart.

Lavatera trimestris
(syn. *Lavatera rosea*)
Mallow (UK/USA)
Height: 60-90cm/2-3ft
Spread: 38-50cm/15-20in

Erect and bushy hardy annual with oval and lobed pale green leaves and flat-faced but trumpet-shaped, rose-coloured flowers up to 10cm/4in wide from mid- to late summer. There are several superb cultivars, including 'Silver Cup' (shown) at 60cm/24in tall.

Full sun or dappled, light shade and well-drained soil. Avoid excessively rich soil as this encourages leaf growth at the expense of flower development. Tall varieties in exposed areas need to be supported by twiggy sticks, inserted when the plants are small, so that shoots and stems grow up and through them. In autumn, pull up and compost the plants.

From early to late spring sow seeds in the positions where they are to flower. Form drills, 12mm/½in deep and 25-30cm/10-12in apart, and sow seeds evenly and thinly. Germination takes two to four weeks. When large enough to handle, thin the seedlings to 38cm/15in apart.
    In mild areas, seeds can also be sown in their flowering positions in late summer and covered with cloches.

Cotula barbata
Pincushion Plant (UK)
Height: 7.5-10cm/3-4in
Spread: 7.5-10cm/3-4in

Half-hardy annual with narrow leaves thickly covered in silky hairs. During mid- and late summer it becomes smothered in yellow, button-like flowers.

Digitalis purpurea
Common Foxglove (UK/USA)
Height: 90cm-1.5m/3-5ft
Spread: 45-60cm/18-24in

Hardy biennial with characteristic stiff, upright stems bearing a profusion of bell-shaped flowers during early and mid-summer. These range in colour from purple, through pink, to red.

Erysimum alpinum
(syn. *E. hieraciifolium*)
Alpine Wallflower (UK)
Fairy Wallflower (UK)
Height: 15cm/6in
Spread: 10-15cm/4-6in

Hardy biennial with dark green, lance-shaped leaves. During late spring it bears a mass of fragrant, yellow flowers, each 12mm/½in across.

Euphorbia marginata
Ghost Weed (USA)
Snow on the Mountain (UK/USA)
Spurge (UK)
Height: 60cm/2ft
Spread: 30cm/12in

Hardy, bushy annual with bright green leaves edged and veined in white. The flowers, which appear in late summer and into early autumn, are white and relatively insignificant.

Hardy annuals, half-hardy annuals and biennials

PLANT NAME AND DESCRIPTION	SITUATION AND CULTIVATION	PROPAGATION

Limnanthes douglasii
Meadow Foam (USA)
Poached Egg Flower (UK)
Height: 15cm/6in
Spread: 15-23cm/6-9in

Low-growing hardy annual with glossy, pale green, deeply cut leaves and masses of scented, funnel-shaped, 2.5cm/1in-wide, yellow flowers with white edges during early and mid-summer. It is ideal in hardy annual borders, mixed borders and rock gardens.

Full sun and ordinary, well-drained garden soil. Choose a warm position. In autumn, pull up and discard the plants. Plants naturally seed themselves. Therefore, once it has been grown one year, it is more than likely that during the following season young plants will appear.

From early to late spring, sow seeds in the positions where they are to flower. Form drills, 3mm/1/8in deep and 15cm/6in apart, and sow seeds evenly and thinly. Germination takes two to three weeks. When large enough to handle, thin the seedlings to 15cm/6in apart.
In mild areas, seeds can also be sown in their flowering positions in late summer and covered with cloches.

Limonium sinuatum
(syn. *Statice sinuata*)
Sea Lavender (UK/USA)
Height: 38-45cm/15-18in
Spread: 25-30cm/10-12in

Hardy perennial, invariably grown as a half-hardy annual. From mid-summer to autumn it bears 7.5cm/3in-long clusters of blue and cream flowers. There are many varieties, which extend the colours to orange-yellow, salmon, rose-pink, red, carmine and lavender.

Well-drained but moisture-retentive soil and an open, sunny position suit it best.
The flowers are often raised for drying and displaying indoors.

Sow seeds 6mm/1/4in deep in seed-trays from mid-winter to early spring. Keep them at 15-20°C/59-68°F. After germination, reduce the temperature and when the seedlings are large enough to handle transfer them to seed-trays and give them wider spacing. When all risk of frost has passed, plant them into a garden.

Linum grandiflorum
Flowering Flax (USA)
Height: 38-45cm/15-18in
Spread: 23-30cm/9-12in

Hardy annual with masses of slender stems, narrow and pointed pale green leaves and rose-coloured, saucer-shaped, 36mm/1¹/₂in-wide flowers during early and mid-summer. The Scarlet Flax (*L. g.* 'Rubrum') is shorter, at 30cm/12in high, with brilliant crimson flowers.

Full sun and well-drained soil. This can range from slightly acid to slightly alkaline. A sunny situation is vital to encourage good flowering. Its wispy nature makes this an excellent partner for Love-in-a-Mist (*Nigella damascena*).
In autumn, pull up the plants and place on a compost heap.

From early to late spring, sow seeds in positions where they are to flower. Form drills, 6mm/1/4in deep and 15cm/6in apart, and sow the seeds evenly and thinly. Germination takes two to three weeks. When large enough to handle, thin the seedlings to 23cm/9in apart. Seedlings of Scarlet Flax, which is lower growing, should be thinned to 15cm/6in apart.
In mild areas, seeds can also be sown in their flowering positions in late summer and covered with cloches.

Lobularia maritima
(syn. *Alyssum maritimum*)
Sweet Alyssum (UK/USA)
Height: 7.5-15cm/3-6in
Spread: 20-30cm/8-12in

A hardy annual usually grown as a half-hardy annual. The densely branched stems bear narrow, grey-green leaves and rounded clusters of white or mauve flowers from early to late summer. There are many varieties, in white, violet-purple, rose-carmine and deep purple.

Full sun and well-drained soil. When growing them as bedding plants in borders, set plants 15-20cm/6-8in apart, depending on their vigour. If grown in a country-garden setting, perhaps in paths where they can sprawl and grow naturally, they should be about 30cm/12in apart. After their first flush of flowers, use hedging shears to lightly clip over them to encourage a further display. In autumn, pull up and discard plants.

Sow seeds thinly and evenly, 6mm/1/4in deep, in seed-trays during late winter to early spring. Keep at 10-13°C/50-55°F. Germination takes seven to ten days. When large enough to handle, prick out the seedlings in clusters into seed-trays. When established, slowly acclimatize plants to outside conditions by first putting them in a cold frame. Plant into a border when risk of frost has passed. Alternatively, sow seeds in flowering position 6mm/1/4in deep in mid- to late spring. Thin to 15-20cm/6-8in apart.

Felicia bergeriana
Kingfisher Daisy (UK/USA)
Height: 15cm/6in
Spread: 15cm/6in

Half-hardy annual, forming a mat of lance-shaped, grey and hairy leaves. From early to late summer it bears a profusion of daisy-like, 18mm/3/4in-wide, light blue flowers, each with a central yellow disc.

Godetia grandiflorum
(now known as *Clarkia rubicunda*)
Height: 23-38cm/9-15in (range)
Spread: 15-25cm/6-10in (range)

Hardy annual with mid-green, pointed leaves and clusters of funnel-shaped, rose-purple, 5cm/2in-wide flowers during early and mid-summer. Colours now include crimson, pink, salmon, cherry red and white, in single and semi-double forms. Some have frilly edged petals.

Gypsophila elegans
Baby's Breath (UK/USA)
Height: 50-60cm/20-24in
Spread: 30cm/12in

Hardy annual with narrow leaves and masses of white flowers from early summer to autumn. There are several superb varieties that extend the colour range to pink, rose-pink, carmine and soft purple.

Helianthus annuus
Mirasol (USA)
Sunflower (UK/USA)
Height: 90cm-3m/3-10ft (range)
Spread: 30-45cm/12-18in

Hardy annual well known for its large, daisy-like flower heads, up to 30cm/12in wide, during mid- and late summer. Wide range of varieties in colours from pale primrose to copper-bronze. The central discs are purple or brown.

PLANT NAME AND DESCRIPTION	SITUATION AND CULTIVATION	PROPAGATION

Malope trifida
(syn. *M. grandiflora*)
Height: 60-90cm/2-3ft
Spread: 23-30cm/9-12in

Hardy annual with a bushy habit and upright stems bearing trumpet-shaped flowers up to 7.5cm/3in wide from early to late summer. The rose-purple flowers are borne amid mid-green, slightly lobed leaves. There are several varieties, extending the colour range to white and shell-pink.

Prefers full sun and light, moisture-retentive soil, although it gives a reasonable display in most conditions. Seeds are sown where they are to flower. When flowering is over, pull up the plants and place on a compost heap.

Sow seeds thinly and evenly in drills 6mm/¹⁄₄in deep and 15-23cm/6-9in apart in early to mid-spring. When the seedlings are large enough to handle, thin them to 23cm/9in apart.

Myosotis sylvatica
Forget-Me-Not (UK/USA)
Garden Forget-Me-Not (USA)
Height: 20-30cm/8-12in
Spread: 15cm/6in

Hardy biennial or short-lived perennial with masses of fragrant, misty blue flowers in lax sprays during late spring and early summer. The related *M. alpestris* is shorter, at 7.5-20cm/3-8in high, and some varieties of this species are ideal for planting in rock gardens.

Partial shade and fertile, moisture-retentive soil, rich in well-decomposed organic material. Avoid heavy, waterlogged soil as this encourages plants to die off in winter. Set plants in borders in late summer or early autumn, spacing them 15cm/6in apart. They need little attention and having flowered are best pulled up and placed on a compost heap.

From late spring to mid-summer sow seed thinly and evenly in drills 6mm/¹⁄₄in deep and 15-20cm/6-8in apart in a well-prepared seedbed. Germination takes two to three weeks. When large enough to handle, thin the seedlings to 10-15cm/4-6in apart. In late summer or early autumn transfer the plants to their flowering positions.

Nicotiana alata
(syn. *Nicotiana affinis*)
Tobacco Plant (UK)
Height: 60-90cm/2-3ft
Spread: 25-38cm/10-15in

Half-hardy annual with erect stems bearing mid-green leaves and loose clusters of heavily scented, white, tubular, 7.5cm/3in-long flowers from early to late summer. Colour varieties include white, cream, pink, crimson, yellow and yellowish green.

Full sun or light shade and fertile, well-drained soil, enriched with well-decomposed compost. Set the plants 20cm/8in to 30cm/12in apart, depending on the variety's vigour. Support tall plants in exposed gardens with twiggy sticks inserted early so that stems and leaves grow up and through them. In autumn, pull up and discard plants.

Sow seeds thinly and evenly, 3mm/¹⁄₈in deep, in seed-trays during late winter to mid-spring. Keep at 16-18°C/61-64°F. Germination takes ten to fourteen days. When the seedlings are large enough to handle, prick them out into seed-trays, so that they are spaced 36-50mm/1¹⁄₂-2in apart. Alternatively, move the seedlings into individual pots. When established, slowly acclimatize plants to outside conditions by first putting them in a cold frame. Plant into a border as soon as all risk of frost has passed.

Nigella damascena
Love-in-a-Mist (UK/USA)
Wild Fennel (USA)
Height: 45-60cm/18-24in
Spread: 15-23cm/6-9in

Hardy annual with bright green, fern-like foliage and cornflower-like blue or white flowers from early to mid-summer. Varieties include 'Miss Jekyll' (semi-double/bright blue), 'Persian Jewel' (colour mixture) and 'Miss Jekyll Alba' (semi-double/white).

Full sun and light, well-drained soil. Remove dead flowers to encourage more to develop. When the last of the flowers fade, pull up and discard plants.

From early to late spring, sow seeds in positions where they are to flower. Form drills, 6mm/¹⁄₄in deep and 20cm/8in apart, and sow seeds evenly and thinly. Germination takes two to three weeks. When large enough to handle, thin the seedlings to 15-23cm/6-9in apart. Alternatively, sow seeds in late summer, placing cloches over seedlings in winter, to produce plants that flower early in the year.

Hibiscus trionum
Bladder Ketmia (UK)
Flower-of-an-Hour (UK/USA)
Height: 60-75cm/24-30in
Spread: 30cm/12in

Hardy annual with coarsely toothed, dark green, oval leaves and primrose-coloured flowers up to 7.5cm/3in across during late summer and into autumn. Each flower has a bright maroon-chocolate centre.

Iberis umbellata
Candytuft (UK)
Globe Candytuft (USA)
Height: 15-38cm/6-15in
Spread: 23cm/9in

Hardy annual with narrow, mid-green leaves and 5cm/2in-wide clusters of white, red or pale purple flowers from early summer until the frosts of autumn. There are many varieties to choose from.

Lobelia erinus
Edging Lobelia (UK/USA)
Trailing Lobelia (UK/USA)
Height: 10-23cm/4-9in
Spread: 10-15cm/4-6in

Half-hardy perennial, invariably grown as a half-hardy annual, with masses of blue, white or red flowers, about 6mm/¹⁄₄in wide, from late spring till autumn. In addition to bushy and compact varieties there are also trailing types.

Lunaria annua
(syn. *L. biennis*)
Honesty (UK/USA)
Silver Dollar (USA)
Height: 45-60cm/18-24in
Spread: 30-38cm/12-15in

Hardy biennial with coarsely toothed, mid-green and somewhat heart-shaped leaves. The fragrant, purple flowers appear from late spring to early summer and are followed by attractive seed pods.

Hardy annuals, half-hardy annuals and biennials

PLANT NAME AND DESCRIPTION	SITUATION AND CULTIVATION	PROPAGATION

Papaver rhoeas
Corn Poppy (USA)
Field Poppy (UK/USA)
Shirley Poppy (UK)
Height: 45-60cm/18-24in
Spread: 25-30cm/10-12in

Hardy annual with deeply-lobed, pale-green leaves and upright stems bearing 7.5cm/3in-wide red flowers with black centres during early and mid-summer. Varieties extend the colour range to pink, rose, salmon and crimson.

Full sun and ordinary, well-drained soil. It is not necessary to support plants.In autumn pull them up and discard.

From early to late spring, sow seeds in positions where they are to flower. Form drills, 6mm/¼in deep and 20-25cm/8-10in apart, and sow seeds evenly and thinly. Germination takes ten to fourteen days. When large enough to handle, thin the seedlings to 25-30cm/10-12in apart.
     When sowing seeds in a wild garden, or to create an area full of native annuals, scatter the seeds thinly over the surface and lightly rake them into the surface soil.

Papaver somniferum
Opium Poppy (UK/USA)
Height: 75-90cm/2½-3ft
Spread: 30-38cm/12-15in

Hardy annual, infamous as the source of opium and having fruits and sap that are poisonous. Nevertheless, with deeply lobed, grey-green leaves and white, pink, scarlet or purple flowers up to 10cm/4in wide, it is excellent for bringing colour to borders during early and mid-summer. Some flowers are double.

Full sun and well-drained soil. It is not necessary to support plants, except in windy and exposed areas. Insert twiggy sticks among young plants, so that stems and leaves grow up and through them. In autumn pull up plants and discard.

From early to late spring sow seeds in positions where they are to flower. Form drills, 6mm/¼in deep and 20-25cm/8-10in apart, and sow seeds evenly and thinly. Germination takes ten to fourteen days. When large enough to handle, thin the seedlings to 25-30cm/10-12in apart.

Petunia x hybrida
Height: 15-30cm/6-12in
Spread: 15-30cm/6-12in

Half-hardy perennial, usually grown as a half-hardy annual, with trumpet-shaped flowers, 5-10cm/2-4in wide, from early to late summer and often until the frosts of autumn. Colour range includes white, cream, pink, red, mauve and blue, as well as bi-coloured forms. It is ideal for planting in flower borders, and in hanging-baskets, tubs and windowboxes.

Full sun and fertile, well-drained soil in a sheltered position. Avoid cold, wet and shady positions. Set the plants 15-30cm/6-12in apart, depending on their vigour. In autumn, pull up and discard plants.

Sow seeds in seed-trays, thinly and evenly on the surface of the compost, from late winter to early spring. Just press the small seeds into the compost. Keep at 15-18°C/59-64°F. Germination takes seven to fourteen days. When the seedlings are large enough to handle, prick them out into seed-trays, spacing them 36-50cm/1½-2in apart. When established, slowly acclimatize plants to outside conditions by first putting them in a cold frame. Plant out after all risk of frost has passed.

Rudbeckia hirta
Black-eyed-Susan (UK/USA)
Height: 45-60cm/18-24in
Spread: 30-45cm/12-18in

Short-lived perennial invariably grown as a hardy annual. The bright-faced, daisy-like, 7.5cm/3in-wide flowers have golden yellow petals and deep, brown-purple cones at their centres. Flowering is from mid-summer to early autumn. The range of varieties is wide.

Full sun and fertile, deeply prepared, well-drained but moisture-retentive soil. Seeds are sown where the plants will flower. After the first flush of flowers, feed the plants and cut them back to encourage a further display. At the end of the season, pull up and discard the plants. It is an excellent plant to use as a cut flower for decorating rooms indoors.

Sow seeds where they are to flower, thinly and evenly in drills 6mm/¼in deep and 30cm/12in apart. Germination takes two to three weeks. When the seedlings are large enough to handle, thin them to 30-38cm/12-15in apart. Alternatively, sow seeds 3mm/⅛in deep in seed-trays in late winter and early spring. Place them in gentle warmth. When large enough to handle, prick out the seedlings to about 5cm/2in apart in seed-trays. Slowly acclimatize the plants to outdoor conditions.

Malcolmia maritima
Virginian Stock (UK/USA)
Height: 25-30cm/10-12in
Spread: 20cm/8in

Hardy annual with slender stems, blunt-topped grey-green leaves and white, cross-shaped, sweetly scented flowers in white, pink, red, lavender and purple. Make sowings every four weeks to produce flowers from late spring through to autumn.

Matthiola bicornis
(syn. *M. longipetala*)
Evening Stock (USA)
Night-scented Stock (UK)
Perfume Plant (USA)
Height: 30-45cm/12-18in
Spread: 30cm/12in

Hardy annual with narrow, greyish green leaves and masses of four-petalled, scented, lilac-purple flowers during mid- and late summer.

Nemophila menziesii
(syn. *N. insignis*)
Baby Blue-Eyes (UK/USA)
Height: 23cm/9in
Spread: 15cm/6in

Hardy annual with feathery, deep-cut, light green leaves and masses of white-centred, sky-blue, saucer-shaped flowers from early to late summer.

Salpiglossis sinuata
Painted Tongue (UK/USA)
Height: 50-60cm/20-24in
Spread: 30cm/12in

Half-hardy annual with slender, branching stems that bear narrow, light green leaves. From mid-summer to autumn they bear funnel-shaped flowers up to 5cm/2in long in many colours, including lavender, yellow, orange, scarlet and crimson.

PLANT NAME AND DESCRIPTION	SITUATION AND CULTIVATION	PROPAGATION

Salvia splendens
Scarlet Salvia (UK/USA)
Height: 30-38cm/12-15in
Spread: 20-25cm/8-10in

Half-hardy perennial, invariably grown as a half-hardy annual, with oval, mid-green leaves and upright spires of scarlet flowers from mid-summer to autumn. There are several superb varieties, including 'Blaze of Fire' (bright scarlet, 30cm/12in high) and 'Laser Purple' (deep purple, 25-30cm/10-12in high).

Full sun and fertile, well-drained but moisture-retentive soil. Set the plants about 25cm/10in apart. When they are 13-15cm/5-6in high, pinch out their growing tips to encourage bushiness. In autumn, pull up and discard plants.

Sow seeds thinly and evenly, 6mm/¼in deep, in seed-trays during late winter and early spring. Keep at 18-20°C/64-68°F. Germination takes two to three weeks. When the seedlings are large enough to handle, prick them out into seed-trays, so that they are spaced 36-50mm/ 1½-2in apart. Alternatively, move the seedlings into individual pots. When established, slowly acclimatize plants to outside conditions by first putting them in a cold frame. Plant into a border as soon as all risk of frost has passed.

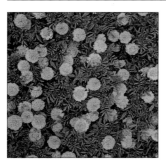

Tagetes patula
French Marigold (UK/USA)
Height: 30cm/12in
Spread: 25-30cm/10-12in

Half-hardy bushy annual with dark green, deeply cut leaves and yellow or mahogany-red flowers up to 5cm/2in wide from early summer to autumn. There is a wide range of varieties, with both single and double-flowered types, as well as dwarf marigolds, which are 15-23cm/6-9in tall.

Full sun and fertile, well-drained soil. Set the plants 15-25cm/6-10in apart, depending on their vigour. Staking is not necessary. It is not essential to remove dead flowers, but it does encourage the development of new ones as well as tidying up plants. In autumn, pull up and discard plants.

Sow seeds thinly and evenly, 6mm/¼in deep, in seed-trays during late winter to early spring. Keep at 15-18°C/59-64°F. Germination takes seven to ten days. When large enough to handle, prick out the seedlings into seed-trays. When established, slowly acclimatize plants to outside conditions by first putting them in a cold frame. Plant into a border when all risk of frost has passed. Alternatively, sow seeds 12mm/½in deep in mid- to late spring where they are to flower. Thin these seedlings to 25cm/10in apart.

Verbena x *hybrida*
Verbena (UK/USA)
Vervain (USA)
Height: 15-45cm/6-18in (range)
Spread: 15-30cm/5-12in (range)

Half-hardy perennial invariably grown as a half-hardy annual. From early summer until the frosts of autumn, bushy plants are smothered in clustered, dome-shaped heads about 7.5cm/3in wide, bearing brightly coloured flowers in pink, scarlet, carmine, blue and white.

Full sun and light, fertile, well-drained soil. Set out the young plants in a border as soon as all risk of frost has passed, spacing them 15-23cm/6-9in apart, depending on their ultimate height. Pinch out the tips of the shoots to encourage bushiness. In autumn, pull up the plants and discard.

Sow seeds evenly and thinly, 3mm/⅛in deep, in seed-trays in late winter or early spring. Keep them at 18-21°C/64-70°F, and keep the compost barely moist. Germination takes between ten and fourteen days. When the seedlings are large enough to handle, prick them out into seed-trays, setting them about 5cm/2in apart. Slowly acclimatize the plants to outdoor conditions and plant into a garden when all risk of frost has passed.

Zinnia elegans
Youth-and-Old-Age (USA)
Height: 15-75cm/6-30in (range)
Spread: 15-38cm/6-15in (range)

Half-hardy annual with oval, light to mid-green leaves and upright stems bearing bright purple flowers, up to 6cm/2½in across, from mid- to late summer. There are many varieties, in colours including white, purple, yellow, orange, red and pink. 'Envy Double' has chartreuse green flowers.

Full sun, fertile and well-drained soil in a wind-sheltered position. Set plants 15-30cm/6-12in apart, depending on their vigour. Pinch out the growing points of young plants to encourage bushiness. Also, remove dead flowers to improve the plants' appearance and to encourage the development of further blooms.

Sow seeds thinly and evenly, 6mm/¼in deep, in seed-trays during early and mid-spring. Keep at 15-18°C/59-64°F. Germination takes seven to fourteen days. When large enough to handle, prick out the seedlings into seed-trays. Slowly acclimatize established plants to outside conditions by putting them in a cold frame. Plant into a border when all risk of frost has passed. Alternatively, sow seeds 12mm/½in deep in late spring where they are to flower. Thin these seedlings to 25-30cm/10-12in apart.

Salvia sclarea
Clary (UK/USA)
Height: 75cm/30in
Spread: 30-38cm/12-15in

Hardy biennial invariably grown as a hardy annual. The large, hairy, somewhat triangular leaves are surmounted in mid-summer by tall stems bearing tubular, pinkish mauve flowers with yellow, purple-blue, petal-like bracts.

Scabiosa atropurpurea
Mourning Bride (UK/USA)
Pincushions (UK/USA)
Sweet Scabious (UK/USA)
Height: 45-75cm/18-30in
Spread: 23-30cm/9-12in

Hardy annual with deeply lobed mid-green leaves and dark crimson flowers at the tops of slender stems from mid-summer to autumn. Several varieties, in blue, red, pink, and white.

Tagetes erecta
Aztec Marigold (USA)
African Marigold (UK/USA)
Height: 60-90cm/2-3ft
Spread: 30-45cm/12-18in

Half-hardy, erect and well-branched annual with glossy, dark green, deeply divided leaves and lemon yellow flowers, 5cm/2in wide, from mid-summer to autumn. Varieties from yellow to orange, some dwarf, at 30-38cm/12-15in high.

Viola x *wittrockiana*
Garden Pansy
Height: 15-23cm/6-9in
Spread: 20-25cm/8-10in

Hardy biennial, well-known for its large-faced flowers up to 7.5cm/3in wide. There are both summer- and winter-flowering strains, in a wide colour range.

Raising and planting biennials

Biennials are plants that produce flowers during their second season of growth. In the first year, seeds are sown in seedbeds and later, in autumn, the young plants are moved to their flowering positions. During the second year, they produce a spectacular display of flowers, mainly during spring and early summer, though some flower throughout most of the summer.

SOWING BIENNIALS

In late autumn or early winter, dig a piece of ground in a warm, lightly shaded, sheltered, well-drained part of a garden to prepare a seedbed for biennials. Do not tread on the bed during winter. As soon as the soil warms up in spring and the surface becomes dry and crumbly, you can prepare the seedbed for sowing. It is important that the seedbed is free from weeds, so thorough preparation is essential.

Rake the area and then systematically shuffle sideways across it to produce an evenly consolidated bed. Then rake the surface level, but take care not to bring lumps of soil to the surface. It is essential to create a deep, even tilth over the entire surface to encourage even germination of the seeds. Insert 30cm/12in-long sticks, 23cm/9in apart, along two opposite sides of the seedbed.

In spring or early summer, stretch a garden line between the pairs of sticks and use a draw hoe to take out drills 12mm/½in deep. Ensure that the base of the drill has a uniform depth.

Sow seeds evenly and thinly in the base of the drill, taking care not to let them fall in clusters. Do not sow seeds directly from the packet; instead, tip a few into one hand and allow them to pass singly between your thumb, index finger and middle finger into the drill. Do not feel obliged to sow a complete packet of seeds in a single drill; this produces seedlings that become congested, etiolated and susceptible to diseases. Place a marker at the end of the row showing the biennial's name and the date of sowing.

Cover the seeds by using a metal rake to push and draw soil into the drill, but take care not to disturb the seeds. Use the head of the rake to firm soil over the drill; it is essential that the soil is in firm contact with seeds as this encourages even germination.

Right: Foxgloves (*Digitalis purpurea*) create spires of bell-shaped flowers on tall stems from early to late summer. They prefer moisture-retentive soil and a woodland or wild garden setting, and are ideal for introducing height into a border.

SOWING BIENNIALS

1 In late autumn or early winter dig a piece of ground to form a seedbed. In spring, rake the bed and systematically shuffle sideways over the area to consolidate the soil. Then rake level.
2 Insert 30cm/12in-long sticks, 23cm/9in apart, along two opposite sides. Stretch a garden line across the bed and use a draw hoe to form a drill 12mm/½in deep.
3 Tip a few seeds into the palm of one hand and then thinly and evenly dribble them along the drill's base. Ensure that they do not fall in clusters.
4 Use a metal rake to push and pull loose surface soil over the seeds, taking care not to move them sideways. Firm soil over them by using the head of the rake.

GERMINATION, THINNING AND REPLANTING

Keep the seedbed free from weeds, both in between the rows and the seedlings. During dry weather, lightly but thoroughly water the soil – do not merely dampen the surface as this will do more harm than good.

When the young seedlings are large enough to handle, either thin them out or transplant to a nurserybed. If the seeds have been sown thinly, and the ensuing plants are relatively small, for example, Daisies (*Bellis perennis*), thin seedlings to 7.5-10cm/3-4in apart. Larger biennials, such as Wallflowers, should be thinned to a distance of 13-15cm/5-6in apart.

Where seeds are sown close together, fork up the young plants as soon as you can handle them and replant them into a nurserybed, spacing them 15-23cm/6-9in apart in rows 30cm/12in apart. A few days before lifting plants for replanting, water both the seedbed where the young plants are growing, and the nurserybed into which you are going to transfer them. Young plants that are put into dry soil seldom succeed, even if you water them generously afterwards.

PLANTING BIENNIALS

Plant biennials into gardens and containers in late summer or early autumn, especially if you are planting them in beds with bulbs such as tulips, which will need to be put into the ground about the same time. (Position both the bulbs and the young biennials on the soil's surface before planting them.) If you are planting a flower bed solely with biennials or, perhaps, if you are placing them between established plants in a border, the timing is not so critical.

In extremely cold areas, planting biennials into their flowering positions is sometimes delayed until spring; leaving plants in the nurserybed provides them with more protection than if you were to plant them out in an exposed border. However, planting biennials in autumn encourages more rapid growth in spring.

A few days before planting biennials in their flowering positions, water the soil. Also, water the nurserybed to ensure that the biennial plants are fully charged with water. If this is neglected, the establishment of the young plants is put at risk, especially if subsequent weather is dry and windy.

BIENNIALS TO CONSIDER

There are many biennials that create colour in borders during spring and early summer – and some throughout summer. These include:

- **Daisy** (*Bellis perennis*): Grows 10-15cm/4-6in high and from spring to late summer produces white, pink or red flowers. Plant them about 13cm/5in apart. This is a hardy perennial, but is invariably grown as a biennial.

- **Forget-me-not** (*Myosotis alpestris*): Grows 10-20cm/4-8in high and creates a wealth of flowers – mainly blue – during late spring and early summer. Space plants 15cm/6in apart.

- **Foxglove** (*Digitalis purpurea*): Grows 90cm-1.5m/3-5ft high and from early to late summer develops spires of bell-shaped flowers. Space plants 45-60cm/18-24in apart.

- **Hollyhock** (*Alcea rosea/Althaea rosea*): Grows about 1.8m/6ft high, with single and double, pink, red, yellow or white flowers peppered on upright stems from mid- to late summer. Space the plants 45-60cm/18-24in apart. This plant is really a hardy perennial, but is usually grown as a biennial.

- **Siberian Wallflower** (*Erysimum x allionii*): Grows 38cm/15in high and from late spring to mid-summer produces orange, scented flowers. Space the plants 25-30cm/10-12in apart. This is a hardy perennial, but is usually grown as a biennial.

- **Sweet William** (*Dianthus barbatus*): Grows 30-60cm/12-24in high and develops dense heads of scarlet, pink or crimson flowers during early and mid-summer. Space plants 20-25cm/8-10in apart. This is a perennial, but is invariably grown as a biennial.

- **Wallflower** (*Erysimum cheiri*): Grows 20-60cm/8-24in high, depending on the variety, and flowers from mid-spring to early summer. Flower colours are mainly red, yellow and orange. Space dwarf varieties 25cm/10in apart and tall ones 30-38cm/12-15in apart. This is a hardy perennial, but is usually grown as a biennial.

Growing herbaceous perennials

Herbaceous perennials develop fresh shoots from ground level each spring. They bear flowers in late spring or summer and with the onset of cold weather in autumn the leaves and stems die down, leaving the root dormant during winter. Some herbaceous borders are completely formed of these plants, while others contain herbaceous perennials, bulbous plants and ever-green and deciduous shrubs.

PREPARING HERBACEOUS BORDER

There is no substitute for digging a border in late autumn or early winter to prepare for planting herbaceous perennials in spring. If the border is newly converted from pasture, double-digging (see pages 38-9) is advisable, but if you are preparing an established border for re-planting, single-digging (see pages 40-1) is sufficient. It is not necessary to break up large clods of soil, as frost, snow and rain will have broken down the surface by early spring.

Do not try to prepare a border for planting too early in spring; rather, wait until the surface is dry and crumbling. If the soil is wet, treading on it will cause compaction, reduce aeration and encourage waterlogging. Also, it is pointless to plant herbaceous perennials too early as their crowns readily decay in cold, wet soil.

When the soil is ready, use a large garden rake to level the surface. The soil will need to be firm and this is best done by systematically shuffling sideways across the border, firming strips about 25cm/10in wide at a time. This process is time consuming, but is more effective than using a garden roller, which does not firm soil evenly. After treading over the border, again use a rake to level the surface.

PLANNING AND DESIGNING A BORDER

Detailed planning is essential; colour harmonies and contrasts need consideration, and you will also need to think about how many plants of each species and variety you will need.

First of all, measure the width and length of the border, then transfer these details to scaled paper, together with the border's shape. Next, draw in the planting areas; these will vary in size and shape according to the size and position of

PLANTING HERBACEOUS PERENNIALS

1 Measure the border and mark its size and shape on graph paper. Design the border on the graph paper, indicating the number of plants in each group and its extent. Then, transfer the outlines on to the border, using either a pointed stick or sand.
2 Position the plants in groups so that they look natural and do not create straight lines.
3 Use a trowel to set each plant in the soil. Spread out the roots and firm soil over and around them.
4 Use a fine-rosed watering-can to thoroughly water the soil. Repeat this several times during the first week after setting the plants in position, but take care not to make the soil too muddy.

Above: Herbaceous borders are seldom just planted with hardy herbaceous plants (those that die down naturally in autumn and produce fresh shoots in spring). Instead, they become a medley of plants, with annuals, biennials and bulbous plants are often also feathered. This one includes dahlias amongst traditional herbaceous type.

the plants. For example, tall delphiniums at the back of a border will need to be spaced 45cm/18in or more apart, while diminutive species, such as the Ice Plant (*Sedum spectabile*), need to be 25-30cm/10-12in apart. The planting areas will need to increase in size towards the back – or the centre, for an island bed situated in a lawn – to accommodate some larger and more dominant plants.

Herbaceous borders often look best when plants are grouped in threes and planted in triangles to produce a dominant display. It is better to plant fewer different species than to produce insignificant displays of more species. You will need to consider the size of your borders – small,

narrow borders cannot accommodate three plants of each species. When you have completed the design on paper, use a pointed stick, or a thin trickle of sharp sand, to transfer the design to the border. (Do not use lime as this may make the soil too alkaline.)

PLANTING A BORDER

Plant herbaceous perennials with care; if you position them too deeply in cold, wet, clay soil they may decay. Conversely, plants positioned shallowly in light soil, which subsequently settles, may be left with their crowns exposed. These then become dry and hard and the entire plant may topple or be blown over.

Some plants, including acanthus, anchusas, Hollyhocks, Oriental Poppies and verbascums, have long tap roots and need to be planted slightly deeper – about 2.5cm/1in – than they were in their planting pots (check the old soil-mark on each stem).

Plants with fibrous roots, such as Michaelmas Daisies, *Achillea ptarmica* and pyrethrums, must not be planted deeply; this especially applies to surface-rooting plants such as London Pride and Lamb's Tongue (*Stachys byzantina*).

Whatever the type of plant, it is essential that its roots are firmly secured in the soil. Use a trowel to form a deep hole so that roots can be spread out and firm soil around and over roots using your fingers. If the soil becomes too compressed, air is excluded and plants suffer. Conversely, if not sufficiently firm, establishment is delayed. Label each plant and thoroughly but gently water the soil to settle it around roots.

STAKING AND SUPPORTING PLANTS

Many tall herbaceous plants have stems that are not sufficiently sturdy to support the leaves and flowers and will need staking. (Most nursery catalogues indicate them.) There are three basic ways to stake herbaceous plants, but whichever method you choose, it is essential to give support early, so that stems grow up and through them.

- **Pea sticks** are the traditional way to support herbaceous perennials. These are inserted into the soil close to a plant, so that stems and leaves grow up and through them. Eventually they become hidden by leaves and flowers. In autumn, at the end of the flowering season, pull them up, clean off soil and plant debris, and store under cover for use during the following year.

- **Three stout stakes** inserted around plants such as paeonies, delphiniums and dahlias – and encircled by strong garden string at several heights – create a strong support. Remove the stakes in autumn, then clean and store them under cover.

- **Proprietary metals supports** with tops that encircle plants are ideal for small plants. These supports can also be made at home from stout wire (the type used to make clothes hangers).

Border flowers

PLANT NAME AND DESCRIPTION	SITUATION AND CULTIVATION	PROPAGATION
 ***Achillea filipendulina*** Fern-leaf Yarrow (UK/USA) Height: 90cm-1.2m/3-4ft Spread: 90cm/3ft Hardy herbaceous perennial with plate-like, 10-15cm/4-6in-wide heads packed with lemon yellow flowers from mid-summer to autumn. There are several superb varieties, such as 'Coronation Gold' (shown) and 'Gold Plate'. The flowers appear above mid-green, fern-like leaves.	Fertile, well-drained but moisture-retentive soil and a position in full sun suit it. In late autumn, cut down stems to soil-level. However, if the area is very cold and likely to suffer severe winter frosts, leave this task until spring. Support plants by inserting twiggy pea-sticks around them while still small. Stems then grow up and through the sticks which are eventually hidden by leaves and flowers.	In early spring, lift and divide congested plants; replant young pieces from around the outside of each clump. Discard the old, central parts. Do not let the fibrous roots become dry while being replanted.
 ***Agapanthus praecox*** (syn. *A. umbellatus*) African Lily (UK/USA) Lily of the Nile (USA) Height: 60-75cm/24-30in Spread: 45cm/18in Half-hardy evergreen perennial with fleshy roots, well known in herbaceous borders for its magnificent umbrella-like heads of bright to pale blue flowers from mid- to late summer. There is also a white-flowered form.	Fertile, well-drained soil and a position in full sun and sheltered from cold winds are essential. Plant new plants in spring and then leave them undisturbed. Ensure that their roots do not dry out during summer. In autumn – or spring in very cold areas – cut down plants to soil-level. Alternatively, cut down plants in autumn and cover them throughout winter with a thick layer of straw.	Lift and divide congested plants in spring. Replant only young pieces from around the outside of a clump. Do not allow the roots to become dry.
 ***Alchemilla mollis*** Lady's Mantle (UK/USA) Height: 30-45cm/12-18in Spread: 38-50cm/15-20in Hardy herbaceous perennial with light green, hairy leaves which have rounded lobes and serrated edges. From early to late-summer it bears a profusion of tiny, sulphur-yellow flowers in loose sprays above the leaves. It is ideal in gardens as well as for flower arrangements indoors.	Moderately fertile, moisture-retentive but well-drained soil and a position in full sun or light shade suit it. Although the plants are relatively low-growing, in exposed areas young plants benefit from twiggy supports. Insert the sticks during early summer while plants are still small, so that leaves and stems grow up and through them. In early autumn, cut back stems to just above soil-level.	It readily increases itself from self-sown seedlings. Transplant them in late summer, taking care to keep the soil moist. Alternatively, lift and divide congested plants in autumn or spring, replanting only the younger parts from around the outside.
 ***Allium moly*** Golden Leek (UK) Lily Leek (UK/USA) Yellow Onion (UK) Height: 25-30cm/10-12in Spread: 20-25cm/8-10in Bulbous plant with an herbaceous nature. Bright yellow, star-shaped flowers up to 18mm/³/₄in wide are borne in small, umbrella-like heads during early and mid-summer. These appear amid greyish green, strap-like leaves.	Full sun and light, well-drained soil suit it. It is ideal for planting in herbaceous borders, as well as among shrubs. It is a spreading plant, often swamping less vigorous neighbours. Plant it in autumn, setting the bulbs about 10cm/4in deep and in small clusters. There is no need to lift the bulbs in autumn; once established, they can be left alone until congested.	Lift and divide congested clumps in autumn, ensuring that the bulbs are not allowed to become dry before replanting.

Acanthus spinosus
Artist's Acanthus (USA)
Bear's Breeches (UK/USA)
Height: 90cm-1m/3-3¹/₂ft
Spread: 60-75cm/24-30in

Hardy herbaceous perennial with handsome, dark green, deeply cut and spiny leaves, creating a distinctive plant. During mid- and late summer it produces tall spires of white and purple flowers.

Aconitum napellus
Helmet Flower (UK/USA)
Monkshood (UK/USA)
Wolf's Bane (UK/USA)
Height: 90cm-1m/3-3¹/₂ft
Spread: 38-45cm/15-18in

Hardy herbaceous perennial with deeply cut, dark green leaves. During mid- and late summer it produces deep blue, helmet-like flowers. There are several varieties. All parts are poisonous.

Allium giganteum
Height: 1-1.2m/3¹/₂-4ft
Spread: 38-45cm/15-18in

Hardy, bulbous-rooted herbaceous perennial with broad, glossy, strap-like green leaves. During early summer the plant develops long, upright stems that bear 10cm/4in-wide, ball-like heads of deep lilac, star-like flowers.

Anaphalis triplinervis
Life Everlasting (USA)
Pearl Everlasting (UK)
Height: 30-38cm/12-15in
Spread: 30-38cm/12-15in

Hardy herbaceous plants with small, white flowers in bunched heads borne above silvery grey leaves from mid-summer to autumn. The variety 'Summer Snow' (also known as 'Sommerschnee') is especially attractive.

PLANT NAME AND DESCRIPTION	SITUATION AND CULTIVATION	PROPAGATION

Anemone* x *hybrida
Japanese Anemone (UK)
Japanese Windflower (UK)
Height: 60cm-1m/2-3½ft
Spread: 38-45cm/15-18in

Elegant, hardy herbaceous perennial with upright stems bearing bright-faced, white to deep rose flowers up to 7.5cm/3in wide from late summer to autumn. The range of varieties is wide; many are sold under the name *Anemone japonica*.

Light shade and fertile, moisture-retentive but well-drained soil. Set the plants about 38cm/15in apart, where they can be left undisturbed for several years. In autumn, cut down the stems to soil-level.

Lift and divide congested plants in autumn or spring. Alternatively, take root-cuttings during late autumn or early winter. Insert them in trays of equal parts moist peat and sharp sand, and place in a cold frame. When shoots appear, put the young plants in a nurserybed until large enough to be planted into a garden.

Aster sediformis
Height: 60-75cm/24-30in
Spread: 38-45cm/15-18in

Hardy herbaceous perennial with clear, lavender-blue flowers, each up to 2.5cm/1in wide and with golden centres, densely borne on bushy plants during late summer and into autumn. The form 'Nanus' is shorter, at 30cm/12in. Other superb asters include *A. amellus*, with varieties in many colours: 'King George' (violet-blue) and 'Nocturne' (lilac).

Fertile, moisture-retentive but well-drained soil and a position in full sun suit asters. Add well-decayed garden compost or manure to the soil to ensure it does not dry out in summer, especially when plants are flowering.
  Stake tall plants with twiggy sticks, inserted when plants are small, so that stems and leaves grow up and through them. In autumn, or spring in cold areas, cut down plants to soil-level.

In autumn or spring, lift and divide congested plants. Replant only younger parts formed around the outside of each clump. Discard old, woody, central parts.

Astilbe* x *arendsii
Height: 60-75cm/24-30in
Spread: 38-50cm/15-20in

Hardy herbaceous perennial with fern-like, deep-green leaves and clouds of feather-like flowers borne in pyramidal heads from early to late summer. Varieties include 'Amethyst' (lilac-rose), 'Bressingham Beauty' (clear pink), 'Fanal' (dark red), 'Federsee' (rose-red), 'Hyacinth' (rose-pink) and 'White Gloria' (white).

Fertile, moisture-retentive soil, with a position in full sun or light shade, suits it. Prepare the soil by digging in peat and well-decayed garden compost or manure to ensure it does not dry out during summer. It is also necessary to water astilbes during dry periods in summer. In autumn, cut down plants to soil-level.

Lift and divide congested plants – usually every three years – in autumn or spring. Ensure that roots do not become dry before plants are replanted.

Camassia quamash
(syn. *C. esculenta*)
Camass (UK)
Comosh (USA)
Quamash (UK/USA)
Height: 45-75cm/18-30in
Spread: 30-38cm/12-15in

Bulbous herbaceous perennial with clusters of star-shaped flowers up to 36mm/1½in wide during early and mid-summer. The flower colour varies, from white to blue and purple.

Full sun or light shade and fertile, moisture-retentive soil – which can be somewhat heavy. Set the individual bulbs about 10-13cm/4-5in apart in small clusters. They can be left undisturbed until excessively congested. Cut off the flower stems after the flowers fade.

Lift and divide congested clumps in autumn. Replant the large bulbs but put the small offsets in a nurserybed for two or three years. Alternatively, sow seeds during mid- to late summer in loam-based compost. Place in a cold frame. It takes up to five years to produce flowering plants from seed.

Aquilegia Vulgaris
Columbine (UK)
Garden Columbine (USA)
Granny's Bonnet (UK)
Height: 45-60cm/18-24in
Spread: 30-38cm/12-15in

Hardy herbaceous perennial with large, grey-green leaves formed of several lobes. During early and mid-summer it bears funnel-shaped, spurred flowers in white, pink, blue, yellow and crimson.

Aruncus dioicus
Goat's Beard (UK/USA)
Height: 1.2-1.8m/4-6ft
Spread: 60-75cm/24-30in

Hardy herbaceous perennial with large, light green leaves formed of several leaflets. During early summer, creamy white flowers appear in lax, terminal plumes. It is ideal for planting in a wild garden or around the edge of a pond.

Astrantia major
Greater Masterwort (UK/USA)
Height: 45-60cm/18-24in
Spread: 38-45cm/15-18in

Hardy herbaceous perennial with mid-green leaves and upright stems bearing rosettes of star-like, white or pink flowers surrounded by small, narrow, pinkish green bracts during early and mid-summer. Each cluster is about 2.5cm/1in across.

Bergenia cordifolia
Height: 25-30cm/10-12in
Spread: 30-38cm/12-15in

Distinctive hardy border plant with evergreen, rounded leaves. During early and mid-spring it produces drooping heads of pale pink, bell-shaped flowers borne on upright stems. The form *B. cordifolia purpurea* has beautiful pinkish purple flowers, with leaves tinged purple. Creates superb ground-cover.

Border flowers

PLANT NAME AND DESCRIPTION	SITUATION AND CULTIVATION	PROPAGATION

Catananche caerulea
Cupid's Dart (UK/USA)
Blue Cupidone (UK)
Height: 45-75cm/18-30in
Spread: 38-45cm/15-18in

Short-lived hardy herbaceous perennial with narrow, lance-shaped leaves and 36mm/1¹/2in-wide, cornflower-like, purple-blue flowers during mid-summer. Varieties include the vigorous 'Major', with deep lavender-blue flowers; it is ideal for cutting for room decoration.

Full sun and light, well-drained garden soil. Space plants 25cm/10in apart in groups of three or five. In exposed areas, support plants with twiggy sticks inserted around them while the plants are still small. The stems and leaves then grow up and through them. In autumn, cut down the plants to ground level.

Increase named varieties by taking root cuttings in early spring. Insert them in boxes of sandy, loam-based compost and place in a cold frame. When rooted, plant into a nurserybed until large enough to be put into a garden.

Chrysanthemum maximum
(now known as _Leucanthemum maximum_)
Max Daisy (USA)
Shasta Daisy (UK)
Height: 75-90cm/2¹/2-3ft
Spread: 30-45cm/12-18in

Hardy herbaceous perennial with bright-faced, daisy-like, white flowers, 6-7.5cm/2¹/2-3in wide, and large, boss-like, golden centres, from early to late summer.

Fertile, well-drained but moisture-retentive, slightly alkaline soil and a position in full sun suit it. Support young plants with twiggy pea sticks, inserted around plants while still small, so that shoots and leaves grow up and through them. Cut down plants to soil-level in autumn. However, in cold, frosty areas leave this task until spring.

Lift and divide congested clumps in early spring – usually every third year. Replant young pieces from around the outside of the clump, not from the oldest part at the plant's centre.

Coreopsis verticillata
Height: 45-60cm/18-24in
Spread: 30-45cm/12-18in

Hardy, long-lived herbaceous perennial with finely divided and fern-like, bright green leaves and masses of clear yellow, 36mm/1¹/2in-wide flowers from early to late summer. There are several varieties, including 'Grandiflora' (finely divided leaves and rich yellow flowers) and 'Zagreb' (golden flowers on compact, 35cm/14in-high plants).

Full sun and well-drained, ordinary garden soil. Set the plants 30cm/12in apart, in groups of three or four. In exposed places, where plants may be buffeted by wind, use twiggy sticks to give support. Insert them early, so that leaves and stems grow up and through them. In autumn or spring, cut plants down to ground level.

Lift and divide congested plants in autumn or early spring. Replant young pieces from around the outside of the clump, and ensure each part has several young shoots.

Delphinium elatum
Height: 90cm-1.5m/3-5ft
Spread: 45-60cm/18-24in

There are two distinct forms of this hardy herbaceous perennial: Elatum types (shown) have stiffly erect spires, tightly packed with large florets, mainly in shades of blue but also lavender, silvery mauve and white, and in a range of heights. Belladona types, in heights from 1-1.3m/3¹/2-4¹/2ft, have lax and graceful spires of cupped florets.

Deeply prepared, fertile, moisture-retentive soil and a position in full sun suit it. Choose a place sheltered from strong prevailing winds.
Large varieties need staking with strong bamboo canes: insert four or five canes around a large plant and loop garden twine around them. After the flowers fade, cut all stems back to just below a healthy leaf. In autumn, or during early spring in exceptionally cold areas, cut the entire plant back to soil-level.

Take 7.5cm/3in-long cuttings from the bases of plants in spring. These are known as basal cuttings and are inserted in pots of equal parts moist peat and sharp sand. Place in a cold frame and when rooted plant into a nurserybed. Move them to their permanent positions in autumn or spring.
Alternatively, lift and divide congested clumps in spring. Replant only young pieces from around the outside of the clump.

Campanula lactiflora
Height: 90cm-1.5m/3-5ft
Spread: 45-50cm/18-20in

Hardy herbaceous perennial with light green leaves. During early and mid-summer it creates a wealth of bell-shaped, light lavender-blue flowers. There are several varieties, including 'Loddon Anna' (soft pink) and 'Pritchard's Variety' (deep lavender-blue).

Crambe cordifolia
Colewort (USA)
Height: 1.8m/6ft
Spread: 1.2-1.5m/4-5ft

Large, hardy herbaceous perennial, forming a mound of enormous, deeply cut, dark green leaves. During early and mid-summer it produces scented, gypsophila-like heads of white, starry flowers.

Crocosmia x _crocosmiiflora_
(syn. _Montbretia crocosmiiflora_)
Montbretia (UK/USA)
Height: 45-60cm/18-24in
Spread: 10-15cm/4-6in (clump forming)

Slightly tender, cormous plant with narrow, arching leaves and funnel-shaped, 36mm/1¹/2in-long flowers from mid- to late summer. There are many superb varieties, ranging in colour from yellow to deep red.

Dicentra spectabilis
Bleeding Heart (UK/USA)
Height: 45-75cm/18-30in
Spread: 45-50cm/18-20in

Hardy herbaceous perennial with grey-green, deeply dissected, fern-like leaves. During early summer it produces rose-red, heart-shaped flowers with protruding white petals.

PLANT NAME AND DESCRIPTION	SITUATION AND CULTIVATION	PROPAGATION

Dictamnus albus
(syn. *D. fraxinella*)
Burning Bush (UK/USA)
Dittany (UK)
Fraxinella (USA)
Height: 45-60cm/18-24in
Spread: 38-45cm/15-18in

Hardy herbaceous perennial with spire-like heads of fragrant, white, spider-like flowers during early and mid-summer. 'Purpureus' is a handsome variety, in pink with red stripes.

Well-drained, slightly alkaline soil and a position in full sun are needed. If the soil is acid, dust it with lime a few weeks before setting new plants in position. Once established, plants are best left alone. In autumn, cut back plants to soil-level; in exceptionally cold areas, leave this job until spring.
The old flower heads are especially rich in oil, which during a hot, still evening can sometimes be ignited.

Sow freshly gathered seeds thinly in a seedbed outdoors during late summer. Even at their seedling stage, plants do not like being moved. Therefore, ensure the seeds are sown thinly so that the seedlings can be left in the seedbed for two years before being moved into their flowering positions.

Echinacea purpurea
Purple Cone Flower (UK/USA)
Height: 90cm-1.2m/3-4ft
Spread: 45-60cm/18-24in

Hardy herbaceous perennial with rough, slightly toothed, mid-green leaves and purple-crimson flowers up to 10cm/4in-wide from mid-summer to autumn. Each flower has a distinctive, cone-shaped, orange centre. Varieties include 'Robert Bloom' (purple-rose) and 'White Lustre' (white).

Deeply prepared, fertile, moisture-retentive but well-drained soil and a position in full sun suit it. Extend the flowering period by cutting off stems that have borne flowers.
In autumn, cut down plants to soil-level. However, in cold, frosty areas leave this job until spring.

Lift and divide congested plants in autumn or spring, replanting young pieces from around the outside of the clump. Discard the old, woody centres.
Alternatively, sow seeds thinly and evenly in a seedbed outdoors in spring. When seedlings are large enough to handle, move them to a nurserybed until large enough to be planted into a border.

Epimedium perralderianum
Barrenwort (UK)
Bishop's Hat (UK)
Height: 20-30cm/8-12in
Spread: 30-45cm/12-18in

Hardy, evergreen perennial with leaves formed of three heart-shaped, oval segments. At first, these are bright green, with bronze-red markings, becoming dark coppery bronze in autumn. Bright yellow, spurred flowers appear during early summer.

Light shade and moisture-retentive soil suit it. It thrives under trees, but only where the soil does not dry out, and is ideal for creating ground-cover, especially at the edges of borders. Set the plants 30-38cm/12-15in apart. Once established, leave them alone for several years, until congested. In early spring, pull off dead leaves but take care not to damage young flowers.

Lift and divide congested plants in autumn or early spring. Alternatively, sow seeds during mid-summer in loam-based compost. Place in a cold frame. When the seedlings are large enough to handle, prick them off into seed-trays, spacing them 36-50mm/1½-2in apart. Plant into a garden during the following spring.

Erigeron speciosus
Fleabane (UK/USA)
Height: 45-60cm/18-24in
Spread: 30-38cm/12-15in

Hardy herbaceous perennial with daisy-like, purple flowers from early to late summer. Varieties include 'Adria' (rich lavender-blue), 'Charity' (light pink), 'Darkest of All' (deep violet-blue), 'Dignity' (violet-blue) and 'Schwarzes Meer' (lavender-violet with yellow centres).

Fertile, moisture-retentive yet well-drained soil and a position in full sun or light shade. In windy positions, support plants with small, twiggy sticks inserted around them while they are still small. Shoots and leaves then grow up and through them.
Cut off dead flowers and in autumn cut down plants to soil-level. In cold and exposed areas, leave this job until spring.

Lift and divide congested plants in autumn or spring. Replant young pieces from around the outside of the clump, discarding old central parts.
Alternatively, sow seeds in seed-trays in spring and place in a cold frame. After germination, and when large enough to handle, move the seedlings to wider spacings in seed-trays, later transferring them to a nurserybed until large enough to be planted into a border.

Geum chiloense
Avens (UK/USA)
Height: 45-60cm/18-24in
Spread: 30-45cm/12-18in

Hardy herbaceous perennial with mid-green leaves. From early summer to autumn it displays bowl-shaped flowers. There are several superb varieties, including 'Lady Stratheden' (double, yellow flowers) and 'Mrs Bradshaw' (semi-double, scarlet flowers).

Hakonechloa macra 'Aureola'
Height: 25-30cm/10-12in
Spread: 75-90cm/2½-3ft

Hardy, cascading, perennial grass with narrow, bright yellow leaves striped in green. The leaves need room in which to spread and the plant creates a superb feature in a raised bed.

Helleborus niger
Christmas Rose (UK/USA)
Height: 30-45cm/12-18in
Spread: 38-45cm/15-18in

Hardy perennial with evergreen, dark green leaves formed of seven to nine lobes. From mid-winter to early spring it bears white, saucer-shaped flowers, up to 5cm/2in across. Each flower has golden anthers.

Incarvillea delavayi
Height: 50-60cm/20-24in
Spread: 38-45cm/15-18in

Hardy herbaceous perennial with deeply incised, mid-green leaves. During early and mid-summer, rose-pink, foxglove-like flowers up to 7.5cm/3in long are borne at right angles to stiff and upright stems.

Border Flowers

PLANT NAME AND DESCRIPTION	SITUATION AND CULTIVATION	PROPAGATION

Filipendula purpurea
(syn. *Spiraea palmata*)
Meadowsweet (UK/USA)
Height: 60cm-1m/2-3¹/₂ft
Spread: 38-45cm/15-18in

Hardy herbaceous perennial with deeply cut mid-green leaves and large, fluffy heads of carmine to pink flowers during mid-summer. There are also white and rosy red varieties. Flowers are borne at the tops of tall, stiff stems and are attractive when cut for room decoration.

Full sun or light shade, and well-drained but moisture-retentive, slightly alkaline soil ensure success. The soil must not dry out during summer. In early summer, form a mulch round the plants to ensure their roots do not become dry. In autumn, cut down stems to soil-level; in extremely cold areas leave this task until spring.
    Support young plants with twiggy sticks, so that their stems and leaves have an early chance to grow up and through them.

In autumn or early spring, lift and divide congested plants. Replant healthy young parts from around the outside of the clump. Discard old and woody parts from the centre.

Geranium endressii
Crane's-bill (UK/USA)
Height: 30-45cm/12-18in
Spread: 38-45cm/15-18in

Hardy herbaceous ground-covering perennial with deeply lobed, mid-green leaves and pale pink flowers, lightly veined in red, about 2.5cm/1in wide and appearing from early summer to autumn. Varieties include 'Wargrave Pink'.

Well-drained soil in full sun or light shade suits this plant. It is an ideal plant to create ground-cover in a lightly shaded position. Plants do not need support from twiggy sticks unless they are in extremely exposed places.
    Cut off faded flowers and their stems, but leave the clump to spread undisturbed.

Lift and divide congested plants in autumn or spring, replanting the younger parts from around the outside. Discard the old, woody, central part.

Gypsophila paniculata
Baby's Breath (UK/USA)
Height: 60-90cm/2-3ft
Spread: 60-75cm/24-30in

Hardy herbaceous perennial with finely divided stems bearing small, usually white flowers during early and mid-summer. The variety 'Bristol Fairy' has double, white flowers. 'Compacta Plena' (shown) develops heads of double, white flowers on plants 45cm/18in high, while 'Flamingo' bears pink, double flowers.

A position in full sun and deeply cultivated soil, well drained and slightly alkaline, assures success. The ground should not dry out during summer. If the soil is acid, apply 50-100g/2-4oz of lime to each square metre/yard in early winter. Support plants by inserting twiggy sticks around them. Cut down stems to ground level in autumn, but in very cold areas postpone this job until spring.

Take 7.5cm/3in-long cuttings from shoots around the plant's base in mid- or late spring. Insert them in pots of equal parts moist peat and sharp sand, and place in a cold frame. When rooted, plant them into a nurserybed; put them into a border during spring or autumn of the following year.

Helenium autumnale
Sneezewort (UK/USA)
Height: 1.2-1.8m/4-6ft
Spread: 38-45cm/15-18in

Hardy herbaceous perennial with daisy-like flowers, 25-36mm/1-1¹/₂in wide, from mid-summer to early autumn. A wide colour range includes yellow ('Butterpat' shown), orange, copper, bronze-red and crimson-mahogany. It is an excellent plant for bringing dominant splashes of colour to borders.

A position in ordinary garden soil and full sun assures success. Support young plants by inserting twiggy sticks around them so that stems and leaves grow up and through them. In autumn, cut down all stems to soil-level, but in exceptionally cold and frosty areas leave this job until early spring. The stems and leaves will then give the roots slight protection from severe winter weather.

Lift and divide congested plants – usually every three years – during autumn or spring. Replant only the younger parts from around the outside of the clump. The pieces at the centre will be old and woody, and will not produce the best shoots.

Iris sibirica
Siberian Iris (UK/USA)
Height: 60cm-1m/2-3¹/₂ft
Spread: 45-60cm/18-24in

Hardy iris with sword-like leaves that die down in winter. It flowers in early summer and it is mainly the hybrids that are grown; these include 'Cambridge' (pale blue), 'Helen Astor' (orchid pink) and 'White Swirl' (pure white).

Liatris spicata
Blazing Star (UK/USA)
Gayfeather (UK/USA)
Height: 60-75cm/24-30in
Spread: 30-45cm/12-18in

Hardy, tuberous, herbaceous perennial with tall, upright, torch-like spikes of pinkish purple flowers during late summer and into autumn. It grows well in moist areas.

Lupinus polyphyllus
Lupin (UK)
Height: 90cm-1.5m/3-5ft
Spread: 45-60cm/18-24in

Hardy herbaceous perennial, well known for its tall flower spires packed with blue or red flowers during early and mid-summer. The most widely grown types today are from the strain known as Russell lupins, in white, red, carmine, yellow, pink and orange.

Lychnis chalcedonica
Jerusalem Cross (UK/USA)
Maltese Cross (UK/USA)
Scarlet Lightening (USA)
Height: 75-90cm/2¹/₂-3ft
Spread: 38-45cm/15-18in

Hardy herbaceous perennial with lance-shaped, mid-green leaves and small, bright scarlet flowers borne in flattened heads up to 13cm/5in wide during mid- and late summer.

PLANT NAME AND DESCRIPTION	SITUATION AND CULTIVATION	PROPAGATION

Hemerocallis thunbergii
Day Lily (UK/USA)
Height: 75-90cm/2¹/₂-3ft
Spread: 60-75cm/24-30in

Hardy herbaceous perennial with large, trumpet-shaped, sulphur-apricot flowers at the tops of tall, stiff stems during early and mid-summer. There are also many superb hybrids, in colours from golden yellow to pink, orange and brick red. Most hybrids are 75-90cm/2¹/₂-3ft high and have flowers 13-18cm/5-7in wide.

Rich, moisture-retentive soil but well-drained in winter, with a position in full sun or light shade suits it. Plant *H. thunbergii* about 60-75cm/24-30in apart, but set the hybrids closer, at 45cm/18in. After flowering, cut down all stems to soil-level. In autumn, remove the leaves, which by then will have died down. Plants do not need to be supported.

Lift and divide congested plants – usually every three years – in autumn or spring. Replant only the young parts from around the outside of the clump. Discard the old, woody parts from the centre.

Hosta fortunei 'Albopicta'
Plantain Lily (UK/USA)
Height: 45cm/18in
Spread: 45cm/18in

Hardy herbaceous perennial, primarily grown for its pale green leaves with their buff-yellow variegation. There are many other species and varieties, including *H. rectifolia* 'Tall Boy' grown for its dominant (1.2m/4ft) height and long spikes of violet-mauve flowers. Some have bluish green leaves.

Full sun or light shade and fertile, moisture-retentive but well-drained soil. Plants benefit from the addition of peat and well-decomposed garden compost. Hostas grown for their variegated leaves develop the best colours when planted in light shade.

Established hostas can be left undisturbed for many years.

Lift and divide congested plants in early spring, just as growth begins. Replant only young, healthy parts from around the outside of the clump.

Kniphofia
Poker Plant (USA)
Red Hot Poker (UK/USA)
Height: 60cm-1.5m/2-5ft (range)
Spread: 38-60cm/15-24in (range)

Hardy herbaceous perennials, with many species and hybrids, all bearing distinctive, poker-like heads. Flowers come in a wide colour range – from cream and yellow to fiery red – from early summer to early autumn.

Full sun and well-drained soil. Avoid soils that become cold and waterlogged in winter, as well as those that have been heavily manured. When setting new plants in a border, ensure that their roots do not become dry. In excessively cold and frosty areas, cover the bases of plants with straw during winter. After the flowers fade, cut back the stems to soil-level. Cut off the remaining stems and leaves in autumn or spring.

Lift and divide congested clumps in early spring, but avoid causing unnecessary damage to the crowns.

Limonium latifolium
(syn. *Statice latifolia*)
Sea Lavender (UK/USA)
Statice (UK)
Height: 45-60cm/18-24in
Spread: 45cm/18in

Hardy perennial with somewhat woody stems and rootstock and leathery, dark green leaves. From mid- to late summer it develops cloud-like heads of tiny, funnel-shaped, lavender-blue flowers.

Full sun and well-drained garden soil. Avoid heavy soils that remain wet during winter. Set the plants 45cm/18in apart. In autumn or early winter, cut all stems down to ground level.

This plant resents root disturbance and therefore is best raised from seeds. Sow them 6mm/¹/₄in deep in seed-trays or pots in late spring or early summer and place in a cold frame. Germination takes two to four weeks. When the seedlings are large enough to handle, prick them into seed-trays, spacing them 36-50mm/1¹/₂-2in apart. Plant young plants them into their flowering positions in autumn or early spring.

Meconopsis betonicifolia
Blue Poppy (USA)
Himalayan Blue Poppy (UK)
Height: 90cm-1.2m/3-4ft
Spread: 38-45cm/15-18in

Hardy herbaceous perennial with oblong, mid-green leaves and clear sky blue to purple flowers up to 7.5cm/3in wide during early and mid-summer. Each flower has distinctive golden stamens.

Monarda didyma
Bee Balm (UK/USA)
Oswego Tea (UK/USA)
Sweet Bergamot (UK)
Height: 60-90cm/2-3ft
Spread: 38-45cm/15-18in

Hardy herbaceous perennial with mid-green leaves and dense heads, up to 7.5cm/3in wide, of bright scarlet flowers from early to late summer. Varieties in pink, lavender, violet-purple and white.

Phlox paniculata
Fall Phlox (USA)
Perennial Phlox (UK)
Summer Phlox (UK)
Height: 45cm-1m/1¹/₂-3¹/₂ft (range)
Spread: 45-60cm/18-24in (range)

Hardy herbaceous perennial with lance-shaped, mid-green leaves and terminal clusters of purple flowers from mid-summer to autumn. There are many varieties, in a wide colour range.

Polygonum bistorta 'Superbum'
Bistort (UK/USA)
Easter Ledges (USA)
Snakeweed (UK/USA)
Height: 75-90cm/2¹/₂-3ft
Spread: 60-75cm/24-30in

Hardy, spreading, herbaceous perennial with a mat-forming habit. During early summer the light green leaves are surmounted by spikes of clear pink flowers.

Border flowers

PLANT NAME AND DESCRIPTION	SITUATION AND CULTIVATION	PROPAGATION

Lysimachia punctata
Dotted Loosestrife (UK)
Garden Loosestrife (USA)
Yellow Loosestrife (UK)
Height: 60-90cm/2-3ft
Spread: 38-45cm/15-18in

Long-lived, vigorous and slightly invasive herbaceous perennial with bright yellow, cup-shaped flowers borne in whorls up to 20cm/8in long from early to late summer. When allowed to form large clumps it creates a dominant feature.

Full sun or partial shade and fertile, moisture-retentive soil. It grows well in heavy soils. Set the plants about 38cm/15in apart. Plants do not need to be staked. In autumn or spring, cut down all stems to ground-level.

Lift and divide congested plants in autumn or early spring. Replant only the younger parts from the outside of the clump.

Perovskia atriplicifolia
Russian Sage (UK)
Height: 90cm-1.3m/3-4¹/₂ft
Spread: 45-60cm/18-24in

Hardy, deciduous, shrubby perennial invariably grown in a mixed or herbaceous border. Grey-green, finely cut, aromatic leaves clad the upright, branching stems which bear lax spires of tubular, violet-blue flowers during mid- and late summer. 'Blue Spire' has larger spires of delicate, lavender-blue flowers.

Full sun or light shade and fertile, well-drained soil. Set the plants 45cm/18in apart, in groups of three or five. This creates an attractive colour theme against which other plants can be planted. No staking is needed. In early spring, cut down the stems to about 30-38cm/12-15in high.

Take 7.5cm/3in-long cuttings in mid-summer and insert them in pots of equal parts moist peat and sharp sand. Place them in a cold frame. Preferably, each cutting should have a heel of the older wood. When rooted, pot up into individual pots and replace in a cold frame. Plant into a flower border in spring.

Rudbeckia fulgida
Coneflower (UK/USA)
Height: 60-90cm/2-3ft
Spread: 45-60cm/18-24in

Hardy herbaceous perennial bearing daisy-faced flowers, 6cm/2¹/₂in wide, with large, purple-brown, cone-like centres from mid-summer to autumn. It creates eye-catching bursts of colour, from yellow to orange. 'Deamii' has yellow flowers, 7.5-10cm/3-4in wide; 'Goldsturm' is yellow and 13cm/5in wide.

Sunny and open position and well-drained but moisture-retentive soil. In exposed areas, support young plants with twiggy sticks. Young shoots and leaves are then able to grow up and through them, while they provide unobtrusive support. Cut down stems to soil-level in autumn, or in spring in cold, frosty and exposed areas.

Lift and divide congested plants in autumn or spring. Replant only the younger parts from the outside, discarding the central old and woody pieces.

Sedum 'Autumn Joy'
(syn. S. spectabile 'Autumn Joy')
Height: 45-60cm/18-24in
Spread: 45-50cm/18-20in

An herbaceous perennial with pale green, somewhat pear-shaped, fleshy leaves. During late summer, it develops 10-20cm/4-8in-wide heads of salmon pink flowers that slowly change through orange-red to orange-brown in mid- to late autumn. S. spectabile 'Variegatum' has variegated leaves.

Light, well-drained, but moisture-retentive soil and a position in full sun suits it. Avoid heavy soils, unless they have been lightened with sharp sand and well-decomposed compost.
   Leave the flower heads on plants until early spring, then snap them off. They look attractive when covered with frost.

Lift and divide congested plants in autumn or spring, replanting young parts from around the outside.

Potentilla atrosanguinea hybrids
Height: 45-60cm/18-24in
Spread: 45-50cm/18-20in

Hardy herbaceous perennials, often short-lived, with grey-green, strawberry-like leaves. From early summer to autumn the plant displays lax flower heads of single or double flowers. Hybrids to consider include 'Etna' (coral), 'Gibson's Scarlet' (bright red) and 'Monsieur Rouillard' (dark copper).

Pulmonaria officinalis
Blue Lungwort (USA)
Jerusalem Cowslip (UK/USA)
Jerusalem Sage (UK/USA)
Height: 30cm/12in
Spread: 30cm/12in

Hardy ground-covering herbaceous perennial with green leaves spotted in white. During late spring and early summer it displays purple-blue, funnel-shaped flowers.

Pyrethrum roseum hybrids
(now known as Tanacetum coccineum)
Pyrethrum (UK/USA)
Height: 75-90cm/2¹/₂-3ft
Spread: 38-45cm/15-18in

Hardy herbaceous perennial with bright green feathery leaves and large, daisy-like flowers during early and mid-summer. Hybrids include 'Brenda' (cerise-pink) and 'Eileen May Robinson' (clear pink).

Sidalcea malviflora
Checkerbloom (UK/USA)
Height: 75cm-1.2m/2¹/₂-4ft
Spread: 45-60cm/18-24in

Hardy, easily grown herbaceous perennial with round to kidney-shaped mid-green leaves. From early summer to autumn, tall, branched stems bear spires of pink flowers. There are several varieties.

PLANT NAME AND DESCRIPTION	SITUATION AND CULTIVATION	PROPAGATION

***Solidago* hybrids**
Golden Rod (UK/USA)
Height: 30cm-1.5m/1-5ft (range)
Spread: 25-60cm/10-24in (range)

Hardy herbaceous perennials in a wide range of forms, some dwarf, others large and dominant. Plume-like, slightly arching heads of tiny yellow or golden flowers appear from mid-summer to autumn. 'Crown of Rays' (shown) has densely packed heads on plants 45cm/18in high.

Full sun or light shade and ordinary, well-drained garden soil. The planting distances depend on the height and vigour of the varieties selected. Tall types need support from twiggy sticks. In autumn, cut down plants to soil-level.

Lift and divide congested plants in autumn or spring. Replant only the younger parts from around the outside of the clump.

Stachys byzantina
(syn. *S. lanata/S. olympica*)
Lamb's Tongue (UK)
Lamb's Ears (UK/USA)
Height: 30-45cm/12-18in
Spread: 30-38cm/12-15in

Half-hardy herbaceous perennial that smothers the ground with leaves densely covered with silvery hairs which create a woolly appearance. During mid-summer it develops spikes of purple flowers. 'Silver Carpet' is a non-flowering form.

Full sun or light shade and well-drained soil. Set the plants 30cm/12in apart to create rapid ground-cover. Remove dead flower stems in autumn, and in spring tidy up plants that have been damaged by wet, cold weather.

Lift and divide congested plants in autumn or spring, replanting only young pieces from around the outside of the clump.

***Tradescantia virginiana* 'Isis'**
(syn. *Tradescantia* 'Isis')
Spiderwort (UK/USA)
Trinity Flower (UK)
Height: 45-60cm/18-24in
Spread: 45-50cm/18-20in

Hardy herbaceous perennial with rich, royal purple flowers up to 36mm/1½in across from early to late summer. They are borne amid dull green, strap-like leaves. Other varieties include 'Osprey' (white) and 'Purple Dome' (rich purple).

Well-drained yet moisture-retentive garden soil with a position in full sun or light shade suits it. Support young plants with twiggy sticks, so that stems and leaves grow up and through them.
In autumn, cut down plants to soil-level. In cold, frosty areas, do not cut down the plants until spring.

Lift and divide congested plants – usually every three years – in spring. Replant only the younger parts from around the outside. Discard the old central parts.

***Zantedeschia aethiopica* 'Crowborough'**
Arum Lily (UK/USA)
Calla Lily (USA)
Trumpet Lily (USA)
Height: 45-75cm/18-30in
Spread: 45-60cm/18-24in

Half-hardy, deciduous, rhizomatous perennial, with deep green, arrow-shaped leaves. 'Crowborough' is slightly hardier than the normal species, and has white, arum-like flowers from early summer.

Full sun or light shade and fertile, moisture-retentive soil. It can also be grown as a water-side plant, with its roots in boggy soil. Plant the rhizomes in spring, so that they are covered with 5-7.5cm/2-3in of soil. Water the soil and keep it moist until shoots appear. In early winter, cover the fleshy crowns with peat, straw, bracken or well-weathered ashes. When grown as a pool-side plant and with its roots shallowly covered by water it will survive all but the severest winters.

Lift and divide congested plants in spring. However, this is not always easy – each new piece must have shoots, which are not apparent until late spring.

Symphytum grandiflorum
Comfrey (UK/USA)
Height: 20cm/8in
Spread: 30-38cm/12-15in

Hardy, fast-growing herbaceous perennial with a ground-covering nature. The mid-green leaves are lance shaped and hairy. During mid- and late spring it develops white flowers in terminal clusters.

Thalictrum aquilegiifolium
Meadow Rue (UK/USA)
Height: 60-90cm/2-3ft
Spread: 38-50cm/15-20in

Hardy herbaceous perennial with glossy, blue-green leaves and fluffy, purple or mauve flowers during early and mid-summer. Varieties include 'Thundercloud', with deep purple flowers.

Tiarella cordifolia
Foam Flower (UK/USA)
Height: 23-30cm/9-12in
Spread: 23-30cm/9-12in

Hardy, low-growing and ground-covering evergreen perennial, ideal for smothering the soil under shrubs and trees. During late spring and early summer the somewhat maple-like, mid-green leaves are surmounted by erect spires of creamy white flowers.

Trollius x cultorum
Globe Flower (UK/USA)
Height: 60cm/24in
Spread: 38-45cm/15-18in

Hardy, moisture-loving herbaceous perennial with round to oval, mid- to dark green leaves. During late spring and early summer it develops large, buttercup-like flowers. There are many handsome varieties.

Planting bulbs and corms

Bulbs and corms are often grouped together, though they are different botanically. A bulb is formed of fleshy, overlapping, modified leaves enclosing a young shoot, while a corm is a thickened stem base, usually covered with a papery skin. At the top is a bud from which new shoots and roots develop. Both bulbs and corms need careful handling when being planted to ensure they are not damaged.

PLANTING GLADIOLI

Gladioli create colourful features in borders; they can be mixed with herbaceous plants and shrubs, or set out together on their own, perhaps in a narrow border. Plant gladioli from early to mid-spring, whenever the soil is workable. Like many bulbs and corms, they are best planted in a group. Use a spade or trowel to create a circular hole 38-45cm/15-18in wide; on medium to heavy soils make the hole 10cm/4in deep, and in light soils 15cm/6in deep to help prevent plants being blown over by wind when they are in full bloom.

Shallowly fork the soil in the hole's base and add sharp sand, then firm the soil. Position the corms 10-15cm/4-6in apart. Gladioli do not generally need to be staked, but large-flowered hybrids in exposed areas benefit from the support of a bamboo cane inserted to the rear of each corm (it will later be obscured by the leaves and flowers). Stakes also indicate where corms have been planted before their foliage appears. Carefully spread soil over the corms, firming, but not compacting, it. Water the soil to settle it around the corms, but avoid watering further until roots have started to form, about eight weeks later.

NATURALIZING DAFFODILS IN GRASS

Groups of daffodils, naturalized in grass, create attractive displays in spring. Plant the bulbs in late summer or early autumn, as soon as they are available. For a natural appearance, scatter the bulbs on the grass and plant them where they fall, but to create a dominant display, ensure they are not more than 10cm/4in apart.

You can use a trowel to plant in grass, but a bulb-planting tool, which is pushed into the soil and takes out a core of turf, makes the job easier.

PLANTING GLADIOLI CORMS

1 Use a spade or trowel to make a circular hole, 38-45cm/15-18in wide. On medium to heavy soil the hole should be 10cm/4in deep, but on light soil make it 15cm/6in deep. Lightly fork the base and add a layer of sharp sand.
2 Insert 1.2m/4ft-long canes 10-15cm/4-6in apart in the hole's base, and then position corms next to them.
3 Carefully place topsoil over the corms, taking care not to disturb them.
4 Firm the soil, but not so that it is excessively compacted.

Above: Grape Hyacinths (*Muscari armeniacum*), which create a wealth of deep blue flowers with white rims during spring, are excellent companions for bright-faced polyanthus. Once established, they can be left alone for several years. The bulbs need lifting and dividing every three or four years; wait until the leaves become yellow before lifting and dividing them.

Each hole should be three times the depth of its bulb (for example, a bulb with a depth of 5cm/2in needs a hole 15cm/6in deep). Ensure that the base of the bulb rests on the soil at the base of the planting hole, and then replace the plug of turf (having removed some of the soil from the turf's base to prevent it standing above the level of the surrounding grass). Firm it into position and lightly water the whole area once you have planted all the bulbs.

PLANTING NARCISSI FOR CUT FLOWERS

Daffodils and other narcissi are ideal for cutting to display indoors in spring. Select an out-of-the way part of the garden that is sheltered and receives plenty of sun to encourage early flowering. Use a spade to take out a trench about 38cm/15in wide and 15cm/6in deep. Lightly fork over the base, then gently firm it level. Space the bulbs 36-50mm/1½-2in apart cover them with friable soil, then gently firm. Mark the corners of the bed, so that you will not inadvertently dig up the bulbs in winter, before they indicate their presence by developing shoots.

When planting narcissi this close, you should lift the bulbs every two years. Always leave the foliage to die down naturally before lifting. You can then replant them during the following late summer or autumn.

PLANTING LILIES

Plant lilies at any time from mid-autumn to early spring, whenever the soil and weather allow. Plant stem-rooting lilies (those that develop roots from their stems as well as from the bulb's base) in holes two-and-a-half times the depth of the bulb; basal-rooting types are best planted slightly less deeply and in autumn.

The Madonna Lily (*Lilium candidum*) is the exception to these rules; plant it with its nose just below the surface. Also, it is best planted or transplanted when the stems have died down – usually in late summer or early autumn.

Most lilies grow well in ordinary garden soil, but many detest lime – a pH of 6.5 suits them all. About a month before planting the bulbs, dig well-decomposed compost into the soil, adding grit or coarse sand to heavy soil. The soil should retain moisture, yet not be waterlogged.

Use a trowel to take out a hole, set the bulb in position and return and firm soil around it. Water the soil to settle it around the bulb and mark the position with a cane.

GROWING LILIES IN POTS

Patios can be given a bright and exotic look with even a few lilies in large pots. Growing them in this way is neither difficult nor expensive.

- As soon as bulbs are available in autumn, plant them singly in pots 15-20cm/6-8in wide, or three in a 25cm/10in wide pot. If you are planting several bulbs in the same pot, keep to the same variety.

- Thoroughly clean the pots, then put drainage material in the base, followed by compost. Position each bulb well down the pot; this allows space for stem-rooting types, as well as for them to be topdressed later.

- Use a well-drained, soil-based potting compost or a mixture of two parts loam, one part sharp sand and two of well-decayed manure.

- After potting, water the compost and place the pot in a cool place (for example, a dark, vermin-proof, airy cellar or shed) to encourage the development of roots. Ensure that the compost does not become dry.

- In spring, when shoots appear, place the pot on a patio and keep the compost moist. Support plants as necessary with bamboo canes, but take care not to insert the stake into a bulb.

Hardy spring-flowering bulbs, corms and tubers

PLANT NAME AND DESCRIPTION	SITUATION AND CULTIVATION	PROPAGATION

Anemone nemorosa
European Wood Anemone (USA)
Wood Anemone (UK)
Height: 15-20cm/6-8in
Spread: 10-15cm/4-6in

Tuberous-rooted, with 2.5cm/1in-wide white, pink-flushed flowers during early and mid-spring. There are many superb forms, including 'Allenii' (silvery pale lavender), 'Robinsoniana' (pale lavender-blue) and 'Royal Blue' (blue).

Full sun to light shade and moisture-retentive but well-drained light soil are essential. It tolerates slightly limy soil and thrives when naturalized in woodland or wild gardens. Plant the young tubers 36mm/1½in deep in autumn.
 It creates an attractive feature when planted with the white-flowered Wake Robin *(Trillium grandiflorum)* and yellow *Erythronium tuolumnense*.

Lift and divide congested clumps after the flowers fade and replant about 36mm/1½in deep.
 Alternatively, during mid- or late summer – as soon as they are available – sow seeds in pots or seed-trays of sandy, loam-based compost and place in a cold frame. When seedlings are large enough to handle, prick them off into seed-trays or pots, later transferring them to a nurserybed.

Chionodoxa sardensis
Glory of the Snow (UK/USA)
Height: 10-15cm/4-6in
Spread: 5-10cm/2-4in

Bulbous plant with two folded, strap-like, mid-green leaves and slender stems bearing 18mm/¾in wide, nodding, sky blue flowers from early to late spring. Flowers are star-shaped, each with six petals and a tiny white centre.
 Other species include *C. luciliae*, with light blue flowers and white centres.

Full sunlight and light, well-drained soil. Avoid heavy, waterlogged soil that remains cold in spring. These bulbs are ideal for planting in rock gardens and at the fronts of borders. They can also be naturalized in short grass.
 Plant the bulbs 5-7.5cm/2-3in deep in autumn. Do not plant them singly, but arrange in small groups, spacing the bulbs 5-7.5cm/2-3in apart. Once established they can be left alone until the group becomes too congested.

Lift and divide congested clumps as the foliage dies down. Alternatively, increase plants from seeds, which germinate freely. Collect the round seed pods in late spring, when ripe – indicated by turning black – but before they open. Sow seeds immediately in friable soil in a nurserybed and transplant young seedlings to their permanent positions about two years later.

Endymion hispanicus
(now *Hyacinthoides hispanica*)
Bluebell (UK/USA)
Spanish Bluebell (USA
Spanish Jacinth (USA)
Height: 25-30cm/10-12in
Spread: 10-15/4-6in

Bulbous plant with strap-like, glossy, mid-green leaves and bell-shaped, purple-blue flowers during spring and early summer. There is also a white-flowered form (shown).

Fertile, moisture-retentive but well-drained soil in light shade suits it. The soil must remain moist during summer.
 Plant the bulbs 10-15cm/4-6in deep as soon as they are available; do not allow them to become dry.

It is easily increased by sowing seeds; scatter them on the surface of soil in the position where they are to grow and become established. Lightly cover them with friable soil and keep the area moist but not waterlogged.

Galanthus nivalis
Common Snowdrop (UK/USA)
Height: 7.5-18cm/3-7in
Spread: 7.5-13cm/3-5in

Bulbous plant with flat, strap-like, glaucous green leaves and white flowers from mid-winter to early spring. Each flower has six petals – three long outer ones and three short inner ones. There are green markings on the inner petals. *G. n.* 'Flore-plena' has double flowers.

Light shade and moisture-retentive but well-drained fertile soil. They are ideal for planting in woodland and naturalized gardens, thriving under deciduous trees and shrubs. It is essential that the leaves receive good light during winter and spring. They are not easy to get established, but once growing strongly need little attention. Plant them 5-7.5cm/2-3in deep in late summer.

Lift and divide congested clumps just after they finish flowering. Carefully separate the bulbs and replant them immediately, so that the roots do not become dry.

Anemone coronaria
Height: 15-25cm/6-10in
Spread: 7.5-10cm/3-4in

Widely known as Florist's Anemones, these have finely dissected, mid-green leaves and during spring produce 36-50mm/1½-2in-wide flowers in shades of white, blue or red. There are two forms; 'De Caen' (single-flowered) and 'St. Brigid' (semi- or double-flowered), with several varieties of each type.

Crocus chrysanthus
Height: 7.5-10cm/3-4in
Spread: 5-7.5cm/2-3in

Well-known cormous plant with cup-shaped, honey-scented, bright yellow flowers during late winter and early spring. The many varieties, include 'Blue Pearl' (pale blue), 'Ladykiller' (purple-blue), 'Princes Beatrix' (clear blue), 'Snow Bunting' (white) and 'Zwanenburg Bronze' (dark bronze).

***Daffodils* trumpet types**
Height: 32-45cm/13-18in
Spread: 7.5-10cm/3-4in

Trumpet daffodils form the first of twelve divisions into which narcisi are divided. They are defined as having the trumpet (corona) as long as, or longer than, the petals. They flower outdoors in spring and drench gardens in yellow or white flowers. The range of varieties is wide.

Eranthis hyemalis
Winter Aconite (UK/USA)
Height: 10cm/4in
Spread: 7.5cm/3in

Hardy, tuberous plant with lemon yellow, buttercup-like flowers up to 2.5cm/1in wide and backed by a distinctive frill of deeply cut green leaves. Sometimes they appear as early as mid-winter, but more commonly during late winter and very early spring.

PLANT NAME AND DESCRIPTION	SITUATION AND CULTIVATION	PROPAGATION

Ipheion uniflorum
Spring Starflower (UK/USA)
Height: 15-20cm/6-8in
Spread: 5-7.5cm/2-3in (clump forming)

Bulbous plant with pale green, grass-like leaves and scented, white to violet-blue, six-petalled and star-shaped flowers, each up to 5cm/2in wide, during late spring. There are several varieties, including 'Wisley Blue' (violet-blue).

Moisture-retentive, well-drained soil and a sheltered position in full sun or light shade suit it. Plant the bulbs about 5cm/2in deep in early or mid-autumn.

As soon as the leaves die down, carefully lift the bulbs, separate them and replant them 5-7.5cm/2-3in apart. If the bulbs are put into store, do not allow them to become either dry or wet.

Muscari armeniacum
Grape Hyacinth (UK/USA)
Height: 20-25cm/8-10in
Spread: 7.5-10cm/3-4in

Bulbous, with narrow, mid-green leaves and upright stems crowned with scented, bright azure blue to deep purplish blue flowers, each with a white rim. Flowers appear during mid- and late spring.
There are several superb varieties, including 'Blue Spike' (mid-blue and double).

Full sun and well-drained soil. Avoid shaded areas, as this encourages excessive leaf growth and reduces flowering. Plant bulbs 7.5cm/3in deep, and at the same distance apart, in late summer and early autumn. Once established they soon spread.
For increased interest, plant Primroses *(Primula vulgaris)* and Polyanthas among them. Alternatively, try a combination of Grape Hyacinths and *Alyssum saxatile* (now *Aurinia saxatilis*) 'Citrinum'.

Lift and divide congested clumps – usually every three or four years – as soon as the leaves turn yellow, and replant immediately. Take care that the bulbs do not become dry.

Trillium grandiflorum
Wake Robin (UK)
Height: 30-45cm/12-18in
Spread: 25-30cm/10-12in

Rhizomatous herbaceous perennial widely grown in woodland and wild gardens. It forms a clump of pale to mid-green leaves, with three-petalled white flowers, later flushed pink, each with golden anthers; flowers appear in spring and early summer. The form 'Roseum' (shown) has pink flowers.

Moisture-retentive, well-drained soil enriched with garden compost. Plant in lightly shaded areas, or in a sunny position so long as the soil is continually moist. Plant the rhizomes in groups and about 10cm/4in deep during late summer or autumn.

Lift and divide congested groups at any time after the leaves have died down (usually in late summer) and until early spring. Replant them in groups; take care not to divide them excessively.
Alternatively, as soon as they are available, sow seeds in seed-trays and then place in a cold frame. It takes up to six years to produce flowering plants.

Tulipa tarda
Height: 15cm/6in
Spread: 7.5cm/3in (clump forming)

A bulb with narrow, mid-green leaves and clusters of up to five flowers on each stem. Each flower is white, but with a dominant bright yellow centre that often spreads over much of the pointed petals.

These low-growing bulbs are ideal for brightening rock gardens and the edges of borders. Plant them 6-7.5cm/2¹/₂-3in apart and 15cm/6in deep in well-drained soil in autumn. Arrange them in groups of nine to twelve bulbs. After flowering and when the stems have died down, remove the leaves and keep the area free from weeds. Bulbs can be left in the ground until they become too congested.

When the bulbs become congested, lift them as soon as the flowers fade and place them, complete with stems and leaves, in a dry, vermin-free shed. When the stems and leaves have died, place the bulbs in dry boxes and store in a dry, airy shed until autumn. Break up large clusters of bulbs, and replant.

Leucojum vernum
Spring Snowflake (UK/USA)
Height: 20cm/8in
Spread: 10cm/4in

Bulbous, with strap-like, shiny green leaves and white, six-petalled, bell-like, 18mm/³/₄in-long flowers during late winter and early spring. The petals are tipped in green.
L. v. 'Carpathicum' is especially attractive, with petals tipped in yellow.

Narcissus bulbocodium
Hoop Petticoat Daffodil (UK/USA)
Height: 7.5-13cm/3-5in
Spread: 7.5cm/3in

Bulbous, with pretty, distinctive and graceful, yellow, 2.5cm/1in-long, funnel-shaped trumpets during late winter and early spring. The green leaves are either thread-like or very narrow.

Narcissus cyclamineus
Height: 15-20cm/6-8in
Spread: 7.5-10cm/3-4in

Bulbous, with narrow, bright green leaves and small, deep yellow trumpets up to 5cm/2in long and with the petals distinctively swept back. Flowers appear in late winter and early spring.
This species has been used to create a wonderful range of varieties, such as 'February Gold', with larger flowers.

Scilla bifolia
Squill (USA)
Height: 15-20cm/6-8in
Spread: 13-15cm/5-6in

Bulbous, with two – or sometimes four – channelled leaves and star-shaped, 12mm/¹/₂in-wide, mauvish blue flowers during early spring. Pure white as well as pink forms are also known.
Other scillas include *Scilla siberica*, with brilliant blue, bell-shaped flowers.

Planting a climber

Climbers introduce a vertical dimension to the garden, clothing dull walls, screening unsightly areas and creating romantic arbours. Few gardens cannot offer a home to at least one climber and even the walls of a small bungalow can be clothed with two or three of them. Furthermore, it does not matter if the aspect is north, south, east or west, there is a climber to suit it.

There is a wide range of climbers, with a variety of climbing habits; some just lean against a support, many have a twining tendency, others have tendrils, while a few are scramblers and, in the wild, are supported by stems and branches of other plants. A range of climbers grown for their flowers or attractive leaves is described on pages 126-9, and details of the soil preferences and climbing nature of each plant are given.

PLANTING A CLIMBER

Whatever the type of climber, it is essential to plant it firmly in well-prepared soil. Most climbers are sold as container-grown plants and can be planted at any time when the soil is not frozen or waterlogged. However, spring is the best time, as plants then have a long period in which to establish themselves before the onset of cold weather.

A few weeks before planting, excavate soil where the climber is to be planted to about 30cm/12in deep. If it is light, add peat or well-decayed compost; if heavy, mix in sharp sand as well as compost. Add a sprinkling of bonemeal to help establishment and root development.

The day before planting, thoroughly water the compost in the container in which the climber is growing. If this is neglected, the climber's establishment will be retarded, especially if the soil it is to be planted in is also dry.

Remove the climber from the container and use a trowel or spade to take out a hole to slightly more than the depth and width of the root-ball. Tease out matted roots around the side of the root-ball. Position the root-ball in the hole and adjust the depth so that its top is just below the surface. This allows for settlement of the soil. Replace soil and firm it around the roots, making sure that the surface is level. Water the soil well to settle it around the roots.

Right: Clematis chrysocoma resembles the Mountain Clematis (*Clematis montana*) but is less vigorous and grows only to about 3m/10ft high. It is a deciduous climber and the single, white, saucer-shaped flowers appear during early and mid-summer. Often flowering continues on new shoots well into late summer and beyond.

PLANTING A CLIMBER

1 The day before planting, water the plant several times.
2 Prepare the soil. Dig a hole 30cm/12in deep and wide and improve the soil by adding well decayed compost. Also, fork in a sprinkling of bonemeal.
3 Remove the container and position the plant in the hole. The top of the root-ball should be fractionally below the surface.
4 Use a trowel to place topsoil around the roots, then gently but firmly compact it.
5 Use a fine-rose watering-can to water the soil. This may need to be repeated several times, especially if the weather is dry.
6 Form a mulch over the soil around the climber; this helps to conserve moisture in the soil and to keep it cool during hot weather.

FAST-GROWING CLIMBERS

Clothing a pergola, fence or dull wall rapidly is often important, especially when establishing a garden or to block out unsightly views introduced by neighbours.

- **Covering a large, bland wall** The self-clinging True Virginia Climber (*Parthenocissus quinquefolia*) and Boston Ivy (*Parthenocissus tricuspidata*) both soon cover walls, as well as bearing leaves that assume rich autumn tints.

- **Pergolas** The deciduous Yellow Hop (*Humulus lupulus* 'Aureus') soon clothes trellises and pergolas with richly coloured leaves during summer.

- **Fences, pergolas and sheds** The Russian Vine (*Polygonum baldshuanicum*), also known as Mile-a-Minute Vine, is a well-known smotherer. But take care – it is very vigorous. The Mountain Clematis (*Clematis montana*) is more decorative.

CLIMBING HABITS

A climber's nature indicates the type of support it needs to allow its shoots to climb. For example, climbers which have adhesive suckers are able to scale walls without any extra help. Whereas those with tendrils need a supporting framework or another plant to which they can cling.

Leaners do not have any visible means of support and in the wild, either lean against a support or scramble through larger plants. In a garden, smaller climbers of this type are given a supporting framework to which they will be tied, while vigorous types are allowed to wander through trees and large shrubs. Leaning climbers include: *Abutilon megapotamicum* (Trailing Abutilon); *Berberidopsis corallina* (Coral Plant); *Jasminum nudiflorum* (Winter-flowering Jasmine); Roses (climbing forms); *Solanum crispum* (Chilean Potato Tree).

Self-supporting climbers are highly successful in the wild, using adhesive suckers and aerial roots to scale walls and trees. They grow equally well in either of these ways in the garden or up house walls. Self-supporting climbers include: *Campsis radicans* (Trumpet Vine); *Hedera* (range of species); *Hydrangea petiolaris* (Climbing Hydrangea); *Parthenocissus henryana* (Chinese Virginia Creeper); *Parthenocissus quinquefolia* (True Virginia Creeper); *Parthenocissus tricuspidata* (Boston Ivy).

Climbers with tendrils or twisting leaf stalks need twiggy hosts around which they can wrap tendrils or hook their leaf-stalks, in the wild. In gardens, they need the support of a framework, or other plants through which to grow. Species include: *Clematis* (vast range); *Lathyrus odoratus* (Sweet Pea); *Passiflora caerulea* (Passion Flower); *Tropaeolum peregrinum* (Canary Creeper); *Tropaeolum speciosum* (Flame Flower); *Vitis coignetiae.*

Twiners are friendly plants, gaining support by closely twining around a neighbour. In a garden, they are usually trained to clamber over a framework of wires or poles. Twiners include: *Actinidia chinensis* (Chinese Gooseberry); *Actinidia kolomikta* (Kolomikta Vine); *Humulus japonicus* 'Aureus' (Golden Hop); *Jasminum officinale* (White Jasmine); *Lonicera* (range of species); *Polygonum baldshuanicum* (Russian Vine); *Wisteria floribunda* (Japanese Wisteria); *Wisteria sinensis* (Chinese Wisteria).

You will probably need to insert a cane for the climber to use before it reaches the supporting frame – or a wall, if it is a self-clinging type. Insert the cane between the root-ball and the wall, taking care not to damage roots, and tie plant's stem to the cane. Do this by first tying a piece of string tightly to the cane, then looping and tying it below a leaf-joint to prevent the stem falling down. Take care not to constrict the stem. Tie the top of the cane to the supporting framework.

Flowering climbers and wall shrubs

PLANT NAME AND DESCRIPTION	SITUATION AND CULTIVATION	PROPAGATION
 ***Ceanothus thrysiflorus repens*** Blue Blossom (USA) Californian Lilac (UK) Height: 1.2-1.5m/4-5ft Compact evergreen shrub, which although normally having a mound-forming nature, can also be trained to grow against a wall, where it spreads to 1.8m/6ft. During late spring and early summer it bears small, light blue flowers in 7.5cm/3in-long clusters. One of the hardiest evergreen Californian Lilacs.	Plant it against a warm, sheltered wall, in well-drained light soil, preferably neutral or slightly acid. Prune by shortening lateral shoots to two or three buds from the previous season's growth after the flowers fade.	Take 7.5cm/3in-long cuttings in mid-summer and insert them in pots of equal parts moist peat and sharp sand. Place in gentle warmth. When rooted, pot up and harden off in a cold frame before planting into a garden.
 ***Clematis montana*** Mountain Clematis (UK) Height: 5.4-7.5m/18-25ft or more Hardy and vigorous deciduous climber with dark green leaves and pure white flowers up to 5cm/2in across during late spring and early summer. There are several superb varieties, including 'Elizabeth' (soft pink and slightly fragrant), 'Tetrarose' (lilac-rose) and 'Alexander' (creamy white and sweetly scented).	Sunny position but with shade available for the roots. Fertile, neutral to slightly alkaline soil enriched with peat or well-decomposed garden compost is essential. Plants need support. In the first year, prune plants by one-third after their initial flowering. When established, cut out old flowering stems in early summer – after the flowers fade – and train shoots on to a framework. Often, however, plants are left to clamber unrestricted over trees or frameworks.	Take 7.5-10cm/3-4in-long stem cuttings from half-ripe shoots during mid-summer and insert them in pots of equal parts moist peat and sharp sand. Place in gentle warmth. When the cuttings have developed roots, pot them into individual pots and place in a frost-free greenhouse or cold frame during winter. In spring, either repot the plants into larger pots, or plant into a nurserybed.
 ***Clematis* large-flowered hybrids** Height: 1.2-4.5m/4-15ft (range) Deciduous climbers with large flowers, usually 13-15cm/5-6in wide. Most varieties are single-flowered and flowers appear during summer, the exact period depending on the variety. The range of colour is wide, with some varieties revealing further shading in bars or stripes down the petals. The variety shown is 'Alice Fisk'.	Sunny position but with shade available for the roots. Fertile, neutral to slightly alkaline soil enriched with peat or well-decomposed garden compost is essential. Plants need support. Pruning requirements vary considerably from one type to another, but the aim is to encourage the development of new shoots.	Take 7.5-10cm/3-4in-long stem cuttings from half-ripe shoots during mid-summer and insert them in equal parts moist peat and sharp sand. Place in gentle warmth. Transfer the cuttings into individual pots when rooted and place in a frost-free greenhouse or cold frame during winter. In spring, either repot the plants into larger pots, or plant into a nurserybed.
 ***Fremontodendron californicum*** (syn. *Fremontia californica*) Height: 1.8-3m/6-10ft Slightly tender, deciduous or semi-evergreen shrub that is ideal for a warm wall. The three-lobed, dull green leaves are covered with a soft, brown down. Cup-shaped, golden yellow and waxy flowers, up to 5cm/2in wide, are borne throughout summer and into early autumn. 'Californian Glory' is particularly free-flowering.	Full sun and well-drained, sandy soil. Plant against a warm, sheltered wall. It is not self-clinging and therefore needs support from a trellis or wires. Tie the trunk and main shoots to it. No regular pruning is needed, other than the removal in mid-spring of shoots damaged during cold winters.	During early and mid-spring, sow seed 3mm/1/8in deep in pots of loam-based seed compost. Keep at 16°C/61°F. When large enough to handle, prick out the seedlings into individual pots and place in a cold frame or a sheltered position. Plant into a garden during the following spring.

Clematis tangutica
Height: 3-4.5m/10-15ft

Slender-stemmed, vigorous, spreading, deciduous climber with grey-green, deeply divided leaves and deep yellow, lantern-shaped flowers up to 5cm/2in wide from mid-summer to early autumn. The flowers are borne singly on 7.5-15cm/3-6in long stems, and are followed by attractive silvery seed heads. Supports are essential.

Jasminum nudiflorum
Winter-flowering Jasmine (UK)
Height: 1.2-1.8ft/4-6ft or more

Deciduous, lax, wall shrub with pliable stems that bear bright yellow flowers, up to 2.5cm/1in across, from late autumn to late spring. The flowers are borne on naked stems; leaves appear later. Given a suitable framework to lean upon, it often spreads to 1.8m/6ft.

Jasminum officinale
Common Jasmine (UK)
Common White Jasmine (UK)
Poet's Jessamine (USA)
Height: 6-7.5m/20-25ft

Hardy, deciduous, sprawling and twining climber with mid-green leaves formed of several leaflets. From early summer to autumn it displays scented, pure white flowers in lax clusters. It needs support.

Lonicera japonica
Japanese Honeysuckle (UK/USA)
Height: 4.5-7.5m/15-25ft

Hardy, slow-growing, evergreen climber with light green leaves. From early to late summer it produces fragrant, white to pale yellow flowers. A supporting framework is essential. The variety 'Halliana' is semi-evergreen, with exceptionally fragrant flowers.

PLANT NAME AND DESCRIPTION	SITUATION AND CULTIVATION	PROPAGATION

Hydrangea petiolaris
(syn. *H. scandens*)
Japanese Climbing Hydrangea (UK)
Height: 9m/30ft or more

Vigorous, deciduous, rambling climber with dark green, deeply serrated leaves and flat heads, up to 25cm/10in wide, of creamy white flowers during early summer. It has aerial roots and freely attaches itself to walls. It often takes up to five years for plants to bear flowers.

Full sun or light shade and fertile, moisture-retentive soil enriched with well-decayed compost or manure. It grows well on cold and exposed walls. Alternatively, it is excellent for clothing tree stumps as well as climbing tall trees.
No regular pruning is needed, other than cutting out damaged shoots in spring.

Take 7.5cm/3in-long cuttings during mid-summer and insert in pots of equal parts moist peat and sharp sand. Place in a cold frame. When cuttings are rooted, pot them up and place outdoors. When established and growing strongly, plant into a garden.

Passiflora caerulea
Blue Passion Flower (USA)
Common Passion Flower (UK)
Height: 1.8-4.5m/6-15ft or more

Slightly tender, scrambling and sprawling, deciduous climber with mid-green leaves and spectacular and intricately formed flowers from early to late summer. The flowers, about 7.5cm/3in wide, have white petals and a blue-purple centre. The form 'Constance Elliot' is pure white and slightly hardier.

Full sun or light shade and well-drained soil. Avoid excessively fertile soils as they encourage the development of leaves at the expense of flowers. A warm, sheltered wall is essential, with a trellis up which the plant can climb. Normally it is a vigorous climber, but this can be reduced by restricting the roots.
Prune in spring, shortening lateral shoots to 15cm/6in from their bases and cutting out dead stems. During severe winters plants may be damaged, but shoots then develop from the base.

Take 7.5-10cm/3-4in-long cuttings in mid-summer and insert in pots of equal parts moist peat and sharp sand. Place in gentle warmth. When rooted, pot up into individual pots and place in a cold frame. Plant into a garden in spring.

Solanum crispum
Chilean Potato Tree (UK)
Height: 3-6m/10-20ft

Bushy, scrambling, slightly tender, semi-evergreen climber with dark green leaves and purple-blue, star-shaped flowers with prominent yellow anthers from early to late summer. The 2.5cm/1in-wide flowers are borne in clusters up to 15cm/6in wide. The form 'Glasnevin' is slightly hardier and more floriferous.

Full sun and a warm and sheltered wall are essential. In cold areas it becomes semi-evergreen, with leaves withered and shoots dying back. It does not naturally cling to a wall and therefore needs the support of a trellis.
Prune in spring, thinning out weak shoots and cutting back those damaged by severe weather. Also, cut back the previous season's shoots to within 15cm/6in of their base.

Take 7.5cm/3in-long cuttings in mid-summer and insert them in equal parts moist peat and sharp sand. Place in gentle warmth. When rooted, pot up into individual pots and place in a cold frame. Later, when established and growing strongly, plant into a garden, preferably in spring.

Wisteria floribunda
Japanese Wisteria (UK/USA)
Height: 7.5-9m/25-30ft or more

Vigorous deciduous climber with light to mid-green leaves formed of twelve to nineteen leaflets. During late spring and early summer it develops large, pendulous bunches of fragrant, violet-blue flowers. There is a white form, 'Alba', while 'Macrobotrys' has lilac-blue and purple flowers in very large clusters.

Full sun and a warm and sheltered position are essential, as is fertile, moisture-retentive but well-drained soil.
Prune in late winter, cutting back all growths that produced flowers during the previous year to two or three buds from their base.

Take 7.5-10cm/3-4in-long cuttings in mid-summer and insert in pots of equal parts moist peat and sharp sand. Place in gentle warmth. When rooted, pot up into individual pots and place in a cold frame.

Lonicera periclymenum
Honeysuckle (UK)
Woodbine (UK/USA)
Height: 4.5-5.4m/15-18ft

Hardy deciduous climber. 'Belgica' (Early Dutch Honeysuckle) has reddish purple flowers, becoming yellow in early summer; 'Serotina' (Late Dutch Honeysuckle) has reddish purple flowers in late summer and autumn. A supporting framework is essential.

Polygonum baldschuanicum
Mile-a-minute Vine (UK)
Russian Vine (UK)
Height: 9-12m/30-40ft

Exceptionally vigorous, deciduous, shrubby climber, often growing 3m/10ft or more in a season. A strong supporting framework – or a large tree through which it can scramble – is essential. White or pale pink flowers from mid-summer to autumn.

Schizophragma integrifolium
Height: 4.5-6m/15-20ft

Hardy deciduous climber with bright green leaves, grey-green beneath. From mid-summer to autumn it produces lax flower heads, about 30cm/12in across and formed of small white flowers and long white bracts. It needs a supporting framework or a tree through which it can sprawl.

Trachelospermum jasminoides
Confederate Jasmine (USA)
Star Jasmine (USA)
Height: 3-4.5m/10-15ft

Hardy evergreen climber with leathery, dark green leaves. During mid- and late summer it bears fragrant, white flowers. 'Variegatum' has leaves edged and mottled in creamy white. It needs a supporting framework.

Climbers with attractive leaves

PLANT NAME AND DESCRIPTION	SITUATION AND CULTIVATION	PROPAGATION

Actinidia kolomikta
Kolomikta Vine (UK)
Height: 2.4-3.6m/8-12ft

Deciduous spreading climber, sometimes as high as 4.5m/15ft but usually about 3m/10ft. Its dark green, slightly heart-shaped leaves, up to 15cm/6in long, are marked at their tips and upper parts in white or pink. White, slightly fragrant flowers are borne in early summer.

Fertile, well-drained, slightly acid or alkaline soil suits it, but avoid shallow and chalky situations. Plant it in full or light shade. It is not self-supporting and therefore needs a framework of plastic-covered netting or wood up which to clamber.
No regular pruning is needed, other than restricting growth and cutting out thin shoots in late winter.
This climber is said to attract cats, so protect plants – especially young ones – from their attentions.

Take 7.5-10cm/3-4in-long cuttings from the current season's shoots in mid-summer and insert them in equal parts moist peat and sharp sand. Place in gentle warmth. When rooted, transfer them to individual pots, later planting into a garden.

Hedera canariensis 'Gloire de Marengo'
(syn. *H. canariensis* 'Variegata')
Height: 4.5-6m/15-20ft

Vigorous evergreen climber with large, thick and leathery leaves, deep green at their centres, merging into silvery grey and with creamy white edges. It creates a dense screen of colourful leaves. This is a variegated form of the Algerian Ivy, also known as Canary Island and Madeira Ivy.

Like all ivies, this is a versatile climber, thriving in most types of soil and most aspects. It is ideal for clothing cold and sunless walls.
Being self-clinging, it does not need to be provided with support. Its eventual size very much depends on the wall on which it is climbing. It can also be used to cover unsightly tree stumps.
No regular pruning is needed, other than cutting back excessively large plants in late winter or early spring. Also, cut out long shoots in mid-summer.

Take 7.5-13cm/3-5in-long cuttings during mid-summer and insert them in pots of equal parts moist peat and sharp sand. Place in gentle warmth. If the plant is to be grown as a climber, take the cuttings from long shoots of the current season's growth. If a bushy, low-growing plant is desired, take them from older shoots. Pot them up into individual pots when rooted, then plant into a garden when established and acclimatized to outdoor conditions.

Hedera colchica 'Dentata Variegata'
Height: 6-7.5m/20-25ft

Vigorous evergreen climber with thick, leathery, bright green leaves edged in creamy white. Their colouring when young is bright creamy yellow. This has the largest leaves of all ivies, up to 15-20cm/6-8in long. It is a variegated form of the Persian Ivy, also known as Fragrant Ivy and Colchis Ivy.

It grows in most soils and conditions, and is hardier than *Hedera canariensis* 'Gloire de Marengo'. It is self-clinging and soon clothes walls, the surrounds of porches or old tree stumps.
No regular pruning is needed, other than trimming to shape in late winter or early spring and cutting out long and straggly shoots during mid-summer.

Take 7.5-13cm/3-5in-long cuttings during mid-summer and insert them in pots of equal parts moist peat and sharp sand. Place in gentle warmth. If the plant is to be grown as a climber, take the cuttings from long shoots of the current season's growth. If a bushy, low-growing plant is desired, take them from older shoots. Pot them up into individual pots when rooted, then plant them into a garden when established and acclimatized to outdoor conditions.

Hedera colchica 'Sulphur Heart'
(syn. *H. colchica* 'Paddy's Pride')
Height: 5.4-6m/18-20ft

Vigorous evergreen climber with large, leathery, broadly oval, deep green leaves splashed and irregularly streaked in bright yellow. Sometimes almost an entire leaf is yellow. As leaves age, they broaden and the yellowing is not so pronounced, instead being sectioned between the veins.

It grows in most soils and conditions, and is hardier than the *Hedera canariensis* 'Gloire de Marengo'. It is self-clinging and soon clothes patio walls, the surrounds of porches, old tree stumps and garden walls. Additionally, it is ideal as a ground-cover plant.
No regular pruning is needed, other than trimming to shape in late winter and cutting out long and straggly shoots during mid-summer.

Take 7.5-13cm/3-5in-long cuttings during mid-summer and insert them in pots of equal parts moist peat and sharp sand. Place them in gentle warmth. If the plant is to be grown as a climber, take the cuttings from long shoots of the current season's growth. If a bushy, low-growing plant is desired, take them from older shoots. Pot them up into individual pots when rooted; plant into a garden when established and acclimatized to outdoor conditions.

Actinidia chinensis
Chinese Gooseberry (UK/USA)
Kiwi Fruit (UK)
Height: 6-7.5m/20-25ft or more

Vigorous deciduous climber with large, heart-shaped, dark green leaves. From early to late summer it has creamy white flowers about 36mm/1½in across. If both male and female plants are present – and in warm regions – succulent fruits are borne.

Celastrus orbiculatus
Climbing Bittersweet (UK)
Oriental Bittersweet (UK/USA)
Staff Vine (UK)
Height: 6-7.5m/20-25ft

Vigorous, hardy deciduous climber with round to pear-shaped, mid-green leaves. During autumn the leaves assume rich yellow tints. Additionally, in autumn the brown seed capsules split, revealing scarlet and orange-yellow fruits.

Hedera helix 'Glacier'
Height: 1.8-3m/6-10ft

A hardy, small-leaved, evergreen ivy with superbly attractive, somewhat diamond-shaped leaves, which are variegated grey-green with irregular creamy white edges. It creates a feast of year round colour.

Jasminum officinale 'Aureum'
Height: 4.5-6m/15-20ft

Hardy, deciduous, sprawling and twining climber with mid-green leaves blotched with creamy yellow. Each leaf is formed of several leaflets. Throughout summer it bears scented, pure white flowers in lax clusters.

PLANT NAME AND DESCRIPTION	SITUATION AND CULTIVATION	PROPAGATION

***Hedera helix* 'Goldheart'**
Height: 3.6-7.5m/12-25ft

Hardy evergreen climber. This small-leaved ivy is strikingly attractive, revealing shiny green leaves centrally and conspicuously splashed with yellow. With age the yellowing fades slightly, but is still attractive.
    This is a form of the Common Ivy, also known in North America as English Ivy.

It grows in most soils and conditions, even brightening north and east-facing walls. It is self-clinging and soon clothes walls. Bright, sunny positions encourage rapid growth and brightly coloured leaves; in shade growth is slow and leaves less colourful.
    Unlike large-leaved ivies, it is not suitable as a ground-cover plant and is normally planted to climb walls. No regular pruning is needed, other than trimming to shape in late winter.

Take 7.5cm/3in-long cuttings from the current season's growth during mid-summer and insert them in pots of equal parts moist peat and sharp sand. Place them in gentle warmth. Pot them up into individual pots when rooted; plant into a garden when established and acclimatized to outdoor conditions.
    Occasionally this plant is grown as a houseplant. When it becomes too large to be grown indoors, place it outside in late spring and slowly acclimatize it to outdoor conditions.

***Humulus lupulus* 'Aureus'**
Golden-leaved Hop (UK)
Yellow European Hop (USA)
Height: 1.8-3m/6-10ft

Fast-growing herbaceous climber with scrambling stems densely clothed in three- to five-lobed, coarsely toothed, bright yellowish green leaves. In winter, this climber dies down to soil-level, surviving winter in a dormant state and sending up fresh shoots in spring.

Fertile, moisture-retentive but well-drained soil in full sun. Rich soil is essential as each year this climber produces a completely new array of leaves.
    Remove dead stems and leaves in autumn. In cold areas, leave this job until spring, so that the stems can protect the roots in winter.
    This climber is superb when trained round a rustic arch over a path or up a tripod in a flower border.

It is easily increased by lifting and dividing congested plants in autumn or spring. Replant only the younger parts from around the outside of the clump.

***Lonicera japonica* 'Aureo-reticulata'**
Variegated Japanese Honeysuckle (UK/USA)
Height: 1.2-2.4m/4-8ft

Evergreen or semi-evergreen climber with oval to oblong, light green leaves with the midrib and veins attractively lined in yellow. It seldom flowers. In exceptionally cold winters the stems and leaves often die back to soil-level, but it usually produces fresh shoots in spring.

Fertile, well-drained soil and a position in full sun or light shade suit this climber. It is not self-supporting and therefore needs support from a wooden trellis or plastic-covered wire netting. In its early stages, train it up a small cane until it reaches the supporting framework.
    No regular pruning is needed, other than occasionally cutting out old shoots after flowering.

Take 7.5-10cm/3-4in-long cuttings in mid-summer from shoots produced earlier in the year. Remove the lower leaves and trim beneath a leaf joint. Insert them in pots of equal parts moist peat and sharp sand and place in a cold frame. After roots have formed, pot up into individual pots of loam-based compost. When established and growing strongly, plant into a garden.

Parthenocissus tricuspidata
Boston Ivy (UK/USA)
Height: 9-12m/30-40ft

Hardy, vigorous, self-supporting, deciduous climber with variably shaped green leaves, usually three-lobed, though leaves on young plants are sometimes formed of three leaflets. The lower and mature leaves can be up to 25cm/10in wide, but are normally only 13cm/5in wide. 'Veitchii' has smaller leaves, tinged purple when young.

Fertile, moisture-retentive soil and a position in sun or partial shade. It generally grows too large to be planted against a house wall and is better suited to scrambling in a tree or sprawling over a garden wall.
    Pruning is usually needed to restrain it. Tackle this job in summer.

Take 10cm/4in-long cuttings in late summer from shoots produced early in the season. Trim off the lower leaves and sever the cuttings below a leaf joint. Insert them in pots of equal parts moist peat and sharp sand and keep at 13°C/55°F. When rooted, pot up individually and place in a cold frame. Later, when established and growing strongly, plant into a garden.

Parthenocissus henryana
Chinese Virginia Creeper (UK)
Height: 6-7.5m/20-25ft

Deciduous, self-clinging climber with three- to five-lobed, dark green leaves, attractively variegated white and pink along the veins and midrib. In autumn the variegation become even more pronounced and the green becomes brilliant red.

Parthenocissus quinquefolia
American Ivy (USA)
Five-leaved Ivy (USA)
True Virginia Creeper (UK)
Virginia Creeper (UK/USA)
Height: 10.5-18m/35-60ft or more

Vigorous, hardy, deciduous, self-clinging climber with dull green, five-lobed leaves that in autumn assume brilliant scarlet and orange shades.

Vitis coignetiae
Crimson Glory Vine (USA)
Japanese Crimson Glory Vine (UK)
Height: 23m/40ft and more

Hardy, vigorous deciduous climber with rounded but lobed, mid-green leaves; the undersides are covered in rust-red hairs. The base of each leaf is heart shaped. In autumn the leaves assume rich colours, first yellow, then orange-red and later crimson.

***Vitis vinifera* 'Purpurea'**
Teinturier Grape (UK)
Height: 4.5-5.4m/15-18ft

Hardy deciduous grape vine with claret-red, rounded and lobed leaves that in autumn deepen to rich purple. It is ideal for covering a large rustic arch.

Planting roses

For many years, roses were sold only in bare-rooted form and were despatched to customers, packed in pyramidal straw bundles tied with string, during winter, when dormant and free from leaves. Nowadays, bare-rooted roses are sent out from nurseries in large, multi-layer paper sacks closed by machine stitching, and roses growing in containers are sold throughout the year. Container-grown roses can be planted whenever the soil is not frozen or waterlogged and are invariably sold by garden centres.

PLANTING A BARE-ROOTED BUSH ROSE

Plant a bare-rooted rose from late autumn to late winter. If you are going to plant the bush within a week of receiving it from the nursery, you can place it unopened in a cool, airy shed, cellar or garage. If you need to delay planting because of the weather, remove all the wrapping and heel-in the roots in a sheltered corner. Dig a 20-25cm/8-10in-deep trench, place the roots in it and cover them with soil. Ensure the soil remains moist.

To plant a bare-rooted rose, dig a hole 50-60cm/20-24in wide and 20-25cm/8-10in deep. Fill the base with equal parts good soil and moist peat and add a sprinkling of bonemeal to encourage root growth. Check that the hole is large enough to accommodate the roots, then form and firm a mound of soil in the base.

Position the bush in the hole and spread out the roots over the mound. Check that the union (just below the lowest stem) between the roots and the varietal part will be about 2.5cm/1in below the surface when the hole is filled in. (Placing a straight stick across the hole will enable you to check the height.) Allow for consolidation of the soil after planting.

Carefully work a mixture of equal parts good soil and moist peat between the roots and sharply lift the stem up and down a few times to ensure this works down between the roots – air pockets left around the roots will reduce the speed of the plant's establishment.

Firm the soil in layers around the roots, using the heel of your shoe – never just fill up the hole with soil and then firm it. After planting, use a garden fork to level the soil, and remove footprints. Ensure that the bush is labelled.

PLANTING A CONTAINER-GROWN BUSH ROSE

1 Water the compost in the container thoroughly during the days before planting it.
2 Dig out a hole 38-45cm/15-18in wide and 25cm/10in deep. Fork the base and add moist peat and a sprinkling of bonemeal to assist in the growth of roots.
3 Place the rose and container in the hole and place a straight stick across the hole to check that the top of the compost is level with the surrounding soil.
4 Carefully remove the container, replace the rose in the planting hole and firm soil and peat around it in layers.

Above: The miniature rose 'Pompon de Paris, Climbing' is one of the few miniature climbing roses. It is ideal for covering a wall up to 2.4m/8ft high with clusters of dainty, small, double rose-pink flowers borne on arching stems. It flowers early in the rose season. Like other climbing roses it is not self-supporting and requires a framework upon which it can lean and be secured.

PLANTING A CONTAINER-GROWN BUSH ROSE

You can plant container-grown roses throughout the year, whenever the soil is workable.

Before removing the rose from its container, make sure that the compost is moist; this may mean watering the plant several times during the preceding days. Take care not to splash water on the flowers or leaves.

Dig out a hole 38-45cm/15-18in wide and 25cm/10in deep. Fork over the base, then firm, and add a 5cm/2in-thick mixture of friable soil, moist peat and a sprinkling of bonemeal. Position the plant and container on top and check that the top of the root-ball is level with the surrounding soil. (Lay a stick across the hole to check this.) Carefully remove the container and place soil around the root-ball. Firm the soil in layers, rather than all at one time. Use a garden fork to level the surface and to remove footprints. Ensure that the plant is labelled.

PLANTING A CLIMBER

When planting a climber, take care that the roots are not too close to a wall, where the soil is dry. Instead, dig the hole no nearer than 38cm/15in to the wall, slope its base away from the wall and mix moist peat or well-decomposed compost with the soil to assist in moisture-retention.

Space out the roots in the planting hole and carefully spread and firm soil over them in thin layers. When planting is complete, water the soil thoroughly and continue to water the soil regularly during the first year.

PLANTING A STANDARD ROSE

Standard roses differ from bush roses in having a long, straight, upright stem between the roots and the plant's head. The length of the stem varies considerably, from miniature standards with stems 20-30cm/8-12in long, to half-standards with 75cm/30in stems, and full-standards at 1.3m/4¹/₂ft.

Standard roses must be planted and supported at the same time. If this is neglected, the top of the rose might snap off during high winds. Lightly clipping off long stems when planting helps to reduce the area buffeted by wind. Later, plants can be properly pruned.

Form a hole 50-60cm/20-24in wide and 25cm/10in deep. Fork over the soil in the base, then firm it to form a slight mound.

Drive a stout stake 30-45cm/12-18in into the soil, positioning it slightly off-centre and towards the prevailing wind. Its top should be slightly below the lowest branch.

Position the roots in the hole and spread them out. Check that the soil mark on the stem is 12-25mm/¹/₂-1in deeper than before to allow for soil settlement. Position the stem on the lee side of the stake, start to replace the soil over the roots and firm it over them in layers. Scarify the surface to remove footprints.

Check that the stake's top is 2.5cm/1in below the lowest branch, then fit tree ties – three for a full-standard and two for a half-standard. Re-check the ties several times during the following season to ensure that they are firm but not strangulating the stem.

Roses for beds, walls and pergolas

TYPE OF ROSE	SITUATION AND CULTIVATION	PRUNING
**Species Roses** *Rosa canina* Brier Rose (UK/USA) Dog Brier (USA) Dog Rose (UK/USA) Height: 1.5-2.1m/5-7ft Spread: 1.2-1.8m/4-6ft Hardy, deciduous shrub with light green leaves and white to pale pink flowers up to 5cm/2in wide during early summer. Forms include 'Abbotswood' (shown) and 'Andersonii' (deep pink).	Full sun and light, well-drained but moisture-retentive, neutral or slightly acid soil. Excessive fertility is not necessary. This is a hardy species and needs good air circulation, but avoid positions in strong wind.	In the second year after planting, cut out dead and thin shoots during late winter. The following autumn again cut out thin and weak growths, as well as dead and diseased wood. In late winter or early spring tip back all vigorous sideshoots. At the same time remove at their base a few old shoots. During the following autumn cut out thin, weak, dead and diseased shoots. Repeat this cycle of autumn and late winter or early spring pruning during the following years.
**Hybrid Tea Roses** Height: 60cm-1.2m/2-4ft (range) Spread: 60-90cm/2-3ft (range) Now properly classified as 'Large-flowered Roses', this group is still popularly known as Hybrid Teas. They originated in 1867 from a cross between a Tea Rose and a Hybrid Perpetual. The flowers of Hybrid Teas are large and shapely, and form a distinctive central cone.	Full sun or light shade and deeply prepared, well-drained but moisture-retentive soil. Dig the soil thoroughly in late autumn or early winter, adding plenty of well-decayed compost or manure. Roses grow best in slightly acid soil, about pH 6.0-6.5. A few weeks before planting, fork in a light dusting of bonemeal. Container-grown plants can be planted at any time when the soil is not waterlogged or frozen, while bare-rooted types are put in from late autumn to early spring.	In the first year cut back the bush to 10-13cm/4-5in above the ground during late winter or early spring. Cut just above outward-pointing buds. The following autumn cut back the ends of shoots, then in late winter or early spring cut out dead or diseased wood. At the same time cut back strong shoots to 23cm/9in long, and weak ones to 15cm/6in. Repeat this cycle of autumn and late winter or early spring pruning during subsequent years.
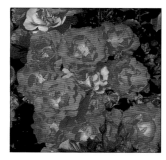**Floribunda Roses** Height: 60cm-1.5ft/2-5ft (range) Spread: 45cm-1m/1¹/₂-3¹/₂ft (range) Now properly classified as 'Cluster-flowered Roses', this group is still best known as Floribundas. They originated in 1924 from a cross between a Polyantha and a Hybrid Tea. Floribundas bear flowers in clusters, with several blooms opening at the same time. The flowers are usually smaller than those on Hybrid Teas.	Full sun or light shade and deeply prepared, well-drained but moisture-retentive soil. Dig the soil thoroughly in late autumn or early winter, adding plenty of well-decayed compost or manure. Roses grow best in slightly acid soil, about pH 6.0-6.5. A few weeks before planting, fork in a light dusting of bonemeal. Container-grown plants can be planted at any time when the soil is not waterlogged or frozen, while bare-rooted types are planted from late autumn to early spring.	In the first year cut back the bush to 15-23cm/6-9in above the ground during late winter or early spring. Cut just above outward-pointing buds. The following autumn cut back the ends of shoots. Then, in late winter or early spring, cut out dead or diseased wood. At the same time cut back old wood to 15-23cm/6-9in long, and laterals (sideshoots) to 10-15cm/4-6in. Repeat this cycle of autumn and late winter or early spring pruning during subsequent years.
**Grandiflora Roses** Height: 1.2-1.5ft/4-5ft (range) Spread: 75-90cm/2¹/₂-3ft (range) Grandiflora is very much an American classification and refers to large floribunda varieties. It does not specifically indicate the size of their flowers, but to the plant's size. It is sometimes used in British rose catalogues to describe varieties such as 'Queen Elizabeth'.	Full sun or light shade and deeply prepared, well-drained but moisture-retentive soil. Dig the soil thoroughly in late autumn or early winter, adding plenty of well-decayed compost or manure. Roses grow best in slightly acid soil, about pH 6.0-6.5. A few weeks before planting, fork in a light dusting of bonemeal. Container-grown plants can be planted at any time when the soil is not waterlogged or frozen, while bare-rooted types are planted from late autumn to early spring.	In the first year cut back the bush to 23cm/9in above the ground during late winter or early spring. Cut just above outward-pointing buds. The following autumn cut back the ends of shoots. Later, in late winter or early spring, cut out dead or diseased wood. At the same time cut back old wood to 23-30cm/9-12in long, and laterals (sideshoots) to 15-23cm/6-9in. Repeat this cycle of autumn and late winter or early spring pruning during subsequent years.

Alba Roses
This group dates back to the Middle Ages and derives from *Rosa alba*, a vigorous, upright, hardy shrub with pink, blush and white flowers, mainly during mid-summer.
Varieties include: 'Alba Maxima' (fragrant, creamy white flowers on bushes 1.8m/6ft high and 1.5m/5ft wide); 'Félicité Parmentier' (densely packed buds opening to clear, flesh pink, on bushes 1.2m/4ft high and wide).

Bourbon Roses
A group with mainly China and Portland roses in their ancestry, together with a touch of a few other Old Roses. The flowers have an Old Rose fragrance.
Varieties include: 'Boule de Neige' (fragrant, double, ivory-white flowers on bushes 1.8m/6ft high and 1.2m/4ft wide); 'Souvenir de la Malmaison' (fragrant, soft pink flowers paling at their edges on bushes 90cm/3ft high and wide).

Damask Roses
A group derived from *R. damascena* and revealing elegant foliage and flowers during mid-summer; flowers are usually scented.
Varieties include: 'Celsiana' (soft pink flowers with golden stamens on bushes 1.5m/5ft high and 1.2m/4ft wide); 'Mme Hardy' (pink-tinged white flowers on bushes 1.8m/6ft high and 1.5m/5ft wide. Flowers have a slight lemony fragrance).

Gallica Roses
These are derived from *R. gallica*. The flowers are large and come in magnificent colours including shades of crimson, purple and mauve.
Varieties include: 'Belle de Crécy' (rich cerise-pink flowers becoming soft parma violet on bushes 1.2m/4ft high and 90cm/3ft wide); 'Empress Joséphine: (large, clear rose-pink flowers veined in deep pink on bushes 90cm/3ft high and wide).

TYPE OF ROSE	SITUATION AND CULTIVATION	PRUNING
 **Climbing Roses** Height: 2.4-9m/8-30ft (range) Spread: 1.8-7.5m/6-25ft (range) Climbing roses embrace a group of hardy deciduous shrubs that bear flowers each year on stiff stems that soon form a more or less permanent framework. The flowers are usually borne singly or in small groups, and some varieties have the ability to produce further blooms after their main flush, which is usually during early summer.	Full sun or light shade and deeply prepared, well-drained but moisture-retentive soil. Dig the soil thoroughly in late autumn or early winter, adding plenty of well-decayed compost or manure. Roses grow best in slightly acid soil, about pH 6.0-6.5. A few weeks before planting, fork in a light dusting of bonemeal. Container-grown plants can be planted at any time when the soil is not waterlogged or frozen, while bare-rooted types are planted from late autumn to early spring.	Climbing roses create a permanent framework of branches, from which flowering shoots arise. Therefore, the purpose of pruning is to encourage the regular development of the young, flowering shoots. Additionally, old and exhausted main shoots may occasionally need to be cut out. Most climbers flower on the current season's shoots; therefore, in spring cut back shoots which flowered during the previous year to two or three buds from the older wood.
 **Rambling Roses** Height: 3.6-9m/12-30ft (range) Spread: 2.4-7.5m/8-25ft (range) Rambling roses embrace a wide group of hardy deciduous shrubs with pliable, long stems that bear masses of small flowers in large clusters during early summer, usually in one single flush. The growth is vigorous and robust, somewhat graceful and able to cover large areas.	Full sun or light shade and deeply prepared, well-drained but moisture-retentive soil. Dig the soil thoroughly in late autumn or early winter, adding plenty of well-decayed compost or manure. Roses grow best in slightly acid soil, about pH 6.0-6.5. A few weeks before planting, fork in a light dusting of bonemeal. Container-grown plants can be planted at any time when the soil is not waterlogged or frozen, while bare-rooted types are planted from late autumn to early spring.	Ramblers have variable growth, depending on their parentage, but in general they annually produce long shoots which bear flowers during the following season. Therefore, in late summer or early autumn, after the completion of flowering, cut back old flowered shoots to their point of origin. Additionally, cut back any lateral shoots to two or three eyes from their base. Train and tie in new shoots to a supporting framework.
 **Miniature Roses** Height: 15-45cm/6-18in (range) Spread: 23-50cm/9-20in (range) True miniatures are derived from *Rosa chinensis* 'Minima', also known as Rouletti Roses after Dr. Roulet who introduced them into Switzerland where at one time they were grown in pots on windowsills. In about 1922, they were rediscovered by Henri Correvon.	Full sun or light shade and deeply prepared, well-drained but moisture-retentive soil. Dig the soil thoroughly in late autumn or early winter, adding plenty of well-decayed compost or manure. Roses grow best in slightly acid soil, about pH 6.0-6.5. A few weeks before planting, fork a light dusting of bonemeal into the soil. Container-grown plants can be planted at any time when the soil is not waterlogged or frozen, while bare-rooted types are planted from late autumn to early spring.	Very little pruning is needed, other than the removal of dead, diseased, thin and spindly growth in spring. Additionally, ensure the bush retains an even and attractive shape. Instead of secateurs, it is usually easier to use sharp scissors.
 **Patio Roses** Height: 45-60cm/18-24in (range) Spread: 38-50cm/15-20in (range) This is a relatively new group of small roses and, correctly, they are low-growing floribundas. They have a bushy stature and repeat-flowering nature, and are hardier and more robust than true miniature roses. In some catalogues, however, they are not distinguished from miniature roses or dwarf polyanthas.	Full sun or light shade and deeply prepared, well-drained but moisture-retentive soil. Dig the soil thoroughly in late autumn or early winter, adding plenty of well-decayed compost or manure. Roses grow best in slightly acid soil, about pH 6.0-6.5. A few weeks before planting, fork in a light dusting of bonemeal. Container-grown plants can be planted at any time when the soil is not waterlogged or frozen, while bare-rooted types are planted from late autumn to early spring.	In the first year cut back each each shoot to 15cm/6in above the ground during late winter or early spring. Cut just above outward-pointing buds. The following autumn cut back the ends of shoots and then in late winter or early spring cut out dead or diseased wood. At the same time cut back old wood to 15cm/6in long and laterals (sideshoots) to 10cm/4in. Repeat this cycle of autumn and late winter or early spring pruning during subsequent years.

Hybrid Musk Roses
These are derived from *R. moschata* (Autumn Musk Rose); flowers appear from late summer to the frosts of autumn.
    Varieties include: 'Buff Beauty' (warm buff to apricot-yellow, scented flowers borne in large trusses on shrubs 1.5m/5ft high and wide); 'Prosperity' (semi-double, ivory-white flowers borne in large trusses on bushes 1.8m/6ft high and 1.2m/4ft wide).

Hybrid Perpetuals
These are derived from China, Bourbon and Portland types. They have cabbage-like flowers from early summer to autumn.
    Varieties include: 'Baron Girod de l'Ain' (large, dark crimson flowers, petals edged in white on bushes 1.5m/5ft high and 1.2m/4ft wide); 'Gloire de Ducher' (fragrant, deep crimson flowers turning purple on bushes 1.8m/6ft high and 1.2m/4ft wide).

Hybrid Sweetbriars
Also known as Penzance Briars, these are hardy, vigorous and free-flowering, with richly scented, semi-double flowers in early and mid-summer.
    Varieties include: 'Amy Robsart' (semi-double, rich rose-pink flowers on bushes 2.4m/8ft high and wide); 'Janet's Pride' (bright, cherry-pink flowers with nearly white centres on bushes 1.8m/6ft high and 1.5m/5ft wide).

Moss Roses
These are natural mutations (sports) of *R. centifolia* 'Muscosa', or hybrids derived from it. They have flowers up to 7.5cm/3in wide during early summer and into mid-summer. They are characterized by having resin-scented mossy glands on the leaf stalks and outer parts of flowers.
    Varieties include: 'Maréchal Davoust' (intense carmine-pink flowers turning to lilac and purple on bushes 1.2m/4ft high and wide).

Constructing a rock garden

Creating a rock garden that will remain attractive for twenty or more years demands good planning and careful construction. Rock garden plants – and especially alpines – need a sunny position and soil that is well drained.

SELECTING A SITE AND ASPECT

Choosing a suitable site for a rock garden is essential to ensure a long life and ease of maintenance. Choose a site that faces the sun for most of the day; slight shade for a few hours is welcome as it prevents plants and the soil becoming too hot. Avoid areas that are constantly in shade.

Avoid positions under trees; both deciduous and evergreen types create shade, and drip water over plants long after a rain shower ceases. In autumn, deciduous trees also blanket soil and plants with leaves. As well as suffocating plants, leaves retain moisture around them which encourages the onset of diseases and the presence of pests.

The soil must be well drained and free from perennial weeds, especially Horsetail and Couch Grass. Also, it should not be contaminated with soil pests such as wireworms and cockchafers, which are present in large numbers in land newly converted from pasture.

A windbreak, perhaps formed of conifers positioned on the cold, windward side, will help to protect plants.

CONSTRUCTING A ROCK GARDEN

Ground with a gentle slope will be relatively easy to make into a home for rock garden plants, but you can also import well-drained soil to create an artificial mound.

Check that the drainage is good and that you don't need to install land drains. If the surface of the slope is slightly sandy and the top 30cm/12in of soil is well drained, you can position rocks directly on the surface, without adding further soil. Usually, however, you will need to improve the soil by removing the top 25cm/10in of soil, but still leaving a gentle slope (an incline of some 10° is about right). On the base, lay and firm a 10cm/4in-thick layer of clean bricks or stones. Cover this with 5cm/2in of sharp sand, then add and firm a 10cm/4in layer of well-drained topsoil.

Right: Rock gardens can be constructed on near flat surfaces by using rocks to form varying levels of raised beds. Here the golden yellow flowers of *Hypericum olympicum* appear during mid-and late summer. Plants grow 23-30cm/9-12in high and with a spread up to 30cm/12in or more.

MAKING A SCREE BED

1 Mark out an area at the base of a rock garden so that it widens gently to form a mushroom shape. Dig out the area to 38cm/15in deep and fill with 15cm/6in of clean rubble. Over this, form a 5cm/2in-thick layer of coarse sand.
2 On top of sand, form a 15cm/6in-thick layer of one part topsoil, one of moist peat and three of sharp grit.
3 Position the rocks, so that they appear to be a small outcrop from the rock garden. This helps to unify the scree bed with the rock garden.
4 Plant the alpines, then spread a 2.5cm/1in-thick layers of shingle or chippings over the surface.

TYPES OF ROCKS

The range of rocks that can be used to construct a rock garden is wide but it is best to use local types so that they blend with the surroundings. The five main types of stone are:

- **Sandstone** Soft and mellow in appearance and available in several colours. Weathering is usually slow.

- **Limestone** Weathers quickly and soon loses angular edges. Unfortunately, it is not suitable for lime-hating plants. There are several forms – usually, but not always, grey.

- **Granite** Weathering is slow and the stone is hard and fine-grained.

- **Slate** Available in several shades, varying from grey to green or purple; weathering is slow, but more rapid than granite.

- **Tufa** Porous rock, a form of magnesium limestone, is not used extensively in rock gardens. Instead, plants are sometimes planted into it to create distinctive features in rock gardens, scree beds, troughs or raised beds.

BUYING ROCKS

Select the type of stone you want and then contact a local supplier. Much of the expense in buying stone is the cost of delivery.

- The amount of stone required depends on the type of rock garden; those with only a slight slope need less than where a steep rise is required. However, a rock garden 3m/10ft square will need about 2 tonnes/4410lbs of stone.

- Agree the cost of stone and delivery charges before buying.

- If practical, inspect the rocks before buying; make sure there is a mixture of large and small pieces.

- If possible, be on site when the stones are delivered; check they are what you ordered.

- Do not economize by taking stones from the countryside. Never use old pieces of concrete.

LAYING THE STONES

Assess the size and shapes of stones by spreading them out. Start positioning them from the bottom of the slope and work to the top. Most rock gardens on a slope are designed to form a sloping terrace, with tiers of stones forming natural-looking strata.

Each stone should tilt backwards slightly, with one-third to one-half of it buried in the soil. This ensures that each stone is firmly held in place and also replicates natural arrangements of stones. Dig out some soil and set the first stone in position, then check it from all angles. When satisfied that it is right, firm soil around it, ensuring that no air pockets remain. The position of the second rock will be determined by the first. Continue with other rocks in the same stratum; each stratum line should follow at the same angle across the slope.

When the first tier is complete, form the second in the same way as the first. Use slightly smaller rocks for each progressive tier. When all the rocks are in place, stand back from the area and check that it looks right from all angles. Then spread topsoil between the rocks, leaving space for the plants and a planting mixture.

MAKING A SCREE BED

Screes naturally occur at the bases of cliffs or gulleys and are formed of a scattering of small, loose stones. In gardens a scree bed will usually be constructed at the base of a rock garden and planted with further alpine plants. A scree bed is a relatively inexpensive feature, as it does not involve buying expensive rocks. However, a few rocks positioned to give the impression of an outcrop from the main rock garden help to unify both features and to prevent the scree bed appearing to have been added as an after thought.

To make a scree bed, mark out a position at the base of a rock garden; increasingly widen the area slightly from the rock garden's base to create a natural appearance. Dig out the area to 38cm/15in deep and fill with 15cm/6in of clean rubble. Compact it slightly and add a 5cm/2in-thick layer of coarse sand or gravel. Over this spread a 15cm/6in-thick mixture of one part topsoil, one of moist peat and three of sharp grit. Plant alpines in this, then add a 2.5cm/1in-thick layer of 6mm/¼in shingle on top to ensure that the surface is well drained.

Plants for rock gardens and dry-stone walls

PLANT NAME AND DESCRIPTION	SITUATION AND CULTIVATION	PROPAGATION

Aethionema armenum 'Warley Rose'
(syn. *A.* 'Warley Rose')
Persian Candytuft (UK)
Height: 10-15cm/4-6in
Spread: 30-38cm/12-15in

Hardy herbaceous perennial with lax, loosely branched stems and grey-green leaves. During mid- and late spring it develops domed heads of deep rose flowers. Other species include *A. grandiflorum* (pink, and flowering

Full sun and light, well-drained soil. Set the plants 30-38cm/12-15in apart. After the flowers fade, remove the dead heads, together with their stems.

Increase the hybrid 'Warley Rose' from 5cm/2in-long cuttings taken in early to mid-summer and insert in equal parts moist peat and sharp sand. Place them in gentle warmth until rooted, then pot up and place in a cold frame until established. Plant into a garden in spring.
    Increase *A. grandiflorum* from seeds sown in pots of sandy compost and placed in a cold greenhouse or cold frame.

Alyssum saxatile
(now known as *Aurinia saxatilis*)
Gold Dust (UK)
Height: 23-30cm/9-12in
Spread: 30-45cm/12-18in

Hardy, shrubby evergreen perennial with grey-green leaves and masses of clustered flowers from mid-spring to early summer. Varieties include 'Dudley Neville' (biscuit yellow), 'Citrina' (bright lemon-gold), 'Compacta' (golden yellow and only 15cm/6in high).

Full sun and well-drained soil suit it. Set the plants 25-30cm/10-12in apart. After the flowers fade, cut back the woody stems to encourage the development of new growth. This also prolongs the life of the plants and keeps them compact.

Sow seeds 6mm/¼in deep in pots of seed compost during early spring. Place in a cold frame or cool greenhouse. Germination takes seven to ten days. When large enough to handle, prick out the seedlings into 7.5cm/3in-wide pots. Slowly harden off and plant into a garden in late summer.
    Alternatively, take 5cm/2in-long cuttings in early summer and insert them in equal parts moist peat and sharp sand. Place in a cold frame. When rooted, pot up into 7.5cm/3in-wide pots.

Aubrieta deltoidea
Height: 7.5-10cm/3-4in
Spread: 45-60cm/18-24in

Hardy, low-growing, evergreen perennial with small, hoary green leaves and masses of cross-shaped flowers up to 18mm/¾in wide, in shades of rose-lilac to purple, from early spring to early summer. There are many varieties, colourful ones include 'Variegata' (purple flowers and white leaf edges) or 'Aurea' (purple flowers and gold leaf edges).

Full sun and well-drained, preferably limy soil. Space plants 30cm/12in apart when used as edgings. It can also be planted to grow in crevices in dry-stone walls and between paving slabs and steps in cottage-garden settings. After the flowers fade, clip back the plants to near ground level to keep them restrained and neat, and to encourage the development of further flowers. However, only lightly cut back the old flower heads of plants grown on walls.

Sow seeds thinly and evenly in a seedbed outdoors, in drills 6mm/¼in deep and 20cm/8in apart, from mid-spring to early summer. Germination take two to three weeks. When large enough to handle, thin the seedlings to 15cm/6in apart. Move them to their flowering positions in late summer. Alternatively, divide congested plants in late summer or early autumn.

Helianthemum nummularium
Sun Rose (UK/USA)
Rock Rose (UK/USA)
Height: 10-15cm/4-6in
Spread: 45-60cm/18-24in

Hardy, low-growing, evergreen shrub with deep glossy green to soft silvery grey leaves and saucer-shaped flowers 12-25mm/½-1in wide during early and mid-summer. The colour range is wide, from white and cream to yellow, orange, scarlet, crimson and pink.

Full sun and light, poor and sandy, well-drained soil. Set the plants about 45cm/18in apart. After the flowers fade, cut down plants by about one-third.

Sow seeds thinly and evenly, 6mm/¼in deep, in seed-trays or pots of seed compost during early to late spring. Keep them at 10-16°C/50-61°F. Germination takes two to four weeks. When the seedlings are large enough to handle, prick them into seed-trays or pots and place in a cold frame. Plant into a garden in autumn or spring. Alternatively, divide congested plants in spring or autumn, replanting only the younger parts.

Arabis caucasica
Rock Cress (UK/USA)
Wall Rock Cress (USA)
Height: 15-23cm/6-9in
Spread: 38-45cm/15-18in

Hardy, spreading rock garden and wall plant with grey-green and hoary leaves. From late winter to early summer it bears white, cross-shaped flowers. 'Flore Pleno' (double flowers), 'Snowflake' (large single flowers).

Arenaria purpurescens
Pink Sandwort (USA)
Sandwort (UK/USA)
Height: 5-7.5cm/2-3in
Spread: 25-30cm/10-12in

Spreading, loosely tufted, prostrate plant with slender, pointed mid-green leaves. During mid- and late summer, star-shaped, purple flowers appear in twos and threes. 'Elliott's Variety' has clear pink flowers.

Armeria maritima
Thrift (UK/USA)
Sea Pink (UK/USA)
Height: 15-25cm/6-10in
Spread: 25-30cm/10-12in

Hardy, evergreen, hummock-forming perennial with grass-like, mid-green leaves. From late spring to mid-summer it has 2.5cm/1in-wide heads on long stalks packed with pink flowers. 'Alba' has white flowers; 'Vindictive' is rose-red.

Linum arboreum
Flax (UK/USA)
Height: 25cm/10in
Spread: 30cm/12in

Hardy, shrubby perennial with narrowly triangular, bluish green leaves. During late spring and early summer it develops golden yellow flowers up to 5cm/2in across.

PLANT NAME AND DESCRIPTION	SITUATION AND CULTIVATION	PROPAGATION

Phlox subulata
Moss Phlox (UK)
Moss Pink (UK/USA)
Mountain Phlox (USA)
Height: 5-10cm/2-4in
Spread: 30-45cm/12-18in

Hardy, spreading and tufted, sub-shrubby phlox that forms mats of narrow, mid-green leaves. During mid- and late spring it develops purple or pink flowers. There are several varieties, including 'Samson' (shown).

Full sun or very light shade and fertile, well-drained but moisture-retentive soil. Set the plants 30-45cm/12-18in apart.

Take 5cm/2in-long cuttings from the bases of plants in mid-summer and insert them in equal parts moist peat and sharp sand. Place in a cold frame. When rooted, pot up into 7.5cm/3in-wide pots and overwinter in a cold frame. Plant into a garden in spring.

Ramonda myconi
Height: 10-15cm/4-6in
Spread: 20-23cm/8-9in

Hardy, rosette-forming evergreen with deep green, deeply tooth-edged and hairy leaves. During spring it develops flat-faced, lavender-blue flowers up to 36mm/1¹/2in wide at the top of each flower stem. 'Rosea' has deep rose flowers, while 'Alba' is white.

Well-drained, moderately fertile garden soil and a cool position against a rock suit it. Avoid positions in strong sunlight and where the soil dries out in summer. Add peat to the soil.

During early and mid-summer, take leaf cuttings. Remove a leaf so that a dormant bud remains at its base, and insert at a slight angle in equal parts moist peat and sharp sand. Place in a cold frame, where roots will develop in five to six weeks. When rooted, pot up into individual pots and replace in a cold frame. Plant into a rock garden in mid-spring.

Saxifraga cotyledon
Height: 30-45cm/12-18in
Spread: 30-38cm/12-15in

Rosettes of dark green leaves, lime-encrusted at their edges, and pure white, 12mm/¹/2in-wide, starry flowers borne in plume-like sprays up to 45cm/18in long. The flowers appear from early to mid-summer. The form 'Southside Seedling' has sprays of white flowers peppered with red spots. Both are ideal for planting in crevices between rocks.

A semi-shaded, sheltered position facing east or west and well-drained, gritty, preferably slighty alkaline soil. Set the plants about 38cm/15in apart. When the flowers fade, cut off the flower stems.

Detach non-flowering rosettes in early summer and insert in pots of equal parts moist peat and sharp sand. Place in a cold frame. Water them thoroughly at first, then sparingly. Pot up the rosettes individually when rooted.

Thymus drucei
(syn. *T. praecox arcticus*)
Wild Thyme
Height: 2.5-7.5cm/1-3in
Spread: 38-45cm/15-18in

Hardy, carpeting shrub with small, grey-green leaves and terminal clusters of rose-purple flowers from early to mid-summer. The range of varieties is wide; colours include white, pale pink, crimson and lilac.

Full sun and light, sandy, well-drained soil. When planted to create a carpet, set plants 25-30cm/10-12in apart. It can also be planted between gaps in paving as well as in natural stone walls. After the flowers fade, lightly cut off the dead heads.

Lift and divide congested plants in spring or late summer. Alternatively, take 5cm/2in-long cuttings, preferably with heels, in mid-summer and insert them in pots of equal parts moist peat and sharp sand. Place in a cold frame. When rooted, pot up and overwinter in a cold frame before planting into a garden in spring.

Lithodora diffusa
(syn. *Lithospermum diffusum*)
Gromwell (UK)
Height: 10cm/4in
Spread: 30-45cm/12-18in

Hardy, spreading, prostrate, shrub-like plant with numerous oblong, dark green leaves and 2.5cm/1in-wide, deep blue and funnel-shaped flowers from mid-summer to early autumn. Varieties include 'Grace Ward' and 'Heavenly

Pulsatilla vulgaris
(syn. *Anemone pulsatilla*)
Pasque Flower
Height: 20-30cm/8-12in
Spread: 25-38cm/10-15in

Hardy herbaceous perennial with mid-green, fern-like leaves and outstandingly attractive, cup-like, 5-7.5cm/2-3in-wide purple flowers with golden centres during mid- and late spring. There are several forms, in various other colours.

Saxifraga burseriana
Burser's Saxifrage (UK)
Height: 5cm/2in
Spread: 25-30cm/10-12in

Hardy, with lance-like, blue-grey leaves that form dense, flat cushions. During late winter and early spring it develops 2.5cm/1in-wide, pure white flowers. There are several forms, including 'Brookside' and 'Gloria' (both with large white flowers).

***Verbascum* 'Letitia'**
Height: 15-20cm/6-8in
Spread: 20-30cm/8-12in

A hardy, twiggy bushlet with lance-shaped, grey-green leaves. From early to late summer it bears yellow flowers in spikes up to 10cm/4in long. It is a hybrid between *V. dumulosum* and *V. spinosum*.

Planting dahlias

Dahlias are superb plants to brighten borders in late summer and into early autumn, as well as providing flowers for room decoration. Both are frost-tender and new plants are raised each year and planted into borders as soon as all risk of frost has passed.

PLANTING AND GROWING DAHLIAS

The dazzling dahlias are tuberous-rooted and, if planted in rich, moisture-retentive soil and a frost-free environment, seldom fail to succeed. Usually, fresh plants are raised from cuttings each spring, but tubers lifted from the soil during the previous autumn and stored in a frost-proof shed in winter can be divided and planted in late spring. The quality of the flowers they produce is not as high as those raised afresh each year from cuttings, but they do develop their flowers a few weeks earlier.

Prepare the ground in winter, digging and adding copious amounts of well-decayed compost or manure (see pages 38-41). Allow frost to break down the surface to a friable tilth and in late spring or early summer – depending on the lateness of frosts in the area – fork a dusting of bonemeal into the surface of the soil.

Dahlias need plenty of room, depending on their vigour. Planting distances are suggested opposite. Don't plant them under trees, where water will drip on them, nor in shade nor near the base of a wall or fence, where soil tends to dry out rapidly. When planting tubers, ensure they are covered by 36-50mm/1½-2in of soil. However, young dahlia plants in pots need to have their surfaces only fractionally deeper than the surrounding soil. Water the soil after planting to settle it around the roots, and continue to water regularly throughout summer.

Stake plants using one strong, stout stake or several canes, taking care not to damage the tuberous roots. About two or three weeks after planting, nip out the growing tip on each plant to encourage development of side shoots; snap the stem sideways just above a strong pair of leaves.

When the plants are established, water the soil thoroughly and form a thick mulch around them, keeping it away from the stems. Regularly tie stems to the stake: first tie a piece of string to the

Right: Single-flowered dahlias are ideal for creating a mass of brightly faced flowers from mid-summer to the frosts of autumn. They are less dominant than the large-flowered dahlias and are ideal for planting in flower borders.

TYPES OF DAHLIAS

1 Single-flowered (shown here: 'Princess Marie Jose')
2 Collerette (shown here: 'Chimboraze')
3 Orchid-flowered (shown here: 'Jescot Julie')
4 Ball (shown here: 'Biddenham Purple')
5 Cactus (shown here: 'Wootton Impact')
6 Decorative (shown here: 'Gay Princess')

1

2

3

4

5

6

PLANTING DISTANCES FOR DAHLIAS

- Bedding: 45-60cm/18-24in.
- Single-flowered: 45-60cm/18-24in.
- Anemone-flowered: 50-60cm/20-24in.
- Collerette: 60-75cm/24-30in.
- Waterlily: 75cm/30in.
- Decorative: Giant and Large types 1-1.2m/3½-4ft; Medium types 90cm/3ft; Small and Miniature types 75cm/30in.
- Ball: Small and Miniature types 75cm/30in.
- Pompon: 75cm/30in.
- Cactus: Giant and Large types 1.2m/4ft; Medium types 90cm/3ft; Small and Miniature types 75cm/30in.

stake, then loop it under a leaf joint and make another knot, sufficiently tight to hold the stem secure but without constricting it. Feed the growing plants every four to five weeks from mid-summer onwards.

To encourage large flowers on long stems, remove all the small buds that appear around the main one. Pick the flowers regularly, especially early in the season, to encourage the development of others.

In autumn, about a week after the first frost has blackened the foliage, cut the stems to 15cm/6in above the soil. Use a garden fork to dig up the tubers, taking care not to pierce them and discarding any that are damaged. Brush off loose soil and place the tubers upside-down in boxes in a frost-proof shed. Once they are dry, turn them the right way up, place in 10-15cm/4-6in deep boxes and pack slightly damp peat around them. During winter, maintain a temperature of 5°C/45°F and keep the peat barely damp to ensure that the tubers do not become shrivelled and dry.

In early spring, re-pack the dormant tubers in shallow boxes, packing equal parts sharp sand and moist peat around them. Keep the compost moist and place in gentle warmth. In two to three weeks, the eyes (dormant buds) on the tubers swell. At this stage, use a sharp knife to divide the clusters of tubers, ensuring each new division has at least one undamaged eye. Dust the cuts with a fungicide. You can then plant the divided parts into a garden.

An alternative method of raising plants is from cuttings. This is done by placing dormant tubers in 10-15cm/4-6in-deep boxes and packing moist peat around them in late winter. Place them where the temperature is 15-18°C/59-64°F and keep the peat slightly moist. Shoots will develop and when they are 7.5cm/3in long, sever them with a sharp knife and use as cuttings. Cut the base of each shoot below a leaf joint, remove the lower leaves and insert the cuttings 36mm/1½in deep in pots of equal parts moist peat and sharp sand. Water the compost and place the pot of cuttings in gentle warmth. When the cuttings are rooted, transfer them into 7.5cm/3in-wide pots. Gradually lower the temperature and plant into a garden when all risk of frost has passed.

CONTAINER GARDENING

Even the smallest garden or paved area can be brightened by flowering plants, small shrubs and colourful conifers in tubs and other containers, while walls can become ablaze with colour from plants growing in wall-baskets, windowboxes and hanging-baskets. While summer is traditionally the best time for colourful flower displays in containers such as windowboxes and tubs, there are also many hardy plants that can be grown in them during winter. Also, in spring they can be brightened with colour from bulbs such as crocuses and diminutive irises. Low-growing daffodils and tulips can also be featured in them. Herbs and even a few vegetables can be grown in containers, while strawberries and some roses are suitable for planting in hanging-baskets.

Planting a hanging-basket

Hanging-baskets transform a house and patio, creating spectacular features at eye-level from early summer to the frosts of autumn. Modern hanging-baskets in a traditional style are formed of a bowl-shaped wire framework 25-45cm/10-18in wide; to ensure long life they are frequently coated in white, black or green plastic.

More recent types are shallower, slightly resembling a plastic washing-up bowl, and up to 38cm/15in wide. A drip-tray is built into the base to catch surplus water; this makes them ideal for use in a lobby, porch or conservatory.

PLANTING A WIRE-FRAMED BASKET

Place a wire-framed basket in the top of a plastic bucket, so that it is held firm. Line the inside of the basket with sphagnum moss or a moisture-retentive foam liner to prevent the compost drying out; this also stops compost escaping from between the wires. An alternative and cheaper method is to line the inside of the wire framework with black polythene – once plants are established they cloak the plastic with flowers and leaves. If you are using plastic, cut a piece approximately to size, press it into the wire framework (forming neat pleats) and use scissors to cut the edge about 5cm/2in above the top of the basket. The weight of the compost, as it fills the basket, will decrease this overlap, which you can then trim further. Fill the bottom half of the basket with compost and firm it with your fingers. Equal amounts of peat-based and loam-based compost will create an ideal mixture. Peat-based compost on its own retains plenty of water, but when dry is difficult to re-moisten; the addition of loam-based compost helps to counteract this defect as well as introducing a greater reserve of plant nutrients. The addition of a sprinkling of Perlite or Vermiculite further helps to retain moisture in the compost.

Put a 5cm/2in-thick layer of compost in the basket's base and make 5cm/2in-long slits in the polythene around its sides. Push the roots of trailing plants through these slits and spread and firm compost over them. Add more compost and plant further trailing plants through the holes, so that eventually the outside of the basket will be completely clothed in flowers and leaves.

Right: Many suitable plants have cascading stems and flowers that create a waterfall of bright colour. Here, a medley of pelargoniums, petunias, lobelia, helichrysum and impatiens combine to create an eye-catching feature framed against the dark timber background.

PLANTING A WIRE-FRAMED HANGING BASKET

1

2

3

4

5

6

1 Place the basket in the top of a bucket and line with black polythene.
2 Fill the bottom half of the basket with compost.
3 Push roots of trailing plants through slits in the plastic and into the compost.
4 Add further plants around the outside, then put in a central plant.
5 Add remaining plants around the central one, then fill up basket with compost to within 12mm/^{1}/2in of the rim.
6 Tuck in a thick layer of sphagnum moss over the surface to conserve moisture, then water the compost thoroughly.

When the compost is 6-7.5cm/2½-3in from the basket's top, set a dominant plant, such as a cascading fuchsia, in the centre. Position a few trailing plants around the central plant, setting them at a slight angle outwards so that their flowers and foliage will trail over the basket's edge.

When planting is complete, the surface of the compost should be 12mm/½in below the basket's rim. Trim off the plastic, 12mm/½in above the rim. This ensures there is sufficient space for water to collect when you water the plants. Finish with a layer of sphagnum moss over the surface to help reduce moisture loss from the compost and to create a neat appearance. Finally, water the compost thoroughly.

If possible, place the basket in a greenhouse until the plants are growing strongly and all risk of frost has passed, then suspend the basket from a strong bracket.

PLANTING A PLASTIC HANGING-BASKET

Wide-based plastic baskets do not need liners, but it is essential that the compost used in them is moisture-retentive. Fill the base of the basket with a 12mm/½in layer of well-washed 6mm/¼in pea-shingle to ensure good drainage, then a thin layer of moist peat. Half-fill the basket with a mixture of equal parts loam-based and peat-based compost, plus moisture-retentive additives such as Vermiculite and Perlite. Gently firm the compost with your fingers.

Start planting the container by positioning a dominant, cascading plant in the centre. Then work towards the outside, add further plants and use trailing types at the edges. Cover the roots with compost; gently firm it around them.

Leave a 12mm/½in space at the top and gently water the compost until water trickles out of the drip-tray in the basket's base. If possible, keep the container in a greenhouse for at least a week before positioning it in a lobby, porch or conservatory. Do not place it outside until all risk of frost has passed.

CHOOSING PLANTS FOR HANGING BASKETS

Many plants are ideal for planting in hanging baskets, but here are a few guidelines that will help ensure success:

- Don't use too many different types. Twelve plants of only four types look better than ten different ones.

- Don't cram in too many plants. Once established, a few big, healthy plants create a better display than masses of crowded and starved ones.

- For plenty of colour, use different colour varieties of the same type of plant. This ensures that plants have similar vigour and will not suffocate and ultimately destroy each other.

- Don't restrict the basket to half-hardy annuals – small variegated, trailing ivies will create colour throughout the year.

- Select flower colours that harmonize with their backgrounds. For example, for white walls choose mainly yellow, gold, scarlet and green flowers; select deep purple, deep blue, pink and red flowers for grey stone walls; and try white, soft blue, silver and lemon flowers against a red brick wall.

Planting a windowbox

Windowboxes are superb for brightening windows throughout the year. In winter they can be filled with a collection of miniature conifers, variegated ivies, dwarf evergreen shrubs and winter-flowering pansies. Small shrubs with colourful berries can also be used. During spring, dwarf evergreen shrubs, miniature conifers, variegated ivies and bulbous plants create superb features, while in summer windowboxes are traditionally packed with colourful bedding plants.

PLANTING SCHEMES

Using a separate inner container for each seasonal arrangement – spring, summer, and winter – in a windowbox will enable you to instantly change displays. For example, in early spring you can take out a display of winter-brightening plants and quickly replace it with an inner box that you planted a few months earlier with spring-flowering bulbs and that is now bursting into colour. And later, as soon as all risk of frost has passed, you can change the spring-flowering box to display summer-flowering plants.

POSITIONING AND SECURING WINDOWBOXES

Windowboxes need not be confined to window sills; they also can be secured on brackets against high walls, or on top of low ones where they help to soften harsh outlines.

When positioning them under windows, take into consideration the type of window, as this will determine the position of the windowbox. If you have sash windows, which slide up and down, you can secure windowboxes with the base of the box level with the sill; otherwise you will need to ensure that the windowbox is low enough to allow you to open the window. Only place a windowbox directly on the sill if the latter is made of concrete; wooden sills soon rot and decay if kept wet by water dripping from the compost, while plastic sills (found in many new homes) are neither strong enough nor large enough to take a windowbox.

For casement windows (where the window is hinged on its outer edge and opens over the sill), you will need to secure the base of the windowbox well below the sill. Strong, windowbox brackets are available and these will need to be securely screwed to the wall. Plan to have the top of the box 15-23cm/6-9in below the windowsill to allow the window to open without touching flowers and leaves as they grow above the top of the windowbox.

Some double-glazed plastic-type windows are hinged across the top or one-third of the way down so that the frame opens over the windowsill. Position the box so that its top is slightly below the sill.

Apart from being very strong, brackets should have a lip to hold the box in position to ensure that it cannot slip or be knocked off. Never underestimate the weight of a windowbox after it has been watered, or the strength of wind when battering a box heavily laden with flowers.

The size of the box is important, as it must hold enough compost to accommodate a good selection of plants. Avoid windowboxes with a depth of less than 15cm/6in; 20cm/8in is only just adequate. The dimension from back to front is less critical – it simply affects how many plants you can use – but 20cm/8in is about right.

SECURING A WINDOWBOX BRACKET

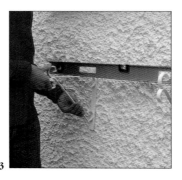

1 Position the bracket on the wall and adjust its height to suit the type of window. Allow for the depth of the box and heights of the plants.
2 Mark the wall and use a masonry drill to make holes. Insert wall-fixings and screw the bracket into place.
3 Position the other bracket and use a spirit-level to check it is level. Drill, insert wall-fixings and screw the bracket into place.

PLANTS FOR A WINTER DISPLAY

Attractive windowboxes in winter are just as important as those festooned with colour in summer. When you remove the inner container holding a winter display in early spring, place it in a sheltered position and stand it on bricks to reduce the risk of slugs and snails gaining access to the plants. The range of plants for winter display is wide and includes:

Miniature conifers:

• Choose small, colourful, slow-growing types. If you want to use faster-growing types, be prepared to discard them or plant them into a garden when they grow too large for a windowbox.

Evergreen shrubs:

• *Hebe pinguifolia* 'Pagei' – Low-growing with small, grey leaves and white flowers in early summer.

• *Calluna vulgaris* – Choose dwarf varieties with brightly coloured foliage.

• *Buxus sempervirens* 'Suffruticosa' – Slow-growing, ideal for a large windowbox.

Evergreen trailers:

• Small-leaved ivies (*Hedera helix*) – Range of variegated leaves, ideal for softening the edges of boxes.

Above: A windowbox planted with brightly coloured dwarf conifers, small evergreen and variegated shrubs and trailing ivies are ideal for bringing colour to gardens from autumn to early spring.

The length of the box is important; if it is more than 1.2m/4ft it will be difficult to handle when filled with compost and planted and may break in the middle. It is better to have two boxes, each 90cm/3ft long, than a single one 1.8m/6ft long.

PLANTING SUMMER-FLOWERING PLANTS

If you are using a plastic inner box and creating both winter and spring arrangements, set the plants directly in compost. However, if you are creating a summer-flowering arrangement, you can either remove the pot from each plant and plant it directly into compost in the container, or leave plants in their pots, placing them in an inner container and just packing peat around them. The advantage of removing pots is that each plant is provided with more compost. On the other hand, if you leave plants in their pots, you will be able to remove individual plants more easily as their display fades and to replace them with fresh specimens.

When planting directly into an inner container, first ensure there are drainage holes in its base. Cover these with pieces of broken clay pots and then a 12mm/1/2in layer of clean pea-shingle. Over this form an 18-25cm/3/4-1in layer of equal parts moist peat-based and soil-based compost. This mixture retains moisture as well as initially providing food, including trace elements. If you know that you will be away from home so that you will not be able to water plants frequently when the weather is extremely hot, you can add Perlite or Vermiculite to the compost to assist water retention.

Position each plant, spread out its roots and firm compost over and around them. Leave a 12mm/1/2in space between the top of the compost and the rim of the box so that you can soak the compost thoroughly with each watering.

When leaving plants in their pots, water the compost in them the day before putting them into the container. Pack moist peat around the pots, positioning pot with its rim 12mm/1/2in below the surface of the peat. Fill the container with peat to within 12mm/1/2in of its rim.

SUMMER-FLOWERING PLANTS

1

2

3

1 Place broken pieces of clay pots over drainage holes in the container's base. Add a 12mm/1/2in layer of pea shingle, then 18-25cm/3/4-1in of moist peat.
2 Form of layer of equal parts peat-based and soil-based compost in the base, and spread out the plants.
3 When the design is right, remove the pots, form holes and firm compost around the plants.

Plants for hanging-baskets and windowboxes

PLANT NAME AND DESCRIPTION	SITUATION AND CULTIVATION	PROPAGATION

Fuchsia
Ladies' Eardrops (UK/USA)
Height: Wide range
Spread: Wide range

Some fuchsias are relatively hardy and can be left in borders throughout winter, but those grown in hanging-baskets and windowboxes cannot be put outside until the risk of frost has passed. Do not select greenhouse varieties, but choose slightly hardier ones. Some have a cascading nature.

Full sun or light shade, a warm and sheltered position and fertile, moisture-retentive but well-drained compost suits it. The compost must remain moist, as fluctuations encourage plants to 'age' and harden, as well as causing the flowers to drop off. Plant bushy types in window-boxes, tubs and troughs, but use a cascading variety as a central plant in a hanging-basket. Pinch off dead flowers to encourage flower development.

Take 7.5-10cm/3-4in-long cuttings from sideshoots in early spring, from established plants growing in greenhouses. Insert them in pots of equal parts moist peat and sharp sand, and place in gentle warmth. Pot up the cuttings when rooted into individual pots and lower the temperature slighty. Pinch out the growing tips of bushy and trailing varieties several times to encourage bushiness. Plant out into containers on a patio when all risk of frost has passed.

***Glechoma hederacea* 'Variegata'**
(syn. *Nepeta hederacea* 'Variegata')
Variegated Ground Ivy (UK/USA)
Height: 7.5-10cm/3-4in then trailing to 60cm/24in or more

Hardy perennial – tends to die back in autumn when grown in a hanging-basket or windowbox – with long stems bearing kidney-shaped, mid-green leaves with soft white markings. It is ideal for creating long curtains of stems clothed in leaves.

Full sun or light shade suits it; avoid heavily shaded positions as the variegations in the leaves will disappear. Moderately fertile, well-drained but moisture-retentive compost suits it. Ensure that the compost remains moist throughout summer; if this is neglected – and the weather is hot – the leaves will shrivel, become unattractive and, eventually, die.

Divide plants in spring, replanting young parts into windowboxes and hanging-baskets. Where plants are in exposed and cold areas, it is essential to position the container in a sheltered position during winter to prevent the roots being killed.

Helichrysum petiolare
(syn. *H. petiolatum*)
Licorice Plant (USA)
Height: 30-45cm/12-18in
Spread: 45-60cm/18-24in

Tender, shrubby perennial with soft, lax, silvery-grey stems and leaves. It sometimes grows up to 1m/3¹/₂ft, but is smaller when raised annually. There is also a yellow-leaved form.

It is frequently planted in hanging-baskets. Full sun or light shade and fertile, well-drained compost suit it. Regularly pinch out the growing tips of the shoots to encourage bushiness and a cascading nature. Plants can be overwintered by putting them in a frost-proof greenhouse in autumn. Usually, however, they are discarded.

During mid- to late summer, take 7.5cm/3in-long cuttings from sideshoots. Remove the lower leaves and insert them in pots of equal parts moist peat and sharp sand. Place them in gentle warmth and when rooted pot up into small pots and move to a cool greenhouse, where they are overwintered. Plant them into containers as soon as all risk of frost has passed.

***Impatiens* hardy hybrids**
Busy Lizzie (UK)
Height: 15-38cm/6-15in (range)
Spread: 20-38cm/8-15in (range)

Tender, half-hardy annual used as a summer-flowering bedding plant as well as in containers on a patio, and in windowboxes. From late spring to autumn, plants are smothered in flat-faced flowers in salmon, scarlet, white, burgundy and lavender. Some varieties have mixed colours.

Full sun or light shade and fertile, well-drained but moisture-retentive compost suit it. Set the plants in containers as soon as all risk of frost has passed, spacing them 20-38cm/8-15in apart depending on the vigour of the variety. In autumn, pull up the plants and discard them.

Sow seeds thinly and evenly, 3mm/¹/₈in deep, in seed-trays during late winter and early spring. Keep them at 16°C/61°F. Germination takes two to three weeks. When the seedlings are large enough to handle, move them into seed-trays, spacing them 36-50mm/1¹/₂-2in apart. Slowly acclimatize the plants to outdoor conditions and plant into their flowering position when all risk of frost has passed.

***Calceolaria integrifolia* 'Sunshine'**
Pouch Flower (UK/USA)
Slipper Flower (UK/USA)
Slipperwort (USA)
Height: 25-38cm/10-15in then cascading

A half-hardy biennial with soft, hairy, mid-green leaves and masses of pouch-shaped, bright yellow flowers from early to late summer. It is ideal for planting in a hanging-basket.

***Campanula isophylla* 'Krystal' varieties**
Falling Stars (USA)
Italian Bellflowers (UK/USA)
Star of Bethlehem (UK/USA)
Height: 15cm/6in then trailing to 45cm/18in

Hardy perennial, with masses of star-shaped, 25mm/1in-wide blue or white flowers from early to late summer.

***Lysimachia nummularia* 'Aurea'**
Height: 5-7.5cm/2-3in then trailing to 45cm/18in or more

A hardy herbaceous perennial and a superb form of the well-known Moneywort or Creeping Jenny. It has rounded, yellow leaves and a wealth of yellow flowers during early and mid-summer. It is ideal for planting in windowboxes and for troughs positioned at the edge of a balcony.

***Nemophila menziesii* 'Pennie Black'**
Height: 5-10cm/2-4in then spreading and trailing to 38cm/15in

The ordinary species of this hardy annual is known as Baby Blue-Eyes, but this variety has a spreading and trailing habit; it is ideal for planting in windowboxes and hanging-baskets. The 18mm/³/₄in-wide, purple to black flowers edged silvery white, appear from early to mid-summer.

PLANT NAME AND DESCRIPTION	SITUATION AND CULTIVATION	PROPAGATION

Pelargonium peltatum
Hanging Geranium (USA)
Ivy Geranium (USA)
Ivy-leaved Geranium (UK)
Height: 10-15cm/4-6in then trailing
45cm/18in or more

Tender perennial, with fleshy, mid-green leaves shaped similarly to those of ivy. From early summer to autumn it bears carmine-pink flowers up to 25mm/1in wide in umbrella-like heads. Several varieties and other colours.

Plant in moderately fertile, well-drained soil-based compost. Do not put plants outdoors until all risk of frost has passed. Keep the compost watered throughout summer and remove dead flowers. In autumn, either discard plants or cut back and place in a frost-proof greenhouse for the duration of winter. Avoid high temperatures and excessive moisture.

During late summer, take 7.5cm/3in-long cuttings and insert them in pots of equal parts moist peat and sharp sand. Place them in a cool greenhouse and cover the leaves with newspaper for about ten days to prevent the cuttings becoming dry. When rooted, pot them up and keep at 7-10°C/45-50°F. Keep the compost barely moist during winter. Pinch out the growing tips to encourage bushiness and plant into containers when the risk of frost has passed.

Pelargoniums Continental Geraniums
Height: 23-38cm/9-15in
Spread: 30-45cm/12-18in

Frost-tender, half-hardy plants – also known as Balcons and Cascade Geraniums – initially widely grown in Europe. Throughout summer they produce clusters of flowers in colours including scarlet, salmon, pink and lilac. With their cascading nature they are ideal for windowboxes and wall-baskets.

Full sun or light shade and well-drained, poor rather than rich compost. Avoid fertile compost as it encourages leaf growth at the expense of flower production. Plant in spring, as soon as all risk of frost has passed, setting plants close together. In hanging-baskets, about five plants are needed, while in windowboxes they should be 10-13cm/4-5in apart. Keep the compost well watered during summer. Discard plants in autumn.

The commercial propagation of these geraniums is controlled by a plant patent and therefore it is only possible to buy new plants from nurseries or seedsmen.

Pericallis x *hybrida*
(syn. *Cineraria cruenta*/*Senecio cruentus*/*Senecio* x *hybridus*)
Florist's Cineraria (UK/USA)
Height: 30-45cm/12-18in
Spread: 25-38cm/10-15in

A half-hardy perennial widely grown as a houseplant, but which, in warm and sheltered areas, can also be used in windowboxes. Large, domed flower heads in single and multi-colours appear from mid-winter to early summer.

Loam- or peat-based composts suit it. Established plants are usually bought just as the flower buds are about to open. Keep the compost moist and ensure plants are not positioned in cold draughts.
Cinerarias are often grown outdoors in windowboxes from late winter onwards, especially in towns and where plants are well sheltered.

Plants can be raised from seeds sown from spring to late summer; spring sowings produce plants for mid-winter displays, while plants from later sowings flower in late spring and early summer. However, when only a few plants are needed it is better to buy established plants. Be prepared to replace them if the weather turns cold and frosty and they become damaged.

Primula x *polyantha*
Polyanthus (UK/USA)
Height: 15-25cm/6-10in
Spread: 15-25cm/6-10in

This hardy, spring-flowering perennial is derived from the Primrose (*P. vulgaris*), Cowslip (*P. veris*) and (*P. juliae*). Polyanthus flowers, up to 36mm/1¹/₂in across, are boldly and brightly coloured in yellow, cream, white, pink, blue and crimson.

Full sun or light shade, a sheltered position and fertile, moisture-retentive loam-based compost are required. Compost must remain moist during dry weather. Space the plants about 20cm/8in apart in windowboxes in late summer or early autumn.

Sow seeds evenly and thinly, 3mm/¹/₈in deep, in seed-trays from early winter to early spring. Keep at 15-20°C/59-68°F. Germination takes between three and six weeks. When large enough to handle, prick out the seedlings into pots or seed-trays. Reduce the temperature and slowly acclimatize the plants to outdoor conditions.

Senecio maritima
(syn. *Cineraria maritima*/*C. bicolor*)
Dusty Miller (USA)
Height: 38-45cm/15-18in
Spread: 25-30cm/10-12in

Slightly tender, evergreen, shrubby perennial, usually grown as a half-hardy annual. The deeply lobed leaves are covered with white hairs, while during summer it develops daisy-like, yellow flowers.

Silene pendula 'Peach Blossom'
Height: 10-15cm/4-6in then cascading to 38cm/15in or more

Half-hardy annual with a spreading and branching nature and masses of double, 18mm/³/₄in-wide flowers throughout summer. They are deep pink when at their bud stage, opening to salmon and maturing to white.

Tropaeolum majus
Nasturtium (UK/USA)
Height: 20-38cm/8-15in (bushy and trailing types)

Hardy annual often climbing to 1.8m/6ft or more high. There are, however, also dwarf types with a bushy or trailing habit that are superb in hanging-baskets and windowboxes. Flower colours include yellow, orange, red and pink.

Viola x *wittrockiana*
Garden Pansy (UK/USA)
Height: 15-23cm/6-9in
Spread: 20-25cm/8-10in

Hardy biennial, with flowers up to 10cm/4in wide and in a range of colours, including yellow, white, red, blue and violet, normally appearing from late spring to mid-summer. There are also winter-flowering forms, blooming from late winter to spring.

Looking after plants in containers

Plants growing in hanging-baskets, windowboxes, wall-baskets and pots are expected to create a wealth of colourful flowers and attractive leaves throughout summer, yet to be able to grow in a relatively small amount of compost. They therefore need more attention than plants growing in beds and borders, where a greater area of soil and larger reserve of moisture is available.

Regular watering, feeding and dead-heading are essential, especially for ephemeral summer-flowering plants such as half-hardy annuals. During winter, shrubs and trees growing in tubs may need protection against excessive rain, severe frost and heavy snow falls.

WATERING PLANTS IN CONTAINERS
Without water, plants soon die, and as those growing in hanging-baskets, troughs and window boxes have so little compost they are vulnerable if given irregular applications of water.

Once compost becomes dry it is very difficult to re-moisten, especially if it contains a large amount of peat. Take down dried-out hanging-baskets and submerge the whole compost area in water until bubbles cease to rise, but take care if plants have only recently been planted, as compost may be washed off the surface. Once roots have penetrated and filled the compost the risk of compost being washed away is diminished.

Wall baskets and windowboxes cannot be immersed in water and you will need to water them several times to re-moisten dry compost; if the compost is exceptionally dry, the first application tends to run straight through the gap between the compost and container, and it is not until the soil expands and cracks close up that thorough watering is possible.

In summer, hanging-baskets, troughs, windowboxes and other small containers need watering two or three times a day. Always water plants in the morning, afternoon or early evening; don't leave the foliage of plants wet at night as they are then likely to be attacked by diseases, especially early or late in the season when the temperature drops rapidly at night.

Container plants are usually easiest to water with a watering-can. However, if you have a large number of plants to water, this is laborious and a

LOOKING AFTER PLANTS IN CONTAINERS

1 Water plants regularly. Groups of tubs and pots, as well as hanging-baskets, are easy to water if you tie the end of a hosepipe to a 1.2m/4ft-long cane.
2 Feed summer-flowering plants regularly, adding fertilizer to water.
3 Pinch out the growing tips of straggly shoots to encourage bushiness.
4 Regularly remove dead flower heads to encourage others to develop and to keep plants tidy.
5 In winter, cover tubs to prevent the compost becoming saturated and roots being damaged.
6 In late autumn, form a tripod of canes and straw over tender plants in tubs to prevent frost damaging shoots and leaves.

PROTECTING PLANTS IN TUBS

Long-lived plants such as trees, shrubs and those with an herbaceous nature need special care.

- Shrubs, trees and conifers in tubs need regular watering in summer, but in winter, when they are inactive, the compost frequently becomes too wet, resulting in roots decaying. Also, during exceptionally cold periods, waterlogged compost is inclined to freeze and further damage roots. To protect these plants, cover the compost with polythene sheeting in early winter. First, place a couple of bricks immediately around the stem, then cut a piece of polythene to the width of the container plus an overlap of 30cm/12in on all sides. On one side, cut the polythene to its centre and place it over the compost; tie its sides to the container.

- Tender evergreen shrubs are likely to have their leaves damaged by severe frost. In early winter – at the beginning of a cold period – insert five 1.5-1.8m/5-6ft canes into the compost and tie them into a tripod. Tie a piece of long string to the top, pack a layer of straw over the canes, and secure it in place by forming a downward spiral of string. Remove the straw and string as soon as the risk of severe frost has passed.

- Tender herbaceous plants, such as agapanthus with its fleshy roots, can be damaged if the compost becomes excessively wet and subsequently freezes. Encapsulating both the compost and container in straw helps to prevent this happening.

Below: Well-drained but moisture-retentive compost is essential for the growth of plants throughout summer. Regularly remove dead flowers and water the compost whenever it starts to look dry. If possible, position the container away from strong, cold winds.

hosepipe is easier, but take care not to create a jet of water that washes away compost. To make watering clusters of plants in pots easier, tie the end of a hosepipe to a 1.2m/4ft-long cane and bend over the top of the hosepipe. You can then dribble water into containers, even those at the back of a cluster of pots. There are also proprietary watering lances that enable you to reach windowboxes and hanging-baskets without having to stand on a stool or step ladder, as well as pulleys and ropes that enable you to lower hanging-baskets and water them at ground level.

If you are out all day, add Perlite or Vermiculite to the compost to help retain moisture and reduce the frequency of watering.

FEEDING PLANTS

There is usually sufficient food in compost to ensure the rapid establishment and growth of summer-flowering, half-hardy annuals in the early part of summer. After this, regular feeding – every two of three weeks – is essential to maintain healthy growth and to encourage a vivid display of flowers. You can add slow-acting fertilizers to the compost at planting time, but you will also need to regularly feed container plants.

Liquid fertilizer diluted in water is the most popular and easiest way to feed plants in containers and you can do this at the same time as watering them. It is essential that the compost is moist before you apply fertilizers; if dry, the mixture of water and fertilizer may pass straight through the compost and be wasted. Also, fertilizers can damage the roots of plants growing in dry compost.

Permanent plants such as small conifers and shrubs do not need regular feeding throughout summer, but a general fertilizer in spring or early summer will encourage growth. Do not apply fertilizers in late summer, as young growth at that stage will be damaged by winter frosts.

DEAD-HEADING AND STOPPING

Removing faded flowers enables further flowers to develop and prevents decaying blooms encouraging the presence of diseases, especially in wet weather.

To remove dead flowers from annual plants, hold the stem firm and nip off the dead blooms. When stems are young and soft, you should be able to nip off flowers without holding the stem. When dead-heading plants such as rhododendrons and azaleas, hold the stem just below the faded flowers and snap the cluster sideways. Always put dead flowers in a box and then on a compost heap; if you leave them on the ground or on top of a plant they will encourage the presence of diseases.

Nip out the growing tips of young half-hardy annuals to encourage bushiness and prevent plants sprawling excessively.

Making a windowbox

Plastic troughs are often used on their own as windowboxes, but you can give a windowbox more visual appeal by using a plastic trough inside an outer box made from wood. Indeed, having three separate plastic inner containers – one for a winter, another for spring and a further one for summer – will enable you to change displays quickly and prepare others in advance (see pages 144-5). Wooden windowboxes are quite easy to make at home.

MAKING A WINDOWBOX

Rather than constructing a wooden windowbox and then searching garden centres for plastic troughs that fit inside it, buy three inner containers of the same size that fit the window. Windowboxes more than 1.2m/4ft long are difficult to handle and when lifted may break with the weight of compost. Even for a 1.2m/4ft-long windowbox it is often best to buy two 60cm/24in-long inner troughs. The inside measurements should ideally be about 20cm/8in deep and wide.

To ensure a windowbox will look right when positioned below a window, make it 10-15cm/ 4-6in wider than the window, so that both sides will extend 5-7.5cm/2-3in beyond the window's edges. Windowboxes that are narrower than the window always looks badly planned; a wider windowbox will appear to form a base for the window. However, if the windowbox is to rest on a concrete sill it should be slightly narrower to allow space on either side for the box to be manipulated into position.

The following information is to make wooden windowbox about 90cm/3ft long, but the measurements can be adjusted to suit other window widths. Measure the length, width and depth of the inner plastic box (or boxes, if the window is large). Make the inside measurement of the wooden windowbox about 25-36mm/1-1$\frac{1}{2}$in longer and wider. This will allow you to easily put in place and later remove the inner containers.

YOU WILL NEED ...

To construct a wooden windowbox 90cm/3ft long and, internally, about 20cm/8in deep and wide, into which to place a trough 80cm/31$\frac{1}{2}$in long, you will need:

MAKING A WINDOWBOX

1 Place the base of the windowbox on a firm surface and mark the positions of the holes. Use a bradawl to mark the drilling positions.
2 Drill and countersink the holes. Ensure the drill is held upright.
3 Smear waterproof glue along the edges before screwing the side into place. Position and screw in the other side.
4 Position each end, drill holes, smear with glue and screw into place.
5 Drill 12mm/$\frac{1}{2}$ in wide holes in the base to ensure water escapes from the box.
6 Screw six pieces of 18mm/$\frac{3}{4}$ in-square wood in the base of the windowbox to prevent the inner box resting directly on the wood.

Above: A wooden window, in which a plastic inner one can be placed, is easily made. As well as creating an attractive outer container, it helps to keep the compost in the inner box cool during summer and warm in winter. Ensure the box is supported on strong brackets.

- Sides: Two pieces of wood 21mm/⁷/₈in thick x 21cm/8¹/₂in wide x 90cm/3ft long.
- Base: One piece of wood 21mm/⁷/₈in thick x 21cm/8¹/₂in wide x 90cm/3ft long.
- Ends: Two pieces of wood 21mm/⁷/₈in thick x 21cm/8¹/₂in wide x 19.5cm/7³/₄in long.
- About forty-four 36mm/1¹/₂in-long, counter-sunk, galvanized or zinc-coated screws.
- Tools: drill, countersink drill, screwdriver, bradawl, set-square, saw, pencil, sandpaper, measuring tape, vice or Workmate bench, waterproof glue, panel pins and outdoor paint.

ASSEMBLING THE WINDOWBOX

When the wood has been cut to size, use a pencil to mark a line 9mm/³/₈in in from one of the sides on each of the 21cm/8¹/₂in wide planks. Mark the drilling positions, 36mm/1¹/₂in from each side, and then at spaces 10cm/4in apart between them. Use a bradawl to make a small hole at each position, then drill and countersink

the holes. Use a vice or work bench to hold the base plank lengthwise and upright, then position one of the other drilled planks so that you can make fixings with screws. First, however, smear the surfaces with waterproof glue. When you have finished, release the two planks from the vice and fix the other side with glue and screws in the same way.

The last job is to fix the ends. Position one of the ends and mark the drilling positions on the outside of the three parts of the box. Then, drill, coat with glue and screw the end into place. Do the same with the other end.

When the glue is set, turn the box upside down, so that the base is uppermost, and drill seven 12mm/¹/₂in holes in it to ensure water can easily escape from the box. If the base of the inner box is flat – and it usually is – cut about six pieces of 18cm/7in-long, 18mm/³/₄in-square pieces of wood that can be secured with panel pins or screws to the inside of the base. Centre them between the sides, so that there is a gap on either side. This ensures water will not be trapped in the box's base, causing it to rot.

Use sandpaper to smooth the surfaces, inside and out, then cover with two or three coats of a non-toxic outdoor paint. Select the colour to suit the window and building.

MAKING A CONTAINER FROM A BARREL

Small beer-barrels or wine-casks, about 45-60cm/18-24in high when standing on end, are easy to convert into attractive and unusual containers for plants by cutting a planting 'window' in them, about 25cm/10in to 30cm/12in square, depending on the size of the barrel.

First, mark the area in pencil. If the lines cross the two inner metal bands these must be cut; the ends that will remain attached to the barrel should be drilled and screwed to the wood before the metal is cut.

Use a 12-18mm/¹/₂-³/₄in drill to form holes at the four corners of the pencilled square; then use a pad-saw to cut out the 'window'. Use a hacksaw to cut the metal bands and smooth the cut ends with a file and sandpaper.

Drill 12mm/¹/₂in-wide holes in the side opposite the 'window' to ensure good drainage when the barrel is filled with compost. A stand for the barrel is essential and the easiest way to provide one is to rest it on several bricks.

CREATING A CONTAINER FROM CAR TYRES

Worn car tyres make unusual containers for plants. Many garages give away old tyres – select four of approximately the same diameter and thickness. Do not be tempted to used very large tyres – an inside diameter of 25-33cm/10-13in is best.

- Place two tyres on top of each other and secure them together with five or six pieces of 15cm/6in-long wire, threaded through their side walls. The easiest way to make holes in the side walls is to use a drill. Add a further two tyres in the same way.

- Select a plastic bucket – one that snugly fits into the hole in the centre of the tyres – and drill four or five 12mm/¹/₂in holes in its base. Place bricks inside the tyres so that the bucket's rim is level with the top of the tyres.

- Fill the base of the bucket with coarse, clean drainage material, then add compost. Plant it with either spring- or summer-flowering plants.

Plants for tubs and urns

PLANT NAME AND DESCRIPTION	SITUATION AND CULTIVATION	PROPAGATION

***Acer palmatum* 'Dissectum Atropurpureum'**
Height: 90cm-1.2m/3-4ft in a tub
Spread: 1.2-1.5m/4-5ft in a tub

Hardy deciduous shrub with finely dissected, bronze-red leaves. The shrub forms a wide dome and creates an impressive feature.
   A. palmatum 'Dissectum' is a green-leaved type with finely divided leaves.

Use loam-based compost and a large tub for this plant, to provide it with a stable base. Take care not to position the tub too close to other plants or buildings, as this spoils the shrub's outline.
   No pruning is needed, other than occasionally cutting out a branch in spring to maintain a neat outline.

With this shrub it is always best to buy an established plant from a garden centre or nursery.

Anthemis cupaniana
(now known as *A. punctata cupaniana*)
Golden Marguerite (UK/USA)
Height: 15-25cm/6-10in
Spread: 30-38cm/12-15in

Short-lived herbaceous perennial, sometimes grown as a biennial, with bright-faced, daisy-like white flowers with bright yellow centres from early to late summer. They appear amid a mound of slightly aromatic, finely dissected, grey leaves. It is ideal in a stone container.

Plant anthemis in well-drained, light soil or loam-based compost, ensuring that the base of the container is filled with coarse drainage material. Position the container in full sun and away from cold winter winds. Once planted, this anthemis will last two or three years before it needs to be pulled up and replaced. Feed it several times during summer and trim off dead flowers.

Remove and divide congested plants in spring, replanting the younger parts from around the outside. Alternatively, take 5-7.5cm/2-3in-long cuttings from the plant's base in late spring or early summer and insert them in pots of sandy compost. Place them in a cold frame and pot up into individual pots when rooted.

***Aucuba japonica* 'Variegata'**
(syn. *Aucuba japonica* 'Maculata')
Gold Dust Plant (USA)
Spotted Laurel (UK)
Height: 1-1.3m/3½-4½ft in a tub
Spread: 90cm-1.2m/3-4ft in a tub

Hardy, bushy, somewhat rounded evergreen shrub with leathery, shiny, dark green, narrowly oval leaves up to 15cm/6in long. In a border it is more vigorous, about 3.6m/12ft high and 2.4m/8ft wide.

In a tub, use well-drained, but moisture-retentive, soil-based compost. A large tub, as well as a large body of soil, is essential to create a firm base, and to provide a long-term home for the plant. Position it in full sun or light shade. No regular pruning is needed, other than in late spring cutting back long stems or those damaged by severe winter frost.

Take 10-13cm/4-5in-long cuttings from the current season's growth in mid- to late summer. Insert them in pots of equal parts moist peat and sharp sand and place in a cold frame. In spring, when rooted, plant them in a nurserybed until large enough to be planted into a container.

***Azalea* Japanese types**
Height: 45-60cm/18-24in
Spread: 60-75cm/24-30in

Small-leaved, bushy evergreen shrubs, some slightly tender, with shallowly funnel-shaped flowers in massed heads during spring. The colour range is wide and includes scarlet, pink and white. Suitable for a tub or large pot.

Well-drained but moisture-retentive, slightly acid soil enriched with moist peat is essential. Position the container in a warm, wind-sheltered position, in light shade; shelter from early morning sun is desirable.

Although plants can be increased from cuttings and by layering low stems, it is better to buy established plants.

***Aegopodium podagraria* 'Variegatum'**
Variegated Gout Weed (USA)
Variegated Ground Elder (UK/USA)
Height: 15-25cm/6-10in
Spread: Forms a clump

Variegated, and less invasive, form of the infamous weed, Ground Elder. It has light to mid-green leaves edged in white and retains its colour even when positioned in light shade.

***Agapanthus* 'Lilliput'**
African Lily (UK/USA)
Height: 45cm/18in
Spread: 25-30cm/10-12in

This slightly tender perennial with fleshy roots has narrow, mid- to dark green leaves 15-20cm/6-8in long. Tall, upright stems bear umbrella-like heads of bright blue trumpet-shaped flowers during mid- and late summer.

***Agave americana* 'Marginata'**
Variegated Century Plant (UK/USA)
Height: 75-90cm/2½-3ft
Spread: 60-75cm/24-30in

Tender succulent with thick, sword-like, grey-green leaves with yellow edges. The ordinary type has plain grey-green leaves. During winter it must be moved into a frost-free greenhouse or conservatory.

***Bergenia* 'Bressingham Ruby'**
Height: 30-38cm/12-15in
Spread: 38-45cm/15-18in

Hardy border perennial with large, glossy green leaves which assume burnished maroon tints in winter. At the same time the undersides become crimson. During spring and early summer it develops spikes of deep rosy red flowers.

PLANT NAME AND DESCRIPTION	SITUATION AND CULTIVATION	PROPAGATION

Begonia x tuberhybrida
Height: 30-45cm/12-18in
Spread: 20-30cm/10-12in

Tender, tuberous plants with mid-green leaves and rose-like flowers up to 13cm/5in wide from early to late summer. Some flowers are single, but invariably it is double ones that are grown. The colour range includes yellow, pink, orange, scarlet and red, as well as white. The form 'Pendula' has smaller flowers and is ideal for hanging-baskets.

Plant in a tub or other large container on a warm, sunny patio and out of cold winds. Use well-drained, loam-based compost. Do not put young plants into containers outdoors until the risk of frost has totally passed. It is usually necessary to support young plants by using split-canes. In autumn, before the first frost, lift the plants and place in a cool greenhouse. After the leaves and stems have died down, place the tubers in moist peat in a frost-proof shed or greenhouse.

In early to mid-spring, put healthy tubers into boxes of moist peat. As soon as they develop shoots, cut up the tubers into several pieces. Each must have at least one healthy shoot.
Alternatively, use 7.5cm/3in-long shoots as cuttings. Take only one or two cuttings from each tuber. Include part of the tuber at each cutting's base and insert them in equal parts moist peat and sharp sand. Place in gentle warmth and when rooted pot up into individual pots.

Camellia japonica
Common Camellia (UK/USA)
Height: 1.5-2.4m/5-8ft in a tub
Spread: 90cm-1.5m/3-5ft in a tub

Hardy evergreen shrub with leathery, glossy, dark green leaves and 7.5-13cm/3-5in-wide flowers in colours ranging from white to pink, red and purple from late winter to late spring. Varieties are available with several types of flowers: single, semi-double, double and anemone- and paeony-flowered.

Slight shade or a sunny position, but where the flowers are shaded from a combination of early-morning frost and strong light. Position the tub away from cold winds. Well-drained, slightly acid compost formed of three parts peat, two of loam and one of sharp sand suits it. Keep the compost moist in spring and summer, but avoid saturating it in autumn and winter.
No regular pruning is needed, other than cutting out in spring shoots damaged by cold weather. Remove faded flowers.

Take 7.5-10cm/3-4in-long cuttings during mid- and late summer. Insert them in pots of equal parts moist peat and sharp sand and keep at 13°C/55°F. When the cuttings fill their pots with roots, pot them up into small pots.

Choisya ternata 'Sundance'
Mexican Orange Blossom (UK/USA)
Height: 75cm-1m/2½-3½ft
Spread: 75-90cm/2½-3ft

Slightly tender evergreen shrub with glossy, golden yellow leaves throughout the year and faintly orange-blossom-scented white flowers in late spring and early summer, and sometimes intermittently throughout summer. The leaves, when bruised, emit the distinctive aroma of oranges.

Full sun in a warm, sheltered corner on a patio. Plant in well-drained, loam-based compost, ensuring that about 5cm/2in of coarse drainage material covers the container's base.
No regular pruning is needed, other than cutting out frost-damaged stems in spring. Feed established plants two or three times from early to mid-summer.
In cold areas, it may be necessary to form a tripod of canes over the plant in winter and to cover it with straw. Remove as soon as the weather improves.

Take 7.5cm/3in-long cuttings in mid-summer and insert them in pots of equal parts moist peat and sharp sand. Place them in gentle warmth. When rooted, pot up into indivual pots and overwinter in a cold frame.

Clematis macropetala
Spread: 1.8-2.4m/6-8ft when planted in a tub and allowed to trail

Slender-stemmed, deciduous and bushy climber with light and dark blue, nodding, bell-shaped flowers up to 7.5cm/3in wide during late spring and early summer. After the flowers fade, it develops a mass of silky, fluffy seed heads. There are two varieties: 'Maidwell Hall' (deep blue) and 'Markham's Pink' (rose-coloured, shaded purple).

Sunny position but with shade available for the roots. Fertile, neutral to slightly alkaline compost.
When planting in a large, tub-like container, use two or three plants so that a good display is produced quickly.
It can also be grown up a trellis, when it reaches 3-3.6m/10-12ft high and 1.5-2.4m/5-8ft wide.

Take 7.5-10cm/3-4in-long stem cuttings during mid-summer and insert them in pots of equal parts moist peat and sharp sand. Place in gentle warmth.

Clematis florida 'Sieboldii'
Height: 1.5-1.8m/5-6ft
Spread: 75-90cm/2½-3ft

Bushy, deciduous, sometimes semi-evergreen climber, ideal for growing in a large pot. The large flowers resemble those of the Passion Flower (*Passiflora caerulea*), with white petals and violet-purple petal-like stamens. Support it with twiggy sticks.

Dicentra 'Snowflakes'
Height: 25-38cm/10-15in
Spread: 38-45cm/15-18in

A diminutive, hardy herbaceous perennial with fern-like, finely divided mid-green leaves and pendulous clusters of white, bee-attracting flowers from early to late summer. It looks its best in a round pot.

Hakonechloa macra 'Aureola'
Height: 25-30cm/10-12in
Spread: 75-90cm/2½-3ft

A hardy, cascading perennial grass with narrow, bright yellow leaves striped in green. When planted in a tub or large pot it creates a fountain of colour throughout summer.

Hypericum olympicum
Height: 20-30cm/8-12in
Spread: 30-38cm/12-15in

Hardy, low-growing evergreen shrub with grey-green leaves and golden yellow flowers up to 36mm/1½in wide during mid-summer. Select a dainty, low container that does not dominate the display.

Plants for tubs and urns

PLANT NAME AND DESCRIPTION	SITUATION AND CULTIVATION	PROPAGATION

Conifers
Height: Wide range, from those with an upright stature to those that are bushy or prostrate.

Choose dwarf or slow-growing conifers that later, when too large for a tub or large pot, can be transferred to a garden. They create colour and interesting shapes throughout the year and are especially welcome in winter, when perhaps there is little other interest in gardens.

Use well-drained soil-based compost in strong wooden tubs or large pots. The compost and container must form a firm base to prevent strong winds blowing over the conifer. Place about 36mm/1¹/₂in of clean rubble in the base of the container to ensure drainage holes do not become blocked with soil.

Most conifers are raised from cuttings, but it is much quicker and easier to buy an established plant that will make an instant display.

***Dimorphotheca ecklonis* 'Prostrata'**
(syn. *Osteospermum ecklonis* 'Prostrata')
African Daisy (UK)
Cape Marigold (USA)
Height: 15-23cm/6-9in
Spread: 30-38cm/12-15in

Bushy perennial with lance-shaped, mid-green leaves and a wealth of daisy-like, 7.5cm/3in-wide, white-petalled flowers with mustard yellow centres during mid- and late summer.

Plant in well-drained but moisture-retentive loam-based compost in spring. Ensure that the base of the container is well-drained. This is an ideal plant for planting in an old stone sink. The normal *D. ecklonis* grows 50-60cm/20-24in high and therefore is less suitable for growing in a container on a patio.
   Plants can be overwinterd by cutting them back in late autumn and placing cloches over them. In wet and very cold areas it is better to plant fresh African Daisies in spring.

Take 5cm/2in-long cuttings from sideshoots during mid-summer. Insert them in pots of sandy compost and place in a cold frame. When they have rooted, pot them up into individual pots and overwinter in a frost-proof frame. Plant into a container in spring.
   Plants can also be raised from seed sown in gentle warmth in early spring.

Dorycnium hirsutum
Hairy Canary Clover (UK)
Height: 30-38cm/12-15in in a container
Spread: 38-45cm/15-18in in a container

A hardy, semi-herbaceous but woody-based dwarf shrub that in a border may grow up to 45cm/18in. Each year it develops shoots with terminal heads of white, pink-flushed flowers during late summer and autumn. The entire plant has a silvery appearance.

Plant it in full sun and light, well-drained compost. Position it on a warm, sheltered patio. Plant in spring and keep the compost moist until the plant is established. The annual growth is usually damaged by frost during winter and the plant invariably dies down after developing flowers and bearing red-tinged seed pods. Therefore, in mid-spring clip over plants to remove the dead growth.

It is best raised from seeds sown in spring, although the progeny may vary greatly in habit. Sow seeds thinly and evenly in seed-trays or pots of sandy compost. When the seedlings are large enough to handle, transfer them into individual pots and place in a cold frame. Later, plant into a garden.

Fatsia japonica
False Castor Oil Plant (UK)
Glossy-leaved Paper Plant (USA)
Japanese Fatsia (USA)
Height: 1.5-2.1m/5-7ft
Spread: 1.5-1.8m/5-6ft

Slightly tender evergreen shrub with large, glossy, hand-like leaves with coarsely toothed edges. White flowers, borne in lax clusters 23-45cm/9-18in long, appear in autumn and often throughout winter.

Use well-drained, light but moisture-retentive soil and a large tub or pot. Fill the base of the container with clean, coarse rubble to ensure good drainage. A warm, wind-sheltered position in full sun or light shade suits it.
   No pruning is necessary, except to cut out straggly shoots in spring.

Detach sucker-like shoots in spring and use them as cuttings. Insert them singly in pots filled with equal parts moist peat and sharp sand and place in a cold frame. When cuttings have rooted, pot them up into large pots and position in a sheltered, warm corner until the following spring.

Ipomoea tricolor
Morning Glory (UK/USA)
Height: 1.5-1.8m/5-6ft in a pot

A half-hardy annual climber, raised from seed each year. From mid-summer to autumn it produces red-purple to blue flowers. It is ideal for growing in a large pot positioned near to a supporting framework. The flowers open during the morning and fade in the afternoon.

***Phormium tenax* 'Yellow Wave'**
New Zealand Flax (UK/USA)
New Zealand Hemp (USA)
Height: 60-75cm/2-2¹/₂ft
Spread: 75-90cm/2¹/₂-3ft

Half-hardy, evergreen perennial with golden yellow, strap-like leaves with green outer markings. Other suitable varieties include "Maori Sunrise', 75-90cm/2¹/₂-3ft high, with pinkish leaves with an apricot band and edged in light bronze.

***Polygonum affine* 'Dimity'**
Height: 15-20cm/6-8in
Spread: Forms a carpet up to 45cm/18in wide

A hardy herbaceous perennial with dark green leaves and spires of deep pink flowers from early to late summer. During autumn, the leaves assume rich autumnal tints. Plant it in a low pot that will not dominate the diminutive nature of the flowers and leaves.

***Prunus incisa* 'Kojo Nomai'**
Height: 1.2-1.5m/4-5ft
Spread: 90cm-1.2m/3-4ft

A hardy deciduous flowering cherry with twiggy, naked branches in winter and red-centred, pinkish flowers that fade to white in spring. In autumn, the fresh-green leaves assume rich autumnal tints of brown, orange and, sometimes, crimson.

PLANT NAME AND DESCRIPTION	SITUATION AND CULTIVATION	PROPAGATION

Hebe x andersonii 'Variegata'
Height: 75-90cm/2½-3ft
Spread: 60-90cm/2-3ft

Slightly tender evergreen shrub with leathery, cream and green variegated leaves. It has the bonus of developing 13cm/5in-long spikes of lavender flowers from mid-summer to early autumn. Although not a dominant patio plant, it creates colour throughout the year and is especially attractive when planted in a large white container.

Plant in a medium-sized wooden tub or a large glassfibre pot. Use well-drained, loam-based compost and set the plant in the container in spring.
No regular pruning is needed, other than cutting out in spring those shoots damaged by cold winter weather. In a severe winter, cover the plant with a tripod of canes with straw wrapped around it. Remove the cover as soon as the weather improves.

Take 7.5cm/3in-long cuttings during mid-summer and insert them in pots of equal parts moist peat and sharp sand. Place them in a cold frame or cool greenhouse. After they develop roots, pot up individually into small pots and place in a cold frame during winter.

Hosta sp.
Plantain Lily (UK/USA)
Height: Choose moderately tall species and varieties, up to 60cm/24in high.

Hardy herbaceous perennials grown for their attractive leaves which may be of one colour or variegated. Some species and varieties have attractive flowers. Hostas look superb when planted in varnished tubs or white pots.

Use well-drained, loam-based compost to which has been added moist peat. It is essential that the compost does not dry out during summer. However, it must not be waterlogged in winter.
Variegated species retain their best colour in light shade.

Divide congested plants in spring, just as growth begins. Some can be raised from seeds, but variegated types do not come true when raised in this way.

Pleioblastus auricoma
(syn. *Arundinaria viridistriata/ Pleioblastus viridistriatus*)
Height: 90cm-1.2m/3-4ft
Spread: Forms a clump 30-45cm/12-18in wide

Hardy bamboo with slender, knitting-needle-like, dark purplish green stems surmounted by dark green leaf blades, which are up to 20cm/8in long and 30mm/1¼in-wide and dominantly striped in rich golden yellow.

Full sun or light shade, fertile, moisture-retentive compost and a position sheltered from cold winds. The roots should not be allowed to become dry, especially in spring and summer. Plant bamboos when the soil is warm, usually in early summer. Never plant them from late autumn to spring. No pruning is necessary.

Divide congested clumps in early summer, replanting each piece before its roots become dry. Keep the compost moist until plants are established – placing them in a greenhouse helps in their establishment.

Yucca sp.
Height: 90cm-1.5m/3-5ft (range)

A group of hardy and slightly tender evergreens with long, stiff, sword-like leaves. Some, such as *Y. filamentosa*, *Y. gloriosa* and *Y. recurvifolia* are relatively hardy, while *Y. elephantipes* (Spineless Yucca) and *Y. aloifolia* (Spanish Bayonet) are normally grown as houseplants in temperate climates, and can be placed outdoors during summer. Choose a warm, sunny corner.

A tub or large pot filled with well-drained, loam-based compost with extra sharp sand added to it is needed. Ensure that the base is filled with clean rubble to prevent the drainage holes becoming blocked. Position the plant in a warm area, away from cold winds.

Remove and pot up rooted suckers in spring. If they are small, place in a cool greenhouse until they are large enough to be planted into a container outdoors.
Yuccas create dramatic features on a patio, but beware of the sharply tipped leaves – especially if young children are present.

Sambucus racemosa 'Sutherland Gold'
Height: 1.8-2.1m/6-7ft
Spread: 1.8-2.4m/6-8ft

Hardy deciduous shrub with handsome, finely divided, golden yellow leaves. Eventually it forms a large shrub, but when young is superb in a large tub.

Stachys olympica
Primrose Heron (UK/US)
Height: 30-38cm/12-15in
Spread: 38-45cm/15-18in or more

Hardy perennial with light grey-green felted leaves suffused in gold for a few weeks. Magenta flowers appear in summer on stems about 30cm/12in high.

Thunbergia alata
Black-eyed Susan (UK)
Black-eyed Susan Vine (USA)
Height: 1.2-1.8m/4-6ft in a pot

Half-hardy annual climber with a climbing and twining nature. From early summer to autumn it becomes drenched in 5cm/2in-wide orange-yellow flowers, each with a dark centre.

Tropaeolum majus
Garden Nasturtium (USA)
Indian Cress (UK/USA)
Nasturtium (UK)
Height: 38-45cm/15-18in (dwarf varieties)

Half-hardy annual with circular, mid-green leaves and faintly scented, orange or yellow flowers up to 5cm/2in across from early summer to early autumn. There are many varieties and colours. Position the pot close to a supporting framework.

Filling and planting a stone sink

Old, shallow, stone sinks form attractive and unusual homes for dwarf conifers, alpine plants and small bulbs; they can be planted up to produce a miniature landscape that creates an eye-catching feature on a patio.

Stone sinks – the type fitted in kitchens and wash-houses not that many generations ago — are best, but although plentiful at one time, they are now prized, expensive and increasingly difficult to find. It is, however, possible to give a glazed white sink an old, rustic appearance by coating it with a peat and glue mixture – the technique is described opposite.

PLANTING UP A STONE SINK

Good drainage is the main need of alpine and other plants in sink gardens, as well as a south- or west-facing position and shelter from cold, northerly and easterly winter winds.

Good light is also necessary, together with a position away from trees; alpines are soon damaged by water dripping on them from rain-soaked branches and leaves. Fallen leaves are also a problem, as they suffocate plants and, when wet, encourage the presence of pests and the rapid spread of diseases.

Position the sink on a firm base, with a slight slope towards the drainage hole in its base. Piers of bricks form the safest and firmest base.

Prepare the sink for planting by thoroughly scrubbing it. Then place a double layer of fine-mesh wire netting over the drainage hole, with a large piece of broken clay pot on top. Form a 2.5cm/1in-deep layer of clean, 6mm/¼in pea shingle in the base. Place a 36mm/1½in layer of moist peat on top, followed by a mixture of two parts loam-based compost and one part sharp sand. Gently firm this mixture until it is about 2.5cm/1in below the rim.

When planting a modified glazed sink – which is likely to be 25-30cm/10-12in deep – increase the thickness of the shingle to 36mm/1½in and the moist peat to 6cm/2½in.

Before setting plants in the sink, arrange them on a piece of paper of a similar size to the sink. Grade the plants in height from the back to the front, using trailing types to soften the sink's edges. Miniature conifers are ideal for creating

Below right: Shallow, old stone sinks create ideal conditions for alpine plants and miniature conifers and shrubs. Good drainage is essential and this is created by a layer of drainage material in the sink's base, porous compost and a layer of grit or pea-shingle on the surface. Small rocks help to create a miniature landscape for the plants.

PLANTING A STONE SINK

1 Stand the sink on bricks to ensure a firm base. Place a couple of layers of wire netting, then a large piece of a broken clay pot, over the drainage hole.
2 Spread a 2.5cm/1in-thick layer of shingle in the base, then 36mm/1½in of peat. (Increase these depths in a deep sink.)
3 Top up and firm well-drained compost to within 2.5cm/1in of the rim.
4 Before setting plants in the sink, arrange them on a piece of paper.
5 Use a small trowel to make the planting holes and spread out the roots; ensure compost is firmed over them.
6 Spread stone chippings over the compost and around each plant. This helps to keep the compost cool and prevents it being disturbed when plants are watered.

PLANTS FOR A SINK GARDEN

The range of plants suitable for sink gardens is wide and includes:

- **Conifers:** Some conifers for planting in sinks are miniature by nature, while slow-growing types are also suitable during their early years. There are many to choose from, including *Juniperus comunis* 'Compressa' (slow growing and, when young, ideal for planting in stone sinks). Many other miniature conifers can be used, but be prepared to move them into a rock garden or scree bed when too large for a sink garden.

- **Miniature plants and alpines:** *Androsace sarmentosa* 'Chumbyi' (deep rose flowers in spring and early summer); *Antennaria dioica* 'Rosea' (deep pink flowers in late spring and early summer); *Campanula cochleariifolia* (blue bells from mid- to late summer); *Edraianthus pumilio* (lavender blue flowers in early and mid-summer); *Erinus alpinus* (bright pink flowers from spring to mid-summer); *Hebe buchananii* 'Minor' (white flowers in early summer); *Lewisia cotyledon* (pink flowers with white veins during late spring and early summer); *Saxifraga burseriana* (white flowers in late winter and early spring).

- **Miniature bulbs for spring display:** *Crocus chrysanthus* (globular flowers in a range of colours, including golden yellow, bronze, mauve-blue, white and deep purple); *Eranthis hyemalis* (yellow, bowl-like flowers with pale green ruffs); *Narcissus bulbocodium* (dainty, yellow, hoop-like trumpets); *Narcissus cyclamineus* (miniature, yellow trumpets and swept-back petals); *Iris danfordiae* (honey-scented, bright yellow flowers); *Iris reticulata* (deep blue, iris-like flowers with gold-yellow blazes on the insides of the lower petals).

height and providing a background for other plants. Although you can use a mixture of plants that do not normally grow together, the design should look natural.

Start by planting one or two small conifers towards one corner. A few small rocks positioned to form a strata at an angle across the sink creates a slight differential in compost height, introducing further interest. Plant cushion-forming plants over parts of the rocks to help them blend in.

When planting is complete, form a 12mm/¹⁄₂in-thick layer of stone chippings over the surface. This creates an attractive background for plants, prevents rain falling on compost and then splashing on plants, keeps the compost cool and moist in summer, prevents the growth of weeds and ensures good drainage around plants.

MODIFYING A GLAZED SINK

Converting an ordinary glazed sink into an attractive feature for a patio is not difficult. Stand the sink on four bricks positioned slightly in from the edges. Ideally, the sink should be raised 10-15cm/4-6in high, so that when it is completed you can place stout poles underneath to move it to its display position. Use soapy water to wash and grime and grease. Rinse with clean water.

Use an old, sharp tool, such as an aged and worn chisel, to scratch all visible surfaces (all over the outside and about 7.5cm/3in down the inside edge). Wash off the dust and allow the surface to dry.

Paint the surface with a PVA bonding glue (available from a builders' merchant or DIY store); use an old brush, as after use it is best thrown away. Allow the glue to become tacky, but not dry, before you apply the 'rustic' coating.

Mix one part sharp sand, one of cement powder and two of fine peat (all parts by bulk, not weight), adding water to create a stiff but pliable mixture. Wearing gloves, spread this mixture to about 12mm/¹⁄₂in thick all over the outer surface and slightly down the insides, pressing it firmly on the glue. Do not tackle this job during frosty or wet weather and protect the sink from strong sunlight, as this encourages the peat and sand mixture to dry unevenly or too quickly.

When the coating is hard – usually after two weeks – move the sink to its final position. Place two strong pieces of timber underneath and ask for the help of a friend to carry it.

Growing vegetables in growing-bags

Compared with most ways of growing plants, growing-bags are a relatively recent innovation. They are basically strong plastic bags of peat-based compost which, when opened and watered, can be used to grow plants. Standard-sized growing-bags are about 1.2m/4ft long, but there are half-sized ones. Check with the instructions on the outside of the bag about preparing it for use: with some, the compost is in the form of a dehydrated and compressed slab that is light and easily transported. Once the bag is set in place, water is added through the growing windows that have to be cut in the plastic and the slab swells to fill the bag with compost.

Most manufacturers do not recommend piercing holes in the bag's base (if they do, this is indicated). With unpierced bags, there is a danger of the compost becoming too wet if excessively watered or after heavy rainfall. If this happens, make a few holes in the bag, so that it can drain.

Bags with pierced bases are able to drain freely. On patios this is no problem, but if the bag is on a balcony, stand it on a tray of shingle to prevent water dripping over the edge.

Plants soon use up the fertilizers originally mixed with the compost, so be prepared to feed them regularly during summer. Use a compound fertilizer containing nitrogen, phosphate and potash, plus trace elements. Thoroughly water the compost, then apply fertilizer diluted in water according to manufaturer's instructions.

Most bags are placed directly on a patio or other surface, but if the area is infested with slugs and snails during summer – or if you may need to move the bag – place it on a board raised above the ground – a pallet-type board is ideal.

ADVANTAGES OF GROWING-BAGS

- Inexpensive way of creating additional areas for growing plants.
- Light weight and so ideal for balconies, as well as patios and terraces.
- Clean compost, free from pests and diseases. If the soil in a greenhouse is contaminated with diseases, a growing-bag isolates the compost and plants.
- Variety of uses, from vegetables and herbs to summer-flowering bedding plants.
- Easily transported home and stored before use.
- Good growth is possible, provided plants are fed regularly once they are established.

Plants such as tomatoes and climbing beans need support; if a growing-bag is positioned against a fence or wall, you can secure wires and strings to it to support plants. If you want to position the bag in the middle of a patio, you will need to use special supports. These are usually formed of a wire framework that fits under the bag and extends upwards for 90cm-1.2m/3-4ft. The weight of the compost in the bag holds the supporting framework secure.

RANGE OF VEGETABLES

Vegetables for growing in growing-bags include:

Aubergines In late spring or early summer, as soon as all risk of frost has passed, put two plants in a standard-sized bag. Water and feed them regularly, pinch out their growing tips when plants are 25cm/10in high and encourage the development of three or four branches on each plant. Plants will need support from strings and wires. Remove all but five or six fruits on each plant and harvest the aubergines when 10-20cm/4-8in long.

PREPARING A GROWING-BAG

1 Shake the bag to loosen the peat-based compost inside. Place the bag on a flat, level surface. If slugs are a problem, place it on a board slightly raised above the ground.
2 Cut windows in the bag (these will be indicated by dotted lines).
3 Thoroughly saturate the compost with clean water.

Above: Tomato plants grown in growing-bags in a greenhouse produce prolific crops of fruits. Plants can be supported in several ways; here, the growing-bag is placed in a strong, polystyrene trough which has a series of holes at its sides in which bamboo canes can be inserted. These can be tied at their tops to create a strong framework of supports.

Courgettes After all risk of frost has passed in late spring or early summer, put two plants in a standard-sized growing-bag. Water and feed the plants regularly. It is essential to keep cutting the fruits when young and tender to encourage more to develop.

Climbing French beans and runner beans During late spring or early summer, as soon as all risk of frost has passed, put four plants in a standard-sized growing-bag. Keep the compost moist and feed plants regularly at fourteen-day intervals once plants are established and growing strongly. Support plants with proprietary wire frameworks. Pinch out the growing point of each stem when it reaches the top of the supporting framework. Start harvesting the beans when they are 16-20cm/6-8in long, before the seeds inside them have started to swell.

Bush French beans These are grown in the same way as climbing French beans, but have a dwarf and bushy nature and therefore do not need to be supported. Place six plants into a standard-sized growing-bag as soon as all risk of frost has passed. Pods are ready to be harvested when they snap when bent; at this stage they will be 10-15cm/4-6in long.

Lettuce It is possible to have fresh lettuces from early to late summer. If you choose small varieties, you can grow eight lettuces in a standard-sized growing-bag.

Potatoes This is a novelty crop for a growing-bag. Choose an early variety and plant in early to mid-spring. Put eight tubers in a bag, setting them a few inches deep. As shoots appear, place more compost over them until slightly mounded.

Tomatoes Standard-sized bags accommodate three or four plants. It is easier to buy healthy plants and to plant them as soon all risk of frost has passed than to raise your own. Plant with the soil-ball level with the surface; remove sideshoots (growths arising from the leaf joints) and pinch out the growing tip when plants reach the eaves. Support with supporting frameworks. There is no need to 'stop' bush types.

GROWING HERBS IN GROWING-BAGS

Herbs in growing-bags are decorative, especially sages and mints with their varied leaf shapes and colours. Also, mint can be constrained in a bag, whereas in a border the plant becomes rampant. Many herbs are either low-growing and bushy or trailing and hide the plastic of the bag.

Culinary herbs to consider for growing-bags include Apple Mint, with pale green leaves covered with white hairs, and Spearmint (also known as the Common Mint), with mid-green, prominently veined leaves. The Common Sage has grey-green, wrinkled leaves, but there are several forms with attractively variegated leaves.

VEGETABLES IN GROWING-BAGS

1 Special supporting frames are available for plants such as beans.
2 Plant three or four tomatoes in a standard-sized growing-bag. Ensure the top of each soil-ball is level with the surface.
3 Lettuces are an excellent crop for growing-bags as they are relatively shallow rooting. Eight small lettuces can be grown in a standard-sized growing-bag.

WATER GARDENING

Water gardens have a magnetism seldom matched by any other area in a garden. Apart from bursting with colourful aquatic and bog plants, they provide a fascinating environment for fish and other water-loving creatures. Ponds can fit into any garden design, whether strictly formal or with a cottage-garden ambience. A flat and spacious patio can be given a vertical dimension with a raised pond, which enables elderly or infirm gardeners to see the fish and plants without having to bend down. Raised ponds are also favoured by those with young children, for obvious safety reasons. Even the smallest patio can accommodate a miniature water garden – made, perhaps, from a large, wooden barrel cut in half.

Making a pond from a flexible liner

Using a flexible liner is one of the most popular ways to make a water feature in a garden; liners are adaptable to many shapes and sizes and no mixing of concrete is involved.

TYPES OF LINER

Liners range in quality and cost; sizes up to 9m/30ft x 6m/20ft are readily available, but larger sizes will have to be ordered. The more expensive liners are thicker and more durable than cheap ones. However, it is more difficult to persuade the thicker liners to assume the shape of acute angles, so consider this when designing the pond. It is false economy to install a cheap liner as after a few years it will need to be replaced, but it may be suitable as an expediency to create a short-term feature. The main materials include the following:

Polyethylene (widely known as polythene) has a limited life of up to three years; when exposed to light it cracks and tears. Consider it only for temporary ponds and use a double layer of 500-gauge sheeting. A few brands of polyethylene are more durable, especially if the water level in the

pond is not allowed to drop and to expose the edges of the liner to sunlight.

PVC (polyvinyl chloride), a material often used to make garden hoses, raincoats and floor tiles, forms a strong pool liner with a lifespan of ten to fifteen years. It is stretchable and more easily adapts to irregularities than polyethylene. It is also about half the cost of butyl (see below). PVC is usually laid in a single thickness, but a double layer is stronger. Some brands are reinforced with netting, to make it extra durable.

Butyl rubber, a form of rubber sheeting frequently used in tyres and insulation, forms the best liner for a pond, but it is the most expensive. Mostly sold in sheets 0.0762cm/0.03in thick, butyl is virtually unaffected by sunlight or low temperatures and has a life expectancy of about fifty years. Because it survives in sunlight, it is the best material to use to create a series of waterfalls from flexible liners.

ASSESSING THE SIZE OF LINER NEEDED

This is not difficult and is best calculated after the pond has been excavated. Measure the width and

MAKING A POND FROM A FLEXIBLE LINER

1 Use a hosepipe or thick rope to form the outline of a pond. At this stage you can easily change the design.
2 Use a spade to cut out the shape on the inside of the hosepipe.
3 Dig out the area to the depth required. Cut the sides at a 20 degree angle.
4 Use a sharp spade to cut a strip about 25cm/10in wide around the pond so that edging stones can be later cemented into position.
5 Form a 36mm/1¹/₂ in-thick layer of soft sand over the base and up the sides; lightly moistening the sand helps it to cling to the slope.
6 Place the liner in the hole. Form pleats around the sides, so that the liner is neat. Use stones at the sides to keep the liner in place as the pond is filled with water. Later, cement edging stones into position.

Above: For a natural-looking pond, allow a lawn to abut the water. Fold the flap of the liner over the edge and then place turf on top. Do not allow the level of the water to fall, or the edge will become unsightly and the lawn will dry out and crumble.

length of the pond (at the widest and longest points), then add twice the depth to each measurement. Also, add 30cm/12in to both length and width to allow for overlaps at the sides.

DESIGNING AND CONSTRUCTING A POND

Getting the pond's shape right, as well as its orientation in relation to the rest of the garden, is not something to be rushed. Use a thick piece of rope or a hosepipe to create the pond's outline; then leave it in position for several days so that you can view it from all positions. When you are sure it is right, you can begin the construction.

Use a spade to cut the outline, just within the hosepipe or rope. Then mark out an area about 25cm/10in wider than the pool. In the outer strip, remove soil to 7.5cm/3in deep to form a base for edging stones; within the central part, dig out soil to about 75cm/30in deep. Try to give the sides a 20° slope. Form a shelf, on which to posi-

tion aquatic plants, immediately within the pool, 23cm/9in wide and deep.

Use a spirit-level to check that all sides of the pond are level and add or remove soil as necessary. Also, check that the base and the shelves are level. Ensure that stones do not stick out of the soil at the sides (they might puncture the liner), then form a 36mm/1¹⁄₂in-thick layer of soft sand over the base and pad out the sides and shelf with moist, soft sand. This prevents the liner puncturing when the water presses upon it.

Place the liner in the hole, taking care not to disturb the sand. Mould it to fit the slopes of the longest sides and, as necessary, form pleats round the bends and corners as you fit the short sides. When the liner is in position, place bricks on the overlap around the pond's edges.

Using a hosepipe, gently fill up the pond with water. As the water level rises, re-adjust the liner to remove creases. When full, remove the bricks from the overlap. Use sharp scissors to trim the overlap to 15cm/6in wide around the pond. Lift up the overlap, form a 2.5cm/1in-thick layer of soft sand beneath it, then fold the flap over it.

Use a mixture of three parts soft sand and one of cement powder to bed in edging stones, which must project 5cm/2in over the water. Use a fairly dry mortar mixture between the edging stones, press it firmly in place and smooth with a trowel. Do not let mortar drop into the pond, or you will need to drain and refill it. Leave the pond alone for about a week so that the edging stones become firm.

REMOVING AND DISPOSING OF EXCAVATED SOIL

Often, the most difficult part of digging a hole to accommodate a pond is disposing of the soil.

If your garden is established, and the pond is something you are adding as an afterthought, the easiest way to get rid of the soil is to hire a skip. You will need a builders' wheelbarrow and strong boards about 23cm/9in wide, on which to run the barrow's wheel. Take care not to damage lawn edges; use a brick or thick piece of wood to build up the level of the border, and then place a plank on top. Do not try to push a wheelbarrow up a ramp and into a skip when the surfaces are wet.

Do not use excavated soil to form the base of a rock garden; the soil is likely to be heavy and badly drained – the opposite of what is required. The topsoil (about 20cm/8in deep) can be used to top-up flower beds.

Aquatic and marginal plants

PLANT NAME AND DESCRIPTION	SITUATION AND CULTIVATION	PROPAGATION

***Iris pseudacorus* 'Variegata'**
Variegated Water Flag (USA)
Variegated Yellow Flag (USA)
Variegated Yellow Flag Iris (UK)
Height: 75-90cm/2½-3ft
Spread: 38-45cm/15-18in

Hardy, water-loving, herbaceous perennial with erect, sword-like, bluish green leaves with yellow stripes. It develops 7.5cm/3in-wide yellow flowers during early summer. These are later followed by brown seed capsules.

Full sun and fertile soil. It grows well in water 15cm/6in deep. Plant the young rhizomes in spring or autumn.

In autumn, cut down leaves and remove them from the pool. If left in the water during winter they decompose and create gases that are toxic to fish, especially if the surface becomes capped in ice.

Lift and divide congested clumps immediately after the flowers fade. Alternatively, divide them whenever the plants are actively growing. If this job is left until the leaves die down it is difficult to trace the positions of the rhizomes.

Lysichiton americanus
Skunk Cabbage (UK/USA)
Western Skunk Cabbage (USA)
Yellow Skunk Cabbage (USA)
Height: 60-90cm/2-3ft
Spread: 60-75cm/24-30in

Moisture-loving, long-lived, hardy, herbaceous perennial which forms a large clump of oval, grass-green leaves up to 90cm/3ft long and with pointed tips. From early to late spring it develops flowers formed of deep yellow spathes.

Full sun or light shade and fertile, moisture-retentive soil at the side of a garden pond or stream. If planting it in a garden pond, build up the soil-level – or use a plastic-mesh water-plant container with its top positioned level with the water's surface. In autumn, remove dead leaves and flowers.

Divide congested clumps by removing young plants that develop around them. Transfer these into large loam-filled pots, keep watered and place in a warm, wind-sheltered position until established, when they can be planted into a pond.

***Mimulus* sp.**
Monkey Flower (UK/USA)
Height: 30-75cm/12-30in (range)
Spread: 25-38cm/10-15in (range)

A group of hardy annuals and herbaceous perennials, well known for their brightly coloured, snapdragon-like flowers throughout summer. These plants are ideal for introducing bright colours to ponds and their surrounds.

These are moisture-loving plants; those within a pond clearly have sufficient moisture, but if planted around the edge they need soil to which has been added plenty of a peat substitute.

M. ringens (Lavender Water Musk/ Allegheny Monkey Flower) grows in water up to 10cm/4in deep, as well as in moist soil around a pond. *M. luteus* can also be grown in water, but not deeper than 5cm/2in, whereas *M. cupreus* and *M. cardinalis* (Scarlet Monkey Flower) are best planted in moist soil around a pond.

Divide and replant herbaceous types (*M. ringens* and *M. cardinalis*) in spring, selecting young parts from around the outside of the clump.

Raise *M. cupreus* and *M. luteus* from seeds sown thinly in a seed-tray in late winter or early spring and keep at 13-16°C/55-61°F. When the seedlings are large enough to handle, transfer them to seed-trays and space further apart. Slowly acclimatize them to outdoor conditions and plant into a garden in late spring or early summer.

***Nymphaea* sp.**
Waterlily (UK/USA)
Height: Water's surface
Spread: 30-75cm/12-30in (range)

Perennial water plant with stems and leaves that die in autumn, fresh ones appearing in spring. The round green leaves float on the surface with the many-petalled, cup-shaped flowers in early and mid-summer, and often into late summer. Colours include white, pink, red, copper and yellow.

Full sun and fertile loamy soil in a plastic-mesh water-plant basket. Waterlilies range in vigour, and in the depth of water that suits them, from 15cm/6in to 1.2m/4ft. When planting a young plant, gently submerge it until the leaves are level with the surface. Stand the container on one or two bricks. As the plant grows, remove the bricks. Little attention is needed, other than removing congested leaves and pulling out dead stems and leaves in autumn.

Divide congested plants in early to mid-spring when the pool is drained. Use a sharp knife to separate the rootstock, and re-plant in separate containers.

***Acorus calamus* 'Variegatus'**
Variegated Sweet Flag (UK)
Height: 45-75cm/18-30in
Spread: 38-45cm/15-18in (clump forming)

Hardy, evergreen marginal plant with erect, sword-like, green leaves with bold cream stripes. It is ideal for planting in water 7.5-15cm/3-6in deep at the edge of a pond.

Aponogeton distachyos
Cape Asparagus (USA)
Cape Pondweed (USA)
Water Hawthorn (UK/USA)
Height: Water's surface
Spread: 38-60cm/15-24in

Hardy aquatic, with white, deeply lobed, vanilla-scented flowers that protrude above the water's surface from early to late summer – sometimes into autumn. Plant it in water 30-45cm/12-18in deep.

Butomus umbellatus
Flowering Rush (UK/USA)
Water Gladiolus (USA)
Height: 75cm-1m/2½-3½ft
Spread: 45-60cm/12-24in

Hardy marginal plant with long, grass-like leaves and tall flower stalks which bear inverted umbrella-like heads of rose-pink flowers during mid- and late summer. Plant in 7.5cm/3in of water, or in very wet soil around a pond.

***Carex elata* 'Bowles' Golden'**
Golden Sedge (UK)
Height: 38-45cm/15-18in
Spread: 15-25cm/6-10in

Tufted marginal plant with yellow leaves narrowly striped green. It is a superb plant, especially for a small pond. Plant in water up to 5cm/2in deep, or in moist soil around a pond.

PLANT NAME AND DESCRIPTION	SITUATION AND CULTIVATION	PROPAGATION

Peltiphyllum peltatum
(now known as *Darmera peltata*)
Umbrella Plant (UK/USA)
Height: 60-90cm/2-3ft
Spread: 45-75cm/18-30in

Hardy, moisture-loving herbaceous perennial, initially developing large heads of pink flowers at the tops of long stems. Later, the bright green leaves appear, eventually growing 30cm/12in wide and changing in autumn to bronze-pink.

Full sun or light shade and fertile, moisture-retentive soil. It grows well in boggy soil at the edge of a stream or pond. Set the plants in position in autumn, about 90cm/3ft apart. Also in autumn, cut down the leaves of established plants.

Lift and divide congested clumps while in their dormant stage.

Pontederia cordata
Pickerel Plant (UK/USA)
Height: 45-75cm/18-30in
Spread: 30-38cm/12-15in

Hardy herbaceous perennial that thrives in water up to 23cm/9in deep. The deep, glossy green, pointed and narrowly heart-shaped leaves create an attractive foil to the terminal, 5-10cm/2-4in-long spikes of purple-blue flowers, each with a yellow eye, that appear during mid- and late summer and sometimes into autumn.

Full sun and fertile compost. Although it can be grown in boggy soil surrounding a pond, it does better when planted in water so that its creeping rhizomes are fully covered. Plant in spring. It quickly establishes itself and then little attention is needed. In autumn, remove dead stems and leaves.

Lift and divide congested plants in late spring and use a sharp knife to cut the rhizome. Re-plant the individual pieces separately in individual plastic-mesh containers and position so that they are covered with about 7.5cm/3in of water. When established, they can be planted in deeper water.

Primula japonica
Japanese Primrose (UK)
Height: 60-75cm/24-30in
Spread: 23-30cm/9-12in

A short-lived, moisture-loving primula with rosettes of pale green leaves and long, upright stems bearing several whorls of magenta-red flowers from late spring to mid-summer. There are several superb forms, including 'Postford White' (pure white with yellow eyes) and 'Miller's Crimson' (bright red).

Full sun or dappled shade and fertile, moisture-retentive, peat-enriched soil suit it. It is essential that the soil should not dry out, and it is often necessary to water these plants regularly during spring and summer. Mulch the soil with peat or similar materials in spring, after first ensuring it is moist.

Lift and divide congested clumps after flowering, separating them and replanting them immediately into their new growing positions. Alternatively, sow seeds thinly and shallowly in seed-trays in spring; place them in a cold frame. Germination is not rapid – usually twenty-one days or more. When large enough to handle, prick out the seedlings into seed-trays, later planting into a garden when established, preferably in spring.

Primula vialii
Height: 25-30cm/10-12in
Spread: 20-25cm/8-10in

Hardy primula with lance-shaped, pale green leaves and 7.5-13cm/3-5in-long spikes of lavender-blue flowers during early and mid-summer. It is ideal for planting in groups alongside a garden pond.

Fertile, moisture-retentive soil is essential; add plenty of a peat substitute to ensure it remains moist in spring and summer. Choose a position in full sun or partial shade.

Large clumps can be divided, but it is more practical to raise new plants from seeds. Sow seeds in seed-trays as soon as they are ripe, barely covering them with compost. Place them in a cold frame. Keep the compost moist and when the seedlings are large enough to handle, transfer them into seed-trays or pots, and give them wider spacings. Overwinter them in a cold frame and plant into a garden when fully established and growing strongly, usually in spring.

***Glyceria maxima* 'Variegata'**
Variegated Reed Sweetgrass (UK)
Height: 75-90cm/2½-3ft
Spread: 75-90cm/2½-3ft

Hardy, grass-like, herbaceous aquatic plant with long, upright then arching, narrow leaves. In spring they have pinkish white stripes, but as the season progresses the pink fades. Plant it in water up to 15cm/6in deep. It can be invasive, so constrain it in a container.

Hydrocharis morsus-ranae
Frog-bit (UK/USA)
Height: 5cm/2in above water's surface
Spread: 15-23cm/6-9in

Floating aquatic, with green, kidney-shaped leaves and short-lived white flowers during mid- and late summer. It is not invasive and is ideal for small ponds.

Nuphar lutea
Brandy Bottle (UK)
Yellow Water Lily (UK/USA)
Height: Water's surface
Spread: 1.2-1.8m/4-6ft or more

Vigorous waterlily-type plant with large, round leaves up to 38cm/15in wide and bright yellow, 5-7.5cm/2-3in wide, brandy-scented flowers that protrude several inches out of the water. Plant it in water 60cm-1.2m/2-4ft deep.

Orontium aquaticum
Golden Club (UK/USA)
Height: 23-30cm/9-12in
Spread: 38-45cm/15-18in

Hardy aquatic plant with blue-green leaves, silver-green below, and pencil-like flower heads formed of pure white flowers during spring. Plant it in water 30-45cm/12-18in deep.

Making a pond from a rigid liner

Using a rigid liner (sometimes called a pre-formed, moulded or ready-made pond) enables you to create a water garden very quickly. Rigid liners are available in a wide range of sizes and shapes.

RANGE OF CONSTRUCTION MATERIALS

Some of the earliest rigid liners were made from galvanized steel. During the first few years they were alright, but rust eventually caused leakage. Nowadays, they are made of rust-proof materials.

Rigid plastic liners are the cheapest, but only semi-rigid. They are usually made of vacuum-formed polythene in a range of colours, including green, brown, blue and grey. Because they are not fully rigid, extra care is needed to ensure that the surfaces are not stressed. With age, ridges and corners often crack, while surfaces exposed to strong sunlight will deteriorate.

Reinforced plastic liners are more rigid, resistant to damaging ultraviolet rays and the best types are guaranteed for ten or more years. The usual depth is 45cm/18in, with a total area up to 7sq m/75sq ft.

Glass-fibre shells are formed of glass fibres bonded with a resin. They are made in several colours, including black, grey, buff, green and blue. These shells are resistant to decay and are not damaged by ultraviolet light. However, they need careful installation to prevent them being stressed when placed on an uneven base. Ensure that the shell allows a water depth of at least 45cm/18in. Because glass fibre is not damaged by ultraviolet rays, it is an ideal material to use for constructing waterfall shells.

INSTALLING A RIGID LINER

When storing or moving a rigid liner, be careful not to stress or drop it, and avoid standing in it, as this causes stress and may crack the material.

Place the shell the right way up in the position where it is to be installed and mark its outline, and the position of the shelves, on the ground. Remove the shell, then add about 7.5cm/3in all the way around the outline to allow for the soft sand to be packed around the shell's edge.

Dig out the soil. Topsoil can be spread over borders, but heavy subsoil is best put in a hired

MAKING A POND FROM A RIGID LINER

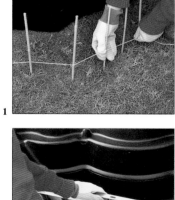

1

4

5

2

6

3

1 Place the rigid liner in position and insert 25-30cm/ 10-12in-long bamboo canes to mark the shell extremities. Wind a piece of string around the canes.
2 Use smaller canes to mark out the area 15-20cm/ 6-8in wide in which the edging stones will be laid.
3 Dig out the central area, so that the shell fits in it; allow a gap of about 7.5cm/3in all the way around it.
4 Place soft sand in the base, position the shell and use a spirit-level to ensure it is level.
5 When the shell is level, insert pieces of wood around it to hold it in position. Then, place soft sand into the gap around the side.
6 Around the sides, form a 12mm/^{1}/2in-thick layer of sand, then cement the edging stones in place.

MINIATURE PONDS

In a courtyard garden or on a patio a sunken pond at may not be possible, but a miniature water garden in a large wooden tub is often practical. In cold areas, where there is a risk that the water will freeze in winter, a miniature pond is a seasonal feature; conversely, in hot climates the water may become too warm – and lack oxygen – during summer.

Creating a miniature water garden

- Check that the tub is clean, strong and watertight. If the timber is dry, small leaks often occur, but if the tub is filled with water for a few weeks the wood expands and leakage stops. If leaks persist, line the tub with thick polythene. Form pleats inside it so that it looks neat, and then fill with water. When full, cut off the polythene level with the tub's top.

- Plant it in late spring or early summer, using miniature waterlilies and other plants. Always put each plant in a separate plastic-mesh container; if the plant is young or small, initially stand this on a brick, which can later be removed. Waterlilies to consider include *Nymphaea* 'Aurora' (first pinkish yellow, later orange, then red) and *Nymphaea* 'Graziella' (orange, with orange-red stamens). Marginal plants include *Carex stricta* 'Bowles Golden' (narrow, golden leaves) and *Scirpus zebrinus* (quill-like stems banded in green and white).

Below: A small pond set in a rock garden is very picturesque. Use waterlilies and other aquatic plants, as well as moisture-loving plants around the sides. Here, the purple-blue-flowered Pickerel Weed (*Pontederia cordata*) creates dominant features on opposite sides of the pond.

skip for removal. Dig the base and shelves 5cm/2in deeper than the depth of the shell. If you are installing the pond in a lawn, ensure that the shell's lip is 5-7.5cm/2-3in below the lawn's surface to allow for edging slabs. Allow for the thickness of the slabs and a 12-18mm/^{1}/$_2$ -^{3}/$_4$in layer of mortar.

Place a straight-edged board across the hole, and measure down with a ruler to ascertain the depth of the hole. Also ensure that the surface of the rigid liner will be level. You may need to try

placing the shell in the hole several times before it fits, leaving space all around it. Finally, ensure that the soil in the hole's base is firm.

Form a 5cm/2in-thick layer of soft sand in the base, then stand the shell on it. Place a long, straight-edged board across the top and position a spirit-level on it to check that the shell is level.

When the shell is level – and there is an equally spaced gap around it – secure it in position by wedging pieces of wood between the hole's sides and the shell. Fill the gap with soft sand, firming it in layers and ensuring that there are no gaps under the shelves and the top lip. Remove the pieces of wood holding the liner in place, then slowly fill it with water.

Finish the pond by forming a layer of paving stones around the edge so that they overlap the sides by about 5cm/2in. Use a mixture of three parts soft sand and one of cement as a bedding mixture for the stones and to cement between them. Do not tread on the stones for at least a week when the mortar should be set, and ensure that mortar does not fall into the water, or you will need to drain, clean and re-fill the pond.

Looking after garden ponds

Like any other garden feature, a pond will need regular attention to ensure it remains attractive. And as fish and plants are an essential part of most ponds, it is important to create the right environment for them to grow and thrive at all times of year.

STRUCTURAL REPAIRS

Leaking ponds are disastrous to fish and plants, as well as creating an unplanned boggy area around a pool. If loss of water occurs suddenly, put the fish and any other pond life into a large container, and the plants in buckets of water, and position them in shade.

Repairs to a concrete pond Cracks and surface damage often appear in concrete through old age, subsidence, frost penetration, tree roots creating pressure, or incorrect construction.

If the surface is being worn away, rub it with a wire brush to remove loose material, then apply several coats of a sealant. For cracks, use a chisel to remove loose mortar and to widen the crack below the surface. This enables a waterproof mastic to adhere firmly to it. If decay and cracks are extensive, the only solution to the problem is to drain and clean the pond and then to install a flexible liner.

Repairs to rigid liners Problems mainly occur if the shell is formed from inferior materials. Vacuum-formed polythene types are especially likely to become twisted and stressed and ultra-violet light will rapidly degrade thin polythene. Dropping a shell may also cause cracks.

Repair kits are available but it is not always easy to locate fine cracks. Tap the shell's surface and listen for a different note.

Repairs to flexible liners Inferior quality liners have a limited lifespan and once they start to decay and leak there is no long-term solution, other than replacement.

Damage can also occur if the liner has been installed on stony ground and has not been laid on a base of soft sand. The roots of nearby trees can cause damage, as can standing in the pond (perhaps to clean it) while wearing spiky shoes.

Proprietary repair kits are available – do not economize on the size of the patch, and follow the instructions carefully.

LOOKING AFTER A POND

1 When filling a pond, do not just put the end in the pond and turn on a tap. Instead, either tie a piece of canvas over the end, or place the end of a hosepipe in a bucket placed in the pond, so water gently trickles out.
2 In autumn, leaves are often blown into the pond and must be removed. Spike a piece of wire-netting on the prongs of a garden fork and pass this through the water.
3 When introducing fish to a pond, place them in a plastic bucket and stand it in the water to allow them to acclimatize. After several hours, lower the bucket and allow the fish to swim out.
4 Emptying a pond can be laborious, but inexpensive pumps operated by an electrically powered drill are available Place a filter over the end of the hose.

CLEANING A POND

If you need to empty and clean a pond, choose a warm day in early summer. First, carefully remove the fish and place them in a prefabricated pond or large buckets in a shaded position. Fill this with the clearest water drawn from near the surface of the pond. Put as much of the other pond life as you can into buckets and lift out the containers of plants and put these, too, into buckets of water.

Pump out the pond – continually checking for any uncaught fish – and drain the water into a sump or ditch. Inexpensive pumps are available that can be powered by electric drills; they pump about 750 litres/200 gallons an hour. Scrub the pond's sides with clean water, rinse and remove water. Then refill with tap water. Do not simply drop the end of a hosepipe into the pond; rather, weight down the end in a bucket placed in the pond or else tie a piece of canvas over the end of the hosepipe, so that the water gently trickles into the pond.

When the pond is full, replace the plants. A sudden change in temperature may kill fish, so place them in a plastic bucket of water and just stand it in the pool with its top slightly above the surface. After three or four hours the water temperature in the pond and bucket will be the same. Lower the bucket so the fish can swim out.

PROTECTING FISH FROM BIRDS

In Law, all birds are protected to some degree and, therefore, it is illegal to cause injury to them. Wire netting attached to a wooden or metal framework covering the pond may be the only way to prevent birds fishing.

PONDS IN AUTUMN

During late summer and autumn, plants cease to grow and their leaves begin to die and drop to the pond's base. Also, leaves fall from trees and if allowed to remain in the water cause toxic gasses. As the leaves of aquatic plants end their life, break them off and remove from the pond.

You can prevent falling leaves from getting into the water by covering the pond with netting. Alternatively you can make an efficient leaf rake to remove recently fallen leaves by spiking a piece of wire netting on the end of a garden fork.

PONDS IN WINTER

Freezing water is the main problem in winter, especially if the pond is small and shallow. It is essential that the fish do not become trapped under the ice; this becomes an especially serious problem, if decaying leaves have been left in the pond, as toxic gasses also become trapped beneath the surface.

Do not use a hammer to knock a hole in the ice; rather, install an electrical pond heater. Most models float on the surface and operate from a mains electricity supply or through a transformer. As the heater floats and creates a open area of water, it must be put in place and turned on before the water freezes.

Some people place a metal kettle full of boiling water on the ice to create a hole initially, but unless this is repeated the area refreezes.

Below: To create a natural-looking pond, allow marginal plants on one side to spill over the pond's edge so that the pond is unified with its surroundings. Here, a variegated iris and a moisture-loving Monkey Flower (*Mimulus*) create a bright edge to the pond.

Making a raised pond

Raised ponds are spectacular features, especially when integrated into patios. They raise the surface level of water, making it easier for fish and plants to be seen, which is a great benefit to the elderly or those in wheelchairs. Also, babies and toddlers are less likely to fall into the water. However, as most children are inquisitive, the only reliable way to make a pond safe is to install a strong wire-netting cover.

Raised ponds can be easier to construct than those at ground level; most importantly, they eliminate the need to get rid of masses of sub-soil (the topsoil can usually be spread on borders). Raised ponds are easier to clean and look after.

Although there are many advantages to a raised pond, there are a few difficulties. During winter there is an increased chance of the water freezing, thereby damaging the pond and killing fish, while in summer the water is likely to become too warm for the fish, especially if the pond is small. In winter, water heaters can be used to ensure the safety of fish (see pages 168-9), but in summer there is little that can be done to reduce the temperature of the water other than planting plenty of oxygenating plants and installing a fountain or waterfall.

CONSTRUCTING A RAISED POND

There are three basic ways to construct a raised pond:

Using bricks and concrete Dig out the topsoil and scatter it on borders, then lay a 15cm/6in-thick raft of concrete over the area. When this is dry, construct 23cm/9in-thick walls from bricks or blocks, and render the inside in concrete. Finally, apply two coats of waterproof pond paint.

This type of construction is efficient and attractive, but a strong base and careful construction are essential, or the pond's life will be limited – especially in a cold climate.

Using a flexible liner Dig out a trench about 23cm/9in deep to support a wall around the pond. Fill the trench with 7.5cm/3in of clean, compacted rubble and then with 15cm/6in of concrete. Construct a 23cm/9in-thick wall to the desired height (usually about 45cm/18in). This needs to be strong to resist the pressure of water as no supporting strength is gained from the

USING A FLEXIBLE LINE TO MAKE A RAISED POND

1 Use strings to mark the area of the trench need for the foundations of the walls.
2 Dig out a trench about 23cm/9in deep and fill the base with compacted, clean rubble. Over this form a thick layer of concrete.
3 Carefully build a wall about 45cm/18in high. Regularly use a spirit-level to check that the wall is upright and the bricks level.
4 Line the inside with 2.5-5cm/1-2in-thick sheets of polystyrene.
5 Form a 7.5cm/3in-thick layer of soft sand over the pond base. Then, place the liner in position and overlap it over the walls, covering the top by about two-thirds.
6 Use mortar to cement capping stones into place over the liner.

Above: A circular, raised pond is unusual and looks particularly effective positioned at the junction of several paths. This one is made more striking with an attractive statue and fountain.

flexible liner. Allow the mortar securing the walls to dry, then line the inside of the walls with sheets of polystyrene about 25mm/1in thick (50mm/2in thick would be even better). This helps to prevent the water freezing in winter. Form a 7.5cm/3in-thick layer of soft sand across the base of the pond. Then install the flexible liner and lap the edges about two-thirds of the way across the top of the brick wall. Cement capping stones in place so that they cover the liner, protruding 5cm/2in over the water and about the same amount over the outer edge of the wall.

Using a rigid liner Build a brick wall in the same manner as for a pool with a flexible liner. The wall does not need to withstand such a high pressure of water as part is supported by the rigid liner, so it need not be so thick. If the liner has shelves at its sides, these will need to be supported by an inner wall. Form a 7.5cm/3in-thick layer of soft sand over the base and then position the rigid liner on it. Check that it is level. Complete by installing capping stones along the top of the wall, so that they extend about 5cm/2in over the inner and outer parts of the wall.

CONSTRUCTING CONCRETE PONDS

Concrete has been used to make garden ponds for many years – usually square and rectangular ones. However, making a formal pond involves casting the shape by pouring concrete into elaborate shuttering. It is easier to make a pond with a simple oval or round shape, and certainly nothing more complicated than a kidney-shaped out-

line as no shuttering is needed. Also, because the pond does not have sharp corners it is stronger and far more able to resist movement in the subsoil. Concreting is best done in late spring and early summer, or late summer and early autumn, when there is no risk of frost and the weather is not excessively hot.

Dig out a hole 15cm/6in deeper and 30cm/12in wider than the desired size. This allows for the thickness of the concrete. Cut the sides with a 45° angle; if steeper, concrete will slip down before it sets. Line the hole with a thick polythene sheet and spread a 10cm/4in-thick layer of concrete over the base and up the sides. Use a mixture of 1 part cement, 1½ of sharp sand, and 2½ of 20mm/⅞ in aggregates. Press wire-netting reinforcement over the sides, extending 30cm/12in into the pond's centre. Cut another piece to cover the base and to overlap with the netting on the sides. Press the netting into the concrete. Lay a further 5cm/2in-thick layer of concrete over the sides and base and smooth the surface.

After laying, concrete takes three or four days to gain any appreciable strength. Many experts say it takes four to five weeks to reach full strength. If the weather is hot during the first week after laying, cover the surface with damp sacking. When dry, apply a surface sealing paint. If this is not used, you will have to empty and fill the pond several times during the first month to remove toxic chemicals released by the concrete. Before adding fish and plants, use a water-testing kit to check that the water is not toxic.

PROPAGATION

Increasing plants is a natural desire for all
gardeners, whether by sowing seeds of annuals,
taking cuttings of dahlias and chrysanthemums or
by layering branches of a shrub.

Some plants which are raised from seeds need
the gentle warmth of a greenhouse or windowsill
indoors to encourage germination, while hardy
annuals can be sown outdoors, directly in the
positions where they are to grow and flower.
Biennials and many herbaceous perennials are
also raised from seed sown outdoors, but in a
nurserybed, from which they are later moved to
their permanent positions.

Many trees and shrubs are easily raised from
cuttings, while low-growing stems can be buried
in soil until roots form on them. So increasing
many plants is therefore inexpensive or even
cost-free as well as satisfying.

Sowing seeds and pricking off seedlings

Many summer-flowering bedding plants can be raised from seeds sown in gentle warmth in greenhouses and conservatories – or on a lightly shaded windowsill – in late winter and early spring. The seedlings are pricked off to give each of them more space and the young plants are planted out in flower borders and containers when there is no risk of damage from frost.

Whatever the type of plant, seeds need three basic conditions to encourage germination – moisture, warmth and air. Also, most seeds germinate in darkness, although a few, such as the Wax Flower (*Begonia semperflorens* – now known as *Begonia* Semperflorens-Cultorum Hybrids), need light.

To create the necessary conditions for germination, sow seeds in a compost that both retains moisture and allows air penetration, and place the sown container either in a greenhouse or on a warm windowsill indoors. Protect the seedlings from strong and direct sunlight. Propagation cases provide warmth with electric cables linked to a thermostat to ensure the maintenance of a uniform temperature. Propagation cases heated by paraffin are also available. Seed packets usually indicate the best temperatures for specific seeds, but in general 16-21°C/61-70°F is needed for germination. When seeds have germinated, lower the temperature slightly. Details of the depth at which seeds should be sown are also given on the packet.

SOWING SEEDS IN SEED-TRAYS

Fill a clean plastic seed-tray with seed compost and firm it with your fingers, particularly around the edges, where compost soon becomes dry when loose, especially if regular watering is neglected. Add more seed compost and strike the surface level by using a straight-edged piece of wood. Then use a flat piece of wood with a small handle attached to it to firm the surface until it is about 12mm/¹⁄₂ in below the rim. Keep the presser clean and dry to ensure an even surface and to prevent seeds and compost sticking to it.

Tip seeds into a folded, V-shaped piece of paper and gently tap the end to encourage them to fall on the compost. Ideally, seeds should be

SOWING SEEDS IN SEED TRAYS

1 Fill the seed-tray with seed compost and gently firm with your fingers, especially at the edges.
2 Add more compost, strike level with a straight-edged piece of wood and firm the surface with a flat-surfaced presser until it is about 12mm/¹⁄₂ in below the rim.
3 Tip the seeds into a folded piece of paper and gently tap them evenly and thinly on to the compost.
4 Cover the seeds with finely sieved compost.
5 Stand the seed-tray in shallow water until moisture seeps to the surface, then allow to drain.
6 Cover with a plastic lid or sheet of glass. Remove every day and wipe away the condensation. If the seeds need darkness to encourage germination, cover with newspaper. Remove when the seeds germinate.

evenly spaced over the surface, but not within 12mm/$\frac{1}{2}$in of the container's sides as this is where the compost tends to become dry – even if well firmed – if watering is neglected. Remember to label the box, with the name of the seeds and the date sown.

Do not be tempted to sow seeds thickly just to use up a packet of them; the result will be thin, etiolated seedlings that are susceptible to diseases and may die back altogether.

Some seeds require light to encourage germination and are sown on the surface, but most need darkness and are covered to three or four times their diameter with finely sieved compost. Fine-meshed horticultural sieves are available, but culinary types can be used.

WATERING AND AFTERCARE

Water the compost by standing the seed-tray in a bowl shallowly filled with clean water. When moisture seeps to the surface of the compost, remove the seed-tray and allow excess water to drain away. Do not water from overhead, as this may scatter the seeds over the surface.

Cover the seed-tray to prevent the surface of the compost drying; this also helps to maintain an even temperature. Proprietary domed, plastic lids are convenient but a sheet of glass can also be used. Take care when using glass – children and animals may be tempted to touch it and could be cut. Remove these coverings daily and wipe away the condensation. To create a suitable environment for darkness-loving seeds, cover with a sheet of newspaper, which also further helps warmth to be retained in the compost.

As soon as the seedlings appear, remove the paper if used and lift off the glass or plastic cover for increasingly long periods each day. This prevents the atmosphere around the seedlings becoming too humid and warm, encouraging the onset of diseases.

PRICKING OFF SEEDLINGS

As soon as seedlings are large enough to be handled they must be moved to give them more space. If not pricked off they become drawn up, weak and spindly. Tightly clustered seedlings are more susceptible to diseases than those spaced out and with a good circulation of air.

Seedlings transplant best when their roots are moist, so water the compost several hours before moving them. Then, allow excess water to drain. Fill a seed-tray or pot with compost and gently firm it, first with your fingers and then with a flat piece of wood (presser). Compost in pots can be firmed with a flat lid from a jar. Do not use unsterilized compost, as it may harbour diseases and pests that soon decimate seedlings. With a small dibber or thick pencil, make 25-36mm/ $1\frac{1}{2}$-1in-deep holes in rows about 36mm/$1\frac{1}{2}$in apart. Do not make them within 12mm/$\frac{1}{2}$in of the container's edges, as this is where compost is likely to dry out first.

Use a small spatula or an old table fork to loosen a cluster of seedlings; place them on damp newspaper to prevent their roots becoming dry. Hold each seedling by a leaf, not its stem, and position it in a hole so that it is about the same depth as before. A dark area on the stem usually indicates the previous depth. Using a dibber, gently lever compost against the roots, taking care not to crush them.

When the seed-tray or pot is full of seedlings, gently tap the edges to level loose surface compost. Using a fine-rosed watering-can, water the seedlings gently from above to settle compost around their roots. Allow excess water to drain.

Return the seedlings to a slightly shaded greenhouse or windowsill and reduce the temperature when they are established and beginning to grow. At this stage, fresh air is vital to encourage strong, healthy growth.

Summer-flowering bedding plants are slowly accustomed to outdoor conditions. A soon as there is no risk of frost the plants can be placed either in a cold frame with increasing ventilation or in the shelter of a south or west-facing wall.

Creating a seedbed for raising plants

Biennials and herbaceous perennials are easily and inexpensively raised from seeds sown outdoors from spring to mid-summer. Hardy annuals are also sown outdoors, but unlike biennials and herbaceous plants that are later transferred to their growing positions, they grow and flower in their sowing positions (see pages 100-7).

Hardy biennials are frost hardy and are sown one year to flower during spring and summer of the following one. Herbaceous perennials are also frost-tolerant plants; they live for several seasons, each year dying down to soil-level in autumn, they survive winter in a dormant state and in spring develop fresh shoots that bear flowers during summer.

PREPARING THE SEEDBED

It is essential to prepare a seedbed where seeds can be sown and the plants allowed to develop until they are ready to be transplanted to their growing positions. Because this takes several months, select an out-of-the-way position that is also sheltered and lightly shaded, with well drained but moisture retentive soil.

Start preparing a seedbed in early or mid-winter, digging the soil and ensuring it is well drained (see pages 38-43). Take care not to leave pieces of perennial weeds in the soil as they develop into plants during the following year. Leave the surface rough but level, so that frost, rain and snow create a crumbly tilth by late winter.

In spring, use the back of a garden fork to further break down lumps of soil. Firmly – and in one action – bang and scrape the back of a fork on large pieces of soil, then rake the surface level. The soil must be evenly firm but not compacted. To achieve this, gently shuffle sideways over the seedbed. Finally, use a rake to level the surface again.

If the ground is very heavy, do not firm it by treading as this will consolidate the soil particles too much and impede drainage. Also, never use a lawn roller to level seedbeds as this invariably creates an unevenly compacted surface.

The precise time for sowing seeds outdoors depends on the soil and weather. Wait until the ground is warm, moist but not waterlogged and the surface soil can be worked into a tilth rather

PREPARING SEEDBEDS AND SOWING SEEDS

1 Dig the soil thoroughly in early winter so that frost and rain break down the surface to a fine tilth by late winter.
2 In spring, break down the surface soil further by knocking it with the back of a garden fork, then rake the surface level. Except in very heavy soils, gently shuffle sideways across the seedbed to consolidate it uniformly. Use a rake again to level the surface.
3 To form straight drills, either use a garden line or a long, straight stick. Hold it in place with a foot, then use a pointed stick to create a shallow, V-shaped drill.
4 Thinly sow seeds along the drill's base, then use the back of a metal rake to carefully cover the seeds with soil. When this is complete, use the back of a rake to firm soil over the seeds.

HARDY BIENNIALS

These are usually sown from mid-spring to mid-summer, in V-shaped drills 15-30cm/6-12in apart. Sow the seeds evenly and thinly and when the seedlings are large enough to handle, thin or transplant them to wider spacings, so that plants are not congested. In late summer or early autumn, or in early spring of the following year if the soil is heavy and cold, move the plants into their growing and flowering positions.

Some plants are grown as hardy biennials although their true nature is perennial. For example, Daisies (*Bellis perennis*) and Wallflowers (*Cheiranthus* x *allionii*, but now known as *Erysimum* x *allionii*) are hardy perennials grown as biennials, while Sweet Rocket (*Hesperis matronalis*) is a short-lived perennial raised as a biennial. These biennials, as well as many others, are described and illustrated on pages 100-7.

HERBACEOUS PERENNIALS

These are usually sown during spring and mid-summer in V-shaped drills 23-30cm/9-12in apart. Sow the seeds evenly and thinly and when the seedlings are large enough to handle, thin or transplant them to wide spacings to give them space in which to develop. In autumn or spring, move them to their growing and flowering positions. These plants are described and illustrated on pages 112-9.

Below: Perennial lupins are often raised from cuttings, but you can also increase them from seeds sown in a greenhouse, cold frame or in a seedbed outdoors in late spring or early summer. They create a superb background for other border plants, as well as being eye-catching on their own.

than sowing seeds too early. Light soil warms up in spring sooner than heavy clay, although if extremely sandy it is usually impoverished and lacks the ability to retain moisture, a fundamental requirement for seed germination.

Stretch a garden line across the seedbed, or use a long, straight stick. Hold it in place with your foot and use the corner of a draw hoe to form V-shaped drills in which seeds can be sown. Alternatively use a pointed stick where a fine tilth has been created. You will need to run the stick down the row several times.

SOWING TECHNIQUES

Do not sow seeds directly from the packet as it is very difficult to control their flow into the drill. Instead, place about a quarter of the seeds in the palm of one hand, take a pinch of them with the other and, thinly and evenly, dribble them into the drill.

After sowing each row, label and mark the ends. Also, keep a record in a notebook of the seeds sown, together with the date. Cover the seeds by straddling the row and shuffling along it. Position your feet in a V-shaped formation and use both heels to guide soil into the drill and over the seeds. Use the back of a metal rake to firm the surface lightly. Then gently level the surface by raking shallowly along the direction of the row; if seeds are dislodged they will not then be scattered between the rows.

An alternative way to cover the seeds is with a metal rake; turn the head so that the prongs are pointing upwards and use the head to push and pull soil over the seeds. Then use the head again to firm soil over the seeds. Regularly water the soil to encourage germination.

Layering trees and shrubs

Layering is an excellent way to increase shrubs with low-growing stems. Trees with a pendulous nature and branches near the ground can also be increased in this way, as can climbers such as wisteria, jasmine, parthenocissus and clematis.

This is an easy way to increase plants, although not rapid: roots usually develop within a year, after which the stem can be severed from the parent plant. However, some shrubs and trees, such as magnolias and rhododendrons, take up to two years before roots develop sufficiently to enable the branch to be severed and planted into a nurserybed or garden. The number of stems or branches that can be easily lowered to soil-level is clearly limited, so only a few new plants can normally be raised from a mother plant at the same time. It is possible to dig up a mother plant, replant it on its side and to layer several stems, but this is a technique best left to nurserymen.

Another variation on layering, used with heathers, ericas and daboecias, especially when they are old and spreading, is to form a mound of light, friable soil in the plant's centre. This is worked in among the shoots. Later, when the roots have formed, the complete plant is dug up and the rooted parts severed and planted out into a nurserybed or border.

LAYERING A SHRUB

Shrubs, trees and climbers can be layered at any time throughout the year, but late summer to early autumn, as well as spring, are best Select a healthy, vigorous, low-growing stem or branch, either one or two years old. The part of the shoot that is bent and pegged into the soil is 23-45cm/9-18in from its tip. The stem at this point must be pliable and able to be easily bent and manipulated. Several weeks before layering the shoot prepare the soil into which it will be buried: dig about 25cm/10in deep, ensuring that the area is well-drained then add moist peat to sandy soils and sharp sand to heavy ones. Gently firm the area but do not compact heavy soil.

Use a trowel to form a sloping trench, which at its deepest – where the stem will be bent – is 7.5-15cm/3-6in deep. Bend the stem down to soil-level and push it into the trench. At the deepest part bend it up, so that the shoot's tip is upright.

Right: Azaleas are easily increased by layering low-growing stems. In spring and early summer, these acid-loving shrubs drench borders with brightly coloured flowers from ground-level to their tops.

LAYERING A SHRUB

1 Select a healthy, low-growing, vigorous shoot up to two-years old. Form a shallow trench that slopes to 7.5-15cm/3-6in deep at its lowest point, some 23-45cm/9-18in from the shoot's tip.
2 Lower the shoot into the depression and bed it tip upright. Wound the stem by making either a tongued cut at the point of the bend, or cut half-way around the stem and remove part of the bark.
3 Use a wooden peg or piece of bent wire to hold the stem in the soil. Firm soil over the stem, so that the surface is level.
4 Tie the end to a strong cane or piece of wood. When rooted, remove the soil and peg and sever the stem. Plant into a border or nurserybed.

A thin stem can be bent back and forth to make the bark softer and make it easier to bend. Thick stems may have to be partly cut at the point of the bend, but take care not to sever them completely. Alternatively, encircle part of the stem with a cut to remove bark. The aim of this bending and cutting is to wound the stem and check the flow of sap, creating a callus and thereby encouraging the development of roots.

Use a wooden peg or piece of strong, bent wire to hold the stem firmly in the soil. Then attach the end of the shoot to a strong cane inserted into the ground to hold it upright. Place sharp sand in the trench at the position where

the stem is bent, then pack soil around it and water the area to settle the soil. During the following twelve months, ensure that the area is kept free from weeds and that the young shoot protruding above the soil is not damaged.

About a year after the shoot is layered, check to see if roots have formed; fresh growth at the shoot's tip is a good indication of this. Gently remove some soil from around the bent stem. If roots are visible, untie the stem, remove the peg or bent wire, and sever the shoot. Transfer the young, rooted plant to a border or, if small, to a nurserybed.

AIR LAYERING SHRUBS AND TREES
Air layering is mostly associated with houseplants such as the tropical *Ficus elastica*, widely known as the Rubber Plant. However, temperate-zone trees and large shrubs can also be propagated in this way. Successful air layering of shrubs and trees depends on keeping the area around the cut stem moist. A sheet of polythene wrapped tightly around the cut makes air layering practical on trees and shrubs outdoors. Even with polythene, air layering is neither an easy nor a widely used technique and is best considered as a novel way to increase shrubs and trees which have branches that cannot be lowered to soil-level.

It is best performed in spring, when sap is starting to flow. Select a young, vigorous and healthy stem. Use a sharp knife to make a cut 20-30cm/8-12in below the shoot's tip. Start the cut from the tree's side and angle it so that it is about 36mm/1½in long and penetrates half-way through the stem. It should form a tongue in which a matchstick can be inserted to ensure that it remains open. Dust the cut surfaces with hormone rooting-powder to encourage the rapid formation of roots.

Form a 20cm/8in-long tube of clear polythene around the cut area and pack damp peat or sphagnum moss in it. Use waterproof adhesive tape to seal the ends of the polythene to the tree. Because the peat or sphagnum moss weighs down the shoot, secure it to a stake. When roots can be seen growing through the moist peat, sever the branch, carefully remove the polythene and transfer the new plant to a large pot. Place it in a cool greenhouse, conservatory or garden frame until established. Do not plant it into a garden until fully established.

SHRUBS AND TREES THAT CAN BE LAYERED

Amelanchier	Daboecia	*Parrotia persica*
Azalea	*Daphne cneorum*	Parthenocissus
Calluna	Erica	Pieris
Camellia	Euonymus	Piptanthus
Chaenomeles	Forsythia	Rhododendron
Chimonanthus	*Garrya elliptica*	Rhus
Clematis	Hamamelis	Stachyurus
Cornus	*Jasminum nudiflorum*	Vaccinium
Cotinus	*Liriodendron tulipifera*	Viburnum
Cotoneaster	Magnolia	Wisteria

Lifting and dividing herbaceous perennials

Hardy herbaceous perennials are easily increased, either by sowing seeds in a seedbed during spring and early summer (see pages 176-7), or by lifting and dividing established and congested plants during their dormant period.

INCREASING FIBROUS-ROOTED PLANTS
Plants of this type can be divided at any time between early autumn and mid-spring provided the soil is not frozen or waterlogged. Usually this means in autumn where the weather is mild, but it is better to wait until spring in extremely cold and frosty areas.

First, cut all stems down to within a few inches of the ground. Clear these away and make sure that the soil is free from debris, including weeds. Use a garden fork to dig up the clump, taking care not to sever too many roots.

To divide the plant, push two garden forks placed back-to-back down through the centre of the clump. Then, lever the handles together to force the roots apart. Ensure that the forks are pushed fully into the clump and both to the same depth. If they are only partly pushed in, the upper part of the clump will rapidly tear away from the base. Two hand-forks can be used to divide small clumps. Select and pull away young parts from the outside of the clump for subsequent planting into borders. Discard the woody, central area, which is the oldest part of the clump. Also, remove roots of perennial weeds.

If the roots are extremely matted, wash them in water and part them gently with a plant label or pointed stick. Replant the new pieces before their roots become dry. If plants cannot be replanted immediately, wrap them in wet sacking. Also, ensure that the soil into which they are to be planted is moist; water it thoroughly several days before planting, so that excess moisture has time to drain away. Water the soil after planting and regularly through the growing season.

If the divided parts are extremely small, plant them into a nurserybed for one or two years before setting them into their permanent positions in a border. Also, if the mother plant is 'choice' and a large number of new plants are needed, pot very small pieces into 7.5cm/3in-wide pots and place in a cold frame until they are

Right: Division is an easy and inexpensive way to increase many hardy herbaceous plants. Once a border is established with these plants it is easy to lift and divide them every three or four years. *Crocosmia* creates a wealth of strongly coloured flowers, from yellow to the deepest red, from mid-summer to autumn. Congested clumps should be divided either just after the flowers fade or before growth begins in spring.

INCREASING FIBROUS-ROOTED HERBACEOUS PLANTS

1 In autumn or spring, cut down all stems so that the crown of the plant can be seen. Use a garden fork to dig up the clump, taking care not to damage roots.
2 Insert two garden forks, back-to-back, into the clump and lever their handles together. Small plants are best divided with a pair of hand-forks.
3 Gently pull the clump into small pieces, but not too small unless a large number of plants are required. Discard the old, woody, central part.
4 Replant the young pieces soon after the clump has been divided. Do not allow the roots to become dry. Cover them with damp hessian if planting is delayed.

TYPES OF HERBACEOUS PLANTS

Herbaceous plants can be divided into several types, depending on their type of growth and roots. These include:

- **Plants with fibrous roots,** such as *Aster novae-angliae* (New England Daisy), *Aster novi-belgii* (Michaelmas Daisy), *Chrysanthemum maximum* (the Shasta or Max Daisy, and now known as *Leucanthemum maximum*), *Helenium autumnale* (Sneezeweed), *Rudbeckia fulgida* (Coneflower) and Solidago (Golden Rod). Increase this type of plant by lifting the complete roots and carefully dividing them, as described earlier.

- **Plants with fleshy roots** and woody crowns, such as *Delphinium elatum* (Delphinium) and *Lupinus polyphyllus* (the Lupin or Lupine). Propagate by lifting the crowns and using a sharp knife to cut through them or alternatively, by taking cuttings from young shoots in spring.

- **Plants with rhizomatous roots,** such as *Iris germanica* (variously known as the Flag Iris, London Flag, Purple Flag and Fleur-de-Lis) have thick, tough roots. Lift the plant and use a sharp knife to divide the young roots around the outside of the clump into pieces 5-7.5cm/2-3in long, each containing a few strong leaves. Dust the cut surfaces with a fungicide. Replant them to the same depth – the dark mark on the stem indicates the previous level. Discard the old, woody, central parts.

large enough to be planted into a garden. This especially applies if the clump is divided in autumn.

KEEPING PLANTS HEALTHY

Slugs and snails soon devastate young herbaceous plants, especially if the weather is moist and warm. Use slug and snail baits alongside the plants to attract and kill them. Pick up and remove dead slugs and snails. Make sure that you place the pellets under tiles so that cats and dogs – as well as wild life such as badgers – cannot reach them.

Woodlice, millepedes and wireworms are other plant-chewing pests that are attracted by soft stems and leaves. They will also destroy the roots and are especially prevalent in soils rich in humus and other plant debris. Dust the soil with an insecticide to keep them at bay.

Increasing plants from cuttings

Cuttings can be formed from leaves, buds and roots, but the most popular way is from stems and shoots. The three main forms are softwood, semi-hardwood and hardwood.

SOFTWOOD CUTTINGS

Softwood cuttings are soft shoot tips, severed from plants while young and relatively immature. Plants increased in this way include houseplants and many perennials, as well as dahlias and chrysanthemums. A few tender shrubs can also be increased from softwood cuttings.

Softwood cuttings taken from greenhouse plants and houseplants can be severed from healthy parents at any time of year. However, spring and summer are the best times as the light is better than in winter and this helps to create stronger plants. Softwood cuttings from outdoor plants are best taken in early and mid-summer. Dahlias and chrysanthemums are mainly outdoor plants, but to encourage growth of soft shoots to provide cuttings early in the year, dormant tubers (dahlias) and roots (chrysanthemums) are placed in gentle warmth in greenhouses.

Because softwood cuttings are young and soft they need gentle warmth to encourage the development of roots. They also need relatively high humidity to prevent them wilting and drying before roots have formed and are able to absorb moisture. The compost into which these cuttings are inserted must be moisture retentive, well drained and aerated. This is usually provided by a mixture of equal parts moist peat and sharp sand.

Professionally, softwood cuttings are inserted in a mist-propagation unit, which prevents them flagging before they have developed roots and are able to absorb their own moisture. Amateur mist-propagation units are available, but when propagating just a few cuttings, a humid and warm environment can be created by putting a transparent plastic bag over a pot of cuttings and sealing it in place with an elastic band. Seed-trays with transparent plastic lids also create a humid atmosphere.

To root just a few softwood cuttings, fill a clean 7.5-13cm/3-5in-wide pot with equal parts moist peat and sharp sand. First, firm it gently with your fingers, then add further compost and firm

TAKING SOFTWOOD CUTTINGS

1 Fill a pot with equal parts moist peat and sharp sand and gently firm it with your fingers. Refill the pot with compost, strike it level with the rim and firm with a round firmer or top of a jar.
2 Use a dibber or thick pencil to make holes 36-50mm/ 1^1/$_2$-2in apart and 25-36mm/ 1-1^1/$_2$ in deep. Do not position them within 12mm/^{1}/$_2$in of the pot's edge.
3 Prepare the cuttings so that they are 6-7.5cm/2^1/$_2$ -3in long; trim their bases below a leaf joint and remove lower leaves.
4 Insert the cuttings and use a dibber to firm compost around their bases. Water the compost. Insert five small, thin canes into the compost around the pot's edge and draw a transparent bag over them. Seal it around the pot with an elastic band.

Many technical terms are associated with cuttings and frequently used in gardening books. These include:

- **Basal cutting** A non-flowering shoot taken from the base of a plant. Occasionally, such a cutting originates from slightly below soil-level. They often occur on chrysanthemums.

- **Internodal cutting** When a stem is severed between two leaf-joints (nodes), rather than just below one. Cuttings normally root more quickly and easily when severed just below a node.

- **Irishman's cutting** A basal cutting which has a few roots. Such cuttings can usually be potted up immediately. Chrysanthemums often produce Irishman's cuttings.

- **Nodal cutting** When the base of a cutting is severed just below a leaf-joint (node).

this with a round firmer or the lid of a jar. The compost's surface should be about 12mm/^{1}/$_2$in below the rim. Dust the surface with sharp sand.

TAKING AND STRIKING SOFTWOOD CUTTINGS

Water the mother plant the day before taking the cuttings. Select healthy shoots and cut them from the parent plant, just above a leaf-joint so that short stubs are not left on the mother plant. Immediately – so that they do not become dry – prepare the cuttings by trimming each one just below a leaf-joint; use a sharp knife to remove the lower leaves close to the stem. Each cutting, when prepared, should be 6-7.5cm/2^1/$_2$-3in long. Dipping their bases in hormone rooting-powder encourages the development of roots. See left for how to root softwood cuttings.

After the cuttings have been inserted and covered with a plastic bag, place the pot in gentle warmth, but out of direct sunlight, which would raise the temperature too high. When fresh shoots start to develop from the cuttings, remove the plastic bag and check to see if roots have formed. If the cuttings are well rooted, put them into individual pots, water and place in light shade and gentle warmth until established.

SEMI-HARDWOOD CUTTINGS

These are riper and firmer than softwood cuttings, but less mature than hardwood types. They are also known as half-ripe cuttings and can be taken from mid-summer to the early part of late summer. They are rooted in lower temperatures than softwood types and take slightly longer to

develop roots. Some will develop roots when inserted in open ground outdoors, but a cold frame or cloche provides protection and a more favourable environment.

These cuttings are taken from young shoots that developed earlier the same year. They are 10-15cm/4-6in long and relatively soft, especially at their tips. The bases are trimmed below a leaf-joint and the lower leaves removed. If the tip of the cutting is especially soft, cut this off too.

The cuttings of some plants root more quickly when they have a small piece of the older wood at their bases. These are known as heel cuttings and are produced by gently tearing a shoot from its stem, so that a piece of the old wood is attached to it. Trim the heel with a sharp knife to remove whisker-like growths from its edges.

Fill a pot with a mixture of equal parts moist peat and sharp sand, firm the compost until its surface is about 12mm/^{1}/$_2$in below the rim, sprinkle sharp sand on the surface and use a dibber to form planting holes 5-7.5cm/2-3in apart. Do not position them nearer than 12mm/^{1}/$_2$in to the pot's sides. Insert each cutting to one-third to a half of its length and firm them in. Water from above with a fine-rosed watering-can, allow to drain and place in a cold frame or under a cloche. Lightly shade the cuttings during periods of strong sunlight and keep the compost moist.

HARDWOOD CUTTINGS

Hardwood cuttings are formed from mature shoots of the current season's growth and are taken from autumn to early spring, when plants are dormant and leafless. They are 23-38cm/9-15in long, depending on the plant, and take up to twelve months to form roots. The rooted cuttings are then dug up and planted in a nurserybed until large enough to be put in a garden.

Prepare a sheltered nurserybed by digging and adding well-decomposed compost or manure. Use a spade to form a V-shaped trench with one vertical side. Trickle sharp sand in its base and stand the cuttings upright in it. Trim each cutting slightly above a bud at its top, and below one at the base. Position each cutting half to two-thirds of its length deep and space them 7.5-15cm/3-6in apart. Firm the soil around them. After periods of severe frost, re-firm the soil around the cuttings using the heel of a boot or shoe. When rooted, plant them individually in a nurserybed.

Increasing plants by budding

Budding is a more specialized way of increasing plants than by seeds or cuttings. With budding, part of the desired variety is positioned in close contact with a rootstock of known vigour, so that they unite and eventually form one plant.

Budding is mainly used to propagate roses but some ornamental shrubs and crab apples are also increased in this way. It is usually carried out from early to mid-summer, but can be continued until slightly later in the season.

Rootstocks are raised from cuttings or seeds, but as this is a lengthy process – especially from seeds – it is better to buy stocks from a nursery and to plant them in a nurserybed during the previous year. The buds of the variety are taken from shoots with healthy, vigorous, plump buds.

BUDDING BUSH ROSES
In autumn, plant the rootstocks. Commercially, they are positioned 38-45cm/15-18in apart in rows with 75-90cm/2½-3ft between them. If the rows are too close there is a danger of developing shoots being knocked off later in the year. When a few roses are being budded by an amateur, similar spacings should be used as plants must not be congested.

Select the varietal part during early and mid-summer, from shoots that earlier produced flowers. They are ready to use when thorns snap off easily under sideways pressure. Sever the shoot low down on the bush and cut off the soft top. Also, cut off all leaves, but ensure 12-18mm/½-¾in of each leaf stalk remains. Keep these shoots – known as bud wood – moist; either place them in a bucket of water or temporarily wrap them in damp sacking.

Prepare the rootstocks by using a trowel to draw soil away from the neck of the stem, then use a budding knife to make a T-cut about 5cm/2in above the ground. First, make a horizontal cut about 18mm/¾in long, then a 36mm/1½in vertical cut to form the base of the T shape. A budding knife has a spatula at one end and this is used to prise open the bark alongside the vertical cut. In hot areas, make the T-cut on the side most protected from strong sunlight; otherwise, the side towards the prevailing wind is best as the bud is not then easily blown off.

BUDDING BUSH ROSES

1 Use a hand-trowel to draw soil back from around the stems of rose stocks. Take care not to damage them.
2 For the varietal part, select a healthy, strong shoot which has just finished flowering and cut off a piece about 30cm/12in long.
3 Cut off the leaves, but leave the leaf-stalks attached to the budding stick.
4 Make a T-cut about 5cm/2in above soil-level, formed of a 18mm/¾ in horizontal cut and a 36mm/1½ in vertical one.
5 Remove the sliver of wood that is behind the bud. Insert the bud into the T-cut and cut its top level with the top of the horizontal cut.
6 Secure the bud in place with raffia earlier soaked in water to make it pliable. Position the knot on the side opposite the bud.

Above: Roses are popular garden plants and although they can be bought as established bushes it is fascinating to bud a few of your own.

Prepare the bud part by inserting a sharp knife about 12mm¹/₂/in below a bud. Then, with a sloping cut, pass the knife under the bud and withdraw it about 2.5cm/1in above. In total, the wood surrounding the bud must be about 12mm/¹/₂in wide and 36mm/1¹/₂in long. Remove the tiny sliver of wood underneath the bud.

Hold the bud by its leaf-stalk and gently slide it into the T-cut then trim the top part of the wood above the bud level with the top of the cut. Tie the bud in place with raffia previously softened by soaking it in water. Tie the ends of the raffia on the side of the stem opposite the bud. Commercially, proprietary rubber ties are avail-

able and these are quicker to use than raffia. About three weeks later, the leaf-stalk will fall off when knocked, but the bud should remain secured to the rootstock. If the bud is plump, carefully cut the raffia at the back of the stem to ensure it is not constricted. There is no need to remove the entire length of raffia.

During later winter of the following year, use sharp secateurs to cut the stem about 2.5cm/1in above the bud. In exposed areas, support new growth with canes. In autumn of the same year transfer the plant to a garden.

BUDDING STANDARD ROSES

The technique of budding standard roses is exactly the same as for bush types. The only difference is that three buds are used and inserted well above the ground: 75-90cm/2¹/₂-3ft for half-standards and 1.2-1.3m/4-4¹/₂ft for standards.

Rootstocks are prepared by allowing a single stem to grow well above the desired height. It is necessary to support it with a strong stake. In late autumn or early winter, sever it about 15cm/6in above the required height. In spring, allow three shoots to develop (rub out the other buds) and in early or mid-summer insert buds into them, close to the main stem. Insert the buds on the upper surfaces of the shoots.

The above method applies when using briar (*Rosa canina*) rootstocks, whereas with rugosa (*Rosa rugosa*) types the buds are inserted directly into the main stem. Later, cut off the stems about 2.5cm/1in beyond the buds, as well as cutting off the main stem of the rootstock slightly above the uppermost stem of the variety.

ROOTSTOCKS FOR ROSES

Several types of rose species are used to create the root part of a rose, although some, such as miniature roses, are raised from cuttings.

- **Seedling Briar (*Rosa canina*)** Raised from seeds, more than 80 per cent of all roses are budded on it. It is a rootstock that transplants well, is long-lived and develops deep roots. Additionally, it is ideal for medium and heavy soils, although not light, sandy ones.

- **Cutting Briar (*Rosa canina*)** Raised from cuttings and ideal on medium soils. Plants do not transplant easily. It is not so widely used now, but good for standard and half-standard forms, as well as weeping standards. Laxa stocks are *Rosa canina froebelii*.

- **Rugosa (*Rosa rugosa*)** Raised from cuttings, these develop a large, coarse root system, but do not last as long as briar stocks. They develop long shoots and are therefore ideal for standards and half-standards.

- **Multiflora (often known as *Polyantha simplex*)** Vigorous and ideal on light, impoverished soil. Raised from cuttings and seeds. It does not transplant well and the roots must be regularly watered until established, as well as in dry weather.

- **Laxa (*Rosa canina froebelii*)** Vigorous and better on heavy soils than Multiflora. Develops practically thornless stems. Popular in Scotland.

Increasing plants by grafting

Like budding, grafting involves uniting a chosen variety with a rootstock of known vigour. However, unlike budding – when only one bud of a selected variety is used – grafting involves the use of shoots with several buds. Fruits like apples and pears, as well as a few shrubs such as lilac, are increased by grafting.

There are many types of grafts, some frequently used, while others are restricted to a few species. New trees of apples and pears are increased by 'whip-and-tongue' grafts, while healthy and vigorous old trees can be changed from one variety to another by the techniques known as topworking and frameworking.

Topworking involves severely cutting the main limbs and creating a completely new branch system. Framework grafting is less rigorous and initially entails leaving branches intact and grafting many scions (varietal parts) on to the trees, using any of a wide range of grafts. After these new shoots and branches have become established, the old ones are cut off.

Grafting is mainly performed at the end of the dormant period which, depending on the loca-tion, varies from late winter to early spring. However, a few grafts are performed a little later as their success depends on the ready separation of the rind from the central wood.

Whatever the type of graft and whenever it is performed, success relies on placing the cambi-um layer (just beneath the bark) of the scion (the varietal part) in contact with a similar layer in the rootstock or tree being rejuvenated.

TOPWORK GRAFTING

Although whip-and-tongue grafting is the main method of producing young apple and pear trees, it is by topworking and framework grafting that old, excessively large trees can be given a new lease of life. Therefore, such techniques are often more useful to home gardeners than whip-and-tongue grafting.

Crown grafting is the major form of topwork-ing and involves cutting all the main branches to within 60-90cm/2-3ft of the crotch of the tree. The stubs of the branches should not be more than 13cm/5in wide, preferably 7.5-10cm/3-4in, as large cut surfaces take much longer to heal than

Right: Apples are an ideal fruit to grow in temperate countries and even just one tree can provide a family with plenty of delicious fruits. There are many varieties to choose from.

CROWN OR RIND GRAFTING

1

2

3

4

5

6

1 Prepare the tree in autumn or winter (see above). Later, pare the surfaces smooth.
2 Make one, two or three vertical cuts, 36mm/1^1/$_2$ in long, down the sides of each branch.
3 Gently prise open the upper edges of each cut.
4 Prepare the scions (varietal part) by cutting above a bud at the top and just above the fourth or fifth bud below it. Make a sloping cut, 36mm/1^1/$_2$ in long, at the scion's base and opposite the lowest bud. Also, make a small sloping cut at the base of the scion on the side opposite the main cut. This helps when inserting the scion. Insert a scion into each cut.
5 Securely tie the scions with soft string.
6 Cover the string and all cuts with grafting wax.

FRAMEWORK GRAFTING

Unlike topworking, when branches are cut back to 60-90cm/2-3ft of the crotch, with frameworking the existing branches and shoots are initially left in place. Only small, lateral shoots and spurs are removed in late autumn or early winter prior to grafting from late winter to early spring.

The objective is to create, through many types of graft, a framework to replace the existing branches. When these grafts are established and growing strongly, the old framework is cut off. The scions are longer than those used in topworking and have seven or eight buds.

The range of frameworking grafts includes *stub-grafts*, *side-grafts*, *oblique side-grafts*, *inverted L-rind-grafts* and *slit-grafts*. They are used to create branches spaced evenly over the tree that will eventually form a natural-looking and attractive feature. Frameworking takes longer to do than topworking, but the tree returns to cropping faster and there is less risk from disease infection.

small ones. Often, branches are cut off to about 1.2m/4ft of the crotch in autumn or winter, and re-cut later to produce freshly cut surfaces for grafting in late winter or early spring, when the sap starts to rise. When topworking exceptionally large trees, leave a few branches intact so that they draw up the sap. Later, they can be either cut out completely or left until the following year and topgrafted.

The varietal parts (scions) should be one-year-old shoots, cut off in winter, labelled and heeled-in to a depth of about 23cm/9in in a well-drained, cool and shaded nurserybed, preferably on the north side of a wall or fence. When they are needed for grafting, wash them thoroughly in cold water to remove soil and any moss-like growth.

Each of these shoots will have a range of buds and will therefore yield several scions, each formed of three or four buds. Do not use the soft tops of shoots.

The success of crown grafting – also known as rind grafting because the scions are inserted between the rind and the wood that forms the main part of the branch – depends on the rind parting readily from the wood, so it is essential to wait until mid- to late spring. The first stage is to pare the freshly cut surface with a knife to make it smooth. Depending on the thickness of the branch, make one, two or three 36mm/1^{1}/2in long, equally spaced cuts downwards from the pared surface. Use the spatula end (or blade) of the knife to ease open the top of each cut.

Prepare each scion by cutting just above a bud at the top and just above the fourth or fifth bud at the base. Then, make a sloping cut about 36mm/1^{1}/2in long on the side opposite the lowest bud. To enable the scion to be easily inserted into the cut, trim off about 6mm/^{1}/4in of the base, cutting diagonally on the bud side.

Gently but firmly insert the scion into the cut, until it is about 36mm/1^{1}/2in deep. Secure the scions by tying them firmly with soft string (which is easier to use than raffia on large limbs). Cover the cuts and pared surface, as well as the top of each scion, with grafting wax. During midsummer, cut the string to prevent it constricting the growth of the grafted scions.

Increasing bulbs, corms and tubers

Bulbs and corms, although botanically slightly different, both develop offsets which eventually form new plants. Bulbs are formed of fleshy, modified leaves closely wrapped around each other and enclosing a young shoot. Offsets, known as bulbils, are produced around the base of each bulb and these can be removed and encouraged to develop roots. Corms are formed of a thickened stem base, usually covered with a papery skin. At the top of a corm is a bud from which new shoots and roots develop. Like bulbils, cormlets can be removed and encouraged to form roots. Several ornamental plants, including dahlias, have root tubers and these can be increased by division.

INCREASING BULBS

Bulbils develop annually around the parent bulbs. After flowering and when the foliage has died down naturally, the bulbs are lifted and bulbils carefully removed. Large bulbils can be replanted with mother bulbs in late summer or early autumn. Small bulbils, however, take two or three seasons before they are large enough to produce

flowers. For this reason they should be planted out in a nurserybed to mature and develop.

In autumn, plant them 5-7.5cm/2-3in deep (depending on their size) in a nurserybed. First, trickle sharp sand into the base of a flat-based drill to ensure the bulbils have good drainage at their base. After a couple of years or so they will have reached flowering size and can be lifted and planted into their flowering positions.

INCREASING CORMS

Gladioli are corms. Towards autumn, the old corm shrivels, leaving a new one that will flower during the following year, together with clusters of small cormlets around the base.

In autumn, carefully fork up the plants and, after the foliage and shoots have died back, cut off each stem about 12mm/½in above the corm. Place the corms in a dry shed and allow them to dry for about a week. Discard the old, shrivelled corm and store the new one in a dry, vermin-proof shed during winter. At the same time, remove the cormlets and also store them in a dry shed during winter.

DIVIDING DAHLIAS

1

2

3

4

1 Lift dahlia tubers in autumn, about a week after their foliage has been blackened by frost. Cut stems to 15cm/6in high, position upside down for a few weeks to ensure they are dry and then place in boxes of damp peat.
2 In early to mid-spring, divide the tubers by cutting upwards through the stem, so that each tuber has at least one healthy bud.
3 Dust the cut surfaces with a fungicide.
4 Plant the individual tubers about 10cm/4in deep once all danger of frost is past.

Below: A mixture of yellow tulips and blue Forget-me-nots creates an eye-catching display in spring and early summer. Both the tulips and Forget-me-nots are planted in early or mid-autumn.

In early or mid-spring, plant the cormlets in a weed-free nurserybed, setting them close together in drills 5cm/2in deep and 30-38cm/12-15in apart. Place them on a layer of sharp sand, as this assures good drainage during wet periods and makes lifting them in autumn much easier.

During summer, keep the seedbed well-watered and free from weeds. In autumn, lift the corms and cormlets, dry and store them during winter. In spring, replant them into a nurserybed. It normally takes about two or three years before the cormlets reach flowering size.

DIVIDING DAHLIA TUBERS

The easiest way to increase dahlias is to divide the swollen roots. Another way to propagate them is by cuttings, but this requires gentle warmth in spring.

Lift the tubers in autumn, about a week after their foliage has been blackened by frost. First, cut down the stems to 15cm/6in above the soil, then use a garden fork to lift the tubers carefully. Remove any soil and place the tubers upside down in boxes in a dry, frost-proof shed, so that moisture drains from the stems and they become dry but not shrivelled.

Then place the tubers, the right way up, in boxes and pack slightly damp peat around them. Place the boxes in a frost-proof and vermin-proof shed. Preferably, the temperature should be about 5°C/41°F. Periodically, check the tubers to ensure they are not shrivelled. If they should shrivel, place them in a bucket of tepid water overnight, then dry them thoroughly and replace in the damp peat.

These tubers can then be treated in two ways: one alternative is to put them in boxes containing equal parts moist peat and sharp sand in late winter and keep them at 15-18°C/59-64°F. If the compost is kept moist, shoots will appear and these can be used as cuttings (see pages 138-9). However, a simpler method is to wait until spring then divide the tubers.

In early and mid-spring, put the dormant tubers into boxes containing a mixture of moist peat and sharp sand. Keep the compost moist and replace in a frost-proof shed. Within two or three weeks the tubers start to swell and young buds become more visible on the stems.

Use a sharp knife to cut up the roots, ensuring that each part has at least one healthy, undamaged bud. Cut upwards, severing the stems, not the tubers. After division, dust the cut surfaces with a fungicide to prevent the entry of disease spores into the plants. These pieces are then planted directly into a border, setting them about 10cm/4in deep. In very cold areas, delay planting for several weeks, as young shoots that later appear will be damaged by frost.

VEGETABLE GARDENING

Growing vegetables, then harvesting and eating them fresh, is the dream of most gardeners, and one which can be fulfilled in almost all circumstances. Even in courtyards and on patios, many vegetables can be grown in containers, but a vegetable plot allows a wider range of crops to be considered. Salad crops, such as lettuces, spring onions and radishes, need only a small area, while potatoes demand more space and a longer growing period. Some vegetables, such as asparagus, have an even longer lifespan and are given a permanent position.

Most vegetables are raised from seeds, sown either directly where they will grow, or first in a nurserybed with young plants later being moved to their growing and maturing positions. Other vegetables, such as potatoes, grow from tubers, which are planted in the ground.

Planning a vegetable garden

Many gardeners, however small their gardens, like to grow vegetables. Sometimes, if only a patio is available, this has to be done in pots, tubs and growing-bags on a patio, but if the garden is large a complete area can be set aside for vegetables. Some crops, such as cabbages, cauliflowers and potatoes, need large areas, whereas others, like lettuces, spring onions and radishes, require relatively little room and are quick-growing. Indeed, these rapid-growing salad crops can be grown between long-term vegetables.

Whatever the situation, soil management, crop rotation and selection of varieties are important and these and other secrets of success are outlined here.

SOIL MANAGEMENT

Soil is a complex mixture of air, water, mineral particles, organic materials, bacteria and other soil organisms. If these are out of balance, plants cease to grow healthily.

Bulky organic materials such as garden compost and farmyard manure are essential to a healthy soil: they are slowly broken down by soil organisms to form humus, a fine, dark material which aids both drainage and moisture-retention and is also a reservoir of plant foods. Garden compost and manure should be dug into the soil every year during late autumn or early winter (see pages 38-41). Additionally, forming mulches of decayed organic material improves the soil and encourages healthy plant growth, as well as conserving moisture in the soil and keeping it cool during summer (see pages 46-7).

Good drainage is essential in a vegetable plot (see pages 42-3) as excess water reduces the amount of air in soil, kills beneficial organisms and makes land cold and slow to warm up in spring, producing a 'late soil' unsuitable for the early sowing of seeds or planting of young plants.

The acidity or alkalinity of soil plays an important part in soil husbandry; most vegetables grow well in a pH of 6.5 to 7.0. Assessing and altering soil acidity is described on pages 38-9. However, it is much easier to make soil less acid by adding lime during winter, than to change alkaline soil to one that is acid. And much depends on the alkalinity of the underlying soil.

CROP ROTATION

1 In year one, grow root crops such as carrots, parsnips and swedes, as well as potatoes.
2 In year two, plant cabbages, cauliflowers, Brussels sprouts, as well as other brassica-related crops.
3 In year three, grow peas and beans, as well as salad crops such as lettuce, spring onions and tomatoes.
4 Some vegetables, such as radishes and lettuces, mature quickly and can be planted between slower-growing types.

GROWING VEGETABLES ORGANICALLY

Increasingly, gardeners are preferring to grow vegetables without the use of artificial chemicals. Here are the keys to success:

- **Improve the fertility** and structure of soil with annual applications of bulky materials such as garden compost and manure. These are broken down naturally by soil organisms into compounds that plants can use.

- **Rotate crops** to control soil-borne pests and diseases.

- **Mulch plants** to conserve soil moisture and to blanket the growth of weeds. Eradicating weeds also helps to prevent them harbouring pests and diseases.

- **Encourage natural predators** to control garden pests. Pesticides frequently kill beneficial insects as well as pests. If chemicals have to be used, select organic types that are non-persistent and non-systemic.

- **Select for disease-resistance** Seed catalogues usually offer advice about specific varieties.

CROP ROTATION

Growing vegetables of the same type on the same plot of land, year after year, results in the depletion of fertility, destruction of the soil's structure and a build-up of pests and diseases. For example, growing brassica crops (cabbages, cauliflowers and Brussels sprouts) continuously on the same piece of land causes a build-up of the fungus disease club-root, while the repeated cultivation of onions adds risk of eelworms.

The solution is to introduce crop rotation which not only helps to prevent disease but also improves a soil's structure. For example, before planting potatoes the soil is deeply prepared and during the crop's growth the surface soil is frequently disturbed when earthing-up shoots. This makes the soil ideal for other types of vegetables during the following year.

Vegetables vary in the amounts of manure and lime they require and growing them in rotation helps to keep this in balance. For example, when preparing for planting potato tubers, neither lime or manure is needed whereas, for brassica crops, lime is essential on acid soils and manure and compost are needed if the land is short of humus. Legumes (peas and beans), together with marrows, lettuce, aubergines, onions and sweetcorn always need liberal amounts of well-rotted manure or compost.

It is therefore convenient, when planning a vegetable garden, to take account of their requirements so that those with similar needs can be grown together and moved from one plot to another from one year to the next.

Vegetables can be arranged by their shared needs into three groups, so divide the vegetable garden into three parts. Each piece will contain one of the following groupings which are rotated in the sequence indicated below:

Group one – Root vegetables beetroot, carrot, chicory, Jerusalem artichoke, parsnip, salsify, scorzonera. Potatoes can also be included here.
Soil preparation: Dig the soil in winter but do not add manure or compost. Also, do not apply lime. About two weeks before sowing or planting, rake a general-purpose fertilizer into the soil.

Group two – Brassicas broccoli, Brussels sprouts cabbage, cauliflower, kale, kohlrabi, radish, swede, turnip.
Soil preparation Dig the soil in winter, adding well-rotted manure or compost, especially if the soil is lacking humus. If the soil is acid, apply lime, but not at the same time as digging in manure or compost. About two weeks before sowing or planting, rake a general-purpose fertilizer into the soil.

Group three – Legumes and other crops aubergine, beans, capsicum, celery, cucumber, endive, leek, lettuce, marrow, onion, peas, spinach, sweetcorn, tomato.
Soil preparation Dig the soil in winter and add copious amounts of well-decayed manure or compost. If the soil is acid, apply lime, but not at the same time as digging in manure or compost. About two weeks before sowing or planting, rake a general-purpose fertilizer into the soil.

ASSESSING VARIETIES FOR THE HOME

The range of varieties on sale in greengrocers or supermarkets is usually restricted to those that are profitable to commercial growers, and this is understandable. However, when growing your own food it is possible to have varieties that specifically suit you and your family.

Seed catalogues frequently give advice about the taste of individual vegetables and after a few seasons of growing your own food you will find you become increasingly specific about your choice. It is always worth growing a number of varieties of each vegetable so as to prolong cropping and avoid a glut with crops all maturing at the same time.

Sowing vegetable seeds

Many vegetable seeds are sown in the positions where they are to germinate, grow and mature. Others, such as cabbages, cauliflowers and Brussels sprouts, are sown in seedbeds. Later, when large enough to handle, young plants are transplanted into a vegetable garden. Young brassica plants can be sown in a seedbed the same way as biennials and herbaceous perennials (see pages 176-7; for the times of sowing specific vegetables, see pages 204-9). Here, however, the technique of sowing seeds directly in a vegetable plot is described.

PREPARING THE SOIL

Firm, friable, well-drained but moisture-retentive soil is essential to encourage seeds to germinate quickly and evenly. This is best achieved by digging the soil in early winter and allowing rain and frost to break down the surface to a fine tilth. Ground that has not been cultivated before (see pages 38-41) is best dug to a depth of two spade blades (double-digging), but soil that has been regularly cultivated need only be dug to the depth of one blade (single-digging).

In late winter, use a garden fork or tined-cultivator to break down the top 7.5-10cm/3-4in of soil. While doing this, try not to bring large clumps of soil to the surface. With a garden fork, use a slicing and banging action, but with a tined-cultivator simply push backwards and forwards.

On heavy clay land, wait until the soil starts to dry out in late winter or early spring before working on it: too early a start will cause it to become compacted. Do not, however, let it dry out and form large, hard lumps before preparing it.

Next rake off large stones, then spread and rake a general fertilizer at a rate of 50-100g per sq m/2-4oz per sq yd into the surface soil. Finally, the land must be evenly consolidated and the best way of achieving this is to shuffle sideways over the surface. If the soil is heavy, just rake it level afterwards but light sandy soil benefits from being systematically firmed, then raked level.

SOWING VEGETABLE SEEDS

The weather and soil influence the precise times when seeds can be sown. It is pointless sowing seeds when the soil is cold and wet, as this will

SOWING SEEDS IN V-DRILLS

1 Break down the top 7.5-10cm/3-4in of soil, add a general fertilizer, firm the surface and rake it level.
2 Stretch a garden line across the plot and use a draw hoe to form a V-shaped drill. To keep the line in the right place, place your foot on it.
3 Most vegetable seeds are sown in a continuous dribble, evenly and thinly, in the base of the V-drill.
4 Cover V-drills by straddling the row and shuffling forward so that loose soil is directed into the drill. Firm the soil with the back of a rake. Then, shallowly rake the surface level by raking along – not across – the row.

Above: When sowing vegetables, do not sow seeds thickly as this is a waste of money and often results in seedlings being more vulnerable to diseases. Plan the vegetable plot carefully, so that the space is fully used.

result in decay rather than germination. When sowing in dry weather, thoroughly water the soil during the previous day, but ensure the surface is not tacky when sowing begins.

The equipment needed for seed sowing includes a metal rake, draw hoe, garden line, measuring rod or tape-measure, spade and labels. There are two main types of drill in which vegetable seeds are sown:

Sowing in V-drills Most vegetable seeds are sown in V-shaped drills formed with the corner of a draw hoe. Start by lightly raking the surface level to eliminate the depressions and bumps that cause uneven germination.

Use a measuring rod or tape-measure to mark out the ends of the rows on both sides of the plot. Then stretch a garden line between the first pair of markers. Use a draw hoe to form a drill to the depth that suits the seeds: onions require drills 12mm/¹/₂in deep, French beans about 5cm/2in (see pages 204-9). Until you have gained

experience at using a draw hoe to form drills, repeatedly place your foot on the garden line to prevent it being forced sideways as you work backwards down the row.

Sow the seeds evenly and thinly. If congested, there is a risk of seedlings becoming diseased, especially after a shower of rain and when moisture cannot readily evaporate from their leaves. Also, seedlings become weak and spindly if sown too thickly. Furthermore, seeds are expensive to buy and should not be wasted.

Do not sow seeds directly from a packet. Instead, put a few into the palm of your hand and then dribble them into the drill between your forefinger and thumb. Most seeds are sown in a continuous line but some larger or irregularly shaped seeds, like beetroot, are sown in clusters of two or three seeds at intervals along the row.

After sowing place a label at each end of the row, then cover the drill by straddling it; position your feet in a V-formation and shuffle forwards. Loose soil earlier removed from the drill is then directed over the seeds. Alternatively, use the back of an iron rake to push and pull soil over the seeds. Use the flat head of a rake to firm the surface, then lightly rake the surface, in the direction of the drill – not across it.

Sowing in flat-bottomed trenches Some vegetables, such as peas, are sown in flat-bottomed trenches. Use a spade or draw hoe to form a flat-based drill 20cm/8in wide and 5cm/2in deep. Seeds are sown 5cm/2in apart in three staggered rows. This is an excellent way to grow peas in small gardens.

SOWING PREFERENCES

Many vegetables are sown where they are to grow and mature: this can be in continuous lines in the base of a seed drill, or else singly or in small clusters equally spaced along a row. Some are also sown in flat-bottomed trenches.

● In continuous lines in V-drills: carrots, lettuces, onions, parsnips, radishes, spinach, turnips.

● Singly spaced at intervals along V-drills: broad beans, French beans, runner beans, Jerusalem artichokes, potatoes.

● In clusters at spaced intervals along V-drills: beetroots,

● In flat-bottomed drills: peas.

Thinning and transplanting young plants

Many vegetables are sown in the positions in which they will grow and mature and are later thinned to prevent overcrowding. Plants may also be raised in nurserybeds and, when large enough to handle, are transplanted as small, bare-rooted plants into their growing positions. Alternatively, some plants are raised in pots and later transferred to a vegetable garden.

If seedlings are left to grow too close together they become thin, drawn up and susceptible to diseases, competing for moisture, nutrients and space. For this reason, as soon as they are large enough to handle they are thinned. This is often done in two stages: first to half the desired spacings and later to the full distance. This ensures that, should a few seedlings die after the first thinning, the spacings can be adjusted at the second stage.

When small plants are transplanted they can be positioned at exactly the desired spacing. Should any of these plants die within a few weeks of being planted, they can be replaced by a few extra plants earlier heeled in at the end of a row.

THINNING SEEDLINGS
Before thinning seedlings, ensure the soil is moist. If the weather is dry, thoroughly water the soil the day before, but do not swamp the area as this could wash the seedlings away.

After using a measuring rod and thinning a few seedlings along part of a row, experienced gardeners can often judge the spacings needed for the others without measuring. Novice gardeners, however, should use a measuring rod or tape measure all the time and stick to the correct spacings (these are indicated on pages 204-9).

As soon as seedlings are large enough to handle, thin them to leave the healthiest and strongest at each position. Always pick up unwanted seedlings and place them on a compost heap. If left on the soil's surface they look untidy and encourage the spread of pests and diseases. After thinning seedlings, always re-firm soil around those that are left. This is especially necessary if seeds have been sown too thickly and produced thick clusters of seedlings. Also, gently water the soil.

TRANSPLANTING YOUNG BRASSICA PLANTS
Brassicas – cabbages, Brussels sprouts and cauliflowers – are the main vegetables that are transplanted. Plants are raised from seeds sown in well-prepared seedbeds and later moved to their growing positions.

Young brassica plants are usually ready for transplanting between five and seven weeks after being sown. They each should have three or four leaves and be about 13cm/5in high. Water the seedbed the day before transplanting. Use a garden fork to dig under young plants to remove them and try to avoid damaging the plants, especially their fine root-hairs. After lifting them, initially place the roots in a bucket of water for twenty minutes, then wrap the plants in damp sacking or newspaper to transport them to their planting positions. Before planting, dip their roots in a proprietary fungicide to reduce the risk of clubroot attacking them.

Stretch a garden line across the plot and use a measuring rod or tape measure to ensure rows are straight and plants are at the correct spacings (see pages 204-9). Although a trowel can be used

Right: Lettuce seeds are sown thinly in shallow drills. Later, the young seedlings are thinned so that each plant has sufficient space in which to grow to maturity.

PLANTING BRASSICAS

1 Prepare the planting positions and stretch a garden line over the soil. Use a dibber to make the holes.
2 Hold a young plant by a couple of leaves, so that its roots dangle in the hole. Then, use the dibber to lever soil around the roots.
3 Water the soil thoroughly, so that water rests in the depression made by the dibber.

THINNED OR TRANSPLANTED?

Vegetables are either sown where they will grow, and then thinned; sown in a nurserybed and planted; or raised in pots and later planted.

- Vegetable seedlings that are thinned to the desired spacings: beetroot, carrots, lettuces, parsnips, spinach, turnips.
- Vegetables that are transplanted with bare roots: Brussels sprouts, cabbages, cauliflowers, leeks.
- Vegetables that are planted as pot-grown plants: aubergines, courgettes, marrows, tomatoes.

to plant brassicas, it is easier to use a dibber (a tool like the shortened handle of a garden spade or fork, 23-30cm/9-12in long and tapering to a blunt point). Form a planting hole by pushing the dibber 13-15cm/5-6in into the soil; rapidly twisting it about a quarter of a turn before pulling it out helps to prevent soil clinging to it.

Hold a young plant by its leaves and lower the roots into a hole, so that it is fractionally deeper than before. Insert the dibber into the soil 5-7.5cm/2-3in from the stem then lever it towards the plant so that soil is forced tightly around the roots. To judge if a plant is firmly held in the soil, tug the tip of a leaf. If it parts from the plant without disturbing the roots, it is firm enough. Do not test all the plants like this, just a few at random. Water the soil to settle it around the roots.

PLANTING POT-GROWN PLANTS

A few days before planting pot-grown plants, thoroughly water the soil in the vegetable plot. This helps to ensure rapid establishment, especially if the weather is dry. Additionally, water the compost in the pot the day before setting the plants into position.

Use a garden line and measuring rod to ensure that rows are straight and spacings between plants are correct; then use a trowel to make a hole large enough to take the soil-ball. Remove the pot and position the soil-ball so that the top of the compost is fractionally below the surface of the soil. This ensures that, after it settles, the soil will be level with the top of the soil-ball. Gently firm soil around the roots, but take care not to disturb the soil-ball. Afterwards, thoroughly water the soil-ball and surrounding soil.

PLANTING LEEKS

 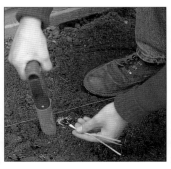 

1 When planting leeks, use sharp scissors or a knife to trim off about one-third of the roots, as well as leaf tips. **2** Use a garden line to ensure the row is straight, and a dibber to make holes about 15cm/6in deep. **3** Just drop one plant in each hole; do not fill it with soil. Then, gently fill the hole with water.

1   2   3

Planting tubers and rooted crowns

The best known vegetables grown from tubers are potatoes and Jerusalem artichokes, while asparagus is planted as rooted crowns earlier raised from seeds sown in a seedbed.

Tubers, together with shoots and stems that develop from them, are soon damaged by late spring frost. However, the energy stored in dormant tubers enables rapid development to take place once they are planted and ensures that growth is completed by the onset of cold weather in autumn. Rooted crowns also give vegetables a major start and have the virtue of being hardier than tubers.

PLANTING POTATOES
Potatoes are stem tubers and are distinguished from root tubers in having dormant buds known as eyes. Potatoes are classified as either 'First Earlies', 'Second Earlies' or 'Main Crop', depending on the variety and when they are planted. The precise time when potato tubers are planted depends on the locality and climate as it is preferable to avoid late frost damaging young, tender shoots. In general, first earlies are planted in early spring, second earlies in mid-spring, and maincrop types from mid- to late spring.

About two weeks before planting tubers, rake the soil level and add a base fertilizer at the rate of 112g per sq m (4oz per sq yd). Stretch a garden line across the plot and, with a spade or draw hoe, form a V-shaped drill about 15cm/6in deep.

Place a measuring rod or tape measure alongside the row and position tubers at the recommended spacings in the drill (see page 208), and with their eyes (buds) upwards. Use a draw hoe to cover the tubers and also to pull up soil over the row to a height of 10-15cm/4-6in. Take care not to damage the tubers by pressing the draw hoe too deeply.

PLANTING JERUSALEM ARTICHOKES
The tubers of Jerusalem artichokes are susceptible to frost, but once planted and established in spring they grow rapidly and shoots often reach 3m/10ft or more high by the end of summer. Indeed, sometimes they are planted to form a screen to hide sheds and compost heaps. In early spring, stretch a garden line across the plot and

PLANTING POTATO TUBERS

1 Stretch a garden line across a plot and use a draw hoe to form a 15cm/6in-deep V-drill.
2 Space out the tubers in the drill, with their 'eyes' upwards. For spacings, see page 208.
3 An alternative method of forming a drill is to use a spade.
4 Use a draw hoe to cover the drill and to form a 10-15cm/4-6in-high ridge.

Above: Potatoes are an important crop in temperate countries. They are easily grown, but require regularly cultivated soil. It is therefore an ideal crop to consider when trying to improve soil, perhaps during the first season after it has been converted from pasture land.

form 15cm/6in-deep V-drills. Place a measuring rod or tape measure alongside the drill and plant individual tubers – each the size of a small egg –at 30-38cm/12-15in intervals.

Remove the garden line and use a draw hoe to cover the drills. Water the soil thoroughly to initiate growth.

PLANTING ASPARAGUS CROWNS

Order asparagus crowns early in the year, so that they arrive in mid-spring. The crowns can be either one-, two- or three-years-old, and although the older ones are larger they do not necessarily establish themselves faster than one-year-old types, which invariably are less expensive.

In the previous winter, dig the soil and mix in well-decayed garden compost or manure. Once established, asparagus beds are maintained for

many years so ensure that perennial weeds are removed as if left – even in small pieces – they will contaminate the bed.

When the rooted crowns arrive, in mid-spring, do not let them dry out before planting. Wrap them in damp sacking and place in a cool, shaded shed. Dig a trench 38cm/15in wide and 25cm/10in deep. Form a slight mound in its base and space the rooted crowns 45cm/18in apart. Ensure that the roots are spread out over the mound, then cover with 5-7.5cm/2-3in of friable soil. Thoroughly water the soil.

During the first summer, keep the area free from weeds and the soil moist. In autumn, cut down the stems to ground level and add a layer of well-rotted garden compost of manure mixed with friable soil. Leave the row with a slight mound.

PLANTING SEAKALE ROOT CROWNS

Seakale is a hardy perennial grown for its succulent, blanched leaf stems. Dig the soil thoroughly in winter, adding plenty of well-decomposed garden compost or manure. In mid-spring, rake the soil level and stretch a garden line across the plot. Place a measuring rod or garden line along the string. Rub out all but the strongest bud on each crown and use a garden trowel to plant them so that their tops are 5cm/2in below the surface and 45-60cm/18-24in apart. Thoroughly water the soil and keep it moist until the crowns are established and develop shoots.

INCREASING PLANTS FROM BULBS

Some vegetables are grown from bulbs, such as:

- **Garlic** is grown from cloves, which are scale-like parts of a 'mother' bulb. Bulbs are split up and individual cloves planted 2.5cm/1in deep and 10cm/4in apart in rows about 20cm/8in apart in late winter or early spring. Their pointed ends must be uppermost. They are harvested in late summer.

- **Onion sets** are partly developed bulbs that are planted in early or mid-spring. Push each set into the ground so that just the top is visible; space them 10cm/4in apart in rows 25cm/10in apart. This is an ideal way to grow onions where the growing season is short.

- **Shallots** are raised from bulbs (see page 209).

Supporting vegetables

Many vegetables, such as carrots, parsnips and potatoes, do not need to have their stems and shoots supported, but for others this is essential. It prevents plants sprawling under their own weight, protects stems and leaves against damage by strong winds and creates more space for crops such as runner beans to bear pods.

SUPPORTING RUNNER BEANS

The traditional way to support runner beans is to push two rows of bean poles into the soil to take a double row of plants. The poles need to be 2.4-2.7m/8-9ft long, so that about 30cm/12in can be inserted into the ground. Space the double rows about 45cm/18in apart, with the poles set 23-30cm/9-12in apart along the rows. Angle the poles inwards, so that they form a tunnel and cross 15-20cm/6-8in from their tops, where a cross-pole is secured to them with strong string. Sow two seeds at the base of each pole.

If the row is oriented east-to-west, most beans will appear on the sunny side; but if it is positioned north-to-south the crop will be evenly borne on both sides.

An alternative method of support uses four to six poles arranged in a circle and tied at the top to create a 1.8-2.1m/6-7ft-high wigwam. Again, sow the bean seeds at the base of the poles after the wigwam has been erected. This is an ideal way to grow runner beans in an ornamental setting or small garden.

A further way is to secure semi-rigid, 1.5-1.8m/5-6ft-high plastic netting between upright posts. String netting can also be used, but it is extremely difficult to remove the old bean stems in autumn.

Where seeds are to be sown in two rows, you can economize on bean poles by stretching wires in two rows, 60cm/24in apart, along the ground. Secure their ends to stakes and hammer metal hooks (about 20cm/8in long and about the thickness of wire coat hangers) into the ground along their length. Form and support a wooden cross-bar, 1.5-1.8m/5-6ft high, between the rows. Tie individual strings, 23-30cm/9-12in apart, to the cross-bar at the top and the wires at ground-level. Sow seeds at the positions where the strings touch the ground.

Right: Wigwams create ideal supports for runner beans, when they are given plenty of light and air. Additionally, they enable runner beans to be grown in relatively small areas.

SUPPORTING VEGETABLES

1 Runner beans are traditionally supported by a series of poles which lean inwards and have a series of poles tied to their tops.
2 Support garden peas by inserting twiggy sticks among the plants when young, so that stems grow up and through them.
3 An alternative way to grow runner beans is to tension netting between poles.
4 To prevent the stems of broad beans splaying outwards, insert strong canes at the edges of the row and encircle the crop with string.

SUPPORTING GARDEN PEAS

Garden peas are traditionally supported useing twiggy sticks. These must be 15-20cm/6-8in longer than the ultimate height of the crop, which varies from one variety to another. These sticks are pushed into the soil alongside plants.

Alternatively, when plants are about 7.5cm/3in high, erect a 45-60cm/18-24-high screen of wire netting along the row, secured at its ends to stout posts and given further support at intervals with strong canes.

SUPPORTING ASPARAGUS PEAS

Asparagus peas need support to prevent the pods trailing on the soil and becoming dirty. Supports also decrease their susceptibility to attack from soil-roaming pests, such as slugs and snails. Insert twiggy sticks alongside each plant.

SUPPORTING STEMS

A few plants need only the support of soil drawn up around their stems when young. Jerusalem artichokes, for example, benefit from this; as well as creating support, it helps to encourage the formation of tubers near the surface. Brussels sprouts, kale and cabbages also benefit from a little soil being drawn up around their stems to protect them from frost and strong winds.

SUPPORTING TOMATOES

Most tomato plants need support, whether in a greenhouse or outdoors. Some varieties have a bush habit, while a few can be grown in hanging-baskets, but most produce a single stem from which the leaves and fruiting trusses develop.

Tomato plants grown in pots on a patio, as well as in vegetable plots, are usually supported with individual canes. Insert these before or soon after plants are planted. Secure the stems to the canes by using strong garden string: first, tie it tightly around the stake, then form a loose loop around the tomato stem, just below a leaf-joint.

Plants in growing-bags cannot be supported by canes, as these would pierce the plastic. Instead, use proprietary supports that are held firm by the weight of the bag and its compost. In greenhouses, a common way to support tomatoes is to secure wires at ground-level, as well as 1.5-1.8m/5-6ft high, and to tie strings between them. As the plants grow, stems can be gently trained in a loose spiral around the strings.

SUPPORTING VEGETABLES

The golden rules for supporting plants are:

- Support plants early in their lives. If left, stems become stiff and difficult to manipulate.
- Don't damage stems, roots or shoots when constructing supports.
- Ensure that the main supports, as well as wires and strings, are strong enough to support the plants when mature and cropping.
- In windy and exposed areas, check that supports for runner beans are extra strong.
- Check supports regularly throughout summer to ensure they are secure. Also, make sure that stems are not constricted.
- In autumn, when plants have matured and died, remove all haulm (spent shoots and leaves) and recycle wires and poles. Remove soil and debris from the wires and poles and wash them in disinfectant before drying and storing.

Harvesting and storing vegetables

Harvesting home-grown vegetables and eating them while still fresh is one of the joys of having your own vegetable plot. Apart from the advantages of being able to select varieties that specifically suit your family's needs and tastes, home-grown vegetables can be harvested at an earlier stage than is economically possible for commercial growers. Many vegetables have a superb flavour when young: carrots can be pulled when no longer than a finger, turnips when the size of a golf ball, and French beans picked when young and especially succulent. Additionally, vegetables harvested early in their life are available at a time when they are at their most expensive to buy in shops.

VEGETABLE HARVESTING

Artichoke – Globe Mid-summer to early autumn; cut heads when green, swollen but unopened, leaving 5-7.5cm/2-3in of stem still attached.

Artichoke – Jerusalem Autumn to early spring; use a garden fork to lift the tubers as required, and in frosty weather cover those left with straw.

Asparagus Spring and early summer; cut spears when 13-15cm/5-6in long, severing them at 5-7.5cm/2-3in below the surface.

Aubergine Mid-summer to early autumn; cut fruits when 13-15cm/5-6in long, before the shine on the surface disappears.

Beans – Broad Mid-summer to late summer or early autumn; start picking when pods are 5-7.5cm/2-3in long and cook whole. Later pick them when beans swell and can be seen through the pod and cook just the beans. Do not leave the pods to become large and tough.

Beans – French Early mid-summer to autumn; start picking when pods are about 10cm/4in long. Test by bending a pod; if it snaps it is ready for harvesting.

Beans – Runner Early part of late summer to mid-autumn; pick when 15-20cm/6-8in long.

Beetroot Early summer to early autumn; the roots are best when young (about the size of a golf ball) – with age the flesh hardens and becomes coarse. Twist off the foliage about 5cm/2in above the bulbous root.

Brussels sprouts Late summer to early spring;

STORING VEGETABLES

1 Tomatoes and spring onions can be stored for about a week in polythene bags in the bottom of a refrigerator.
2 Cabbages can be stored for up to a week in a refrigerator by first wrapping them in plastic cling film.
3 Store bulbing onions and shallots in wooden trays in a cool, airy, vermin-free place.
4 Store potatoes in a cool, dark place. Put them in strong paper sacks. New potatoes can be stored for about a couple of weeks in polythene bags placed in a refrigerator.

MAKING AN ONION ROPE

Tying onions together so that they form a 'rope' is the traditional way to store and display onions. The rope can be hung up in a light, dry, frost-proof place where the bulbs will remain in good condition throughout winter.

Making a rope of onions is not as difficult as it may seem. Use only well-ripened and undamaged bulbs. Grade them into sizes, so that the larger ones can be placed at the bottom with the smaller ones towards the top.

Onion ropes can be made without a central core, but it is easier for a beginner to use a thick piece of rope about 60cm/24in long as a core. Bunch together three or four large bulbs and, holding their stems, position at the base of the rope. Twist string round the stems to secure them in position (sometimes the stems of the onions are wrapped around the stems to secure them, but this needs experience, and, unless well done, does not allow the onions later to be removed individually). Gather a further three or four bulbs and position them slightly above the first ones. Secure them into position. Proceed like this until the rope is complete.

pick the sprouts (buttons) individually, when tightly closed and the size of a walnut, picking upwards from the stem's base.

Cabbage – Red Autumn to early winter.

Cabbage – Spring Spring.

Cabbage – Savoy Mid-autumn to late winter.

Cabbage – Summer Mid-summer to early autumn.

Cabbage – Winter Late autumn or early to late winter.

Use a sharp knife to cut the stems of all types of cabbage just above soil-level.

Carrots Latter part of early summer to mid-autumn; lift when young and succulent. Take care not to bruise them.

Cauliflowers Winter varieties from late winter to late spring; summer varieties from early summer to early autumn; autumn varieties from early autumn to early winter. Start cutting them while still small, and cut them early in the morning when they are covered with dew, but wait until midday if they are frosted.

Celery – Self-blanching Late summer to mid-autumn; carefully dig up plants as needed. Ensure stems of adjacent plants that become exposed are covered with soil or straw.

Celery – Trench type Early autumn to late winter; carefully dig up plants as needed, replacing soil around exposed stems.

Cucumber – Ridge type Latter part of mid-summer to late summer; use a sharp knife to cut the fruits when 15-20cm/6-8in long. Do not wait for them to become excessively large.

Leeks Late autumn to mid-spring; use a garden fork to carefully dig them up.

Lettuce Range of types, enabling cutting throughout the year. Use a sharp knife to cut the stems of heart-forming types when they feel firm (use the back of your hand to test them). Loose-leaf types do not produce hearts and individual leaves can be picked when ready.

Marrows and courgettes Mid-summer to early autumn; harvest courgettes when 10cm/4in long, and marrows when 20-25cm/8-10in long. A ripeness test for marrows it to push a fingernail into the surface, near the stalk; if it goes in quite easily the fruit is ready for cutting. Cut the stem before moving the fruit.

Onions – Bulb Late summer and early autumn, depending when seeds were sown. Fully ripen onions before lifting (see pages 206-7).

Onions – Spring types Early summer to early autumn; harvest before the bases swell. Use a garden fork to lift them carefully from the soil.

Parsnips Late autumn and throughout winter; use a garden fork to ease them from the soil. They can be lifted and stored as soon as the leaves die down in autumn.

Peas Late spring to autumn, depending when seeds were sown; pick pods when well filled with peas and while there is still space between each pea. Pick the pods regularly.

Potatoes 'First earlies' in early summer; 'second earlies' in mid-summer; 'main crop' in late summer for immediate use, or early autumn for storing. If possible, use a wide-tined potato fork to lift them from the soil.

Radishes Summer varieties in late spring or early summer to late summer; winter varieties from mid-autumn onwards. Take care not to bruise the roots.

Shallots Mid-summer. Stored bulbs will keep for about eight months if kept in a cool, dry place.

Spinach Summer varieties from early summer to mid-autumn; winter varieties from mid-autumn to spring. Cut the tender, young outer leaves at each picking. Regular picking encourages the growth of further leaves.

Sweetcorn Late summer and early autumn (see pages 208-9 for details of harvesting).

Tomatoes – Outdoor Late summer and into early autumn. Pick the fruits when ripe and fully coloured.

Turnips Throughout much of the year. Harvest early turnips while still small and succulent; later ones can be allowed to become slightly larger, but no larger than a cricket ball in size.

Vegetables

VEGETABLE	SITUATION AND SOWING	CULTIVATION AND HARVESTING

Artichoke – Globe

Globe artichokes are relatively short-lived herbaceous plants with succulent flower heads. Plants are grown for three years, discarded and the plot replanted with young ones. These are raised from seeds, or from sucker shoots.

Varieties include: 'Green Globe' (widely available as seeds, moderately hardy); 'Purple Globe' (hardier than 'Green Globe', but not so well flavoured); 'Vert de Laon' (good flavour).

Full sun or light shade and deeply prepared, well-drained but moisture-retentive, fertile soil with a pH of 6.5-7.5, enriched with copious amounts of well-rotted garden compost and manure.

Sow seeds in spring, thinly and evenly in 2.5cm/1in-deep V-drills spaced 30cm/12in apart. Thin the seedlings to 15cm/6in apart and plant into a vegetable garden during the following spring. Also, sucker-like growths can be severed from parent plants in spring and planted 60-75cm/24-30in apart each way.

During the first year, cut off all flower heads before they turn purple and in late autumn cut down plants to soil-level. In spring of the second year, feed with a general fertilizer.

Harvest the flower heads from mid-summer to early autumn. In the following year, allow a further crop to develop. In the fourth year, the quality decreases: use the plants' sucker shoots to create further plants.

Asparagus

Asparagus is grown for its young, succulent shoots that appear from mid-spring to early summer. Although frequently considered as a luxury vegetable, it is easily grown. Once established, an asparagus bed produces 'spears' for ten or more years.

Varieties include: 'Connover's Colossal' (long, fat spears); 'Lucullus' (heavy cropping); 'Larac' (early spears); 'Martha Washington' (heavy cropping, long spears).

Full sun or dappled shade and light, fertile, well-drained soil with a pH of 6.5-7.5 suits it. Dig the soil in early winter, adding garden compost or manure.

Sow seeds 12-18mm/½-¾in deep in a seedbed in mid-spring. It takes three years before plants are ready for planting into a garden. Alternatively, buy established plants in mid-spring and place them 38cm/15in apart in a 25cm/10in-deep and 38cm/15in-wide trench with a slight mound in its base. Cover them with 5-7.5cm/2-3in of soil.

In the autumn after planting, cut down the 'fern' stems to ground level, add a layer of manure or garden compost and form a mound of soil over the trench. During the second year, add fertilizer in spring, cut down the fern in autumn and, again, mound up the ridge. During the following spring and early summer, the spears can be cut (severing about 5cm/2in below the surface) when 13-15cm/5-6in tall. In autumn, again cut down the fern and add a light covering of soil to the mound.

Aubergine

Aubergines, often called Eggplants, are sub-tropical, frost-tender plants usually grown in greenhouses but also grown outdoors on warm patios in summer.

Varieties include: 'Black Enorma' (prolific cropper, large fruits); 'Black Prince' (early cropping, heavy cropping); 'Easter Egg' (small, oval fruits, white skinned); 'Elondo' (very early cropping, shiny, purple fruits, vigorous plants).

Full sun on a wind-sheltered patio. Grow in containers holding fertile compost or use growing-bags.

Sow seeds evenly and thinly, 3mm/⅛in deep, in early spring and place in gentle warmth. Cover with a sheet of glass topped with newspaper. After germination, prick out the seedlings individually into 7.5cm/3in-wide pots, still keeping them in gentle warmth. Slowly acclimatize plants to outside conditions and plant into growing-bags or large pots once risk of frost has passed.

Before setting young plants outside, warm up the compost by placing cloches over it for several weeks, and keep in position for three weeks after planting. Pinch out the growing points when plants are about 30cm/12in high and support them with canes or a special framework for use with growing-bags. Outdoors, allow only five or six fruits to develop – pinch off all other flowers.

Harvest the fruits when they have an even colour and while still glossy. Cut the stems with a knife or scissors.

Beans – Broad

Broad beans are grown for their large pods of succulent beans. Young pods are frequently picked when 7.5cm/3in long and cooked whole, but usually the pods are left to grow larger, then picked and shelled to remove the beans.

Varieties include: 'Aquadulce Claudia' (ideal for early crops, sow in autumn or mid-winter); 'Express' (fast maturing); 'The Sutton' (dwarf); 'Witkiem Major' (heavy cropping).

Full sun and light, well-drained, fertile soil with a pH of 6.0-7.0, to which has been added well-rotted farmyard manure.

Sow seeds 13cm/5in apart in V-drills 7.5cm/3in deep in late winter or early spring. Sow the seeds in double rows 30-38cm/12-15in apart; 23cm/9in for dwarf varieties. Make further sowings in mid- or late spring. Additionally, make sowings in late autumn for plants that can be overwintered and which produce beans early in the following year. Choose varieties such as 'Aquadulce Claudia'.

In mid-spring, insert strong stakes around the crop and surround the plants with strong garden twine. Hoe off weeds, water freely during dry weather and snap off sideways the tender growing tips when the plants begin to flower; remove about 10cm/4in of growth. This encourages the development of pods and helps to prevent the plants becoming infested with black bean aphids.

Pick the mature pods regularly and do not allow them to become large and tough.

Artichoke – Jerusalem

These are edible stem tubers that are harvested from autumn to early spring. They can be left in the soil, but cover with straw to protect from frost.

Plant tubers 15cm/6in deep and 30cm/12in apart in rows 90cm/3ft apart during early spring. During summer, support plants and regularly water the soil. In autumn, cut down stems to 15cm/6in above soil-level.

Asparagus Pea

Also known as Winged Pea, this is grown for its 2.5cm/1in-long, winged pods, which are eaten whole. They are harvested from mid- to late summer.

Sow seeds 2.5cm/1in deep and 10cm/4in apart in drills 30cm/12in apart during late spring, or when danger of frost has passed. Support plants with twiggy sticks.

Broccoli

Purple sprouting broccoli is harvested from mid-winter to late summer; white types in spring.

Sow seeds in a seedbed, in drills 12mm/½in deep and 15cm/6in apart, in mid-spring. Transplant young plants when about 13cm/5in high, setting them 45-60cm/18-24in apart in each direction.

Cabbages – Spring

Spring cabbages are sown in mid- to late summer for harvesting in spring of the following year. 'Spring greens' are the same plants, planted closer together and harvested before they form hearts.

Sow seeds in a seedbed, in V-drills 12-18mm/½-¾in deep and 15cm/6in apart. Transplant young plants in early to mid-autumn. Young plants can also be bought.

	VEGETABLE	SITUATION AND SOWING	CULTIVATION AND HARVESTING

Beans – French

French beans produce masses of bean pods on low-growing plants, although there are climbing forms, which are described with runner beans (see below). The succulent pods and beans are picked when young, and cooked sliced or left whole.

Varieties include: 'Masterpiece' (heavy cropping, stringless); 'The Prince' (long and oval pods, ideal for freezing); 'Radar' (can be cooked without slicing).

Full sun and moisture-retentive but well-drained, fertile soil with a pH of 6.5. Dig in plenty of organic material such as garden compost and farmyard manure in winter. Fork a general fertilizer into the surface soil a few weeks before sowing seeds.

Sow seeds 5-7.5cm/2-3in apart in V-drills 5cm/2in deep in late spring and until mid-summer. Space the rows about 45cm/18in apart.

Keep the soil hoed and water copiously during dry weather. The secret of success with French, as with runner, beans is plenty of sun and moisture-retentive soil. Mulch around plants to help conserve moisture. Most French beans are self-supporting, but during heavy rain storms and when the crop is heavy there is a chance of plants being knocked over. Therefore when plants are young insert twiggy pea-sticks around them. Cut down the tops of plants to soil-level in autumn, but leave roots in the ground.

Beans - Runner

Runner beans develop succulent pods, which are sliced and cooked, on climbing plants. Similar to runner beans are the climbing French types. These plants are quickly damaged by frost and therefore cannot be sown until all risk of frost has passed.

Varieties include: 'Streamline' (heavy cropping, long supple pods); 'Lady Di' (stringless, early cropping).

Full sun and moisture-retentive but well-drained, fertile soil with a pH of 6.5. In winter, dig a 30cm/12in-deep trench and fork in plenty of organic material such as garden compost and farmyard manure. A few weeks before sowing seeds, fork into the surface soil a general fertilizer.

Sow seeds 15cm/6in apart in V-drills 5cm/2in deep in late spring. Space the rows 60cm/24in apart if the plants are to be grown in double rows.

The secret of success is plenty of sun and fertile soil that retains moisture. Mulch around plants to conserve moisture. The plants need support, provided either by poles in double rows that lean inwards and are secured to a cross pole, or by vertical strings tied to wires stretched between posts at ground level and about 1.8m/6ft high. Alternatively, wigwams of poles can be used.

The pods are picked while still young and tender. Aged pods become tough and stringy.

Beetroot

Beetroots are grown for their swollen roots – some globe shaped, others long-rooted – which are usually red. They can be boiled and eaten cold in summer salads, although they can also be served as a hot vegetable or made into soup.

Varieties include: 'Boltardy' (globe, sweetly flavoured, ideal for early sowing); 'Burpee's Golden' (globe, golden yellow roots, does not bleed); 'Cylindra' (long-rooted, ideal for slicing).

Full sun and deeply prepared, well-drained soil that has not had fresh manure added to it. A pH of 6.5-7.5 suits it. Prepare the soil early in spring and if poor add a general fertilizer.

Sow seeds in V-drills 18mm/³⁄₄in deep and 30cm/12in apart (45cm/18in for long-rooted types) from mid-spring to mid-summer. Soak the seeds in water for an hour before sowing, then place groups of two or three seeds at 10-15cm/4-6in intervals along the row. Later, thin the seedlings to one at each position.

Keep the soil free from weeds and water during dry weather. Pull up, or use a garden fork to harvest early beetroots as soon as they are large enough. Beetroots from late sowings can either be forked up in autumn, their leaves cut off and the roots stored in boxes of sand placed in a dry, frost-proof shed, or left in the ground and their tops covered with straw. In cold, wet areas it is better to store the roots under cover.

Brussels Sprouts

Brussels sprouts are grown for their buttons, densely and tightly formed of overlapping leaves, that cluster up the main stem. They mature and can be picked from late summer to spring.

Varieties include: 'Fortress' (mid-winter to early spring cropping, frost resistant); 'Peer Gynt' (late summer to early winter cropping).

Full sun or light shade and deeply prepared but firm, fertile soil enriched with well-decayed manure or garden compost during the previous year. A pH of 6.5-7.5 is needed.

Sow seeds in a seedbed from early to mid-spring in V-drills 18-25mm/³⁄₄-1in deep and 15cm/6in apart. Plants can also be bought. Put young plants into their growing positions from late spring to early summer, setting ordinary varieties 75cm/30in apart each way.

Thoroughly water plants to establish them in the soil and during early summer treat the plants to control cabbage root fly. Hoe off weeds and during mid-summer use a draw hoe to pull soil around the bases of plants. In late summer pull off any yellow leaves.

As soon as the buttons are firm, pick them individually – the ones at the base of the stem will be ready first.

Cabbages – Summer

Summer cabbages are sown in mid-spring for harvesting from late summer until autumn of the same year.

Sow seeds in a seedbed, in V-drills 12-18mm/¹⁄₂-³⁄₄in deep and 15cm/6in apart. Transplant young plants in late spring and early summer. Young plants can also be bought.

Cabbages – Winter

Winter cabbages are sown in mid- to late spring for harvesting from the following late autumn to late winter.

Sow seeds in a seedbed, in V-drills 12-18mm/¹⁄₂-³⁄₄in deep and 15cm/6in apart. Transplant young plants in early and mid-summer. Established plants can be bought.

Calabrese

This is also known as Green Sprouting Broccoli and is harvested in late summer and autumn. It is less hardy than either purple or white sprouting broccoli.

Sow seeds in spring, where the plants are to grow as they do not transplant very well. Sow them 12mm/¹⁄₂in deep in drills 30cm/12in apart. Sow three or four seeds in each position; later, thin to the strongest.

Capsicum – Sweet

These peppers have a mild flavour and are increasingly popular for harvesting outdoors during late summer. Plants grown under cloches are ready earlier.

Sow two seeds 3mm/¹⁄₈in deep in a small pot and place in 16-18°C/61-64°F during early spring. After germination, remove the smaller of the two seedlings; lower the temperature slightly and plant out in early summer.

Vegetables

VEGETABLE	SITUATION AND SOWING	CULTIVATION AND HARVESTING

Carrots

Carrots are grown for their swollen roots – whether short-rooted (ideal for early crops), intermediate-rooted (medium-sized and blunt-ended) or long-rooted (long, tapering, pointed and ideal for late sowings). Roots are either cooked or grated and eaten raw in salads.

Varieties include: 'Early Nantes' (short-rooted, early sowing); 'Amsterdam Forcing' (short-rooted, cylindrical).

Full sun, an open situation and deeply prepared, well-drained, stone-free soil that has not had fresh manure added to it. Prepare the soil in winter; if poor, fork in a general fertilizer in spring.

Sow seeds thinly and evenly, in V-drills 12-18mm/1/2-3/4in deep and 15-23cm/6-9in apart, from early spring to mid-summer. Later, thin the seedlings to about 5cm/2in apart for early crops, and progressively to 10cm/4in, or slightly more, for main crop and later sowings.

Keep the soil moist and free from weeds. Carrot flies are the main pest and these are attracted when the seedlings are thinned. Reduce the risk of infestation by thinning during damp weather, in the evenings, and removing the thinned seedlings.

Pull up early carrots as needed, but in autumn fork up the remaining roots, twist off the foliage and store in boxes of dry sand in a cool, frost-free shed.

Cauliflowers

Cauliflowers are grown for their large heads, tightly packed with white, immature flowers known as 'curds'. Cauliflowers mature throughout the year.

Varieties include: 'All The Year Round' (summer maturing, milky white heads); 'Snowball' (summer maturing, compact); 'Dok-Elgon' (late summer and autumn maturing, large heads); 'Purple Cape' (winter and spring maturing, hardy).

Full sun or light shade and deeply prepared, firm, fertile soil enriched with manure or garden compost during the previous year. A pH of 6.5-7.5 is needed.

Sow seeds of summer-maturing types 3mm/1/8in deep in seed-trays in mid-winter and keep at 13°C/55°F. Prick them out into small pots when large enough to handle and place in a cold frame. Sow seeds 12mm/1/2in deep in a seedbed, in mid- and late spring for late summer and autumn maturing types, and in late spring for winter maturing types.

Keep the soil free from weeds and water plants thoroughly in dry weather. Bend a few outer leaves over maturing curds in summer to protect them from strong sunlight, as well as in winter to decrease the risk of damage from frost.

The curds are ready for harvesting when they are firm but not yet starting to open.

Celery – Trench type

Celery is traditionally grown in trenches to produce crisp, blanched stems that are ready for eating from early autumn to late winter.

Varieties include: 'Giant Pink' (firm, crisp, pale pink stems, superb flavour); 'Giant White' (extremely hardy, white stems); 'Giant Red' (resistant to low temperatures, shell pink stems, lasts to the end of winter).

Full sun or light shade and well-drained but moisture-retentive, fertile soil with a pH of 6.5-7.5. Prepare the soil in winter by digging a trench 38cm/15in wide and 30cm/12in deep. Fork garden compost and manure into the base and fill to within 7.5cm/3in of the surface.

Sow seeds thinly and evenly in seed-trays in early to mid-spring and place in gentle warmth. When large enough to handle, prick off the seedlings to about 5cm/2in apart in seed-trays. Slowly acclimatize plants to outdoor conditions.

In late spring or early summer, set the young plants in the trench, 23cm/9in apart and in two rows. During mid-summer, tie the stems loosely just below the leaves and wrap thick, brown paper around them. Draw up soil around the stems and continue to do this as the plants grow.

Harvest the plants from early autumn to late winter, using a trowel to draw away soil from the stems. Protect celery left in the ground until mid- and late winter with straw.

Cucumbers – Ridge type

Ridge cucumbers are so-named because they are often grown on a mound or ridge of soil outdoors. They are easier to grow, as well as hardier, than cucumbers grown in garden frames or greenhouses.

Varieties include: 'Burpless Tasty Green' (tender-skinned fruits, good flavour); 'Kyoto' (ideal in containers, good flavour); 'Tokyo Slicer' (vigorous, heavy cropping, excellent flavour); 'King of the Ridge' (almost spineless fruits).

Full sun, sheltered position and light, moisture-retentive, fertile soil. Prepare the planting positions in mid-spring. Dig out holes about 30cm/12in deep and square and fill with well-decayed garden compost or manure. Place compost on top to form a mound and allow to settle.

Sow seeds in late spring or early summer (do not sow too early or the plants may be damaged by frost). Sow two seeds 18mm/3/4in deep and 5cm/2in apart and place a small glass jar on top. Later, remove the weakest seedlings.

Keep the area free from weeds and water during dry weather. When each stem has about six leaves, pinch off the growing tip just above a leaf. Spread out the shoots. Spread a thin mulch over the soil to conserve moisture.

During mid- to late summer, cut off the cucumbers when they are 15-20cm/6-8in long.

Cardoon

Cardoons are related to globe artichokes and are grown for the fleshy stems of their inner leaves.

Sow seeds in groups of three, about 5cm/2in deep and 45cm/18in apart, in rows 75cm/30in apart during mid-spring. After germination, thin to the strongest seedling. From late summer to early autumn, blanch the stems by wrapping them in black polythene.

Celeriac

Also known as Turnip-rooted Celery, celeriac is grown for its swollen roots which are harvested in mid-autumn and stored in a frost-free shed.

Sow seeds in small pots, 6mm/1/4in deep and three to a pot, in early spring at 18°C/64°F. After germination, remove the weakest seedlings and harden off. Plant out in early summer; set plants 30cm/12in apart in rows 38cm/15in apart.

Chicory

A perennial with roots used for forcing. Sow seeds in late spring in drills 12mm/1/2in deep in rows 30cm/12in apart. Thin the seedlings 20cm/8in apart. Dig up roots in early winter and store in dry sand in a frost-proof shed. From mid-winter to early spring, pot up roots vertically, keep at 7-13°C/45-55°F and cover with black polythene to encourage the development of young shoots.

Corn Salad

Also known as Lambs Lettuce, this 15-23cm/6-9in-high hardy annual is grown for its young leaves, harvested for use in winter and spring salads.

Sow seeds during late summer and early autumn (alternatively in spring) in drills 12mm/1/2in deep and 15-20cm/6-8in apart. Plants can be harvested when they have developed three or four pairs of leaves.

VEGETABLE	SITUATION AND SOWING	CULTIVATION AND HARVESTING

 **Lettuce**
 	
There are several types of lettuce.
  Cabbage types include Butterheads (soft-leaved and globular), with varieties such as 'All The Year Round', and Crispheads (round, crisp heads) with varieties such as 'Webb's Wonderful'.
  Cos are upright, with crisp hearts, and varieties include 'Little Gem'.
  Loose-leaf types have no hearts, and masses of leaves that can be harvested individually.
	Full sun and fertile, moisture-retentive but well-drained soil with a pH of 6.5-7.5. Dig the soil in winter and add well-decomposed garden compost and manure. Although lettuces can be sown in late summer and overwintered outdoors for spring maturing, most home gardeners sow seed in spring for maturing in summer.
	  Sow seeds of summer-maturing types 12mm/^{1}/2in deep in drills 25cm/10in apart from early spring to mid-summer. Later, thin to 23-30cm/9-12in apart.
		Keep the soil free from weeds and water thoroughly during dry weather. Lettuces mature from early summer to early autumn. Test their readiness for harvesting by pressing hearting types with the back of a hand. If firm, use a sharp knife to cut the stem.

 **Marrows and Courgettes**
 	
Marrows and courgettes are fast-growing, frost-tender plants with a bushy or trailing habit. Courgettes resemble miniature marrows, and some varieties can be grown as marrows and courgettes.
  Varieties include: 'Early Gem' (marrow, bushy); 'Gold Rush' (courgette, bushy); 'Green Bush' (marrow, bushy); 'Zucchini' (courgette, bushy, heavy cropping); 'Long Green Trailing' (marrow, trailing).
	Full sun, warm site and well-drained, moisture-retentive, fertile soil.
	  Sow seeds in gentle warmth in mid- to late spring; put two seeds 18mm/^{3}/4in deep in a 7.5cm/3in pot. After germination, lower the temperature and remove the weaker seedling. It takes five to six weeks to produce a plant ready for setting in a garden, after all risk of frost has passed. Alternatively, in late spring or early summer sow two seeds in growing position. Cover with a glass jar, and, later, remove the weakest plants.
		Bush types do not need to have their growing tips removed (stopping), but trailing forms do. When the sideshoots are about 45cm/18in long, nip them out. Keep the soil moist during summer and feed plants every three weeks when the fruits begin to swell. In cold weather and early in the season, assist pollination by picking off a male flower (smaller than the female, and without a small, undeveloped fruit behind it) and brushing it into a newly opened female one. Pick the fruits regularly.

 **Onions – Bulbing**
 	
Bulbous onions are grown from two main sowings – 'spring' (mature in autumn and are stored for winter use) and 'late summer' (mature during the following summer).
  Varieties include: 'Bedfordshire Champion' (sow spring, heavy cropping); 'Buffalo F1 Hybrid' (sow spring or late summer, heavy cropping); 'Senshyu Semi-Globe Yellow' (sow late summer, bridges gap between seasons).
	Full sun and light, well-drained, deeply prepared, fertile soil with a pH of 6.5-7.5. It is possible to grow onions on the same piece of land for several years.
	  Sow seeds evenly and thinly, 12mm/^{1}/2in deep and in rows 23-30cm/9-12in apart, during early spring. Sowings can be made a few weeks early, but need to be covered with cloches. Sowings can also be made in late summer, as for spring-sown types, but with seeds slightly thicker in the rows to allow for winter losses.
		Thin spring-sown seedlings, first to about 5cm/2in apart, later to 7.5-10cm/3-4in. The thinnings can be used as salad onions. Thin late summer sown types to about 5cm/2in apart and later, in spring, to 10cm/4in.
		  Ripening onions is essential; in mid- and late summer, for the spring-sown types, bend over their stems. A few weeks later fork under the bulbs to lift them from the soil and lay them on the soil, ideally with their bases facing the sun.

 **Onions – Spring**
 	
Spring onions – also known as salad or bunching onions – are superb in salads.
  Varieties include: 'Ishikura' (white and straight, thin stems, long harvesting period); 'Santa Claus' (ready for harvesting in six weeks from a spring sowing); 'White Lisbon' (widely used and readily available, quick-growing); 'White Lisbon Winter Hardy' (very hardy, early cropping); 'Winter White Bunching' (ideal for late summer sowing).
	Full sun and light, well-drained, deeply prepared, fertile soil with a pH of 6.5-7.5 are needed.
	  Sow seeds at three- to five-week intervals from early spring to late summer. Those sown during early and mid-summer can be harvested in six to eight weeks. Late summer sowings of hardy varieties overwinter outside and can be pulled up in spring. Sow seeds, thinly and evenly, 12mm/^{1}/2in deep in V-drills 15cm/6in apart in narrow beds; or 30cm/12in apart in open plots.
		Keep the soil free from weeds and water the plants during dry weather. Thinning is not usually needed unless the seeds have been sown too thickly.
		  Salad onions are harvested before their bases begin to swell. In cold, northerly areas it is necessary to cover overwintered spring onions with cloches from late autumn onwards.

Endive

A hardy annual with stems that are blanched and used in salads.
  Sow seeds, in drills 12mm/^{1}/2in deep and 30cm/12in apart, from mid-spring to late summer for curly-leaved varieties, and mid-summer to early autumn for broad-leaved types. Thin seedlings to 23cm/9in apart for curly-leaved types and 30cm/12in for broad-leaved types. Blanch plants twelve weeks after sowing.

Florence Fennel

Also known as Sweet Fennel or Finocchio, this is grown for its bulb-like base.
  Sow seeds in drills 12mm/^{1}/2in deep and 45cm/18in apart between mid-spring and mid-summer. Thin seedlings to 20-30cm/8-12in apart. Do not let the soil dry out during summer, and draw up soil around the base of each plant so that the bulbous part becomes blanched.

Kale

Hardy brassica, a source of winter and spring greens and eaten from early winter to mid-april.
  Sow seeds in a seedbed in 12mm/^{1}/2in-deep drills spaced 15cm/6in apart during mid-and late spring. Thin seedlings and when 10-13cm/4-5in high transplant to their growing positions. Space them 45cm/18in apart within a row, with rows the same distance apart.

Kohlrabi

A brassica grown for its large, swollen and bulbous-looking roots, which are ready for harvesting from late summer to early winter.
  Sow seeds from mid-spring to mid-summer, 12mm/^{1}/2in deep, in drills 30cm/12in apart. Thin the seedlings first to 7.5cm/3in apart, later to 15cm/6in. Keep the soil moist during dry weather.

Vegetables

VEGETABLE	SITUATION AND SOWING	CULTIVATION AND HARVESTING

Parsnips

Parsnips are swollen roots for harvesting in late autumn and throughout winter. Their flavour is improved by frost.

Varieties include: 'Avonresister' (small roots, resistant to canker); 'Improved Hollow Crown' (long roots, good flavour); 'Gladiator' (F₁ hybrid, early maturing, sweet flavour); 'Tender and True' (long rooted, resistant to canker).

Full sun and deeply prepared, well-drained, fertile, light soil with a pH of 6.5-7.0 are essential.

Sow seeds during late winter and early spring, in V-drills 12-18mm/^{1}/₂-^{3}/₄in deep and 25-30cm/10-12in apart. Sow three seeds every 15cm/6in along each row. When the seedlings show their first true leaves, thin each cluster to the strongest plant. When growing exhibition parsnips, use a crowbar to form holes 75-90cm/2^1/₂-3ft deep. Fill with compost, sow three seeds and later thin to one.

Keep the soil clear of weeds and water the plants during dry weather. Fluctuating levels of moisture in the soil tend to crack the roots. When hoeing between the parsnips, take care not to damage their shoulders, which are only just below the surface.

Harvest the roots from autumn onwards, using a garden fork to ease them from the soil.

Peas

Garden peas, tender and sweet, are a traditional vegetable and a wide range of varieties makes it possible to have fresh peas from late spring to autumn.

Varieties include: 'Daybreak' (early, heavy cropping); 'Feltham First' (early, very hardy); 'Kelvedon Wonder' (second early, good flavour, reliable crops); 'Hurst Green Shaft' (second early); 'Onward' (main crop, heavy cropping, sweet); 'Alderman' (main crop, heavy cropping).

Full sun or light shade and deeply prepared, fertile, well-drained but moisture-retentive soil with a pH of 6.0-7.0. Dig well-decayed garden compost or manure into the soil in late autumn or early winter.

Sow seeds in a flat-bottomed trench 20cm/8in wide and 5cm/2in deep from early spring to mid-summer. Space the seeds in three rows, with the centre one staggered, 5cm/2in apart. Cover each row with a hoop of wire netting to prevent birds digging up the seeds.

Keep the soil free from weeds and thoroughly water the plants during dry weather. They soon suffer if the soil is allowed to become dry. The plants need support, either from twiggy pea sticks inserted along the rows or from wire netting up which plants can climb. Insert the pea sticks or erect the netting when the plants are about 7.5cm/3in high.

Pick the pods when young but when well filled with peas.

Radishes

Radishes are grown for their swollen, globular or cylindrical, crisp, pepper-flavoured roots. They are usually eaten fresh and raw in summer salads (although large, winter types can be cooked as a vegetable).

Varieties include: 'Cherry Belle' (globe, fast-growing); 'French Breakfast' (cylindrical, mild and sweet); 'Prinz Rotin' (globe, survives neglect).

Full sun, open situation and fertile, well-drained but moisture-retentive warm soil that has not had fresh manure added to it recently. Rake in a dressing of a general fertilizer in spring.

Sow seeds thinly and evenly – and at three-week intervals – in V-drills 12mm/^{1}/₂in deep and 15cm/6in apart, from early spring to mid-summer. If sown thinly, the seedlings need little thinning, but if congested, thin them to 2.5cm/1in apart.

Early sowings take six to eight weeks to mature, while later ones can be pulled after three or four weeks. During dry weather, keep the soil moist to encourage rapid growth. Also, keep the soil free from weeds.

Spinach

Spinach, one of the most nutritious vegetables, is grown for its leaves, which are usually cooked but sometimes eaten raw in salads. There are two types of spinach: summer and winter.

Varieties include: 'Long Standing Round' (thick, fleshy leaves, winter variety); 'Monnopa' (low oxalic acid content, winter variety); 'Sigmaleaf' (summer or winter variety).

Full sun or light shade in moisture-retentive but well-drained, fertile soil with a pH of 6.5-7.5 suits it. Dig in plenty of well-decayed garden compost or manure in late autumn or early winter.

Sow seeds of summer spinach from early to late spring or early summer for harvesting eight to ten weeks later. Sow the winter type in late summer or early autumn, cover with cloches and harvest twelve to fifteen weeks later. Sow seeds in V-drills 12-18mm/^{1}/₂-^{3}/₄in deep and 30cm/12in apart.

When the seedlings are large enough to handle, thin them first to 7.5cm/3in apart, later to 15cm/6in. These 'second' thinnings can be eaten. Keep the soil free from weeds and water the plants during dry weather. Harvest the leaves by snapping off their stalks. Do not tear off the stalks as this damages the plant's base. Harvesting the plants regularly encourages the development of further leaves.

Leeks

Leeks are grown for their thick stems formed of tightly packed leaves; they mature from late autumn to mid-spring.

Sow seeds thinly and evenly in a seedbed, in 12mm/^{1}/₂in deep drills about 15cm/6in apart, during early and mid-spring. Thin the seedlings and, when pencil thick, plant into 15cm/6in-deep holes. Drop a plant into each hole and add water. Do not firm soil around them.

Potatoes – Early

'First Earlies' (harvested in early summer) or 'Second Earlies' (harvested a few weeks later).

Plant tubers (known as 'seed potatoes') in early spring, 30cm/12in apart in 15cm/6in deep V-drills. Space the rows about 60cm/2ft apart. Space the second early types about 40cm/16in apart in the rows. Use a draw hoe to cover the tubers, forming a 10-15cm/4-

Potatoes – Main Crop

Potatoes are an especially useful crop for clearing land and producing a fine tilth for further crops.

Plant tubers (known as 'seed potatoes') 40cm/15in apart in 15cm/6in-deep V-drills from mid- to late spring. Space the rows about 75cm/30in apart. Use a draw hoe to cover the potatoes, at the same time drawing up soil to form a 10-15cm/4-6in-high ridge.

Rhubarb

Although frequently considered to be a fruit, rhubarb is usually grown in a vegetable garden. It has a perennial nature and yields stalks from late spring to mid-summer each year. Replace plants every five to seven years.

Plant new roots (old ones lifted and divided, each having at least one bud) from late winter to early spring, or earlier in mild areas.

VEGETABLE	SITUATION AND SOWING	CULTIVATION AND HARVESTING

 **Shallots**
 	
Shallots are related to onions, but have a milder flavour. They are also easier to grow and keep better when stored. Instead of being grown from seeds, plants are raised from small bulbs known as offsets. These are saved from the previous year's crop, or bought.
    Varieties include: 'Dutch Yellow' (popular variety); 'Hative de Niort' (well-shaped bulbs, deep brown skin).
	Full sun and light, well-drained, deeply prepared, fertile soil with a pH of 6.5-7.5 suit it. It is possible to grow shallots on the same piece of land for several years.
	    Plant young bulbs in late winter or early spring, 15cm/6in apart in rows 23cm/9in apart. Although they can be pushed into the soil (if light and well-prepared) so that their tops are just visible, it is just as easy to use the tip of a trowel to form the holes. Firm soil around them.
		Until established, protect the bulbs from birds by placing hoops of wire netting over the rows. Also, keep the soil moist. Use a small hoe to keep the soil free from weeds, and during mid-summer use a finger or small label to scrape soil from around the bases of the bulbs. This helps to hasten the ripening process. From mid-summer onwards, use a garden fork to lift the bulbs from the soil, as soon as their leaves turn yellow and begin to shrivel. Store them in a cool, frost-free shed.

 **Sweetcorn**
 	
Sweetcorn is grown for its heads packed with bright yellow seeds. Cook or freeze the heads as soon as possible after cutting from a plant.
    Varieties include: 'Sweet 'N' Tender' (high yields, good quality); 'Early Xtra Sweet' (very sweet, excellent in coastal areas and where the growing season is short).
	Full sun, a wind-sheltered site and fertile, deeply prepared, well-drained but moisture-retentive soil with a pH of 5.5-7.0 are essential.
	    Sow seeds outdoors in late spring, putting two seeds 2.5cm/1in apart and 12mm/½in deep at 38cm/15in intervals along each row. Space the rows 45cm/18in apart. After germination, thin to leave the strongest seedling. Alternatively – and in cold areas – sow seeds in small pots in mid-spring and plant out once risk of frost has passed.
		Sweetcorn must be grown in blocks, rather than single lines, to encourage pollination. Keep the plants free from weeds and water them during dry periods. Remove sideshoots growing from the bases of plants when they are about 15cm/6in long.
		    The heads are harvested when the tassels become brown and withered. Pull back the brown outer sheath to expose the seed – if pricked with a knife, ripe heads exude a milky liquid. Harvest the heads by twisting downwards.

 **Tomatoes – Outdoor**
 	
Tomatoes are fruits but are invariably grouped with vegetables. There are two main types of outdoor tomatoes: cordon varieties are supported with canes and their sideshoots removed, while bush types do not need support, or the removal of sideshoots.
    Varieties include: 'Tumbler' (bush); 'Shirley' (cordon); 'Matador' (cordon); 'Golden Sunrise' (cordon); 'Sweet 100' (cordon).
	Full sun, a warm and wind-sheltered position and fertile, light, moisture-retentive but well-drained compost.
	    Sow seeds during early to mid-spring, 3mm/⅛in deep in seed-trays. Cover with glass and newspaper and keep at 18°C/64°F. Remove after germination, prick out seedlings to about 5cm/2in apart and pot on into small pots. Slowly harden off for planting into containers or growing-bags on a warm patio in early summer, as soon as all risk of frost has passed.
		Support cordon types with canes or special frames, and remove sideshoots. Also, for cordon varieties, pinch out the growing tip above the second leaf above the fourth truss. Pick fruits as they ripen and in late summer cut plants from their supports and cover with cloches to ripen the remain fruit.

 **Turnips**
 	
Turnips, when home-grown and eaten fresh, are tender and succulent, and if you select the right varieties, they can be harvested throughout much of the year. The key to the production of tender roots is to grow them quickly.
    Varieties include: 'Snowball' (globe-shaped, summer type); 'Tokyo Cross F₁' (superb taste, summer type); 'Manchester Market' (winter type).
	Full sun or slight shade in light, well-drained but moisture-retentive soil with a pH of 6.0-7.0 suits them. Avoid land that has been freshy manured as this causes roots to fork.
	    Sow seeds in early spring for an early crop; in mid- and late spring for summer crops and in mid-summer for autumn and winter crops. Sow seeds thinly and evenly 12mm/½in deep and in rows 30cm/12in apart.
		When the seedlings are large enough to handle, thin mid-summer-sown crops first to 7.5cm/3in apart and later to 15cm/6in (for winter-maturing types thin to 23cm/9in apart). Keep the soil free from weeds. Harvest spring-sown crops when young and tender; harvest those sown in mid-summer and autumn when the leaves have turned yellow. Roots can be lifted and stored in boxes of dry sand or peat and placed in a frost-free shed.

Salsify and Scorzonera

These vegetables have long, tapering roots; those of salsify are white-skinned and the flesh has an oyster-like taste, whereas scorzonera has black skin and the flesh is not so strongly flavoured.
    Sow seeds 12mm/½in deep in groups of two or three in rows 30cm/12in apart during mid-spring. Later, thin to the strongest seedling in each cluster. Mulch and water the plants in summer.

Seakale

This is a hardy perennial, grown for its edible stems, which need to be blanched.
    Plant young crowns (also known as thongs) in early spring, 5cm/2in deep and 38cm/15in apart, in rows 45cm/18in apart. During autumn remove the yellow leaves and in the following mid-winter cover the dormant crowns with a large, light-proof pot. Cover the pot with straw. Harvest blanched shoots in spring.

Swedes

A much underrated winter vegetable with superly flavoured, bulbous roots that are harvested from early to late winter.
    Sow seeds during late spring to early summer, in drills 12mm/½in deep and 38cm/15in apart. Thin the seedlings in several stages so that plants are eventually 23cm/9in apart.

Welsh Onion

Sometimes known as Japanese Bunching Onion, this perennial forms a clump of hollow leaves up to 60cm/24in high. Use them like spring onions or chives.
    Sow seeds in early to mid-spring, 12mm/ ½in deep, in drills 30cm/12in apart. Thin the seedlings to 23cm/9in apart and pick leaves as needed. Divide clumps every three or four years and replant.

Creating a herb garden

In the past, culinary herbs were necessary not just for flavour but to conceal the taste of decaying in food, making it acceptable to taste-buds. Today, herbs can be grown to enhance our food but many also make attractive garden plants. Mint, Parsley and Thyme are well-known and popular culinary and garden herbs but there are others that are well worth growing, including Angelica, Balm, Chives, Fennel, Marjoram, Rosemary and Sage (see pages 212-5).

Most herbs are warmth-loving plants; many are native to Mediterranean regions and therefore demand a sunny, wind-sheltered position and light, well-drained soil. The majority of culinary herbs are grown close to a house and near the kitchen door, which is very convenient provided the site is suitable; small types, and especially when young, are well suited for planting in window-boxes, or in troughs and tubs on a patio. Alternatively, on a larger and grander scale, complete borders can be designed and dedicated to them and surrounded by small, regularly clipped hedges formed of Edging Box (*Buxus semper-virens* 'Suffruticosa').

Most new herb gardens are planted in spring or early summer from pot-grown plants. Prepare for this by digging the area in early winter and mixing in well-decayed garden compost and manure (see pages 38-41). Additionally, if the area is poorly drained install drains (see pages 42-3) and add sharp sand to the top 15cm/6in of soil. By early spring, when the herb garden is being created, the soil's surface will have broken down to form a fine tilth.

CHESSBOARD DESIGNS

This is an ideal and novel way to grow herbs, especially those with a low-growing nature. The aim is to form a chessboard-like arrangement of 45-60cm/18-24in-square paving slabs and to plant herbs in the spaces between them. This design has the great advantage of making all the herbs accessible from a firm surface. The design can be given even more eye-appeal by surrounding the area with an edging of stone chippings or pea-gravel. By using variegated herbs, as well as green-leaved types, attractive patterns of colour can be created to compleiment the 'hard areas'

CREATING A CARTWHEEL HERB GARDEN

1 Dig the soil thoroughly in early winter and add well-decayed garden compost or manure. Ensure the drainage is good. In spring, mark out the area by tying a string to a central peg and inscribing a circle.
2 Mark the positions of the 'spokes', then place pebbles or rustic poles along them.
3 At the centre, use pebbles to form a circle in which a dominant plant can be positioned. If the planting areas are too large for one type of plant, divide them into two sections by using a row of pebbles. Marking every other spoked area in this way creates a regular design.
4 After planting, lightly but thoroughiy water the plants.

Above: Large cartwheels provide ideal homes for herbs, especially relatively low types. Spread pea-shingle over the areas not covered by plants. This helps to prevent the growth of weeds and keeps the soil cool during hot summers.

of paving stones and gravel. Gravel can also be used to mulch the soil to conserve moisture as well as creating attractive backgrounds for plants.

When forming this chessboard arrangement, use paving slabs with ribbed, rustic textures: coloured slabs with shiny, smooth, richly coloured surfaces do not harmonize with herbs and are better suited for use in ultra-modern patios and around swimming pools.

HERB BEDS

Herbs are frequently grown in beds cut out of lawns. Although this design initially looks attractive – with neatly trimmed lawn edges and soil contrasting with the leaves – within a season, the more vigorous plants will start to trail over the lawn's edges. Eventually this creates bare patches in the grass at the bed's edge. If, however, the bed is edged with paving slabs or a 30-45cm/12-18in-wide strip of crazy-paving, it can be easily maintained and kept neat at all times.

GROWING HERBS IN CONTAINERS ON PATIOS

Small, non-invasive culinary herbs grow well in window-boxes, troughs and pots on a patio. Larger herbs such as Rosemary can be grown in large tubs, but need to have their growing tips removed several times when young to encourage bushy growth. Invasive types such a Mint need separate pots and if planted in a border or cartwheel herb garden should be confined in a container buried to its rim.

Culinary herbs for containers include Chervil, Chives, Parsley, Pot Marjoram, Summer Savory, Sweet Basil and Thyme. Sage and Rue can also be grown, but need to be regularly trimmed to size and removed from the container and planted out when too large.

CARTWHEEL HERB GARDENS

Cartwheel herb gardens are eye-catching and distinctive features, never failing to draw attention. They are designed to make it appear as though the herbs are planted between spokes of a cartwheel. Few people are fortunate enough to have a cartwheel in which a herb garden can be created, but by using pebbles or rustic poles the illusion of spokes can be created. Cartwheel herb gardens look best when created in an island bed where they can be seen from all sides. They can also be formed in flower beds and surrounded on all but the front side by herbaceous plants.

Where the wheeled design can be seen from all sides, grade the heights of the herbs with the lowest at the outside and the tallest towards the centre, with a dominant plant such as Bay (*Laurus nobilis*) right in the middle. If the design is to be viewed solely from the front then grade the heights upwards from the front to the back.

Where a cartwheel garden is designed within a real wheel, the basic design is provided. But where the 'wheel' has to be created from pebbles or rustic poles, push a peg into the position where the hub would be and, with a string the length of the radius, mark out the circumference of the circle in the soil surface.

Use large pebbles or rustic poles to create the spokes, forming separate areas each 30-45cm/12-18in wide at the outer edge. At the centre, use more pebbles to form a small circle, 38-45cm/15-18in across, into which a dominant, rounded, hub plant can be positioned.

Culinary herbs

PLANT NAME AND DESCRIPTION	SITUATION AND CULTIVATION	PROPAGATION

Angelica
(Angelica archangelica)
Height: 1.5-2.1m/5-7ft
Spread: 90cm-1m/3-3¹/₂ft

A short-lived perennial grown as a hardy biennial. It forms a dominant plant with thick, ridged, tough stems and deeply dissected, aromatic leaves. The yellow-green, umbrella-like flower heads appear in mid- and late summer. The stems are candied and used in cake decoration.

Full sun or light shade and fertile, deeply prepared, moisture-retentive but well-drained soil suit it. Dig in plenty of well-decomposed garden compost or manure in winter. During early or mid-spring, set young plants into their growing positions, about 90cm/3ft apart. During their first season, remove the flower heads and keep the soil free from weeds; in the following year, harvest the stems in early summer while still tender. Harvest side growths in mid-summer.

Sow seeds thinly and evenly in a seedbed outdoors in spring, in drills 6mm/¹/₄in deep and 30cm/12in apart. When they are large enough to handle, transplant the seedlings to 30cm/12in apart in rows similarly spaced. Keep the soil free from weeds and transfer plants to their growing positions during the following spring. Disturb the roots as little as possible.

Balm
(Melissa officinalis)
Height: 60cm-1.2m/2-4ft
Spread: 30-45cm/12-18in

A hardy herbaceous perennial, widely grown for its lemon-scented, wrinkled-surfaced, somewhat nettle-like, heart-shaped green leaves. The Golden Balm (*M. o.* 'Aurea'), which has gold-and-green leaves, can also be grown as a culinary herb. The leaves are used fresh or dried in iced drinks and fruit salads.

Full sun and light, moisture-retentive but well-drained soil are essential. Set young plants into their flowering positions in autumn or spring, spacing them 30-45cm/12-18in apart.
 Keep the soil free from weeds and cut back plants with variegated leaves to 15cm/6in high in early summer to encourage the development of new leaves. In autumn, cut all plants down to soil-level. In extremely cold areas, cover the plants with straw.

Lift and divide congested plants in autumn or spring, replanting the younger parts from around the outside. Alternatively, sow seeds 6mm/¹/₄in deep in rows 30cm/12in apart in mid- to late spring, where the plants are to grow. Thin the seedlings to 30cm/12in apart when they are large enough to handle. Seeds may also be sown in spring in a seedbed and transfered, when large enough, to their growing positions.

Basil
(Ocimum basilicum)
Height: 45cm/18in
Spread: 25-38cm/10-15in

Also known as Sweet Basil, this half-hardy annual has bright green leaves, grey-green below. White flowers appear in late summer, but it is the strongly clove-flavoured leaves which are used to flavour food. These are used fresh or dried in omelettes, minced meat, soups, fish dishes and salads.

A warm, sheltered position in good light is needed. Well-drained but moisture-retentive soil is essential; it is often necessary to water the soil during summer.
 Regularly pinch off the flowers to encourage the development of young, healthy leaves. Harvest the leaves while young and fresh.

During late spring, sow seeds thinly and evenly in 6mm/¹/₄in-deep drills spaced 38cm/15in apart. Germination takes two to three weeks. When the seedlings are large enough to handle, thin them 30-38cm/12-15in apart.
 Alternatively, in early spring sow seeds 6mm/¹/₄in deep in seed compost in seed-trays. Keep at 13°C/55°F. When the seedlings are large enough to handle, transfer them to small pots. When plants are sturdy and growing strongly, plant into a garden.

Bay
(Laurus nobilis)
Height: 1.8-3.6m/6-12ft
Spread: 1.8-3.6m/6-12ft

Also known as Bay Laurel and Sweet Bay, this well-known evergreen tree has aromatic, glossy, mid- to dark green leaves which are used to flavour cooked meals. Often, this tree is grown as a half-standard in a large tub, when it can eventually reach about 1.8m/6ft high.

Well-drained, light soil and a sheltered position in light shade or full sun suits it. In cold, wind-swept positions the leaves become damaged.
 Pick young leaves as required, but avoid spoiling the shrub's shape and appearance.

During mid- and late summer, take 10cm/4in-long cuttings from sideshoots. Trim the base of each cutting to just below a leaf-joint, and remove the lower leaves. Insert cuttings 36-50mm/1¹/₂-2in deep in pots of equal parts moist peat and sharp sand, and place in a cold frame. When they have rooted, transfer them to individual pots and when established plant into a garden or large container.

Aniseed
(Pimpinella anisum)
Height: 45cm/18in
Spread: 30-38cm/12-15in

Also known as Anise, this hardy annual forms a dainty plant with brilliant green, finely divided and toothed leaves and umbrella-like heads bearing small, white flowers during mid- and late summer. The seeds are used to flavour drinks, soups, cakes and sweets.

Caraway
(Carum carvi)
Height: 60-75cm/24-30in
Spread: 38-45cm/15-18in

A hardy biennial, with aromatic, fern-like, mid-green leaves. During early and mid-summer small flowers appear, and later seeds. These are dried and used to flavour breads, cakes, cheeses and salads. Additionally, they are sprinkled on pork and lamb for roasting.

Chervil
(Anthriscus cereifolium)
Height: 30-45cm/12-18in
Spread: 30-38cm/12-15in

A hardy biennial with bright green, fern-like, aniseed-flavoured leaves that resemble Parsley in appearance and are used as a garnish. They give flavour to salads and sandwiches, as well as soups, egg and cheese dishes and sauces. Dried leaves are used in stuffings.

Coriander
(Coriandrum sativum)
Height: 23-30cm/9-12in
Spread: 15-20cm/6-8in

A hardy annual with dark green, somewhat feathery and fern-like leaves. Pink-mauve flowers appear during mid-summer, followed by the seeds, which are used to flavour curries and stews. The leaves are added to soups and meat dishes.

PLANT NAME AND DESCRIPTION	SITUATION AND CULTIVATION	PROPAGATION

Borage
(Borago officinalis)
Height: 45-90cm/1½-3ft
Spread: 30-38cm/12-15in

A hardy annual with somewhat oval green leaves covered in silvery hairs. From early to late summer it reveals clustered heads of five-petalled, blue flowers. There are also pink and white-flowered forms. The young leaves are used to flavour salads and fruit cups.

Well-drained soil and a sunny position suit it best. However, it grows quite well in most soils as long as they are not waterlogged and cold.
  Harvest the leaves while young for adding to food and drying.

Raise fresh plants each year. From mid-spring to mid-summer, sow seeds evenly and thinly in shallow drills 30cm/12in apart, where the plants are to grow and mature. When the seedlings are large enough to handle, thin them 25-38cm/10-15in apart. Sow seeds at four to six-week intervals to produce a regular supply of young leaves during summer.

Chives
(Allium schoenoprasum)
Height: 15-25cm/6-10in
Spread: 25-30cm/10-12in

Hardy perennial with a bulbous nature and masses of grass-like, tubular, mid-green leaves. During early and mid-summer it develops globular heads, up to 36mm/1½in across, formed of rose-pink, starry flowers. The chopped leaves are used to give a mild onion-like flavour to soups, salads and omelettes.

Full sun or light shade and fertile, moisture-retentive but well-drained, light soil are needed. It is often grown in window-boxes or in containers on a patio. Set new plants into containers, or out in a garden, in autumn or spring, about 25cm/10in apart. Plants die down in autumn and develop fresh leaves in spring.

Lift and divide congested plants in autumn and replant young parts from around the outside. Alternatively, sow seeds thinly and evenly in seed drills 12mm/½in deep and 25-30cm/10-12in apart in a well-prepared seedbed in early spring. When large enough to handle, thin the seedlings to 15cm/6in apart. Later, transfer them to their growing positions.

Dill
(Anethum graveolens)
Height: 60-90cm/2-3ft
Spread: 30-38cm/12-15in

A hardy annual with upright, ridged stems and blue-green, feathery and thread-like, anise-flavoured leaves. From early to late summer it reveals small, yellow, star-like flowers in umbrella-like heads up to 7.5cm/3in across. The leaves are used to flavour fish, salads, boiled potatoes, poultry, peas and beans.

Well-drained, fertile soil is essential, and so is a sunny position. Harvest the leaves while young and fresh. The leaves are difficult to dry and during winter it is better to use seeds, which are often added to sauces. When growing plants mainly to produce seeds, cut down stems when the seeds turn brown, in late summer.

Raise fresh plants each year. In late spring or early summer, sow seeds evenly and thinly in shallow drills 38-45cm/15-18in apart. Germination is not rapid, but as soon as the seedlings can be handled, thin them to 30-38cm/12-15in apart.
  If seeds are desired from the plants, sow seeds in early spring.

Fennel
(Foeniculum vulgare)
Height: 1.5-2.4m/5-8ft
Spread: 45-75cm/18-30in

Hardy perennial with upright stems bearing thread-like, bluish green leaves that, like the rest of the plant, emit an aniseed aroma. During mid- and late summer it bears small, golden yellow flowers. Leaves are used fresh or dried to flavour cheese dishes, fish, sauces and pickles.

Full sun, a warm and sheltered position and well-drained soil that does not dry out during summer are essential. Set young plants in their growing positions in spring. If seeds are not required, pinch off the flower stems as soon as they develop.

Lift and divide congested plants in spring, as soon as young shoots develop. Replant young pieces from around the outside of the plant, setting them 45-60cm/18-24in apart. Alternatively, sow seeds evenly and thinly in V-drills 6mm/¼in deep and 45cm/18in apart in spring or early summer. Thin the seedlings to 30cm/12in apart.

French Sorrel
(Rumex scutatus)
Height: 30-45cm/12-18in
Spread: 25-38cm/10-15in

A hardy perennial, also known as Garden Sorrel and Buckler-shaped Sorrel, with fleshy, mid-green leaves which have a lemony flavour. They are usually used fresh, but can be dried or frozen, and added to sandwiches, salads and soups.

Garlic
(Allium sativum)
Height: 30-75cm/12-30in
Spread: 23-30cm/9-12in

A hardy, bulbous plant related to onions and with a distinctively strong aroma and flavour. Cloves (the separate parts of a bulb) are planted in spring for harvesting in late summer. Garlic is used to flavour many foods, including salads, fish and meat dishes.

Ginger
(Zingiber officinale)
Height: 60-90cm/2-3ft
Spread: 30-38cm/12-15in

A tropical perennial usually grown in a heated greenhouse in temperate countries. Alternatively, it can be grown in a container outdoors on a patio during summer, and taken into a greenhouse in winter. The roots are used to flavour meat, fish, rice and vegetable dishes.

Horseradish
(Armoracia rusticana)
Height: 45-60cm/18-24in
Spread: 30-45cm/12-18in

Also known as Mountain Radish, Red Cole and Great Raifort, this hardy perennial has roots which, when washed, are crushed, grated or minced and simmered with milk, vinegar and seasonings to make a peppery sauce to flavour meat, fish and salads.

Culinary herbs

PLANT NAME AND DESCRIPTION	SITUATION AND CULTIVATION	PROPAGATION
**Marjoram – Sweet or Knotted type** *(Origanum majorana)* Height: 45-60cm/18-24in Spread: 30-38cm/12-15in A slightly tender perennial invariably grown as an annual, developing bright green leaves and clusters of tubular, mauve, pink or white flowers from early to late summer. The whole plant is sweetly aromatic and slightly hairy. The young shoots and leaves are used in fish, meat and tomato dishes.	Full sun, a warm and sheltered position and well-drained but moisture-retentive soil are essential. Plants will survive winter in warm areas, but usually they are pulled up and fresh plants raised each year and planted in spring, about 30cm/12in apart.	Sow seeds evenly and thinly 3mm/¹/₈in deep in seed-trays during late winter or early spring. Keep them at 50-59°C/ 10-15°F. When large enough to handle, prick out the seedlings first into seed-trays, then into their growing positions. Alternatively, sow seeds 6mm/¹/₄in deep in V-drills 23-30cm/9-12in apart during late spring and early summer. Later, thin the seedlings to 23-30cm/ 9-12in part.
**Mint – Common or Spearmint** *(Mentha spicata)* Height: 45-60cm/18-24in Spread: 30cm/12in Herbaceous perennial with aromatic leaves which have a distinctive spearmint flavour. They are used in mint sauce and jelly, as well as for flavouring vegetables such as peas and potatoes. The leaves of Apple Mint *(M. rotundifolia)* have an apple aroma and are also used in kitchens.	Slight shade, a warm and sheltered position and light, fertile, moisture-retentive but well-drained soil are needed. Dig in plenty of well-decayed compost or manure in winter. The plants have invasive roots and are often planted in containers. Every three years, dig up plants in autumn and replant in spring, setting the plants about 25cm/10in apart.	During early summer, take 10cm/4in-long cuttings and insert them in equal parts moist peat and sharp sand. Place in a cold frame until rooted. Alternatively, lift congested plants in spring and replant young pieces directly into their growing positions. Keep the soil moist until the plants are established.
**Parsley** *(Petroselinum crispum)* Height: 30-60cm/12-24in Spread: 23-38cm/9-15in Hardy biennial invariably grown as an annual, with branching stems bearing curly, moss-like, mid-green leaves. If left to grow, it develops greenish yellow flowers, but these should be removed as soon as they appear. The leaves are widely used to garnish fish dishes and sandwiches, as well as to flavour sauces.	Full sun or light shade, a warm position and light, fertile, well-drained but moisture-retentive soil are essential. It is often grown in pots of soil-based compost on a patio. Gather leaves from mid-summer onwards.	Sow seeds thinly and evenly, 6mm/¹/₄in deep in pots on a patio, or in seedbeds in a vegetable garden, from early spring to mid-summer. The seeds are slow to germinate. Initially thin the seedlings in open soil to 7.5cm/3in apart, later to 23cm/9in. If you want to keep the plants in containers, set one or two plants in each pot.
**Rosemary** *(Rosmarinus officinalis)* Height: 1.5-2.1m/5-7ft Spread: 1.2-1.5m/4-5ft Hardy, evergreen shrub with aromatic, mid- to dark green leaves. During mid- and late spring – and sporadically until late summer and often into early winter – it bears mauve, white or bright blue flowers. The leaves are used fresh or dried to flavour roast meat and added to sauces and stuffings.	Full sun and light, well-drained but moisture-retentive soil are essential. Plant young plants in spring. Cut out dead shoots in spring, as well as any that are long and straggly. Old plants can be rejuvenated by cutting all shoots back by half in spring.	Take 7.5-10cm/3-4in-long cuttings in mid-summer and insert them in pots of equal parts moist peat and sharp sand. Place in a cold frame. When rooted, transfer them individually into small pots and overwinter in a cold frame. Plant into a garden or container on a patio the following spring.

Hyssop *(Hyssopus officinalis)* Height: 45-60cm/18-24in Spread: 30-38cm/12-15in A hardy, partially evergreen perennial with aromatic, narrow, mid-green leaves. Young leaves are best for culinary use. They have a mint-like bouquet and are used fresh in salads, as well as fresh or dried in stuffings and soups. Often, they are used to 'balance' oily fish.	**Lemon-scented Verbena** *(Aloysia triphylla)* Height: 90cm-1.5m/3-5ft Spread: 90cm-1.2m/3-4ft Tender deciduous shrub with pale to mid-green leaves that emit a strong lemon scent when crushed. They are used chopped in stuffings or to flavour chicken and fish. They can also be added to jellies and jams.	**Lovage** *(Levisticum officinale)* Height: 90cm-1.2m/3-4ft Spread: 60-75cm/24-30in Hardy perennial with leaves that have a slightly nutty, celery-like flavour. They are chopped and used in salads, stews and broths.	**Rue** *(Ruta graveolens)* Height: 60-75cm/24-30in Spread: 45-60cm/18-24in Hardy, evergreen shrub with deeply divided, blue-green leaves that have an acrid bouquet. When picked young they are finely chopped and added to salads. It is an attractive plant and is frequently planted at the front or corner of a flower border.

PLANT NAME AND DESCRIPTION	SITUATION AND CULTIVATION	PROPAGATION

Sage
(Salvia officinalis)
Height: 45-60cm/18-24in
Spread: 45-60cm/18-24in

Evergreen, slightly tender sub-shrub with grey-green, wrinkled, aromatic, oval leaves and tubular, violet-blue flowers during early and mid-summer. The leaves are ideal for flavouring meats and stuffings. There are also forms with coloured or variegated leaves that are popular for borders.

Full sun, a sheltered position and light, fertile, well-drained but moisture-retentive soil. After about three years, pull up and replace old plants with new ones; old specimens often become leggy and woody.

Take 7.5cm/3in-long cuttings from the current season's growth in late summer and insert them in equal parts moist peat and sharp sand. Place in a cold frame. Pot them up into individual pots when rooted and replace in a cold frame during winter. Plant into a garden in spring.

Summer Savory
(Satureja hortensis)
Height: 30cm/12in
Spread: 23cm/9in

A hardy annual with a bushy habit; spicily flavoured, dark green leaves are borne on square-sectioned, hairy stems, which are also aromatic. The leaves are used to flavour meat, fish and soups, as well as egg and cheese dishes, drinks and stuffings. Small, lilac flowers appear from mid-summer to autumn.

Well-drained, fertile soil and a position in full sun or partial shade suit it. This is an annual and plants are discarded at the end of summer. There is also a Winter Savory, which has a perennial nature (see below).

Raise plants from seeds sown during mid-spring. Form drills 6mm/^{1}/4in deep and 23cm/9in apart and sow seeds evenly and thinly. Germination takes two to three weeks and when the seedlings are large enough to handle they should be thinned to 15-23cm/6-9in apart.
Fresh plants of Winter Savory are raised in the same way, but thin them 23-30cm/9-12in apart.

French Tarragon
(Artemisia dracunculus 'Sativa')
Height: 45-60cm/18-24in
Spread: 38-45cm/15-18in

This fairly hardy perennial herb is also known as True Tarragon to differentiate it from Russian Tarragon (*Artemisia dracunculus* 'Inodora') which is inferior in flavour to the French type. This has narrow, grey-green leaves, used in tarragon vinegar and in *sauce tartare* and French mustard.

Light, well-drained soil and a sheltered position in full sun or light shade suit it. The roots are vulnerable to severe frost and therefore must be covered in very cold areas. Although this is a perennial, plants should be replaced every three or four years.
To encourage the development of leaves, pinch out flowering stems as soon as they appear.

Raise new plants by lifting and dividing established plants in early or mid-spring. Replant only the young pieces from around the outside of the clump, spacing them 30-38cm/12-15in apart and setting them 5-7.5cm/2-3in deep.
New plants can also be grown from seeds, but plants raised in this way are said not to have such aromatic leaves.

Thyme – Common or Garden type
(Thymus vulgaris)
Height: 10-20cm/4-8in
Spread: 23-30cm/9-12in

Hardy, evergreen shrub with aromatic, long and narrow, dark green leaves. During early summer, small, mauve flowers appear in the leaf-joints. The spicy, sweet-flavoured leaves of this popular herb are used fresh or dried in stuffings for meats, in fish dishes and in casseroles, as well as in soups.

Full sun, a warm and sheltered position and light, well-drained soil. Unfortunately, plants often become straggly and need to be replaced after three or four years. Pick the leaves at any time, preferably when young and fresh.

Lift and divide congested or old plants in spring. Replant only younger parts from around the outside of the clump. Alternatively, take 5-7.5cm/2-3in-long cuttings from the current season's growth in early summer. Insert them in pots of equal parts moist peat and sharp sand, and place in a cold frame. Pot up when rooted.

Southernwood
(Artemisia abrotanum)
Height: 60-90cm/2-3ft
Spread: 60-90cm/2-3ft

Also known as Lad's Love and Old Man, this is a hardy deciduous or semi-evergreen shrub with downy, hoary green, finely divided leaves, which emit a strong scent when crushed.

Sweet Cicely
(Myrrhis odorata)
Height: 1-1.2m/3^1/2-4ft
Spread: 75-90cm/2^1/2-3ft

Hardy herbaceous perennial with bright green, fern-like leaves which have an anise flavour and are used fresh or dry in salads. Additionally, the thick taproot can be eaten raw or cooked.

Tansy
(Tanacetum vulgare)
Height: 90cm-1m/3-3^1/2ft
Spread: 45-60cm/18-24in

Hardy perennial with dark green leaves and yellow, button-like flowers from mid- to late summer. The leaves can be shredded and used in omelettes and cheese dishes. They have also been used traditionally in puddings and cakes.

Winter Savory
(Satureja montana)
Height: 30cm/12in
Spread: 23-30cm/9-12in

Hardy, almost evergreen perennial with woody, branching stems and small, grey-green leaves that are used to flavour food in winter, when those from Summer Savory (see above) are not available.
From mid-summer to autumn it bears small, rose-purple flowers.

FRUIT
GARDENING

Fruit trees are traditional features of old gardens, where often they grew too large, dominating the area and producing fruits which were difficult to reach and pick. Nowadays, dwarf rootstocks enable apple and pear trees to be grown in even the smallest garden.

Soft fruits such as strawberries, raspberries, gooseberries and blackcurrants are easily grown and have always been popular. Some, such as raspberries, blackberries and hybrid berries, need to have their canes supported by tiers of wires strained between posts. Most soft fruits, however, need only a warm position and soil that is moisture retentive but not waterlogged.

Soft fruits are best eaten soon after they are picked, but some apple varieties can be stored for several months.

Planting and growing apples

Apples are the most popular tree fruit in countries with temperate climates and they are mainly planted in bush forms. In earlier years, bush apples grew 6m/20ft high or more, making it difficult to prune and spray them, as well as to pick the fruits. Nowadays, a mature dwarf bush apple (on an M27 rootstock) will grow about 1.8m/6ft high and produce about 5.4-7.2kg/12-16lb of fruit each year. An ordinary bush has a much higher yield – 27-54kg/60-120lb of fruit every year – but in small gardens may be too large. There are other dwarfing rootstocks that produce trees slightly larger and heavier cropping than M27 – in the region of 18-27kg/40-60lb of fruit each year.

SOIL PREPARATION

Choose a frost-free site in full sun and sheltered from blustery, strong winds, especially in spring when pollinating insects are active. Apples flower in the early part of late spring and it is at this time that they are most susceptible to frost. In cold areas, plant varieties that flower late in the season. Sun is essential for dessert varieties to produce highly coloured fruits.

The soil should be well-drained, especially for dessert varieties; culinary types can be grown in heavier soil. Prepare the planting site in early autumn by digging and adding compost or manure. Where the soil is extremely light and sandy, add as much well-decayed organic matter as possible; mulching and regular watering will also be necessary.

PLANTING AND STAKING

Plant bare-rooted trees between late autumn and early spring; container-grown types can be planted at any time of year provided the soil is workable, which means that it is not frozen or waterlogged. Space ordinary bushes 4.5m/15ft apart and dwarf ones 1.8-2.7m/6-9ft apart.

When planting a bare-rooted tree, dig out a hole large enough to take the roots. Knock a stout stake about 45cm/18in into the hole, slightly off centre and towards the prevailing wind. This prevents the trunk being blown against the stake, causing chafing and damage. The top of the stake should be about 5cm/2in below the lowest branch.

STORING APPLES

1 Pick apples carefully to avoid bruising them. The best test to see if fruits are ready is to hold an apple in the palm of your hand and to gently raise and twist it; if the stalk easily parts from the tree, the fruit is ready.
2 Traditionally, fruits are placed slightly apart on slatted staging in a cool, airy, dark, vermin- and frost-proof shed. Regularly inspect stored fruits to ensure that they are not starting to decay.
3 If the air is dry, wrap each fruit individually in oiled paper and place folded side downwards.
4 Alternatively, place 1.8kg/4lb of apples of the same variety in a polythene bag punctured with holes. Fold over the bag's top and turn it upside down.

PICKING AND STORING APPLES

The exact time when apples are picked depends mainly on the variety. Some varieties, such as 'Early Victoria' and 'Vista Bella' can be picked in mid-summer, 'Beauty of Bath' and 'Epicure' in late summer, while 'Crispin' and 'Bramley's Seedling' are picked in mid-autumn. A few varieties of apples are ready to be eaten within a few weeks of being picked; others several months later and some can be kept into mid-spring of the following year.

Pick apples with care as they can easily be bruised, causing the onset of decay and reducing the time they can be stored. A test for ripeness for picking is to lift the fruit in the palm of your hand and gently turn it and if the stalk easily parts from the tree it is ready for picking. Another indication is when the first windfalls appear on the ground around the tree. Also, the fruits of some varieties will have started to change colour, particularly with dessert types. Not all fruits on a tree ripen at the same time and frequent inspection over a few weeks is necessary.

Store apples on wooden slats in an airy, dark, frost- and vermin-proof shed. Do not store chemicals or paraffin in the same place as this will taint the fruit. To save space, they can also be placed in shallow boxes which can be stacked. Also, polystyrene and purpose-made papier-mâché trays are available. If the humidity is low, wrap each fruit in oiled paper and place folded-side downwards to prevent them drying out. Inspect the fruits every week and remove any that are starting to decay.

Polythene bags with holes punctured in them can also be used to store apples. Place about 1.8kg/4lb of apples of the same variety in a plastic bag, handling them carefully; keep the bag closed by folding over the top and inverting the bag. Place in a cool, dark shed.

Below: Espalier-trained apples are ideal for growing alongside a path. This method of training a fruit tree ensures that the fruits have plenty of light and air.

Before planting the bush, soak the roots in a bucket of water for a few hours. Also, use a sharp knife or secateurs to cut off the long taproot, as well as broken roots.

Form and firm a slight mound in the hole's base and spread the roots over it. The main stem should be 5-7.5cm/2-3in away from the stake. Place a straight piece of wood across the hole to check that the union between the rootstock and the varietal part (scion) is at least 10cm/4in above the soil's surface. This prevents the varietal part developing roots. The tree should be planted slightly lower than before (indicated by a dark mark on the stem) to allow for slight settlement of the soil during the first few weeks after being planted. This prevents roots becoming exposed.

Spread out the roots and work good soil among them; lifting the stem several times moves the roots so that soil can get between them. Add soil and firm it, then add more and firm again. Do not attempt to fill the hole and firm the soil in one go.

Tie the stem to the stake; bushes need only one tie, positioned about 2.5cm/1in below the top of the stake. Re-check the tie regularly every few months after planting to ensure that it is secure but not choking the tree.

Finally, thoroughly water the soil and add a 7.5cm/3in thick mulch of well-rotted garden compost or manure. Leave a 5-7.5cm/2-3in space between the trunk and the mulch.

When planting a container-grown bush apple, dig out a hole about 15cm/6in wider and 7.5cm/3in deeper than the container. Water the compost in the container the day before planting the bush.

Spread and firm a 7.5cm/3in-thick layer of good soil mixed with moist peat in the hole's base. Carefully remove the container then place the bush in the hole. The top of the soil-ball should be slightly below the soil's surface. Ease out matted roots and work soil around the soil-ball. When planting is complete, water the soil thoroughly.

Rather than using a vertical stake which, if inserted after planting, would damage the roots, it is better to use an oblique or H-shaped stake. An oblique stake is knocked at an angle of 45° into the soil, so that the top of the stake (which should face into the prevailing wind) is just below the lowest branch. An H-shaped stake is best used on standards, where there is a long, bare stem. Two stout posts are knocked about 45cm/18in into soil, about 45cm/18in apart and on either side of the trunk. Then a 60cm/24in pole is tied to the two upright posts at about 5cm/2in below the lowest branch. The trunk can then be attached to the support using a tie. Check the tie regularly to ensure it is secure.

Planting and growing pears

Pears are nearly as popular as apples. However, because they flower slightly earlier a more sheltered position is essential to prevent frost damage to the blossoms. Although there are dwarfing rootstocks for pears, their influence is limited and most grow 3-5.4m/10-18ft high and when mature produce 9-18kg/20-40lb of fruit each year. Yields from an ordinary (non-dwarf) bush types could be double this amount. Pears can also be grown as fans, espaliers, cordons and standards.

The ideal site is one that is well-sheltered from cold winds, especially early in the year, not in a frost pocket, and with plenty of sunshine. The soil must be moisture retentive as pears are not so resilient to drought as apples, although they do grow better in heavier soils. They dislike both light, sandy soil and chalk. In coastal areas the foliage and fruits can be damaged by salt spray. The range of varieties is not as wide as with apples, and it is best to select dessert types.

PLANTING AN ESPALIER

Prepare the planting position in early autumn, adding copious amounts of well-decayed garden compost or manure. Plant bare-rooted trees between late autumn and early spring; container-grown types can be planted at any time when the soil is not frozen or waterlogged. In cold regions, an espalier pear is best grown against a sunny wall, while in warmer areas it can be free-standing, perhaps alongside a path or lawn.

An espalier is formed of a central stem from which arise horizontal tiers of stems 38-45cm/15-18in apart. These horizontal branches are supported by strong, galvanized wires strained between strong posts. The tiers or branches are built up systematically over several years, but before planting and forming an espalier it is essential to construct a supporting framework. If you are starting with a one-year-old bare-rooted tree, it can be pruned to ensure that the tiers of branches fit the positioning of the horizontal training wires. Sometimes, however, container-grown espaliers can be bought with two or three tiers already established. If planting a ready-formed espalier, ensure that the spacings of the wires suit the tiers. If these do not coincide, it is very difficult to secure individual branches.

Right: Training an espalier requires more time and skill that for a bush type. However, it is an ideal way of growing pears in small gardens, when they can be grown against a wall or fence.

PICKING AND STORING PEARS

1 Hold the fruit in the palm of your hand and at the same time gently lift and twist it. If the stalk parts easily from the tree, the fruit is ready to be picked.
2 Early varieties, if left too long on the tree, become soft and mealy. These fruits can be picked before they are completely ready by cutting the stalk with scissors or secateurs.
3 Place the fruits on slatted trays and regularly inspect them for the onset of decay. Remove decaying fruits at the earliest possible stage.
4 Some gardeners like to wrap the fruits individually, but although this helps in their storage, it prevents the onset of decay being readily noticed.

TRAINING AN ESPALIER

Plant a bare-rooted maiden pear tree between late autumn and early spring. Cut the stem back to a healthy bud, just above the bottom wire. There should be two other healthy buds just below it. Later, the top bud will extend growth upwards, while the other two are trained laterally in opposite directions to form the bottom tier of branches.

From early to late summer these buds grow and develop shoots; tie the central one to a cane firmly secured to the wires. Tie the two sideshoots to individual canes which are secured at 45° to the horizontal wires. During mid- or late autumn, cut off the leading shoots just above the next wire and, at the same time, lower the two side branches so that they are horizontal. Remove the canes and tie the branches to the wires. Shorten them by one-third, to a downward-pointing bud. Additionally, cut off any small laterals at the plant's base to three buds long.

During the following summer, train the central stem upwards and use canes at 45° to support the shoots that will form the second tier. Additionally, cut back shoots growing between the first and second tier to three leaves long, and prune sideshoots on the bottom tier to three of four leaves long. In the following mid- or late autumn, cut back the central stem to just above the next tier of wires. Also, lower the second tier to the horizontal, remove the canes and secure the stems to the wires. Tip back the ends of the shoots that form the lower tier and cut back the second tier by one-third.

Use the same system to create further tiers. When the top wire is reached, cut off the leading shoot and train stems to create the top tier. When each arm of the espalier reaches the end of the supporting wire, cut off the end. Also, in early summer cut back sideshoots to three leaves, and sub-laterals (growing off these) to leave one leaf.

Espalier-trained fruit trees are ideal for creating backgrounds for other plants, from flowers to vegetables, herbs and soft fruits. In small gardens, espaliers are invaluable when planted against a wall or fence. Alternatively, position them where they can create divisions within a garden, perhaps alongside a path that separates ornamental plants from fruit or vegetable gardens; allow 45-60cm/18-24in between the path's edge and the espalier.

PICKING AND STORING PEARS

Pears have a far more limited storage life than apples and the correct time for picking is more difficult to judge. Some varieties such as 'Beth' and 'Jargonelle' can be picked in late summer, and 'Louis Bonne de Jersey', 'Conference' and 'Onward', in early autumn. 'Doyenne du Comice', 'Joséphine de Malines' and 'Packham's Triumph' are picked in mid-autumn. However, unlike some apple varieties which keep well into spring, only a few, including 'Winter Nelis' and 'Packham's Triumph', keep until early winter.

Pick pears in the same way as recommended for apples; hold the fruit in the palm of your hand and gently lift and twist it. If the stalk parts easily from the tree, it is ready to be picked. As an indication of ripeness for picking, the ground colour on the skin changes from dark to light green. However, do not leave early varieties (those normally picked in late summer and early autumn) on trees until they are fully ripe as they then become soft and mealy, with brown centres. Instead, use scissors or secateurs to cut through the stalk.

Store pears in a cool (3-7°C/37-45°F), dark, dry, airy vermin-proof shed. The temperature can be a little higher and the atmosphere slightly drier than for apples. Place the fruits on slatted trays, leaving space between them. Regularly inspect the fruits to check if they are developing rot and remove any that are. Some gardeners like to wrap the fruits individually, but this prevents them being easily inspected for decay. The final stages of ripening can be hastened by taking the fruit into a warm room for a day or two.

Planting and growing peaches and nectarines

Peaches and nectarines are closely related succulent tree fruits. Indeed, the nectarine is a smooth-skinned sport (mutation) of the peach, which has a downy or furry skin and slightly smaller fruits.

Nectarines are not easy to grow outdoors in temperate climates and therefore are best grown in only the mildest areas – even then, they should be planted against a warm, sunny wall. Peaches tolerate moderately cold winters, but the summers must be warm to ripen the fruits. Therefore, for both these fruits, select the warmest position and one that is sheltered from cold wind, bathed in sun during summer and free from frost in spring. Growing peaches – and especially nectarines – as fans is a practical way to ensure good crops.

SOIL PREPARATION

Well-drained but moisture-retentive soil is essential. In early autumn, prepare the soil by digging about 45cm/18in deep over an area 1m/3ft square. If the soil is badly drained, dig slightly deeper and place brick rubble and chopped turves in the base of the hole. Sharp sand can be added to help to lighten heavy soil.

Plant bare-rooted plants in late autumn or early winter. Container-grown plants can be planted whenever the soil and weather allow, but are best when put in during autumn.

Dig a hole so that the main stem is 15-23cm/6-9in from the wall. Ensure that the hole is large enough to accommodate the roots when spread out. Position the trunk so that it is slightly deeper than before to allow for natural slight settlement of the soil after planting. Incline the trunk slightly towards the supporting wires (see below). Firm soil in layers over the roots.

SUPPORTING, TRAINING AND PRUNING

While the fan-tree is still young, erect a supporting framework of wires. Starting 30cm/12in above the ground, secure horizontal tiers of strong galvanized wire every 15cm/6in and held 5-10cm/2-4in out from the wall or fence. This allows for a flow of air around the branches and leaves.

Probably the best way of establishing a fan is to plant a feathered maiden (a central stem with

PICKING AND STORING PEACHES

1 Peaches are ready for harvesting when their stalks part easily from the plant. Test each fruit individually; hold it in the palm of your hand and lift and twist gently. If ripe, it will come away quite easily.
2 Another indication that the fruit is ripe and ready for picking is when the flesh around the stalk is soft and the skin has a reddish flush.
3 Store peaches for about a week in a cool place; line a box with tissue paper, but leave the fruits unwrapped.
4 Peaches can be frozen, but first remove the stones.

Below: As well as growing peaches as fans against a warm and sheltered wall, there are several dwarf varieties that are ideal for growing as bushes. Here is 'Garden Annie', a relatively new variety.

young shoots growing from it) and by regular pruning to control its development. It is also possible to buy a two- or three-year-old fan which is partly trained with eight or more established arms, although this is more expensive than starting with a maiden tree.

Never prune peaches and nectarines in early to mid-winter, during their dormant period, as diseases such as bacterial canker are more likely to enter cuts made then than those made when the sap is rising in spring and summer.

In late winter or early spring after planting a feathered maiden, cut back the main stem to about 60cm/24in above the ground and slightly above a strong lateral shoot. At the same time, cut back all lateral shoots to one bud from their base. By early summer a few shoots will have developed. Cut out all but the top one and two others lower down and, preferably, opposite each other. The two lower shoots will form the initial arms of the fan, while the upper one is left temporarily to encourage sap to rise. During the latter part of mid-summer cut it back to slightly above the two arms. Tie these two arms to individual canes, which are each tied at a 45° angle to the supporting wires, as for an espalier.

During late winter or early spring of the following year, as soon as growth begins, use sharp secateurs to cut back the two arms of the espalier to 30-45cm/12-18in from the main stem. Cut just beyond a growth bud (sometimes known as a wood bud and identified as being small and pointed) or to a triple bud, which is formed of two growth buds either side of a fruiting bud.

Young shoots will develop from the buds at the ends of the arms, as well as along them. Select four strong shoots – two on the lower side and two on the upper part – of each of the arms. Then, cut off all other sideshoots, but leaving one leaf at the base of each one. Tie each of these selected shoots to individual canes and secure them to the supporting wires. In early spring of the following year, cut back each of these arms by about a third, making the cuts slightly above a downward-pointing growth bud.

In the following summer, shoots develop on each of the arms; allow three to form on each arm and tie them first to canes, then to the wires. Also, rub out (using a thumb) buds growing towards the wall or fence. During late summer, when these shoots are 45cm/18in long, nip out each growing point.

In late spring and early summer – and at the same time every subsequent year – cut out shoots growing towards the wall or fence. Those with flower buds at their bases can be cut to leave two leaves. Young shoots that were produced during the previous year will bear fruits during the current season.

PICKING AND STORING PEACHES AND NECTARINES

The annual yields of fruits from a mature bush peach vary from 11-18kg/25-40lb (sometimes slightly more), while a fan yields about half of this amount, and a nectarine bears even lighter crops.

Both these fruits are ready for picking when the skin reveals a reddish flush and the flesh around the stalk is soft. Hold the fruit in the palm of a hand and gently lift and twist it. If the stalk parts easily from the tree, it is ready to be picked. Handle fruits with care as they easily become bruised. They are best eaten at once, but can be stored unwrapped in a cool place for about a week. Place them on tissue paper.

Planting and growing plums

Plums are popular and easily grown stone fruits. Gages are similar, but slightly less hardy and with smaller and sweeter fruits. Damsons are also close relatives; they are hardier and succeed where the weather is too cold for plums.

Plums and gages are some of the earliest fruit trees to flower and are therefore vulnerable to damage from spring frost and need a sheltered, frost-free site. Dessert plums, especially, need a warm, sunny position to gain a good flavour.

SOIL PREPARATION

Well-drained but moisture-retentive soil is essential. In early autumn, dig the soil deeply and add generous amounts of well-decayed garden compost or manure, especially if the soil is light.

Plant bare-rooted trees between late autumn and early spring, although early winter is considered best. Container-grown trees can be planted whenever the weather and soil are suitable.

TYPES OF PLANTS

Plums can be grown in a wide range of forms, including standards and half-standards, bushes, fans and pyramids. In a small garden, a fan grown against a wall or fence is one of the best choices, when 5.4-10.8kg/12-24lb can be expected from an established plant. Grown as a pyramid, an established plant yields 13-22kg/30-50lb a year. Standard trees are higher yielding (22-44kg/50-100lb), but are too large for small gardens.

LOOKING AFTER PLUMS

In spring, remove all weeds, sprinkle a general fertilizer over the soil and thoroughly water the area. Then form a 7.5cm/3in-thick mulch over the soil. It is essential – especially when the tree is young – that the soil does not become dry. Regularly water the area throughout summer, thoroughly soaking the soil at each application. When weeding, take care not to damage the roots as this encourages the development of suckers. If these do arise, carefully remove soil around them and pull them up, rather than severing with a spade or knife. Apart from the initial application of a general fertilizer, no other fertilizers are needed until the tree starts to bear fruits. In late winter dust the soil with sulphate of

Right: Plums and gages are not suitable for growing as cordons, but are ideal when trained as fans. Regular pruning is essential to ensure the fan shape is maintained.

PICKING AND STORING PLUMS

1 Plums are ready for picking when the fruit parts easily form the tree. The stalk is usually left on the tree. Take care not to squeeze and bruise the fruits.
2 Dessert plums will keep for a few weeks in a cool place if picked while unripe and with their stalks attached.
3 Store the fruits in slatted boxes lined with tissue paper. Inspect them daily to check they are not decaying.
4 Before freezing plums, remove the stones.

potash at 15g per sq m/¹/₂oz per sq yd, followed in spring by a similar application of sulphate of ammonia. Alternatively, apply a general fertilizer in spring at 70g per sq m/2oz per sq yd every two or three years.

If frost is forecast when wall-trained trees are in flower, drape fine-mesh plastic netting over them, suspending it just clear of the branches.

PRUNING

Like other stone fruits, plums, gages and damsons must not be pruned during early and mid-winter, when they are dormant. Cuts made at this time encourage diseases to enter. Instead, wait until the sap starts to rise in spring. Once established, they need little pruning, other than cutting out dead and crossing branches in spring.

Plums and gages are not suitable for growing as cordons and espaliers, but can be trained as fans. For this, they are pruned and trained in the same way as for fan-trained peaches (see pages 222-3). Once the fan is established and bearing fruits, all that is needed is in spring to rub out with the thumb any shoots growing towards the wall or fence and in mid-summer to pinch out the tips of young shoots that are not needed to form the framework.

Pyramid forms are popular for small gardens. They differ from bush shapes in having sideshoots arising over a much longer area of trunk, and are pruned as follows. In late winter or early spring after planting a feathered maiden, cut back the leading shoot to 1.5m/5ft above the ground. Then cut out close to the main stem all lateral shoots within 45cm/18in of the ground. Prune back each of the remaining shoots by half, cutting to a downward-pointing bud. This framework of branches will eventually form a pyramid.

During the latter part of mid-summer of the same year, shorten the current season's growth to 20cm/8in long, cutting to a downward-pointing bud. Additionally, cut back sideshoots to 15cm/6in long. Do not prune the leading shoot.

In early spring of the following year, prune the central shoot by about two-thirds of the growth it made during the previous year. This can be repeated during the following springs until the stem reaches the desired height. Thereafter, annually cut back the leading shoot to 2.5cm/1in.

Planting and growing blackcurrants

Blackcurrants are widely grown bush fruits that produce juicy, black fruits for picking during the latter part of mid-summer and sometimes into late summer. This is one of the easiest soft fruits to grow and once planted, apart from mulching and watering, the major task is pruning.

PLANTING BLACKCURRANT BUSHES

Plant bare-rooted bushes during their dormant period; preferably in early winter, but in cold and exposed areas late winter and early spring are better. However, plants established in containers can be planted at any time of year when the soil is not frozen or waterlogged. Position each plant about 5cm/2in deeper than before (the old soil-level mark can be seen on the stem); this allows for settlement of the soil after planting and encourages the development of new shoots from below ground-level.

With bare-rooted plants, firm soil around and over the roots; sharply lifting and lowering the plant in the planting hole a few times encourages fine soil to trickle between the roots. Firm the soil in layers, rather than in one go.

For a container-grown plant, ensure that the plant is at the right depth, that the hole is large enough and that matted roots around the outside of the soil-ball are teased out.

After planting, in both cases, cut back all stems to about 2.5cm/1in above soil-level. This drastic pruning encourages the development of fresh, young shoots from the plant's base. If this initial pruning is neglected, the quality and quantity of fruit will be radically diminished.

FEEDING AND MULCHING

Blackcurrant bushes are gross feeders and need regular feeding and watering throughout summer. In early spring, shallowly hoe around bushes to remove weeds and to scarify the surface. Sprinkle a general fertilizer around the bushes and thoroughly water the soil. Then form a 7.5cm/3in-thick mulch of well-decayed manure or garden compost around bushes. Keep the soil moist and when the fruits start to swell apply a potash-rich liquid fertilizer. Throughout summer, shallowly hoe around bushes, taking take not to damage roots, or pull up weeds by hand.

PLANTING A CONTAINER-GROWN BLACKCURRANT

1 Before planting a container-grown blackcurrant, thoroughly water the compost several times.

2 Dig a hole large enough to accommodate the root-ball and use a straight-edged stick to check that the top of the compost is slightly lower than the surrounding soil. This allows for subsequent soil settlement.

3 Draw soil around the root-ball.

4 Firm the soil in layers. Then level the surface to remove all depressions.

Above: The nature of a blackcurrant is to form a bushy plant with several stems arising from the surface of the soil. The whole purpose of pruning is to encourage the annual production of fresh, young shoots.

ANNUAL PRUNING

By late summer or early autumn – after planting during the previous winter or early spring – bushes will have developed young shoots. At this stage, no radical pruning is needed other than cutting back thin and spindly shoots to their base. The shoots that remain will bear fruits during the following season.

During the following year, the yearly cycle of pruning begins. Many experts recommend pruning as soon as the fruits have been picked, but at that stage it is usually difficult to differentiate between the old and new shoots. It is better to wait until late autumn or early winter or, in very cold areas, until early spring.

REJUVENATING AN OLD BLACKCURRANT BUSH

If neglected, blackcurrant bushes become increasingly congested and eventually cease to produce any worthwhile fruits. Bushes that are totally congested with old, black stems are best dug up and burned. Those that have been neglected for a few years can be rejuvenated by radical pruning.

- Cut back ALL stems to their bases in late summer or early autumn. This encourages the development of young shoots from ground-level during the following season. However, pruning in this way means that fruit will not be produced for one season.

- To encourage the development of young shoots, feed, water and mulch.

- During the following autumn or early winter, cut out about a third of those shoots which produced fruits. Thereafter, resume the normal sequence of pruning.

Pruning is necessary because blackcurrants produce their best fruit on shoots that developed during the previous year, although some fruits are borne on slightly older wood. The purpose of pruning, therefore, is to cut out most of the older wood that has borne fruit and to encourage the development of young shoots. Pruning in this way also helps to prevent the bush becoming congested, which leads to the onset of diseases.

Cut out about a third of the old wood to its base. Also, cut out weak and spindly shoots; this allows more air to penetrate into the bush. From about the fourth year after planting, cut out more of the old wood each year. Ensure that no wood is left which is more that four years old.

HARVESTING THE FRUITS

Not all the fruit on a bush of a particular variety ripens at the same time, so check regularly to make sure that fruits do not pass the optimum stage for picking. The fruit is ready for picking about a week after turning blue-black. Do not wait until the berries shrivel. The fruits at the top of each strig (bunch) ripen first and can be picked individually. However, for show purposes the whole strig is cut off, using scissors. The individual berries are said to keep better when picked complete on a strig. After picking, place the fruits in a cool, airy place. They can be stored in a refrigerator for about a week.

Planting and growing red and white currants

Red and white currants are closely related and both need the same treatment and cultivation. Unlike blackcurrants, which develop a large number of stems from ground level, red and white currants are grown on bushes which have a 'leg'. This is a woody stem 15-20cm/6-8in long which connects the roots with the branches. When grown as bushes, red and white currants have a life-span of about twelve years and produce 3.6-4.5kg/8-10lb of fruit each year.

Red and white currants produce their fruits on short spurs which develop on the old wood, as well as in clusters at the base of young growths formed during the previous year.

PLANTING RED AND WHITE CURRANTS

Plant bare-rooted bushes during their dormant period, from late autumn to late winter. Container-grown plants can be planted at any time when the soil is not waterlogged or frozen. Position the plant only fractionally lower than before; this allows for the natural settlement of soil after planting but retains the bush on a leg. Most red and white currants are planted as two-year-old bushes. During late winter of the first few years after being planted, check that the soil has not been loosened by the action of frost. If it has, firmly tread around the bush and over the root area.

FORMATIVE PRUNING

Immediately after planting, completely cut out thin and spindly shoots. Also cut out shoots that cross the bush's centre, then prune each branch back by half to an outward-pointing bud. This helps the bush to develop a strong framework.

During the plant's next dormant period, again cut all leading shoots back to half of the growth they made during the previous season. Always cut the shoots to just above an outward-pointing bud, and cut lateral shoots back to about two buds from their base.

FEEDING AND MULCHING

In spring of each year, use a hoe to remove surface weeds and lightly scarify the surface. Sprinkle a general-purpose fertilizer around the bush, then water the soil thoroughly and form a

PICKING AND STORING RED CURRANTS

1 When fully coloured, pick red currants in clusters, complete with their strigs (small stems).
2 Carefully remove the individual fruits from the strigs, taking care not to squash them. Although time consuming, this task is essential when fruits are to be eaten within a week.
3 For short-term storage (up to about a week) put the fruits in plastic containers and place in a refrigerator.
4 If fruits are to be frozen, leave them on their strigs and form a thin layer in a shallow, plastic container. These fruits, when de-frozen, are not suitable for used as a dessert, but are ideal for flavouring puddings.

GROWING RED AND WHITE CURRANTS AS CORDONS

Planting red and white currants as cordons is not just an attractive and unusual method of growing them; it is an ideal way to fit them into a small garden, and an established single cordon produces about 0.9-1.4kg/2-3lb of fruit every season. Pruning these cordons is slightly more complicated than pruning a bush.

During their dormant period, from late autumn to late spring, plant a row of one-year-old plants, spacing them about 38cm/15in apart. At this stage, each plant will have an upright stem with about four sideshoots growing from it. Immediately after planting, shorten the central stem by between one-third and half of its length; cut it slightly above a bud facing outwards from the row. Additionally, cut back the lateral shoots to one bud from their base, but cut out completely any that are within 10cm/4in of the ground. Stake the plants, but avoid damaging the roots.

During the early part of mid-summer of the following year, prune back the current season's sideshoots to four or five leaves from their base. At this stage, do not prune the leading shoot. However, ensure that the new growth is tied to the stake.

During the second year, prune cordons in winter, cutting back the leading shoot to slightly above a healthy bud and removing all but 15cm/6in of the new growth. In later years, cut back the leading shoot in winter to leave only one bud of new growth, and cut back all lateral shoots that were pruned during the previous year to leave 2.5cm/1in of new growth.

In the following summer – and every subsequent year – cut back sideshoots to leave four or five leaves of growth produced earlier during the same season. Do not prune the leading shoot (it will be cut back during the following winter).

dampening the surface does more harm than good, so be sure to water thoroughly.

ANNUAL PRUNING

From the fourth year onwards it is only necessary each year to cut back the new growth on leading shoots by 2.5cm/1in. Continue to prune lateral shoots to form new fruiting spurs. Also cut out thin and spindly shoots, as well as those that cross the plant's centre. Do this pruning during the plant's dormant season.

Additionally, during each summer – some time around the end of early summer – cut back new lateral shoots to about five leaves from their bases, but do not prune the leading shoots.

HARVESTING THE FRUITS

Fruits are mainly ready for picking during mid-summer, when well coloured and shiny. Pick entire clusters (strigs) to avoid damaging individual berries, and go over the bush several times, selecting those that are ready. The fruits are best eaten soon after picking, but they can be stored in a refrigerator for about a week.

Below: In addition to being grown as bushes and as cordons, red currants can be trained as fans. They create an unusual feature, with plenty of light and air reaching the fruits.

7.5cm/3in-thick mulch of well-decayed manure or garden compost over the soil but not in contact with the leg. This helps to prevent the growth of weeds. It also add nutrients to the soil and reduces the loss of water.

During dry periods, and especially when the fruits are swelling, generously water the soil. Just

Planting and growing strawberries

Strawberries are the most popular of all soft fruits. There are several forms (see pages 238-9) and the one described here is the ordinary, summer-fruiting type. Once planted, strawberry plants are usually left in position for three or four years, so prepare the site well. However, some gardeners grow strawberries as an annual crop; this produces high-quality fruits but not such a large yield as established plants, two- or three-years old. An established plant will produce 225-275g/8-10oz of fruit each year.

SOIL PREPARATION

Choose a sunny, frost-free position with well-drained soil and, preferably, a slight southerly slope. In late spring or early summer, dig the soil and add well-decayed garden compost or manure. Ensure that all perennial weeds are removed. Slightly acid soil is desirable, about pH 6.0-6.5; test the soil (see pages 38-9) and, if necessary, add lime or chalk to reduce acidity – but not at the same time as digging in manure. Just before planting (see below), rake in a general fertilizer at about 70g per sq m/2oz per sq yd. On heavy land, planting strawberry plants on ridges about 7.5cm/3in high and 38cm/15in wide helps to improve drainage around roots, as well as encouraging the soil to warm up.

PLANTING STRAWBERRIES

Plant bare-rooted strawberry plants during mid- and late summer or, at the latest, in early autumn. However, early planting encourages a better crop during the following year. It is also possible to plant bare-rooted plants in early and mid-spring, but this does not allow plants to produce a large crop during the first year. Container-grown plants can be planted at any time when the soil is not frozen or waterlogged.

Thoroughly water the soil the day before setting the plants in position. The technique of planting bare-rooted plants is to use a trowel to form a hole wide and deep enough to accommodate the roots. Then, form and firm a small mound in the hole and spread the roots over it. Ensure that the plant's crown is level with the surface – it decays if buried. Firm soil around and over the roots, then thoroughly water the soil.

PLANTING STRAWBERRIES

1 Bare-rooted strawberry plants can be planted at several times throughout the year (see above). Use a trowel to make a hole wide and deep enough for the roots, then form and firm a mound in the centre. Place the plant on top; the crown should be level with the soil's surface. Firm soil over and around the roots.
2 When planting container-grown plants, water the compost the day before planting. Make a hole and fill its base with moist peat. Place the soil-ball on top; its surface should be slightly below soil-level, but the crown should not be buried.
3 Firm soil around the roots; do not damage the crown.
4 Gently but thoroughly water the plant.

Above: After the fruits have been picked, strawberry plants grow strong and produce masses of runners. The plant above is growing on black plastic laid on a slight mound.

When planting container-grown plants, water the compost in the container the day before. Use a trowel to take out a hole about 7.5cm/3in wider and about 5cm/2in deeper than the soil-ball. Form and firm a 5cm/2in-thick layer of moist peat in the hole's base. Remove the container and position the soil-ball in the hole; the top of the soil-ball should be slightly lower than the surrounding soil, but not so much that the crown is buried. Firm soil around the soil-ball and then thoroughly water the soil.

Space plants 45cm/18in apart in rows 75-90cm/2½-3ft apart. Position the rows so that they run up and down a slope, and not across it. Where strawberries are grown as an annual crop, space the plants 30cm/12in apart and in rows 60-75cm/24-30in apart.

SEASONAL CARE

Keep newly planted strawberries well watered to ensure rapid establishment. Continue to water them throughout summer, but take care not to splash the berries. Always water plants in the morning, so that moisture on leaves has dried by evening. This helps to prevent the spread of fungus diseases.

Pull up all weeds; shallow hoeing is possible, but take care not to damage roots or the plant's crown. During mid-spring, sprinkle a general fertilizer at 70g per sq m/2oz per sq yd. Water the soil regularly, and add a mulch of straw when the fruits are starting to swell. Tuck it up under the plants to keep the soil moist, prevent the growth of weeds, and keep the fruit clean by stopping heavy drops of rain falling on bare soil and then splashing fruits with soil.

Slugs can be a problem; scatter pellets along the rows. Birds are also troublesome and the best way to prevent them reaching the fruits is to cover the rows with cloches. Alternatively, make a cage of plastic netting.

HARVESTING

Strawberries are ready to pick during early and mid-summer. Inspect the plants daily and pick the fruits which have reddened all over. Pick them in the morning once the fruits are dry; they should be picked complete with their stalks. Place them in a punnet and take care not to bruise them. The fruits are best eaten as soon as possible; they are not suitable for freezing, unless small, unripe fruits are selected.

END OF SEASON CLEAN-UP

As soon as all the fruits have been picked, cut off old leaves. At the same time, cut off excess runners; tuck those that are left under plants. During the following seasons, runners can be left to form a blanket between plants within a row. However, it is still necessary to leave space between the rows by removing the runners. As soon as possible after the fruits are picked, remove all the straw that formed the mulch and burn it. If left, it encourages the presence of pests and diseases.

GROWING STRAWBERRIES ON PLASTIC SHEETING

Instead of using straw to mulch strawberry plants and to keep the fruits clean, you can grow plants through black polythene. This also produces an earlier crop of fruits.

Prepare the soil and form it into a ridge about 7.5cm/3in high and 45cm/18in wide. Water the soil and roll a 75cm/30in-wide strip of 10-gauge black polythene along the ridge. Form 15cm/6in-deep slits in the soil at the side of the ridge and push in the edge of the polythene. This secures it and prevents wind ripping it up. If you are forming several rows of polythene, leave 15cm/6in gaps between the strips to enable rain to moisten the soil.

Make slits in the polythene, 45cm/18in apart and at the top of the ridge. Into these, put strawberry plants. Firm soil around the roots.

Planting and growing raspberries

Raspberries are the second most popular soft fruit after strawberries. Summer-fruiting ones are the most popular and established plants yield 680-900g/1½-2lb of fruit for each 30cm/12in of row. Autumn-fruiting varieties yield much less, and about 225g/8oz for every 30cm/12in of row can be expected. Planting and growing summer-fruiting strawberries is described here; autumn types are featured on the opposite page.

SOIL PREPARATION

A position in full sun and sheltered from cold wind is essential, as is a moisture-retentive but well-drained soil. Slight shade is acceptable for part of the day, but do not position raspberries under trees or in frost pockets. When planting on a slope, orient the rows down, not across it so as not to trap frost.

In early autumn, dig out a trench 25-30cm/10-12in deep and 90cm/3ft wide. Fork over the base and mix in plenty of well-decayed garden compost or manure. When the soil is returned to the trench it will bulk up, but later it settles. Ensure that perennial weeds are removed.

PLANTING CANES

Plant bare-rooted canes during late autumn and early winter, or in early spring. Container-grown plants can be planted at any time when the soil is not frozen or waterlogged. When planting in late autumn, ensure that the soil was dug at least five weeks earlier so that the soil has sufficient time to settle prior to planting.

Use a spade to form a trench 7.5-10cm/3-4in deep and 30-38cm/12-15in wide in the prepared soil. If only a few weeks have elapsed since the soil was prepared, systematically tread over it before making the planting trench. Spread out the roots of each cane, spacing them 45cm/18in apart. Position the old soil mark on the stem fractionally lower than before; this allows for natural settlement of the soil after planting. Firm soil in layers over the roots; do not just fill the trench with soil and then firm it. If more than one row is being planted, space rows 1.8m/6ft apart.

After planting, cut down all canes to 23-30cm/9-12in above the soil; cut slightly above a healthy bud. Water the soil thoroughly, so that it settles around the roots.

SUMMER-FRUITING RASPBERRIES

1 The usual way to support raspberries is to train them against a series of wires strained between two posts. The young canes that develop one year produce fruits during the following season.
2 Other ways to support the canes involve training one season's canes to one side of a row, and the young ones the following year to the other side.
3 When the fruits are fully coloured but still firm, pull them off; leave the plug attached to the cane.
4 To freeze the fruits, choose those that are firm and space them in a shallow plastic container. Once frozen, the fruits can be transferred to polythene bags.

SUPPORTING THE CANES

Erect supports for the canes while they are still small. There are several ways to provide support, but the most common is to drive (or concrete) a stout, 10cm/4in-square post into the soil at either end of the row. About 1.8m/6ft of post should protrude above the soil. Then strain tiers of strong galvanized wire between the posts, at 75cm/30in, 1m/3½ft and 1.6m/5½ft above the soil. Do not make the row more than 3.6m/12ft

long, as strong winds blowing against the canes may cause the supporting posts to collapse.

TRAINING AND PRUNING

During the first spring after the young canes are planted, shoots will develop from ground level and these will bear fruits during the following year. As soon as these shoots appear, cut down to just above ground level the old stem of each plant (which was earlier cut to 23-30cm/9-12in high at planting time). During summer, space out new shoots and tie them to the supporting canes. Do not allow more than eight canes to develop on each plant, although in the first year it is unlikely that this number will develop. In late winter, cut off the tips off the canes, about 15cm/6in above the top wire. Sever them just above a healthy bud.

During the following summer, fresh canes will develop from the plant's base and these will produce fruits the following year. This cycle of one-year-old canes fruiting and young ones developing repeats every year. As soon as the fruits have been picked, during mid- and into the early part of late summer, cut out at their base all canes which produced fruits. This will leave the young canes, which can be spaced out and tied to the supporting framework. Later, in winter, their tops will be cut off, about 15cm/6in above the top wire.

FEEDING AND MULCHING

In spring, pull up all weeds and lightly scarify the soil's surface. Avoid damaging roots, which will be near the surface. Sprinkle a general fertilizer on the soil at about 70g per sq m/2oz per sq yd. Thoroughly water the soil and then form a 7.5cm/3in-thick mulch of well-decayed garden compost or manure along the row. It is essential that the soil is sufficiently fertile to encourage the growth of stems each year.

HARVESTING THE FRUIT

Fruits are ready for picking during mid- and into late summer. The berries should be fully coloured yet still firm. Pick them, leaving the stalk and plug attached to the plant. Inspect the plants daily and pick fruits as soon as they are ready. If left – and especially if it rains – they soon decay. Fruits are best when eaten fresh, but they can be frozen fairly successfully.

AUTUMN-FRUITING RASPBERRIES

These are less popular than the summer-fruiting type, but they provide fresh fruits from late summer to mid-autumn, depending on the variety. Autumn-fruiting raspberries bear fruits on the tips of canes produced earlier during the same season, and for this reason the pruning is simpler than for the summer type.

In late winter of each year, cut all the canes to ground level. In spring, fresh shoots develop from the plant's base and as these grow they should be trained and tied to the supporting tiers of wires. Cut out canes which are growing away from the rows, as they are difficult to train. Feed and mulch the plants in the same way as recommended for the summer-fruiting types.

The fruits are less easy to pick than summer types, as they do not readily part from the plug. However, because they appear late in the season, they are not often attacked by birds.

Planting and growing gooseberries

The style in which gooseberries are grown very much resembles that of red and white currants, where each bush is grown on a 'leg' – a stem about 15cm/6in long. Gooseberries develop a permanent framework of branches and can be grown as bushes and as single, double or triple cordons.

Gooseberries are prickly plants and this sometimes puts gardeners off growing them, but if gloves are worn while pruning them there is little risk of hands being scratched. This is a long-lived fruit and if regularly pruned, bushes remain productive for twenty or more years. A mature bush produces 2.3-3.6kg/5-8lb of fruit each year – sometimes slightly more.

PLANTING AND INITIALLY PRUNING BUSHES

Choose a warm, sunny, wind-sheltered position and well-drained fertile soil. Slight shade is permissible, but avoid positions under trees. Also, avoid low-lying areas into which frost drains, as this could damage the early spring flowers. Dig the soil in early autumn and add plenty of well-decayed garden compost or manure.

Plant bare-rooted bushes in late autumn or early winter, or during late winter and early spring. Container-grown plants can be planted at any time when the soil is not frozen or water-logged. Plant bushes 1.5m/5ft apart. Plant one-year-old (maiden) gooseberry bushes. Two-year-old bushes are also available, but it is easier to establish young ones.

Before planting a bush, use sharp secateurs to cut back branches between the old soil-level mark on the stem (indicated by a black mark) and 15cm/6in above it. This will leave a clear stem. Also, pull off sucker-like shoots close to their point of origin.

Dig out a hole large enough to accommodate the roots. Form and firm a slight mound in the hole's base, then spread out the roots on it. The old soil mark on the stem should be fractionally below the soil's surface; this allows for natural slight settlement of the soil after planting. Firm soil in layers over and around the roots. Do not simply fill the hole and then firm it.

Immediately after planting, prune back each main branch by a half, cutting to an upward-

Right: In addition to growing gooseberries as bushes and cordons, plants can also be trained as standards. Use strong stakes to support the stem and the head.

LOOKING AFTER GOOSEBERRY BUSHES

1 In spring, remove weeds growing around bushes. If left, they choke plants, encourage the presence of pests and diseases, and rob plants of food.
2 Water the soil and form a mulch on soil surrounding the plant.
3 During summer, keep plants well watered to encourage the development of large berries. This is especially important when the berries are beginning to swell.
4 In addition to pruning in winter, in the latter part of early summer, cut back all lateral shoots that were produced during the current season to five leaves long.

pointing bud. Sometimes this has already been done by the nursery, as it makes packaging and transporting the plant easier.

FEEDING AND MULCHING

In spring, shallowly hoe around bushes to remove weeds and to scarify the surface soil. Then sprinkle general fertilizer at 70g per sq m/ 2oz per sq yd around each bush; water this well into the soil and then apply a 7.5cm/3in-thick mulch of well-decayed garden compost or manure. This prevents the growth of weeds, keeps the soil moist and helps to feed the bush.

ANNUAL PRUNING

By late autumn or early winter after planting, strong shoots will have grown from the branches which were cut back by half at planting time. Now, shorten the new growth back by a half, cutting to outward-facing buds for upright varieties, or inward-facing buds for spreading and drooping types. Sideshoots should be cut back by a half. Cut out any shoots which are growing from the leg.

By the following autumn, the bush will be well formed. Shorten all leading shoots by a half, cutting to a bud facing in the direction in which the shoot is to grow. Also cut out congested shoots in the bush's centre, and remove diseased and damaged shoots. To create fruiting spurs, cut back lateral shoots to 5cm/2in long.

On established bushes, both winter and summer pruning are needed. In the latter part of early summer (slightly later in cooler areas) prune all lateral shoots that were produced during the current season to five leaves long. Do not prune leading shoots at this stage. During the following winter, prune back leader shoots by a half and all laterals (those which were pruned during summer) to about two buds from their base.

HARVESTING THE FRUITS

Towards the end of early summer, start picking the berries before they are fully ripe. Remove every other berry, so that the remaining ones have more space in which to develop. These early pickings can be cooked and used in pies and tarts. The other fruits will continue to develop and should be picked when fully coloured and slightly soft when squeezed. Pick over the bush several times.

GROWING CORDON GOOSEBERRIES

When planting cordon gooseberries, use one-year-old plants and space them 45cm/18in apart. Double and triple cordons are sometimes grown, but here we describe the pruning of the single type.

Plant them during their dormant period, from late autumn to early spring, but not when the weather is extremely cold. Immediately after planting, prune back the central, leading shoot by one-half. At the same time, completely cut out all shoots that are growing from the main stem and are within 15cm/6in of the ground. Cut all the others to about 2.5cm/1in long and just beyond a bud.

During the latter part of early summer (slightly later in cold areas), cut back to four or five leaves long all sideshoots produced earlier in the season. At this stage, do not prune the central, leading shoot. However, tie it to a cane inserted into the soil.

During the following winter, cut back the leading shoots to leave about 15cm/6in of new growth. At the same time, cut back all sideshoots to leave 2.5cm/1in of new growth. Cut to just beyond a bud. In subsequent years, and as the cordon increases in height, cut the leading shoot to leave 2.5cm/1in of new growth. Summer pruning is also necessary during all subsequent years; cut back sideshoots to leave four or five leaves. Leave pruning the leading shoot until winter.

Summer fruits

FRUIT	SITUATION AND PLANTING	CULTIVATION

Apples

Apples are perhaps the most reliable and widely grown tree fruit in temperate regions. Depending on the variety, they provide fruits that can be eaten from late summer of one year to late spring or early summer of the following one.

Varieties: There is a wide choice, and many apples that have a superb flavour are not grown commercially; these are well worth growing in home gardens.

A warm, sun-facing, gentle slope, where there is little chance of early blossom being damaged by spring frost, is best. Avoid a cold slope, and the lower parts of slopes, into which frost drains, damaging the blossom. In cold areas choose late-flowering varieties. Well-drained but moisture-retentive, slightly acid soil is preferred.

Plant bare-rooted trees or bushes in early spring, or in winter if there is little risk of frost.

To ensure that soil does not dry out, especially in spring, thoroughly soak the ground and then apply a mulch.

Trees and bushes, as well as pyramids and cordons, need to be pruned annually during their dormant season. The technique is influenced by the variety, rootstock and age. However, the objective is to build up and to shape a tree, to encourage the formation of fruit buds and to control their number and position.

Blackberries

The garden blackberry of today is a marked improvement on the Bramble in hedgerows. The range of blackberry varieties is wide, producing fruits between mid-summer and early autumn.

Varieties include: 'Ashton Cross' (heavy cropping); 'Black Satin' (thornless); 'Fantasia' (large fruits, vigorous); 'Merton Thornless' (good flavour, thornless); 'Oregon Thornless' (thornless, vigorous).

Fertile, well-drained but moisture-retentive soil in full sun or partial shade suits it. It is, however, quite tolerant of most soils and, as it does not flower until early summer, can be grown in cold areas.

Plant bare-rooted canes in late autumn or early winter or, alternatively, in early spring. Container-grown plants can be planted whenever the soil and weather allow. Space plants 2.4-3m/8-10ft apart, depending on the variety's vigour.

Feed, water and mulch plants in spring, forming a 7.5cm/3in-thick layer.

Plants need to be trained against tiers of wires, 30cm/12in apart and between 90cm/3ft and 2.1m/7ft high. Blackberries bear fruit on canes (shoots) produced during the previous year. Therefore, cut down canes each year to just above soil-level after their fruit has been picked. This leaves young canes that will bear fruits during the following season.

Blackcurrants

Blackcurrants are easily grown on bush-like plants which have many shoots growing directly from soil-level. Fruits are ready for picking mainly in mid-summer, although some varieties continue into late summer.

Varieties include: 'Baldwin' (latter part of mid-summer); 'Ben Lomond' (latter part of mid-summer); 'Ben Sarek' (small bush, mid-summer); 'Tsema' (early part of mid-summer).

Moisture-retentive, fertile soil and a position in full light or partial shade, with shelter from cold wind, suits them.

Plant bare-rooted, two-year-old plants, certified free from reversion or big bud mite, in early winter, or in late winter and early spring. The old soil mark on the stem must be 5cm/2in below the surface. Cut all stems to an outward-pointing bud, 2.5-5cm/1-2in above the surface. Plant container-grown plants whenever soil and weather allow.

In spring, refirm soil around roots and cover bushes with sacking or netting when frost is forecast. Remove during the day. Feed plants in spring, water the soil and add a mulch. Between late autumn and early spring (but preferably as soon as fruiting finishes), cut out dead, weak and diseased shoots. Then completely cut out from half to all the shoots that produced fruits; this makes room for the development of new shoots, which bear the best fruits.

Cherries – Sweet

This is the well-known dessert cherry, which yields soft, juicy fruits from the latter part of early to late summer, depending on the variety.

Varieties include: 'Compact Stella' (compact tree, dark red, latter part of mid-summer); 'Early Rivers' (large tree, nearly black, early summer); 'Stella' (self-fertile, dark red, mid-summer); 'Sunburst' (black, mid-summer).

At one time, cherry trees grew too large and were not suitable for small gardens. Today, small varieties such as 'Compact Stella' have changed this. Dwarfing rootstocks have also made cherry trees more practical for small gardens. Moisture-retentive but free-draining, deeply prepared soil and a sheltered position in full sun suits them. Preferably plant in late autumn or early winter.

Protect the blossom from frost damage by draping hessian over the branches, but avoid damaging the blossom. Birds damage buds; the only way to prevent this is to grow cherries within a wire cage. Keep the soil moist – but not waterlogged – during dry summers. However, irregular application of water causes fruits to split. Do not prune cherries in winter when they are dormant; wait until the sap starts to rise. On established trees, cut out dead, diseased and congested branches.

Apricots

This stone fruit is not fully hardy outdoors in temperate regions and is sometimes grown in greenhouses. However, outdoor cultivation is possible if a warm position against a wall is available. Well-drained, moisture-retentive, but not excessively fertile, soil is needed.

Varieties include: 'Farmingdale' (good outdoors); 'Moorpark' (reliable).

Blueberries – Highbush

This acid-loving, hardy, deciduous shrub grows about 1.5m/5ft high and produces round, blue-black berries with a waxy white bloom that are ready for picking in late summer or early autumn.

Varieties include: 'Bluecrop' (widely grown); 'Earliblue' (early fruiting); 'Herbert' (noted for its flavour); 'Jersey' (attractive berries).

Cherries – Acid

Also known as sour or culinary cherries and widely used for cooking, making into jam, bottling and making wine. They are ready for picking during late summer.

Varieties include: 'Morello' (near black, self-fertile); 'Nabella' (near black, relatively new variety, self-fertile).

Cranberries

Only attempt to grow this fruit where the soil is exceptionally acid, about pH 4.5. The globular or pear-shaped, red berries are borne in late summer and early autumn on wiry stemmed, prostrate, evergreen bushes (*Vaccinium oxycoccos*). The fruits are used for making cranberry sauce.

FRUIT	SITUATION AND PLANTING	CULTIVATION

Figs

This is an easily grown fruit but it does require a warm, sunny position, especially when planted in a temperate climate. Figs do not need a pollination partner.

Varieties include: 'Brown Turkey' (purple fig, harvesting late summer to early autumn); 'White Marseilles' (green fig, harvesting late summer to early autumn).

Roots must be constricted in a pit 60cm/24in square and deep; this prevents excessive growth and encourages fruiting. Dig a pit, fill the base with 25cm/10in of clean rubble, then top up with soil, coarse stones and a dusting of bonemeal.

The best time for planting is in early spring. In warm areas, planting can be slightly earlier. Figs are usually grown as fans and trained against a wall.

Water plants regularly and thoroughly throughout summer, especially when fruits are swelling. The fruits attract birds and in some areas it is necessary to protect ripening fruits with nets. Prune established trees in early summer by pinching back young shoots to leave only five leaves. In spring, cut out branches damaged by severe frost, and protect young shoots in winter by covering with straw.

Gooseberries

These luscious berries gain their name from their use a sauce to accompany goose. It forms a bush with a permanent framework supported by a single, leg-like stem.

Varieties include: 'Careless' (culinary, large berries); 'Golden Drop' (dessert, small berries): 'Leveller' (culinary/dessert, large berries); 'Whinham's Industry' (culinary/ dessert, medium-large berries).

Well-drained but moisture-retentive soil and a sheltered position in full sun or light shade suit it. Plant bare-rooted bushes during their dormant season, preferably in late autumn or early winter. Container-grown plants can be planted at any time when the soil is not frozen or waterlogged.

In spring, apply a general fertilizer, water the soil thoroughly and apply a 7.5cm/3in-thick mulch. If crops are heavy, gradually thin out berries during late spring and early summer until they are 36-50mm/1½-2in apart. Prune established bushes between early winter and early spring: cut back the new growth at the ends of leading shoots by half. Cut back sideshoots to 5cm/2in long. In early summer, cut back sideshoots produced earlier in the year to four or five leaves.

Grapes – Outdoor

In temperate climates, outdoor grapes are only really successful in warm, sunny and wind-sheltered areas. Warm countries, with good light and long periods of sunshine, assure success. White varieties usually produce a better crop than black ones when planted outdoors.

Varieties include: 'Madeleine Angevine' (dessert/winemaking, white); 'Madeleine Sylvaner' (dessert/ winemaking, white,

Good drainage and a warm, sheltered position against a wall are essential. Avoid excessively fertile soils, but ensure well-decayed garden compost or manure has been added to sandy soils to assist in moisture retention.

Plant new canes (rooted plants) in autumn or from late winter to early spring. Protect early planted canes by covering them with straw.

Support plants by erecting tiers of wires 30cm/12in apart, from 45cm/18in high and 23cm/9in from a wall.

Apply a light dressing of fertilizer around the plant's base in spring, then water thoroughly and form a 7.5cm/3in-thick mulch.

Pruning begins when a cane is planted: cut back to 60cm/24in high and cut sideshoots to one bud. During the first summer, cut off tips of shoots just beyond the fifth leaf. In autumn, cut back the central shoot by half, and lateral shoots to two buds.

Kiwi Fruits

These are the large, rough-skinned fruits of *Actinidia chinensis*, also known as Chinese Gooseberries. Male and female flowers are borne on separate plants; therefore, plant one of each close together. Fruits are ready in early autumn. Temperate regions do not produce good fruits.

Varieties include: 'Hayward' (late flowering and therefore avoiding damage from frost, large and well-flavoured).

Well-drained, moisture-retentive soil and a sheltered position in full sun. Plants are usually planted against a warm wall. This is a tender plant, soon killed by frost.

Plant a container-grown plant in spring, and with tiers of wires for support. Plant males and females close together, so that they intertwine.

In spring, shallowly fork in a light dressing of a general fertilizer. Then thoroughly soak the soil and form a 7.5cm/3in mulch. Keep the soil moist, at least until the onset of late summer. To aid pollination, transfer the pollen from male flowers into female ones.

Form tiers of shoots by annually cutting back leading shoots to just above a supporting wire and allowing one shoot to grow upwards and the other sideways, on each plant.

Damsons

These are close relatives of the plum and are more successful in areas of high rainfall and less sun. Also, they are more hardy and because flowers appear later they are not damaged by frost. The fruits have a tart but spicy flavour.

Varieties include: 'Merryweather' (blue-black); 'Shropshire Damson' (ideal for small gardens).

Elderberries

These are the fruits of Elder *(Sambucus nigra)*, a hardy deciduous shrub. Creamy white flowers appear in early summer, followed by shiny black berries, which are harvested in early autumn. These are frequently made into a rich, purplish red wine. Elderflower wine is made from the flowers, and can be still or sparkling.

Gages

These are a type of plum, but smaller, sweeter and rounder. The yields are smaller than those of a plum and they require a warmer and more favourable position, perhaps against a sunny wall.

Varieties include: 'Early Transparent Gage' (dessert, yellow spotted red); 'Oullin's Golden Gage' (dessert/culinary, golden yellow).

Hybrid Berries

These are increasingly popular and although their parentage consists mainly of Blackberries, many are derived from crossings involving Dewberries, Raspberries and other related fruits. They bear fruit between early summer and early autumn.

Types include: Boysenberry, Dewberry, Loganberry, Silvanberry, Tayberry, Tummelberry and Youngberry.

Summer fruits

FRUIT	SITUATION AND PLANTING	CULTIVATION

Melons

These are succulent fruits, easily damaged by frost. They are too tender to be grown outdoors without protection in temperate regions and therefore grown in greenhouses or cold frames.

Types: There are three types – Cantaloupe (ideal for greenhouse and cold frames); Netted or Musk (needs a warm greenhouse, Winter or Casaba (needs a warm greenhouse).

In a greenhouse, grow plants in growing-bags or 25cm/10in-wide pots up a cane tied to a series of tiered wires, 30cm/12in apart and 38cm/15in from the glass.

In a cold frame, plant into a mound of fertile soil about 20cm/8in high.

Plant greenhouse types in mid-spring, and those under cold frames in early summer, or as soon as the risk of frost has passed.

Train greenhouse plants up a cane; remove all lateral shoots below the lowest wire, but train others along wires. Pinch out their tips when five leaves have developed. Later pinch out each shoot two leaves beyond a fruit. When the main stem reaches the top tier, pinch out its tip.

For cold frame types, pinch out the growing tip just beyond the fifth leaf. Allow only four main shoots; later, pinch each back to two leaves beyond a fruit.

Nectarines

This originated as a smooth-skinned mutant (sport) of the peach; there are now several varieties, all less hardy than peaches. In temperate regions it is not totally successful as it flowers early and blossom is often damaged by late frost.

Varieties include: 'Early Rivers' (late mid-summer); 'Lord Napier' (late summer); 'Pine Apple' (early autumn).

Well-drained but moisture-retentive soil and a warm, frost-free position suit it. For preference, grow it against a sunny, wind-sheltered wall.

Plant bare-rooted specimens in early winter, or container-grown ones in autumn. Fan-trained nectarines grown against a wall will need the support of tiers of wires up to 1.8m/6ft high and 25cm/10in apart. Each part of the fan is tied first to a cane, then to a wire.

Protect blossom in early spring by lightly draping netting or hessian over the fan or bush. It must be removed during the day to allow access for pollinating insects. Shallowly fork in a dusting of a general fertilizer in spring, then water and add a 7.5cm/3in-thick mulch.

To reduce the risk of entry of silver leaf and bacterial canker into a tree, do not prune during winter.

Peaches

The fruits have rough, hairy skin and succulent flesh. Like the nectarine, it is not totally successful in temperate regions as the blossom is early and easily damaged by frost.

Varieties include: 'Duke of York' (latter part of mid-summer); 'Peregrine' (late summer); 'Rochester' (late summer).

Well-drained but moisture-retentive soil and a warm, frost-free position suit it. For preference, grow it against a sunny, wind-sheltered wall.

Plant bare-rooted plants in early winter, or container-grown ones in autumn. Fan-trained peaches grown against a wall need support from tiers of wires up to 1.8m/6ft high and 25cm/10in apart. Each part of the fan is tied first to a cane, then to a wire.

Protect blossom in early spring by lightly draping netting or hessian over the fan or bush. It must be removed during the day to allow access for pollinating insects. Shallowly fork in a dusting of a general fertilizer in spring, then water and add a 7.5cm/3in-thick mulch.

To reduce the risk of entry of silver leaf and bacterial canker into a tree, do not prune during winter.

Pears

A widely grown fruit in temperate climates, with both dessert and culinary varieties. Depending on the variety, pears provide fruits that can be eaten from late summer to mid-winter.

Varieties: The choice is wide, from 'Jargonelle' which is picked and eaten in late summer, to 'Winter Nelis', picked in mid-autumn for eating in mid-winter.

Well-drained but moisture-retentive soil and a position sheltered from cold wind are essential. Because pears are not quite so hardy as apples, they are often grown as espaliers and in the shelter of a sun-facing wall, especially in cool areas.

Plant bare-rooted trees during their dormant period, and container-grown types when the soil is workable.

Ensure soil does not dry out, especially in spring; thoroughly soak the ground and then apply a mulch. Pears can be grown in several forms; trees, bushes, fans, dwarf bushes, pyramids and cordons.

Medlar

These are fruits of a hardy, European tree (*Mespilus germanica*). Fertile, well-drained soil and an open, sunny position are needed. Fruits are ready for picking in late autumn, but they must be stored in trays for several weeks until ready for eating.

Varieties include: 'Dutch' (large fruits); 'Nottingham' (most popular, small, richly flavoured fruits).

Mulberries

These are fruits of the Black Mulberry (*Morus nigra*), a hardy, deciduous, slow-growing tree. By late summer or early autumn, dark red, berry-like fruits are ready for picking; they are best harvested by spreading a cloth under the branches and shaking them. The fruits have a slightly acid flavour.

Passion Fruit

Also known as the Purple Granadilla, this is the fruit of *Passiflora edulis*, a tropical climber. It likes warmth and grows in several Mediterranean countries, as well as in its native Brazil. Fruits are the size of an egg and become purple when ripe, when they assume an aged and wrinkled appearance.

Pineapples

A tropical South American fruit (*Ananas comosus*) grown only in greenhouses in temperate climates. In cool countries it is grown as a houseplant. In warm countries it is grown commercially, with plants being replaced with young ones after two or three years. The fruits are very sweet and rich in vitamins A and C.

	FRUIT	SITUATION AND PLANTING	CULTIVATION
	**Plums** Plums are ideal for planting in temperate climates and there are both culinary and dessert varieties. Many of them are self-fertile and do not need the presence of another variety. Varieties include: 'Czar' (culinary, self-fertile); 'Edwards' (culinary, not self-fertile); 'Sanctus Hubertus' (dessert/culinary, partly self-fertile); 'Victoria' (dessert and culinary, self-fertile).	Well-drained but moisture-retentive soil suits them. Because plums flower early in spring, they should not be planted in a cold and exposed position; avoid areas where cold, frost-laden air travels down slopes and collects at the base. Plant bare-rooted trees in early winter.	In spring, fork a nitrogen-rich general fertilizer into the soil, water thoroughly and then form a 7.5cm/3in-thick mulch. Birds feast on growth and fruit buds, as well as the fruits; therefore, if possible cover the trees with netting. During early summer, use scissors to thin congested fruits to about 7.5cm/3in apart. Do not prune plums during winter; wait until the sap is rising.
	**Raspberries – Summer Fruiting** This popular fruit is ideal for temperate zones, and once planted the canes remain productive for eight or more years. The fruits are ready for picking during mid- and late summer. Varieties include: 'Glen Clova' (high yields); 'Glen Moy' (aphid resistant); 'Malling Admiral' (spine-free canes); 'Malling Jewel' (tolerant of virus infection).	Fertile, moisture-retentive but well-drained soil and on a gentle slope facing the sun suits it best. Avoid frost pockets and plant canes down, rather than across, slopes to prevent frost being trapped. Plant bare-rooted canes in early winter or early spring. Container-grown plants can be planted whenever the soil and weather allow. Space plants 45cm/18in apart in rows 1.5-1.8m/5-6ft apart.	Feed plants with a general fertilizer in spring, water the soil thoroughly and form a 7.5cm/3in-thick mulch. Keep the soil moist throughout summer, especially when the fruits are forming. Prune established canes immediately after the crop has been picked. Cut down to their base all canes that have produced fruits; retain young shoots produced earlier in the year. In late winter, cut back the tops of canes to 15cm/6in above the top wire.
	**Redcurrants** These are succulent fruits, little seen in shops or at pick-your-own farms and therefore ideal for planting by home gardeners. Fruits are ready for picking during mid- and late summer. Varieties include: 'Laxton's No. 1' (widely grown); 'Red Lake' (heavy cropping); 'Redstart' (relatively new variety, late cropping); 'Stanza' (new variety, compact habit).	Moisture-retentive but well-drained soil and a wind-sheltered position in full sun or light shade suit it. Additionally, do not plant redcurrant bushes in frost pockets. Plant bare-rooted bushes in late autumn to early winter. Alternatively, plant in late winter or early spring. Plant container-grown bushes at any time when the soil and weather allow.	Apply a general fertilizer in spring, thoroughly water the soil and apply a 7.5cm/3in-thick mulch. Harvest fruits when ripe, picking whole clusters rather than individual berries. Prune established bushes between early winter and early spring: cut back new growth at the ends of leading shoots by half. Cut back sideshoots to about 5cm/2in long. In early summer, cut back sideshoots produced earlier in the year to four or five leaves.
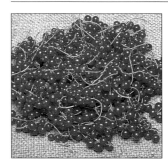	**Strawberries – Summer Fruiting** Summer-fruiting strawberries are popular and produce fruits during early and mid-summer. Others include 'Perpetual' types with fruits during early summer and late summer to autumn, and 'Alpines' (see below). Summer-fruiting varieties include: 'Bogota' (heavy cropping, mid-summer); 'Cambridge Favourite' (reliable crops, early to mid-summer); 'Tantallon' (heavy cropping, early to mid-summer).	Moisture-retentive but well-drained, fertile soil and a wind-sheltered site suit it. A gentle slope towards the sun is desirable. To produce a worthwhile crop of berries, at least twenty plants are needed. Plant summer-fruiting, bare-rooted plants between mid-summer and autumn. If plants are planted earlier, remove their flowers to encourage strong growth. Plant container-grown types whenever the soil and weather allow.	Eradicate all weeds. Apply a general fertilizer in spring, thoroughly water the soil. As fruits start to swell, spread straw between plants, as well as pushing it under them. Water newly planted and established plants regularly, especially during dry weather, but avoid splashing the fruits. As needed, put down slug pellets.

Quinces	**Raspberries – Autumn Fruiting**	**Strawberries – Alpine**	**White Currants**
These are borne on the hardy shrub or small tree *Cydonia oblonga*, known earlier as *C. vulgaris* and commonly as Quince and Common Quince. Pear- or apple-shaped fruits are ready for harvesting in early or mid-autumn, before severe frosts can damage them. Varieties include: 'Champion' (apple-shaped); 'Portugal' (pear-shaped); 'Vranja' (pear-shaped, popular variety).	These have a different fruiting habit from the summer type (see above); instead of canes that develop during one season and produce fruits in the following one, autumn-fruiting types bear fruits during late summer and autumn on canes produced during the same year. Varieties include: 'Autumn Bliss'; 'Fallgold'; 'Heritage'; 'September'; 'Zeva'.	Also known as Wild Strawberry, this has small, succulent but not juicy fruits that are sweet and aromatic and ready for picking from mid-summer to autumn. Varieties include: 'Alexandria' (bright red fruits); 'Baron Solemacher' (popular variety, dark red fruits borne over a long period).	These are borne on bushes similar to those of Redcurrants. The fruits are ready for harvesting in mid-summer. Varieties include: 'White Dutch' (pale golden fruits, heavy cropping); 'White Grape' (white, large fruits); 'White Versailles' (heavy cropping, popular variety).

GREENHOUSE GARDENING

Greenhouses introduce a further dimension to gardening and enable a wide range of tender plants to be grown. They also provide ideal conditions in which seeds can be sown early in the year, and in which plants such as dahlias and chrysanthemums can be increased from cuttings. Greenhouses also form the perfect environment for growing tomatoes and cucumbers in summer. In an unheated greenhouse, small propagating frames, heated by either electricity or paraffin, make the propagation of plants possible. Greenhouses also create ideal environments for growing tomatoes and cucumbers in summer.

Garden frames are useful adjuncts to greenhouses, enabling half-hardy summer-flowering bedding plants to be hardened off before being planted out. Frames can also be used to grow melons during summer months.

Choosing a greenhouse

When choosing a greenhouse, its size, shape and structural material are the main considerations. The size of the greenhouse must be chosen to suit the site and the range of plants you expect to grow in it. It is false economy to buy a greenhouse that suits only your present needs, as invariably after a few years it will prove to be too small. Instead, buy the largest one you can afford and have room for.

RANGE OF GREENHOUSES

Greenhouses range in shape from those with an even span to those that are hexagonal. Each has its advantages and disadvantages, and some may suit the style and shape of particular gardens better than others.

Even-span greenhouses (also known as full-span) have traditional outlines, with a ridge along the top and glass sloping to an eave on both sides. Early types had a timber framework and bricks or wooden panels up to about 75cm/30in high. Modern, aluminium-framed ones, however, are usually glazed from ground-level to each of the eaves.

Even-span greenhouses up to about 2.4m/8ft wide have one central path, usually 60cm/24in wide. This leaves 90cm/3ft-wide spaces on either side, which can be used for greenhouse staging or left as areas in which crops such as tomatoes or cucumbers can be grown during summer. Greenhouses only 1.8m/6ft or 2.1m/7ft wide have narrower staging and growing areas, as the width of the path usually remains at 60cm/24in.

Lean-to types vary in width and length to suit the wall or house they are constructed against. Most have wooden or brick bases to the side walls, up to 75cm/30in high, with a timber or aluminium framework to support the glass. Traditional types are 1.8m/6ft or 2.4m/8ft wide. The floor area is partly occupied by a 60cm/24in-wide path, while the rest of the space is either occupied by staging or left open to allow large plants to be grown in pots on the ground.

Some lean-to greenhouses are large enough to function as conservatories and sunrooms, forming warm, comfortable, relaxing areas for people, with plants growing in pots helping to create a restful ambience.

TYPES OF GREENHOUSE

1

2

3

4

1 Lean-to, conservatory-style greenhouses are increasingly popular both as leisure areas and for growing plants.
2 Wooden greenhouses have a natural appearance which harmonizes with plants. Those constructed of Western Red Cedar are very durable. Instead of being painted, the wood is coated in linseed oil.
3 Hexagonal greenhouses have an attractive, novel outline that harmonizes with ornamental areas.
4 Even-span greenhouses (also known as full-span) are the most widely seen type.

SITING A GREENHOUSE

Choosing the right position for a greenhouse can save a lot of money in fuel bills each year. Orient full-span greenhouses so that the ridge runs from west to east. During winter this enables low winter rays to pass through the glass. Position lean-to greenhouses so that they face south. If this is not possible, a west aspect is acceptable, but avoid north- or east-facing situations. Position doors on the side away from the prevailing wind. A sliding door should open first on the southerly side. If it has hinges, these should be on the northerly side so that the door opens with a southerly aspect.

Full-span greenhouses benefit from a hedge on the cold, northerly side. This is better than a wall, which would cause strong eddies of wind around the greenhouse. A hedge 2.4m/8ft high reduces the wind's speed by 75 per cent up to a point 4.5m/15ft from it. During winter and early spring, when a greenhouse might be used for sowing seeds, this saves a lot of money on heating costs.

Avoid positions under overhanging trees, which both block out light and drip water over the roof, long after a shower of rain has finished. Choose a site that is not waterlogged in winter, as this makes access difficult. A water tap in or near the greenhouse is an advantage, while the installation of a mains electricity cable (which must be installed by a competent electrician) allows the greenhouse to be heated by electricity. Electrically heated propagators are also useful.

Above: Mini greenhouses are popular and ideal for small gardens, where they can be positioned against a warm wall. They are not deep enough to walk into, but do enable a wide range of plants to be grown.

Hexagonal greenhouses are a more recent design and allow the sun's rays to enter from a wide range of angles. They have a decorative shape and suit a position encircled by flower beds, as well as one in a vegetable garden.

Some hexagonal greenhouses have glass from floor to eaves, while others have a wood or brick framework to about 75cm/30in high.

Plastic tunnels are made from heavy-gauge, clear polythene or PVC sheeting stretched over strong metal hoops about 1.8m/6ft high and often 3m/10ft or 3.6m/12ft wide. Polythene has a life of two or three years, while PVC is more durable but more expensive.

Plastic tunnels are mainly used commercially, although enthusiastic amateur gardeners find them useful. The main problem is the rapid heat loss, with accompanying condensation on the inside. Also, because the plastic forms a continuous tunnel, ventilation is a problem; the only way to get air into the tunnel is to open the doors .

Miniature greenhouses are increasingly popular and can be fitted into most gardens – or even just on a patio, where they can be positioned against a wall or fence. Plant houses (the smallest lean-to greenhouses) are about 60cm/24in in depth, 1.5m/5ft to the eaves and 1.8m/6ft to the ridge. In length they range from 1.2m/4ft to 1.8m/6ft. They are not deep enough to walk into but a sliding door at the front provides access to the plants. Some models have hinged ventilators in the roof.

WOOD OR METAL?

Traditionally, greenhouses were made of wood, but aluminium is becoming increasingly popular. Here are a few points to consider.

Timber The life expectancy of a timber-framed greenhouse depends on the type of wood used, the way it is used and its maintenance. Extremes of temperature and high humidity soon cause wood to deteriorate on both the inside and outside of the greenhouse. If the wood deteriorates and warps, the ventilators and door may not fit properly, allowing draughts to enter. Baltic redwood, also known as yellow deal, is often used but needs regular painting as well as initial treatment with a wood preservative. Western red cedar is more durable and, instead of being preserved with coats of paint, is coated in linseed oil. Oak and teak were used in Victorian conservatories, but are now prohibitively expensive.

Aluminium Most greenhouses are now made of extruded aluminium, which gives additional strength to the metal and provides gaps into which shelving and insulation brackets can be fitted. Also, because the glazing bars tend to be narrower than those made of wood, they do not exclude so much light.

Equipping and maintaining a greenhouse

Successful greenhouses are more than just glass-covered structures; to make full use of the space and to benefit from all-year-round protection staging, paths, methods of heating, shading and ventilators are also vital ingredients.

GREENHOUSE STAGING

Usually at least one side of a full-span greenhouse is equipped with staging to enable plants to be displayed, seeds sown and plants potted or repotted at hip or waist height. Most staging is permanent, but, increasingly – and especially in aluminium greenhouses – a type that is hinged and can be lowered is found so that plants can also be grown at ground level. This means that, for example, summer-flowering bedding plants can be sown and raised on the staging, then tomato plants grown in growing-bags or pots placed on the greenhouse floor.

The range of staging is wide and includes the following:

Wooden, slatted staging is the traditional type, with about 2.5cm/1in gaps between slats 5cm/2in wide. This enables air to circulate around the pots and plants, which is especially important in winter when moisture lingering on leaves might encourage the spread of diseases. The slatted base also allows water to drain from the pots.

Solid staging consists of a firm, continuous base covered with a shallow layer of pea-sized gravel chippings. It is ideal in summer, as gravel chippings retain moisture which evaporates gradually to create a buoyant atmosphere around leaves. It also reduces the rate at which compost dries out.

Alpine plants are often plunged to their rims in shingle, while other plants are just stood on top. Alternative base materials include expanded clay particles and grit.

Small-mesh, galvanized or plastic-covered netting creates a base with good air circulation. Unfortunately, after a few years – and depending on the weight of the pots placed on it – it tends to sag between the supports. Nevertheless, it is easy and quick to construct.

Temporary shelving is often needed from late winter to early summer to enable more half-hardy bedding plants to be grown. The extra

VENTILATION AND SHADING

1 The cheapest way to shade a greenhouse is to paint a white strip down the central two-thirds of each pane of glass. Use a proprietary whitening material.
2 It is usually only necessary to paint the shading on the sunny side of a greenhouse.
3 Automatic ventilators close and open according to the temperature. They are operated by a chemical which expands or contracts in response to the temperature.
4 Fine-mesh plastic netting can be draped over the outside of a greenhouse to provide shade. It can be easily and quickly removed during dull weather.

space needed can be provided by suspending long, narrow shelves from the glazing bars. In wood-framed greenhouses, screw wires to the glazing bars and suspend the shelving from them. In aluminium-framed greenhouses, proprietary fittings are available.

When watering plants on these shelves, take care that water does not splash on plants beneath. Also, remember that areas close to the glass are the first to experience a rapid temperature drop during winter and early spring. It may be necessary to cover seed-trays with sheets of newspaper at night when frost is forecast; remove these during the day.

Tiered staging is frequently used to display plants such as orchids.

GLAZING

Glass has proved to be the best material for covering greenhouses. The total weight of glass used in a greenhouse is considerable and gives the framework extra rigidity. Early greenhouses had panes of glass 30cm/12in or less wide, but when glass-making techniques improved 45cm/18in glass panes became popular and now they are frequently 60cm/24in across. The use of larger pieces of glass became possible through the construction of aluminium-framed greenhouses; extruded aluminium is stronger and lighter than wood. Individual panes of glass are secured to wooden glazing bars by putty and brass sprigs,

while those in aluminium-framed greenhouses are secured in position by proprietary clips, sometimes formed from stainless steel.

Only 75 to 80 per cent of available light passes through glass, even when clean; if dirty, this figure is dramatically reduced. In summer, this is not a problem, as the glass will probably be covered with shading; in winter and spring all available light is needed, so keep the glass clean.

SHADING

Strong sunlight damages some plants and dramatically increases the temperature inside the greenhouse. There are several ways to provide shading: the cheapest method is to coat the outside of the glass with a proprietary whitener which is applied with a brush. Paint the central two-thirds of each pane. Weather often removes the paint during summer and fresh applications may be necessary. In autumn or early winter, wash it off completely.

Roller blinds are more expensive than coating glass with paint, but can be rolled up or down according to the weather. Venetian blinds and roller blinds can be fitted to the insides of conservatories and sunrooms, but are not practical for greenhouses. Some of these blinds are horizontal, while others are vertical and therefore do not trap dust so easily. A quick and relatively cheap blind can be created by draping a sheet of fine plastic mesh over the outside of the greenhouse. This can be quickly removed when the sun goes in and light levels drop.

VENTILATORS

Ensure there is at least one ventilator in the greenhouse roof; if possible, there should be ventilators on both sides of the roof. This enables a selected ventilator to be opened so that cold winds do not blow directly into the greenhouse. Ventilators at the side of the greenhouse are also beneficial. Some ventilators open and close automatically as the temperature changes; a chemical within them expands and contracts, thereby controlling the ventilator.

EXTRACTOR FANS

These are sometimes fitted into the gable ends of a greenhouse. Controlled by thermostats, they extract hot air from the roof area. Louvres on the outside prevent cold air blowing in.

Heating a greenhouse

Greenhouses in temperate regions need to have some form of heating; conversely, for those in warm climates the main problem is to reduce the temperature. However, the information here is for greenhouses in countries with a temperate climate, where heating and conserving warmth are major considerations.

Unless the greenhouse is home to a range of tropical and sub-tropical plants, when it needs heating throughout the year, in a temperate climate it is likely to need heating only during late winter and spring, when summer-flowering bedding plants are being raised from seed or softwood cuttings rooted.

METHODS OF HEATING

The method of heating depends on the size of the structure, and whether it is a greenhouse or conservatory.

Paraffin (kerosene) heaters are relatively inexpensive to buy and inexpensive to operate. Also, they are versatile and can be moved within a greenhouse or from one structure to another. The heat they create is controlled by the size of the heater and the length of wick which is allowed to burn. However, if the length of wick is excessive, large amounts of smoke and fumes are produced. Because of the problem from fumes, paraffin heaters are better suited for use in greenhouses than in conservatories. Single and double burners are available in a wide range of sizes. Some are fitted with hot-water pipes, so that the heat-emitting area is increased.

When this type of heater is in use, oxygen is consumed and carbon dioxide given off. Therefore, it is essential to open a ventilator to allow fumes to escape. Ventilation also allows the additional moisture created by the burning of paraffin to escape; it is estimated that when paraffin is burnt it produces an equal volume of water vapour.

If the wick is trimmed properly and is not excessively long, and the fuel tank is checked regularly to ensure that the paraffin is not about to run out at night, paraffin heaters are very reliable.

Electricity is a clean – but expensive – way to heat a greenhouse or conservatory. By the use of a thermostat the temperature can be precisely

Right: By ensuring that a greenhouse is not overshadowed by trees, is not in a frost pocket, and is sheltered from cold winds, the cost of heating can be dramatically reduced. Also, ensure that the door and ventilators fit their frames and do not allow cold air to enter the greenhouse.

HEATING AND INSULATING A GREENHOUSE

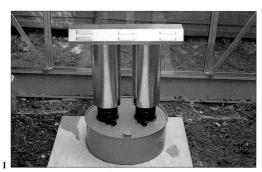

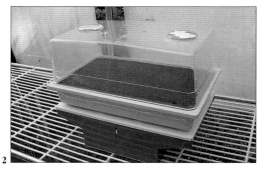

1 Regularly trim the wick on a paraffin heater to ensure it is not too long or it will create black smoke and fumes.
2 Propagation frames heated by paraffin enable plants to be increased even when electricity is not installed in a greenhouse.
3 Electrically powered propagation frames provide the correct environment for seeds and cuttings to be created, without the entire greenhouse having to be heated.
4 Bubble glazing is an efficient way to reduce the heat loss from a greenhouse. Secure it to the inside of the glass.

CONSERVING WARMTH

Heating is one of the largest expenses in operating a greenhouse. Therefore, anything that can be done to conserve warmth is important. Positioning a greenhouse and giving it the right orientation are fundamental, and providing a hedge to create shelter from cold winds can help considerably (see pages 242-3).

Insulation to conserve warmth is essential, especially when a greenhouse is used during winter and spring. There are many proprietary materials available, including bubble glazing which is formed of three layers of plastic with air bubbles between them. It can be held in place inside a greenhouse by a range of fittings, including double-sided adhesive pads, drawing pins in wooden greenhouses, and special clips in aluminium types. Both white and green bubble glazing are available; during winter, the green type can make a greenhouse too dark, although if left in place during summer it provides shading. Other forms of insulation include polythene sheets reinforced with wire mesh.

Warped ventilators and doors allow cold air to blow into a greenhouse; in autumn, check these and correct them if badly fitting. Also, fit a draught excluder around the door.

Creating the optimum temperature is essential. The cost of heating a greenhouse does not rise in direct proportion to the temperature; instead, it rises dramatically. Therefore, assess the optimum temperature required to suit all the plants, install a thermometer and adjust the heating accordingly.

controlled, thereby keeping costs to a minimum. However, the installation of electrical heaters does require the advice and services of a competent electrician. Water and electricity are a deadly duo and the slightest mistake in the installation of an electrical heating system could prove to be lethal. There are safety devices which can be incorporated into the system and these should never be omitted.

There are two basic forms of electrical heater to consider. Tubular heaters are invariably fixed to a wall and positioned about 25cm/10in above the ground. They produce a gentle flow of warm air. If installing one under a solid-topped bench, ensure that a gap of 10-15cm/4-6in is left at the back of the bench so that heat can rise and circulate. Fan heaters create warmth and good air movement, which helps to prevent diseases, but avoid directing hot blasts of air on plants as this will damage them. Do not use domestic fan heaters as they are unsafe in the humid atmosphere found in most greenhouses.

Domestic heating systems can sometimes be extended into conservatories and sunrooms. However, as heating systems in most houses are turned down at night – when plants are most vulnerable to low temperatures – this is not practical unless an electrical fan-heater is also present.

HEATED PROPAGATION CASES

These help to create the right conditions for seeds to germinate and for cuttings to develop roots. Most are heated by electricity, a few by paraffin and these are useful where it is difficult to install electrical cables. Both produce the correct temperature around seeds and cuttings, without the temperature having to be increased throughout the entire greenhouse. It is easier to control the temperature in the electrical types which often have thermostats.

Cloches, cold frames and polythene tunnels

When compared with greenhouses, cloches, frames and polythene tunnels are not only cheaper but also have far more uses in a vegetable garden. They are widely used in temperate climates to warm up soil in late winter and spring, so that early crops can be sown and planted, and the growing season extended in late summer and autumn.

TYPES OF CLOCHES

In earlier years, cloches were chiefly made of glass, but more recently both polythene sheeting and corrugated PVC have been introduced. Whatever cloches are made of, they must be able to retain warmth and transmit light. Additionally, they should allow a flow or air over the plants and therefore must not be completely airtight. But neither should they act as wind tunnels which result in plants being cooled by funnelling air. If cloches do not have built-in ventilators – and few do – they need to be positioned slightly apart when placed end to end to form rows.

Glass cloches These allow more light to enter and reach plants than those made of plastic; they also conserve more warmth. However, they are more expensive and likely to be broken than plastic types. Nevertheless, they are quite resilient, even in high winds.

There are several types of glass cloche. The most popular is the barn cloche, formed of four sheets of glass clipped together, with two forming the sides and the other two the roof. This is an ideal type for placing over crops up to about 30cm/12in high. The other main type is the tent cloche, formed of two sheets of glass that, when placed on the ground and linked by special wire clips, form a triangle shape.

Corrugated PVC This type combines great strength with lightness, and although these cloches do not transmit as much light as glass, they are much less likely to break. Additionally, they are not such a danger to children and animals. Because of their light weight they need to be well anchored in the soil; use strong spikes.

Bell-jars These traditional covers are made of glass. Modern adaptations are formed of transparent plastic – some rigid, others like umbrellas that can be opened and placed over plants.

TYPES OF CLOCHES AND GARDEN FRAMES

1 Glass cloches are the traditional type of cloche. They allow more light to reach the plants than those made of plastic.
2 Some plastic cloches have opaque sides and ends, with clear plastic in the middle. These are less likely to be broken than are those made of glass.
3 Corrugated PVC cloches are light and strong. Also, they are cheaper than cloches made of glass and do not break if knocked.
4 Garden frames help to harden off seedlings in spring. Low-growing vegetables can also be grown under them.

Above: Cloches are an essential part of a vegetable garden, enabling seeds to be sown earlier and plants to be matured and harvested later.

Large clear plastic bottles with their bases cut off, as well as glass jars, can also be used to give seeds an early start when inverted and placed over them. Before throwing any plastic container away, consider its potential to be adapted to form a bell-jar or cloche.

POLYTHENE TUNNELS

These are formed of metal hoops anchored in the ground with clear polythene sheeting stretched over them to form a tunnel, and provide a cheap way of protecting plants. The polythene usually needs replacing every two years as it deteriorates when exposed to sunlight, tears easily and becomes dirty.

PROTECTING VEGETABLES

Cloches, glass-jars, frames and tunnels have several uses in vegetable gardens: Placing cloches and tunnels over bare soil in late winter and early spring encourages it to warm up quickly so that seeds can be sown earlier. Cloches can be used to protect plants from low temperatures in early spring, enabling them to be sown early. To give the plants extra protection at night, cover the frames with hessian. Plants can be covered with cloches in late summer and early autumn to encourage maturity and ripening. Tomato plants, for example, can be detached from their supports in autumn, laid on straw and covered with cloches to encourage fruits to ripen. Placing glass jars over newly sown seeds of frost-tender plants, such as ridge cucumbers, is an inexpensive way to encourage early and rapid germination. Garden frames help to raise plants such as lettuces early in the year. They are ideal in spring for hardening off young vegetable plants. Summer-flowering bedding plants can also be hardened off under them. Additionally, those frames with a wooden, boarded surround can be used to grow self-blanching celery; the wooden edges prevent the sideways entry of light.

These tunnels are an ideal way to protect long rows of low-growing plants and even though the polythene is continuous it can be easily pulled away at one side to allow access to plants. The ends are secured by drawing them together and pegging them to the soil, while plants are ventilated by temporarily lifting up one side.

GARDEN FRAMES

Garden frames retain heat better than cloches and wind has a less cooling effect on them, although they are less flexible as they cannot be rapidly moved around a vegetable plot to cover a crop or assist in the preparation of soil before sowing seeds or planting crops.

The modern garden frame is about 1.2m/4ft long and 60cm/24in wide, and formed of one large piece of glass. The glass is mounted in a wooden frame and positioned on a wooden or brick structure measuring 30-45cm/12-18in high at the back and 15-30cm/6-12in at the front. These frames should be oriented so that the sloping side faces south or south-west, ensuring the maximum amount of light can reach the plants. There are also proprietary aluminium frames clad with glass or rigid, clear plastic. They are 1.2-1.5m/4-5ft wide and about 1.8m/6ft long, tent-like and with a ridge down the centre.

Frames are ventilated by lifting up the lower end and placing a brick of piece of wood underneath to keep the top propped open. Frames can be hinged at the top edge to make ventilating the plants easier.

Growing tomatoes in a greenhouse

Tomatoes are a popular crop for greenhouses in temperate climates. They fit into the cycle of greenhouse use after summer-flowering bedding plants have been raised early in the year. Tomato plants are easily damaged by low temperatures. Therefore, unless some form of heating is available, do not plant them too early.

WAYS TO GROW TOMATOES

There are several ways in which tomato plants can be grown in greenhouses:

Directly in border soil When a greenhouse has only recently been erected, the border soil is usually clean and free from diseases. This enables plants to be planted directly into it. Commercially, planting directly into a border is continued year after year, as soil sterilization equipment is available to kill harmful pests and diseases that can accumulate in the soil. Chemical sterilants are available for use in an amateur's greenhouse and these are watered on to soil which has been loosened by digging. It is more usual to separate the compost from the ground beneath before sterilizing.

In pots about 25cm/10in wide, filled with fresh compost. This is a good method, although during very hot days the compost dries out rapidly. Frequent watering is essential.

Ring culture is a popular method; it involves digging a trench in the greenhouse border 10-15cm/4-6in deep and 38cm/15in wide and lining it with polythene. The area is filled with clean, 6mm/¼in pea shingle, and a 23cm/9in-wide and 20-25cm/8-10in-high bottomless ring is placed on top and filled with a loam-based compost. Plants are put into the compost and, eventually, their roots grow down into the gravel, which must be kept moist.

Growing-bags are popular; they can be placed directly on border soil and plants put into the peat-based mixture they contain. Since the amount of compost is relatively small, the plants must be fed and watered regularly.

WHEN TO SOW SEEDS

From sowing seeds, it takes between eight and ten weeks to raise tomato plants ready for planting into a greenhouse. It is possible to plant

GROWING TOMATOES IN A GREENHOUSE

1 If the border soil in a greenhouse is full of pests and diseases, the best way to grow tomatoes is in growing-bags. Strong, polystyrene troughs enable growing-bags to be held firm as well as providing a way to support the plants.
2 Simple metal frames (which are held firm by the growing-bag) provide another way to support plants.
3 Keep the stems of plants well secured to their supports, but ensure that they are not constricted.
4 Regularly remove shoots growing from between the main stem and a leaf joint. Snap them off sideways while they are still young.

TOMATO VARIETIES FOR THE GREENHOUSE

The range of tomato seeds offered by seed companies is wide and each year many new varieties are introduced. All the varieties suggested here are of the cordon type and require sideshooting and stopping (see main text).

- **'Alicante'** A non-hybrid type, ideal for growing both outdoors and in a greenhouse. It produces heavy crops of high quality fruits.

- **'Dombito' F1 Hybrid** Ideal for a heated or cold greenhouse; produces heavy crops of large, beefsteak-type fruits.

- **'Matador' F1 Hybrid** Can be grown outdoors or in a greenhouse and produces medium to large, semi-beefsteak-type fruits.

- **'Shirley' F1 Hybrid** Ideal for a heated or cold greenhouse, with heavy crops of medium-sized fruits. It is also excellent for growing in polythene tunnels.

- **'Sungold' F1 Hybrid** Can be grown outdoors or in a greenhouse, where it produces small, cherry-like fruits.

- **Tigrella'** A non-hybrid type, ideal for outdoors and in a greenhouse, where it produces heavy crops of brightly striped fruits with a rich, tangy flavour.

tomato plants into a heated greenhouse as early as late winter or early spring, but heating the structure to an acceptable temperature can be expensive. With cold, unheated greenhouses in temperate regions, the best time for planting is between the latter part of mid-spring and early summer. Much of this timing depends on the availability of space in the greenhouse and fitting the tomatoes in with raising summer-flowering bedding plants.

SOWING TOMATO SEEDS

The seeds are sown in seed-trays. Fill and firm either soil- or peat-based compost to within 6mm/¼in of the container's top. Space out individual seeds about 12mm/½in apart over the surface, avoiding the edges, which dry out first if watering is neglected. Cover the seeds with 3mm/⅛in of sieved compost, then gently firm it. Stand the seed-tray in a bowl shallowly filled with water and wait until moisture seeps to the surface of the compost. Then remove and allow excess water to drain. Cover the seed-tray with a sheet of glass, then with newspaper. Provide a temperature of 18°C/64°F. Every day, turn and wipe dry the glass. Germination takes between seven and ten days, after which the glass and paper can be removed. Place the seed-tray in light shade and away from draughts.

PRICKING OFF SEEDLINGS

When the seedlings are 18-25mm/¾-1in high they can be transferred singly into individual pots. Water the seedlings the day before pricking off. Fill a 6-7.5cm/2-3in-wide pot half full with potting compost. Carefully remove a cluster of seedlings and place them on damp newspaper, to keep their roots moist. Hold a seedling by one of its seed leaves and position it in the pot, so

that when compost is firmed around the stem it will be at about the same depth as it was before.

Water the compost, allow to drain and replace in 18°C/64°F. Shade from direct sunlight until established, then place in good light and reduce the temperature to 15°C/59°F. As the seedlings grow, space the pots further apart.

PLANTING YOUNG PLANTS

Plant tomato plants when the flowers on the first truss are opening. At this stage, plants will be 15-23cm/6-9in tall. Use a trowel to dig out a small hole and position the top of the soil-ball level with the surrounding soil. If planting directly into border soil, space plants 45cm/18in apart. Water the soil-ball and surrounding soil thoroughly. Standard-size growing-bags are large enough to accommodate two plants.

SUPPORTING TOMATO PLANTS

The usual way to support tomato plants in an amateur's greenhouse is by inserting a long, strong bamboo cane about 7.5cm/3in away from a plant's stem. The top of the cane is tied to a wire which has been tensioned between stakes at either end of the row.

To secure a stem, first tie a piece of string securely around the cane, then loosely around the plant just below a leaf-joint. Plants in growing-bags can be supported with proprietary wire frames that do not necessitate piercing the bag.

STOPPING, DE-SHOOTING AND DE-LEAFING

Sideshoots develop from the main stem at the axis of leaf-joints. These need to be removed while young (called sideshooting); hold each sideshoot firmly and snap it sideways. This is best done in the morning, when the plant is turgid.

When plants are about 1.2m/4ft high, use a sharp knife to cut off the lower leaves; this helps the lower fruits to ripen. It also increases the circulation of air around plants, thereby reducing the incidence of disease.

When plants have developed six or seven trusses of fruits, the tops will be reaching the roof of the average greenhouse. Snap off the growing tip just above two leaves beyond the top truss (called stopping).

Pick the fruits when ripe, removing each one complete with its calyx (green, spider-like stem). Take care not to bruise or squash them.

General index

Page numbers in **bold** indicate major references (including accompanying photographs).
Page numbers in *italics* indicate captions to other illustrations.
Less important text entries are shown in normal type.

Species index

Page numbers in **bold** indicate major references (including accompanying photographs).
Page numbers in *italics* indicate captions to other illustrations.
Less important text entries are shown in normal type.